Roster of the People
of
Revolutionary Monmouth County
[New Jersey]

by
Michael S. Adelberg

CLEARFIELD

Copyright © 1997 by Michael S. Adelberg
All Rights Reserved.

Printed for
Clearfield Company, Inc. by
Genealogical Publishing Co., Inc.
Baltimore, Maryland
1997

Reprinted for
Clearfield Company, Inc. by
Genealogical Publishing Co., Inc.
Baltimore, Maryland
2003

International Standard Book Number: 0-8063-4677-9

Made in the United States of America

Foreword

The stark everyday realities of war belong to ordinary men and women. Both the lives of those who participated in the military and those who did not are irrecoverably changed by war. Michael Adelberg's research on the American Revolution in Monmouth County is grounded in thorough and detailed investigation of the lives of ordinary individuals. Through publishing, lecturing, and creating resources like this one for fellow researchers, he has made a significant contribution to our knowledge of the American Revolution in Monmouth County and the people who experienced it. This *Roster of the People of Revolutionary Monmouth County* is a natural result of his research methodology and his interest in presenting the human side of wartime.

A review of names and activities that appear in the *Roster of the People of Revolutionary Monmouth County* hints at the variety of ways in which the war dominated the social and economic interests of all levels of society. Monmouth County and its residents felt the full impact of the ideological, economic, and political issues that the Revolution brought. Several factors, including a long-standing and strong allegiance to the British Crown in many neighborhoods, created a climate of civil conflict not seen elsewhere in the colonies.

For genealogists, the *Roster of the People of Revolutionary Monmouth County* offers a valuable resource for more detailed investigation and documentation. In addition, for those who are fortunate enough to locate ancestors in the Roster, it may provide a personal link to the past and a deeper understanding of the chaotic times in which they lived.

Lee Ellen Griffith, Ph.D.
Freehold, N.J.

Roster of the People of Revolutionary Monmouth County

Introduction

It is probable that no county anywhere in the Thirteen Colonies hosted either the same quantity or variety of violent incidents during the American Revolution as Monmouth County, New Jersey. Throughout the Revolution, most Americans suffered through one or two of the four kinds of violence produced by the war: (1) the plundering and destruction that accompanied the campaigns of the major armies, (2) civil warfare between local factions of patriots and tories, (3) foraging and punitive raids launched from British-held cities against the American countryside, and (4) increased violent crime caused by economic troubles and disaffection to the new government. In contrast to those who suffered through one or two varieties of violence, Monmouthers endured all four of these types of violence. Further, Monmouth County was stricken by the latter three types of violence nearly constantly from the fall of 1776 into the summer of 1782, long after the war had ceased in most areas.

Monmouth County was unique. Few areas produced so many active loyalists or covert tories. Throughout 1776, Monmouth County was rocked by a series of loyalist uprisings -- and when the last of the formal loyalist associations was broken up in early 1777, Monmouth loyalists continued their resistance by comprising two of the five battalions of the loyalist New Jersey Volunteers. Along the Atlantic shore from Deal to Tuckerton, entire neighborhoods successfully resisted the new government by refusing to muster into militia companies or pay taxes. These same shore neighborhoods also harbored infamous pine robber gangs and shadowy groups of contraband traders. All of these expressions of defiance against the new government were supported by the British, who continuously occupied the Sandy Hook peninsula -- at the tip of northeast Monmouth County -- from April 1776 through the end of the war (longer than any other piece of the Thirteen Colonies).

For the supporters of the new government in Monmouth County, the Revolutionary War was unusually dangerous. Militia service typically consisted of tedious marches along the shoreline, punctuated by almost random clashes with Tory partisans. Prominent patriots were in constant danger, and most of the leading supporters of the Revolution in the eastern half of the county were either kidnaped or plundered during the war. The constant exposure to danger and the large number of disaffected inhabitants pushed many of Monmouth's

Roster of the People of Revolutionary Monmouth County

patriots to radical extremes. A number of suspected tories were imprisoned, beaten, or even murdered by vigilante patriot gangs, including those of the outlaw Association for Retaliation. For other Monmouthers, the Revolution represented economic opportunity, and a number of Monmouthers invested their fortunes in risky privateering and salt-making ventures.

This roster of the people of Revolutionary Monmouth County and their actions provides abundant evidence of all the activities discussed in the preceding paragraphs. Readers will probably be surprised to see how many Monmouthers opposed the new Revolutionary government at some point during the war. These readers should remember that the Revolutionary War lasted six years in Monmouth County, and many of the people who opposed the new government at one point supported it at another time. The Revolution was a confusing time for all, and local antagonisms and short-term self-interest generally influenced individual actions at least as much as ideological attachment or disaffection to the Revolutionary cause.

It should also be noted that determining a person's ideological attachment (or disaffection) to the Revolutionary cause based on one or two bits of information is a reckless proposition. For example, a great many disaffected persons were coerced into serving in the militia. Conversely, a great many people with pro-Revolutionary feelings still evaded paying taxes at various times. Even veterans of the Continental Army should not necessarily be treated as zealous patriots, since most enlisted men were lured to serve more by bounties than by ideology. In short, readers should not put too much value in any one fact. Only when a string of facts can be put together for an individual is it safe to assume a person's attitudes on the Revolution. For a more complete discussion of the value and shortfalls of the documents used to compile this roster, an annotated list is provided at the back of this roster.

Historical interpretations aside, this roster is of great value as a genealogical resource. It is by far the most comprehensive roster of eighteenth-century Monmouth County (listing about six thousand of the roughly twelve thousand Revolutionary period inhabitants of the county), and few localities have had comparable rosters compiled. The roster contains the names of nearly every white male adult in Monmouth County at this time. The white male emphasis is unavoidable because of the bias inherent in eighteenth-century documents. Nevertheless, this roster also lists a great many women, African-Americans, and a handful of children and others. Unfortunately, this roster cannot possibly list everyone in Monmouth County at the time of Revolution since many people are simply missing from the historical record.

Even with these limitations in mind, the value of this roster as a genealogical and historical resource should not be underestimated. For genealogical researchers, this roster offers an unprecedented opportunity to gather information on the inhabitants of Revolutionary Monmouth County. For historical researchers, this roster provides the opportunity to assess the level of popular support for the Revolution, the zealousness of local leadership, and the pervasiveness of anti-Revolutionary and anti-social activity in a troubled county. For both genealogical and historical researchers, this roster serves as an example of how the disciplines of genealogy and history can compliment each other. It is the author's fervent wish that rosters and other projects that bridge history and genealogy will become more common.

Acknowledgments

I would like to thank some of the people who helped make the completion of this roster possible. No one was a greater help than Barbara Carver Smith, C.G. Barbara's years of tutoring on Monmouth County genealogy and geography were invaluable, as was her thorough editing of this roster. Also extremely helpful were two members of the historical community, David J. Fowler, Ph.D., of the David Library of the American Revolution, and Betty Epstein, of the New Jersey State Archives. Both David and Betty frequently alerted me to obscure manuscripts and assisted me in gathering information on Monmouth County.

Others who deserve my thanks include the entire staffs of the Monmouth County Historical Association and the Monmouth County Archives. The members of both staffs deserve recognition for their good humor and flexibility in the face of my many requests for photocopies and extended research hours. Also a great help was Judy Adelberg, my mother, whose critical proofreading helped sharpen the focus of this roster. To Joseph Donohue, I offer special thanks for compiling the information from numerous muster rolls. Without Joe's efforts, this roster would still be months from

Roster of the People of Revolutionary Monmouth County

completion. Finally, I would like to thank Doranne Brown, Richard Walling, James Raleigh, and the many others who continue to patronize my research on Revolutionary Monmouth County.

Note on the Documents Used to Compile This Roster

This roster compiles the information contained in about 150 documents or sets of documents, each of which lists a great many residents of Revolutionary Monmouth County. These documents -- including petitions, muster rolls, tax lists, and court records -- give important genealogical and historical information on large numbers of specific individuals. An annotated list of these documents is provided at the end of the roster.

When deciding which documents to include or omit from this roster, the author based his decision on whether the document in question provided important information on a large number of individuals. Only those documents (or sets of documents) that provide information on ten or more individuals are included in this roster.

Other manuscript sources (such as letters, diaries, newspaper reports, and veteran recollections) contain excellent information on some of the people listed in this roster, but these sources have been left out of this roster because they are too numerous to include. However, even with these types of documents excluded, the author firmly believes that this roster is by far the most comprehensive Revolutionary era roster compiled for any county in the Middle Colonies.

Of course, serious researchers should check the letters, diaries, newspaper reports, and veteran recollections relating to Revolutionary Monmouth County. Those interested in checking these types of documents should consult the author's research database, a copy of which is in the library of the Monmouth County Historical Association, 70 Court Street, Freehold, New Jersey 07728. This database contains information relating to the American Revolution in Monmouth County compiled from thousands of manuscripts and hundreds of published sources. To further assist researchers, the database provides numerous indexes and finding guides.

Note on the Dates Listed in This Roster

For each person listed in this roster, the information on that person is arranged chronologically by date. For many people, such as militiamen who served their bimonthly tours continuously throughout the war, dates are not listed. The dates that are listed have been abbreviated in the modern format, so that all dates are listed by month/day/year. When the day of the month is unknown, only the month and year are listed. All years listed in the roster are from the 1700s. Examples follow:

- 6/5/79   indicates the date, June 5, 1779
- 9/80   indicates the date, September 1780

Note on the Accuracy of Family Names

Anyone who has waded through the confusing spellings found in old documents will appreciate the difficulties associated with compiling a roster from multiple sources. In addition to the problems inherent in reading old, handwritten documents (damaged paper, archaic symbols and abbreviations, etc.), it must be remembered that the writers of these documents were frequently barely literate themselves. The result is that a great many names are spelled idiosyncratically, and ethnic Dutch, German, and Irish names are often Anglicized.

Unfortunately, some family names are spelled as many as four different ways. Whenever possible, the author has attempted to place names under the most common eighteenth-century spelling. In addition, the author, with the invaluable assistance of Barbara Carver Smith (a certified genealogist with extensive Monmouth County roots), has made every attempt to cross-reference confusing spellings so that readers will be able to find their ancestors when these people are listed under unfamiliar spellings. Still, it is probable that some unusual spellings eluded thorough cross-referencing. If there is any doubt about the names listed in this roster, the documents used in compiling this roster are listed and annotated in the back of this publication.

A

Able, William
   Signer, Petition Favoring Quick Division of Prize Money, 12/79
Abraham, George
   Laborer, Pennsylvania Salt Works, intermittent 8/76-6/77
Ackman, Peter   Middletown
   Corporal, Militia
Adams, Thomas   Upper Freehold
Adams, William   Upper Freehold
Aiken, Abiel   Dover
   Militia Volunteer, Prior to the First General Militia Muster, 6/76
   Signer, Petition to Better Defend Toms River Area, 5/18/77
   Coroner, 1778
   Signer, Petition for Stricter Militia Law, 5/31/79
   Signer, Articles of Retaliation, 6/79
   Justice of the Peace, 1780-3
   Signer, Petition Encouraging Free Trade, 5/12/81
   leased horse team to Continental Quarter Master 12/81
   Signer, Petition Against Association for Retaliation 12/81
   Signer, Petition Urging Action Against the Pine Robbers, 12/27/81
Aiken, Timothy   Shrewsbury
   recipient of poor relief
Aiken, William
   Private, Militia, captured 2/13/77
Aikers, William
   Private, Militia
Airey, Cornelius
   Private, New Jersey Volunteers, enlisted 4/1/77   dead 7/6/77
Akin, see Aiken
Albert, Aaron   Upper Freehold
Alexander, James   Upper Freehold
   deceased prior to 1779
Allen, Adam   Shrewsbury
   indicted for Misdemeanor, 1/81
Allen, Andrew   Shrewsbury
   of Squan
   indicted for Misdemeanor, 5/82
Allen, Andrew, Jr.   Shrewsbury
   indicted for Misdemeanor, 5/82
Allen, Benjamin
   convicted of Misdemeanor 6/3/78, went to Phila. without pass

Allen, Caleb			Shrewsbury
   recipient of poor relief
Allen, David
   Private, New Jersey Volunteers, enlisted 11/23/76 deserts 6/23/77
   Private, Militia, delinquent 8/80
   Convicted of Misdemeanor, 1/23/81
Allen, Ebenezer			Shrewsbury
Allen, Ephraim			Shrewsbury
   Private, Militia
Allen, Gabriel			Shrewsbury
Allen, George			Shrewsbury
   indicted for Misdemeanor, 1/81
   indicted for Misdemeanor, 11/81
   Signer, Petition Against Association for Retaliation 12/81
   leased horse team to Continental Quarter Master 12/81
Allen, George
   deceased prior to 1779
Allen, Hannah			Shrewsbury
   Delegate, Friends' Quarterly Meeting, 1774-82
Allen, Henry			Upper Freehold
Allen, Isaac			Upper Freehold
   estate inquisitioned for Forfeiture, 4/5/79
   estate confiscated
Allen, Jacob			Dover
   Corporal, Continental Army
   Signer, Petition Against Association for Retaliation 12/81
Allen, Jacob			Freehold
   Sergeant, Militia
   present at the capture of the British ship, Britannia, 12/31/79
   Signer, Articles of Retaliation, 6/79
Allen, Jacob			Middletown
   Private, Militia, serves as substitute 2/10/78, delinquent 3/11/78
   Signer, Petition Opposing the Return of Tories 6/10/83
Allen, Jacob
   Private, New Jersey Volunteers, enlisted 12/3/76 dead 3/22/77
Allen, James
   Private, New Jersey Volunteers
Allen, James			Shrewsbury
   Private, Militia
Allen, Jedediah			Shrewsbury
   exempt from Militia service, 2/10/78
Allen, Jeremiah			Dover

Militia Volunteer, Prior to the First General Militia Muster, 6/76
Laborer, Pennsylvania Salt Works, intermittent 8/76-6/77
Allen, John   Dover
    Private Militia
Allen, Jonathan
    arrested for Disaffection, 1/77
    joins Continental Army in exchange for Pardon, 5/23/77
    Private, New Jersey Volunteers, 4/78
Allen, Joseph   Dover and Shrewsbury
    Militia Volunteer, Prior to the First General Militia Muster, 6/76
    sells good to Pennsylvania Salt Works, intermittent 8/76-10/76
    Captain, Associated Loyalists
    Convicted of High Treason, 4/25/82
    Refugee in New York, 1782
    estate confiscated
Allen, Judah
    Private, Militia
Allen, Lydia   Shrewsbury
    sells produce to Continental Army, 7/80
    Delegate, Friends' Quarterly Meeting, 1781
Allen, Mary
    indicted for Misdemeanor, 8/79
    indicted for Misdemeanor, 5/82
Allen, Nathan   Shrewsbury
    arrested for Disaffection, 11/76
    accused of being active in Tory Rebellions of 12/76
    deceased prior to 1779
Allen, Nathan   Upper Freehold
    Private, Militia
Allen, Obadiah   Shrewsbury
Allen, Samuel   Shrewsbury
    indicted for Misdemeanor, 5/82
    indicted for Misdemeanor, 11/82
Allen, Samuel, Jr.   Shrewsbury
    Private, Continental Army
Allen, William   Upper Freehold
    plundered by Tories, 12/76
    Private, New Jersey Volunteers
Allison, John
    Private, State Troops, enlists 5/81
Alward, *see* Alwood
Alwood, John

Signer, Articles of Retaliation, 6/79
indicted for Deceit, 8/79
indicted for Deceit, 5/82
Signer, Petition Supporting Quick Division of Militia Prizes, no date

Amey, *see* Arney

Anderson, Abraham   Dover
    Militia Volunteer, Prior to the First General Militia Muster, 6/76

Anderson, Abraham   Upper Freehold

Anderson, Abraham, Jr.   Upper Freehold
    Private, Militia

Anderson, David
    Captain, Militia
    indicted for Misdemeanor, 1/81
    Signer, Association for Opposing the Return of Tories, 1783

Anderson, Elias   Dover
    Private, Militia

Anderson, Elijah   Dover
    Signer, Association for Opposing the Return of Tories, 1783

Anderson, George
    Captain, Militia

Anderson, James   Freehold

Anderson, John   Freehold
    Adjutant, Militia
    Signer, Petition Calling for Action Against the Disaffected, 2/21/77
    Signer, Petition for Settlement of Quartermaster Debts, 9/6/77
    Signer, Petition for Stricter Militia Law, 5/31/79
    Judge of the Court of Oyer and Terminer, 8/79
    sells produce to Continental Army, 5/80
    Signer, Articles of Retaliation, 6/79
    Signer, Petition Favoring Quick Division of Prize Money, 12/79

Anderson, John   Dover
    Private, Militia

Anderson, John, Jr.   Freehold
    Militia Volunteer, Prior to the First General Militia Muster, 6/76
    Private, Militia
    Signer, Petition for Stricter Militia Law, 5/31/79
    Signer, Petition Supporting Retaliation, 9/17/80
    sells produce to Continental Army, 5/80
    Signer, Association for Opposing the Return of Tories, 1783

Anderson, Joshua   Upper Freehold
    witness at Monmouth Court, 6/78

Anderson, Joshua   Freehold

    Signer, Petition for Stricter Militia Law, 5/31/79
Anderson, Kenneth   Freehold
    Adjutant, Militia
    Clerk of the Monmouth County Courts, 1776-1782
    Signer, Petition Urging Action Against the Disaffected, 3/14/77
    Signer, Articles of Retaliation, 6/79
    sells produce to Continental Army, 5/80
    Signer, Petition Supporting Retaliation, 9/17/80
    Grand Juror, Court of Oyer and Terminer, 11/82
Anderson, Mary   Upper Freehold
    household head
Anderson, Matthew (Mathias)   Freehold
    Signer, Articles of Retaliation, 6/79
Anderson, Thomas
    Lieutenant, Militia
    Signer, Petition Encouraging Free Trade, 5/12/81
Anderson, Tunis   Middletown
    Private, Militia
    present at the capture of the British ship, Britannia, 12/31/79
Anderson, Walter   Middletown
Anderson, William   Middletown
    Private, Militia
    Private, State Troops, enlists 6/80
Anderson, William   Middletown
    Signer, Articles of Retaliation, 6/79
    Signer, Petition Favoring Quick Division of Prize Money, 12/79
Andrews, Isaac
    Private, New Jersey Volunteers
Andrews, John   Upper Freehold
    Signer, Petition Urging Action Against Disaffected
        & Favoring Retaliation, 5/12/81
Andrews, Joseph   Freehold
    Private, Militia, captured 2/13/77
    Private, State Troops, enlists 9/77
Ansley, Ozias
    Private, New Jersey Volunteers
Antonides, John   Freehold
    house burned by British Army, 6/28/78
    Signer, Petition for Stricter Militia Law, 5/31/79
    Signer, Articles of Retaliation, 6/79
    Grand Juror, Court of Oyer and Terminer, 5/82
Antrum, Isaac   Upper Freehold

Applegate, Anthony
   sells produce to Continental Army, 5/80
Applegate, Bartholomew   Dover
   Militia Volunteer, Prior to the First General Militia Muster, 6/76
   Laborer, Pennsylvania Salt Works, intermittent 8/76-6/77
Applegate, Daniel   Dover
   Militia Volunteer, Prior to the First General Militia Muster, 6/76
Applegate, Daniel   Freehold
   Private, Militia
   Private, State Troops, enlists 5/81
   Private, Continental Army
Applegate, David
   Signer, Association for Opposing the Return of Tories, 1783
Applegate, Ebenezer   Freehold
Applegate, Ebenezer   Shrewsbury
   Private, Militia
   indicted for Misdemeanor, 5/82
   indicted for Misdemeanor, 11/82
Applegate, Henry   Upper Freehold
   substitute, Militia, 2/10/78
   Private, Militia
   sells produce to Continental Army, 5/80
Applegate, Jacob   Dover
   Signer, Petition Supporting Issuing of New Jersey Currency, 1771
   Militia Volunteer, Prior to the First General Militia Muster, 6/76
   Township Overseer of the Poor, 1783
Applegate, James   Upper Freehold
   Private, Militia
Applegate, John   Freehold
   Private, Militia
   indicted for Riot, 1/81
Applegate, John, Jr.   Freehold
   indicted for Riot & Trespass, and Misdemeanor 1/20/78
Applegate, Joseph
   sells produce to Continental Army, 5/80
Applegate, Obadiah   Upper Freehold
Applegate, Richard   Middletown
   Signer, Petition Opposing the Return of Tories 6/10/83
Applegate, Robert   Freehold
   Private, Militia
   Private, State Troops, enlists 9/77
Applegate, Sylvester   Dover

Roster of the People of Revolutionary Monmouth County

Applegate, Sylvester
    Militia Volunteer, Prior to the First General Militia Muster, 6/76
Applegate, Sylvester   Shrewsbury
    Private, Militia
Applegate, Sylvester   Upper Freehold
Applegate, William
    Private, Militia
Appleton, Thomas
    Private, New Jersey Volunteers, enlisted 3/15/77 deserts 6/23/77
Armstrong, James   Shrewsbury
    Private, Militia, delinquent 8/80
Armstrong, John   Freehold and Upper Freehold
    Private, Militia
    Signer, Petition Urging Action Against Disaffected
    & Favoring Retaliation, 5/12/81
Arney, David   Middletown
    Private, Militia
    Private, Continental Army, Jonathan Forman's Company, 10/77
Arney, Elizabeth   Middletown
    household head
Arney, Joseph   Upper Freehold
Arnold, William   Middletown
    Signer, Petition Opposing the Return of Tories 6/10/83
Arnold, Zibe   Middletown
Arwin, James   Freehold
    Private, Militia
    Private, State Troops
Arwin, John
    Private, Militia
    Private, State Troops
Ashley, Rachel   Middletown
    household head
Ashmore, Joseph   Upper Freehold
    Militia Volunteer, Prior to the First General Militia Muster, 6/76
Ashton, John   Upper Freehold
Ashton, John, Jr.   Upper Freehold
Ashton, Joseph   Upper Freehold
    Laborer, Pennsylvania Salt Works, intermittent 8/76-6/77
    convicted of Assault, 1/20/78
Ashton, Robert
    Private, Militia
    Private, State Troops
Ashton, Thomas

    Private, Militia
    Private, State Troops
Atchison, *see* Atkinson
Atkinson, John   Upper Freehold
    Signer, Petition Urging Action Against Disaffected
        & Favoring Retaliation, 5/12/81
Atkinson, Robert
    Laborer, Pennsylvania Salt Works, intermittent 8/76-6/77
Attin, Jacob
    Private, Militia
Attison, Robert   Dover
Auger, *see* Aulger
Aulger, Benjamin   Shrewsbury
    Private, Militia, delinquent 8/80
Aulger, Joseph   Shrewsbury
    Private, Militia, delinquent 8/80
Aulger, William   Shrewsbury
    Private, Militia, delinquent 8/80
Aumack, Jacob   Middletown
    Signer, Petition Opposing Slave Manumission, 2/2/74
Aumack, John
    Private, Militia
    Signer, Articles of Retaliation, 6/79
Aumack, John   Middletown
    Private, Militia
    Signer, Articles of Retaliation, 6/79
    present at the capture of the British ship, Britannia, 12/31/79
    Signer, Petition Favoring Quick Division of Prize Money, 12/79
Aumack, Stephen   Shrewsbury
Aumack, Tunis   Dover
Aumack, Tunis   Middletown
    Sergeant, Militia
    Signer, Petition Opposing Slave Manumission, 2/2/74
    present at the capture of the British ship, Britannia, 12/31/79
Aumack, William
    Private, Militia
    Signer, Articles of Retaliation, 6/79
    present at the capture of the British ship, Britannia, 12/31/79
Aumonck, Aumuch, *see* Aumack
Ayres, Bennajah   Shrewsbury
Ayres, Jesse
    Private, New Jersey Volunteers, enlisted 1/3/77 deserts 3/28/77

Roster of the People of Revolutionary Monmouth County

Ayres, John — Shrewsbury
Ayres, Richard
   Private, Militia
Ayres, William
   Minister
Ayres, Zephaniah — Shrewsbury

B

Babcock, Simeon (Simon) — Shrewsbury
   accused of being active in Tory Rebellions of 12/76
   refuses Militia service
   twice arrested
Babcock, Thomas — Shrewsbury
   Private, Militia, delinquent 8/80
Backus, John — Upper Freehold
   accused of being active in Loyalist Rebellion of 12/76
Bacon, Aaron
   Private, New Jersey Volunteers
Bacon, Hannah
   indicted for Misdemeanor, 7/83
Bacon, John — Stafford
   indicted for Misdemeanor, 1/81
   indicted for High Treason, 11/81
   pine robber
Bagley, Jem
   Private, New Jersey Volunteers
Bailey, Elias — Middletown
   Baptist
   estate inquisitioned for Forfeiture, 7/4/77
   Refugee in New York, 1782
   estate confiscated
   Signer, Petition Opposing Slave Manumission, 2/2/74
Bailey, James
   Private, New Jersey Volunteers
Bailey, Jesse
   Private, New Jersey Volunteers
Bailey, John
   Private, Militia, drafted into Continental Army 5/78
Bailey, Jonathan
   son of Nathaniel
   Private, Militia

Roster of the People of Revolutionary Monmouth County

    present at the capture of the British ship, Britannia, 12/31/79
    indicted for Misdemeanor, 1/81
    indicted for Misdemeanor, 11/81
Bailey, Joseph   Middletown
    estate inquisitioned for Forfeiture, 7/4/77
    estate confiscated
    Signer, Petition Opposing Slave Manumission, 2/2/74
Bailey, Joseph
    convicted of Misdemeanor, 6/3/78
    indicted for Misdemeanor, 5/82
Bailey, Nathaniel
Bailey, Patrick   Middletown
    Private, State Troops, enlists 6/80
    Signer, Articles of Retaliation, 6/79
Bailey, Patrick
    Private, New Jersey Volunteers, deserted 1/8/78
    convicted of Misdemeanor, 1/23/81
Baird, Barzilla   Freehold
    Signer, Articles of Retaliation, 6/79
    Signer, Petition Encouraging Free Trade, 5/12/81
    Signer, Petition for Renewing Guard at Toms River, 12/10/81
    Grand Juror, Court of Oyer and Terminer, 11/82
Baird, David   Upper Freehold
    Signer, Articles of Retaliation, 6/79
    sells produce to Continental Army, 5/80
Baird, David   Upper Freehold
    Captain, Militia
    Signer, Articles of Retaliation, 6/79
    Signer, Petition Supporting Retaliation, 1780
    Signer, Petition Supporting Retaliation, 9/17/80
    sells produce to Continental Army, 5/80
    Juror, Court of Oyer and Terminer, 5/82
        fined for missing jury duty
Baird, James
    Signer, Petition Urging Compensation for Inflated Money, 5/22/83
Baird, John   Freehold
    Militia Volunteer, Prior to the First General Militia Muster, 6/76
    Signer, Articles of Retaliation, 6/79
    Signer, Petition Supporting Retaliation, 1780
    Grand Juror, Court of Oyer and Terminer, 12/80
    Juror, Court of Oyer and Terminer, 5/82
    Signer, Association for Opposing the Return of Tories, 1783

Baird, John, Jr.   Freehold
Baird, Joseph
   Signer, Petition Urging Compensation for Holders of Inflationary Money, 5/22/83
Baird, Obadiah   Freehold
   Private, Militia
Baird, Zebulon   Freehold
   Signer, Petition for Settlement of Quartermaster Debts, 9/6/77
   sells clothing to Continental Army, 3/78
   Signer, Articles of Retaliation, 6/79
   Signer, Petition Supporting Retaliation, 9/17/80
   Grand Juror, Court of Oyer and Terminer, 12/80
   Signer, Petition Urging Compensation for Inflated Money, 5/22/83
Baker, Jeremiah
   Laborer, Pennsylvania Salt Works, intermittent 8/76-6/77
Baker, John   Shrewsbury
   Signer, Association for Opposing the Return of Tories, 1783
Baley, see Bailey
Ball, Sylvanus
   Private, New Jersey Volunteers
Balser, William   Shrewsbury
Bangs, Richard   Shrewsbury
   Private, Militia
Banks, Joseph
   Sergeant, New Jersey Volunteers, captured 8/22/77
Barber, Edward   Freehold
Barber, Hugh
   Private, New Jersey Volunteers
Barber, John
   Private, New Jersey Volunteers, enlisted 12/30/76 deserts 2/21/77
Barber, James
   arrested for Disaffection, 11/76
Barber, Peter   Freehold
Barber, Peter   Middletown
   Private, Militia, delinquent 11/29/78, delinquent 6/11/80
Barber, Thomas   Freehold
   Surgeon, Militia
   Signer, Articles of Retaliation, 6/79
   Signer, Petition Against Loyalist Auction Commissioners, 3/24/79
Barclay, George
   indicted for Misdemeanor, 5/82
Barclay, James

Private, New Jersey Volunteers, captured 8/22/77
Barclay, Thomas
    indicted for Misdemeanor, 5/82
Bard, Samuel, Dr.   Shrewsbury
    flees to Staten Island
    estate inquisitioned for Forfeiture, 7/2/77
    estate confiscated
Barkalow, Arthur   Upper Freehold
    plundered by Tories, 12/76
    sells produce to Continental Army, 5/80
    Juror, Court of Oyer and Terminer, 11/82
Barkalow, Cornelius   Freehold
    Private, Continental Army
    Signer, Articles of Retaliation, 6/79
    sells produce to Continental Army, 5/80
Barkalow, Daniel   Freehold
    sells produce to Continental Army, 5/80
    sells produce to Continental Army, 7/80
    indicted for Misdemeanor, 5/82
Barkalow, David   Upper Freehold
    Private, Militia
    sells produce to Continental Army, 5/80
Barkalow, Derrick   Freehold
Barkalow, Derrick   Upper Freehold
    witness at Monmouth Court, 6/78
    sold sheep to Continental Commissary 7/80
    Juror, Court of Oyer and Terminer, 11/82
Barkalow, John   Freehold
    Signer, Articles of Retaliation, 6/79
    Signer, Association for Opposing the Return of Tories, 1783
Barkalow, John
    Signer, Articles of Retaliation, 6/79
    Signer, Association for Opposing the Return of Tories, 1783
Barkalow, Obadiah   Middletown
    Baptist
Barkalow, Richard   Upper Freehold
    plundered by Tories, 12/76
Barkalow, Samuel   Freehold
Barkalow, Stephen   Freehold
    Signer, Articles of Retaliation, 6/79
Barkalow, William   Upper Freehold
    Militia Volunteer, Prior to the First General Militia Muster, 6/76

Barker, Michael
    Private, New Jersey Volunteers
Barker, Nathaniel   Shrewsbury
    estate confiscated
Barkley, see Barclay
Barnaby, John
    Private, New Jersey Volunteers, dead 7/1/78
Barnett, Christian
    Private, New Jersey Volunteers, enlisted 5/2/77 dead 9/3/77
Bart, Abram
    Private, New Jersey Volunteers, enlisted 1/13/77 dead 5/2/77
Barrett, Caleb
    Sergeant, New Jersey Volunteers
Barrett, James
    Private, New Jersey Volunteers
Barrett, Thomas
    Private, New Jersey Volunteers
Barton, Gilbert   Upper Freehold
    tavern keeper
    sells produce to Continental Army, 5/80
    leased horse team to Continental Quarter Master 12/81
Barzilla, Joseph   Upper Freehold
    estate confiscated
Bass, Thomas   Upper Freehold
Bates, James
    Private, Militia
Bates, Richard   Middletown
Bay, George
    Private, New Jersey Volunteers
Beagle, see Bedell
Beakes, Abraham   Upper Freehold
    Militia Volunteer, Prior to the First General Militia Muster, 6/76
Beakes, Edmund   Upper Freehold
    Militia Volunteer, Prior to the First General Militia Muster, 6/76
    plundered by Tories, 12/76
    Juror, Court of Oyer and Terminer, 11/82
        fined L8 for missing jury duty
Beamhem, see Benham
Beck, William
    Private, Militia
Bedell, Israel   Middletown
    flees for New York, June 1778

estate inquisitioned for Forfeiture, 6/8/78
Bedell, Joel   Middletown
   Signer, Petition Opposing Slave Manumission, 2/2/74
   Highway Surveyor, 1778
   Signer, Articles of Retaliation, 6/79
   present at the capture of the British ship, Britannia, 12/31/79
   Juror, Court of Oyer and Terminer, 5/82
      fined for missing jury duty
Bedell, Joel, Jr.   Middletown
   Private, Militia
   indicted for Misdemeanor, 5/82
Bedell, John
   accused of being active in Tory Rebellions of 12/76
Bedell, Thomas   Middletown
   Private, Militia
   Signer, Petition Opposing Slave Manumission, 2/2/74
   present at the capture of the British ship, Britannia, 12/31/79
Bedle, Beedell, see Bedell
Beekman, Gerardus   Shrewsbury
   refuses Militia service
   estate inquisitioned for Forfeiture, 7/4/77
   estate confiscated
Beers, Benjamin   Upper Freehold
Beers, John   Upper Freehold
Beers, Joseph   Middletown
Beers, Nathan   Middletown
   Signer, Petition Opposing the Return of Tories 6/10/83
Bell, David
   indicted for Misdemeanor, 1/20/78
Bell, James   Shrewsbury
   arrested for Disaffection, 11/76
   accused of being part of Samuel Wright's Tory Association 11/76
   accused of being active in Tory Rebellions of 12/76
   indicted for Horse Stealing, 1/81
   indicted for Misdemeanor, 5/82
Bell, Jeremiah
   indicted for Counterfeiting, 1/81
   indicted for Misdemeanor, 5/82
Bell, John
   Private, Militia
   Private, Continental Army
Bell, Mary

indicted for Misdemeanor, 11/82
Bell, Richard
    indicted for Felony, 11/81
Benham, Hannah   Freehold
    household head
    Signer, Petition for Stricter Militia Law, 5/31/79
Benham, John   Freehold
    house burned by British Army, 6/28/78
    Signer, Petition for Stricter Militia Law, 5/31/79
    Grand Juror, Court of Oyer and Terminer, 11/82
Benham, Richard
    Private, Militia
Bennam, see Benham
Bennett, Aaron
    indicted for Misdemeanor, 5/82
    indicted for Misdemeanor, 7/83
Bennett, Barnes (Barnts)   Middletown
    Lieutenant, Militia, court martialed, 2/21/81
    Signer, Articles of Retaliation, 6/79
    Juror, Court of Oyer and Terminer, 5/82
        fined for missing jury duty
Bennett, Benjamin
    Private, New Jersey Volunteers, enlisted 12/15/76
        pressed into British Navy
Bennett, David   Stafford
    indicted for Misdemeanor, 5/82
    indicted for Misdemeanor, 11/82
Bennett, Edward   Shrewsbury
    Private, Militia
Bennett, Elisha
    indicted for Misdemeanor, 7/83
Bennett, Garret   Shrewsbury and Middletown
    sells produce to Continental Army, 5/80
    Constable, 1783
    helps keep the poor
Bennett, Gerardus   Shrewsbury
    helps keep the poor
Bennett, Henry   Shrewsbury
    recipient of poor relief
Bennett, Hendrick   Middletown
    indicted for Misdemeanor, 1/81
    indicted for Misdemeanor, 11/81

Bennett, Hendrick			Shrewsbury
Bennett, Jacob			Middletown
   Signer, Petition Opposing Slave Manumission, 2/2/74
   Signer, Articles of Retaliation, 6/79
   Juror, Court of Oyer and Terminer, 5/82
      fined for missing jury duty
Bennett, Jacob			Middletown
   Private, Militia
Bennett, Jared			Shrewsbury
   helps keep the poor
Bennett, Jeremiah		Shrewsbury
   Private, Militia, drafted into Continental Army 5/78
   Private, State Troops
   Private, Continental Army
   arrested for Disaffection, 11/76
   accused of being part of Samuel Wright's Tory Association 11/76
   accused of being active in Tory Rebellions of 12/76
   Signer, Petition Urging Action Against the Pine Robbers, 12/27/81
Bennett, John			Middletown
   blacksmith
   Overseer of Highways, 1774
   sells produce to Continental Army, 5/80
   Juror, Court of Oyer and Terminer, 5/82
      fined for missing jury duty
   Signer, Petition Opposing the Return of Tories 6/10/83
Bennett, John, Jr.		Middletown
   Private, Militia
   accused of being active in Tory Rebellions of 12/76
   Signer, Petition Favoring Quick Division of Prize Money, 12/79
   present at the capture of the British ship, Britannia, 12/31/79
   sells produce to Continental Army, 5/80
   Signer, Petition Opposing the Return of Tories 6/10/83
Bennett, Joseph
   accused of being active in Tory Rebellions of 12/76
   indicted for Murder, 8/79
   Signer, Petition Against Association for Retaliation 12/81
Bennett, Joshua			Shrewsbury
   Captain, Militia
   Signer, Petition to Better Provision Militia, 2/25/78
Bennett, Joshua
   arrested for Disaffection, 11/76
Bennett, Mary			Shrewsbury

recipient of poor relief
Bennett, Michael   Stafford
  Private, Militia
  Laborer, Pennsylvania Salt Works, intermittent 8/76-6/77
Bennett, Nathaniel   Dover
  Signer, Petition Urging Action Against the Pine Robbers, 12/27/81
Bennett, Samuel   Dover
  Signer, Petition Urging Action Against the Pine Robbers, 12/27/81
Bennett, Samuel   Stafford
  Private, Continental Army
Bennett, Theodore, Jr.
  arrested for Disaffection, 11/76
Bennett, Theophilus (Theodore?)
  accused of being active in Tory Rebellions of 12/76
Bennett, Thomas   Shrewsbury
Bennett, Thomas, Jr.   Shrewsbury
  Private, Militia
  arrested for Disaffection, 11/76
  indicted for Murder, 8/79
Bennett, Tobias
  Private, New Jersey Volunteers
Bennett, William   Middletown
  Signer, Petition Opposing Slave Manumission, 2/2/74
  Overseer of Highways, 1776
  sells clothing to Continental Army, 3/78
  Juror, Court of Oyer and Terminer, 8/79
    fined L30 for missing all or some of jury duty
  sells produce to Continental Army, 5/80
  Juror, Court of Oyer and Terminer, 12/80
    fined L3 for missing all or some of jury duty
  Constable, 1781
Bennett, William   Middletown
  Private, Militia
Bennett, William   Shrewsbury
Bennett, Winnant   Middletown
Bennington, Israel   Stafford
  Private, Militia
Bentley, John
  Signer, Petition Supporting Retaliation, 9/17/80
Berkeley, Charles
  sells produce to Continental Army, 5/80
Berdine, *see also* Bodine

Berdine, John
    Private, New Jersey Volunteers
Berdine, Walter   Middletown
    Private, Militia
    Private, State Troops
Berdine, William
    Signer, Petition Favoring Quick Division of Prize Money, 12/79
Berry, George
    Signer, Association for Opposing the Return of Tories, 1783
Berry, Henry
    Private, Militia
    Signer, Articles of Retaliation, 6/79
Berry, John   Freehold
    Private, Militia
    Private, Continental Army
    Signer, Articles of Retaliation, 6/79
Berry, William   Freehold
Bethel, John
    indicted for Misdemeanor, 11/82
Bigelow, Daniel
    Laborer, Pennsylvania Salt Works, intermittent 8/76-6/77
Bigelow, Samuel   Dover
    Lieutenant of Militia Volunteers, Prior to the First General Militia Muster, 6/76
    Captain, Militia
    Signer, Petition to Better Defend Toms River Area, 5/18/77
    Signer, Articles of Retaliation, 6/79
Billenger, Jacob
    Private, New Jersey Volunteers
Billenger, John
    Private, New Jersey Volunteers
Billenger, Jonathan
    Private, New Jersey Volunteers
Billinghouse, *see* Boltenhouse
Bills, Rachel   Freehold
    household head
Bills, Silvanus
    Private, New Jersey Volunteers, enlisted: 12/23/76 dead: 2/9/77
Bills, Thomas   Freehold
    estate confiscated
Bills, William   Freehold
Bills, William   Freehold

Roster of the People of Revolutionary Monmouth County

Bird, Henry
    Private, New Jersey Volunteers, deserts 6/28/78
Bird, James   Dover
    Private, Militia
Bird, John   Dover
    Private, Militia
Bird, John, Jr.   Dover
Bird, Jonathan
    Private, Militia
    present at the capture of the British ship, Britannia, 12/31/79
Bird, Richard
    Private, New Jersey Volunteers, enlisted 1/15/77 deserts 2/1/77
    Pine Robber
Bird, William   Dover
    Private, Militia
Birdsill, Uriah   Dover
    Militia Volunteer, Prior to the First General Militia Muster, 6/76
Bishop, Joseph   Shrewsbury
    Sergeant, Militia
    Signer, Petition Supporting Retaliation, 9/17/80
Bishop, Noah   Upper Freehold
    Private, Militia, delinquent 8/80
Black Mingo   Upper Freehold
    African-American house holder
Black Sam
    sells produce to Continental Army, 5/80
Black, William
    Private, New Jersey Volunteers, deserts 7/2/77
Blackney, William   Upper Freehold
    plundered by Tories, 12/76
Blackwood, George
    indicted for Misdemeanor, 11/81
Blackwood, John
    Private, New Jersey Volunteers, enlisted 3/13/77 dead 4/16/77
Blair, William   Middletown
    Baptist
    Signer, Petition Against Confiscation Commissioners, 5/8/79
    Signer, Petition Encouraging Free Trade, 5/12/81
    Juror, Court of Oyer and Terminer, 11/82
    donates to Charity Fund for Stevenson Family, 5/83
    Signer, Petition Opposing the Return of Tories 6/10/83
Blake, John

Blake, Thomas   Upper Freehold
    Lieutenant, Militia
Blake, William   Upper Freehold
Blassom, *see* Bloricum
Bloodgood, Joseph
    Laborer, Pennsylvania Salt Works, intermittent 8/76-6/77
Bloricum, David   Shrewsbury
    Militia Volunteer, Prior to the First General Militia Muster, 6/76
Boannin, John
    Private, New Jersey Volunteers
Bodine, *see also* Berdine
Bodine, Abraham   Upper Freehold
Bodine, Walter
    Private, Militia
Bogart, Cornelius
    Private, New Jersey Volunteers, enlisted for bounty 4/79
Bogart, Samuel
    Private, Militia
Boggs, James   Shrewsbury
    Doctor
    Surgeon, New Jersey Volunteers
    Vestryman, Anglican Christ Church, 1770-6
    Signer, Petition Opposing Slave Manumission, 2/2/74
    estate inquisitioned for Forfeiture, 3/31/79
    estate confiscated
Boggs, Mary   Shrewsbury
    household head
Boice, Adam   Freehold
    Signer, Articles of Retaliation, 6/79
Boice, Adam, Jr.   Freehold
Boice, Jane   Freehold
    household head
Boice, Jonathan
    Private, New Jersey Volunteers
Boler, Philip
    Private, New Jersey Volunteers, deserts 7/27/77
Boltenhouse, Bedford   Upper Freehold
    Private, Militia
    Private, State Troops, enlists 5/81
Boltenhouse, Samuel   Upper Freehold
    Militia Volunteer, Prior to the First General Militia Muster, 6/76
Bolton, John   Upper Freehold

Private, Continental Army
Bolton, William
  Private, New Jersey Volunteers
Boman, see Bowman
Bonham, Jeremiah   Shrewsbury
  Private, Militia
Bonham, Jeremiah, Jr.   Shrewsbury
  Private, Militia
Bonham, John
  Private, New Jersey Volunteers, enlisted: 4/15/77 dead: 6/3/77
Bonham, Malacia
  Private, New Jersey Volunteers
Bonham, Richard
  substitute, Militia, 2/10/78
Book, George
  Private, New Jersey Volunteers
Borden, Amos
  indicted for Misdemeanor, 8/79
Borden, Francis   Upper Freehold
  Juror, Court of Oyer and Terminer, 8/79
    fined L30 for missing all or some of jury duty
  convicted of Misdemeanor, 1/81
  Signer, Petition Against Association for Retaliation 12/81
Borden, James   Upper Freehold
  indicted for Misdemeanor, 5/82
Borden, Jesse
  Private, Militia
Borden, Jo Boy   Upper Freehold
  Free Black householder
Borden, Joel   Shrewsbury
Borden, John   Shrewsbury
  estate inquisitioned for Forfeiture, 4/1/80
Borden, John, Jr.   Shrewsbury
  rented Confiscated Tory estate
  Private, Militia
  indicted for Misdemeanor, 8/79
Borden, Joseph   Shrewsbury
Borden, Philip   Shrewsbury
  convicted of Misdemeanor, 6/3/78
Borden, Richard   Shrewsbury
Borden, Samuel   Shrewsbury
  Militia Volunteer, Prior to the First General Militia Muster, 6/76

Borden, Thomas   Shrewsbury
   indicted for Misdemeanor, 1/81
Borden, Thomas, Jr.   Shrewsbury
Borden, William   Freehold
   Private, Militia
   Private, State Troops
Bordine, *see* Berdine *and* Bodine
Bordsill, *see* Birdsill
Borne, Thomas   Upper Freehold
   Militia Volunteer, Prior to the First General Militia Muster, 6/76
Bostick, William
   Militia Volunteer, Prior to the First General Militia Muster, 6/76
   Private, Militia
Boughner, Henry
   Private, New Jersey Volunteers
Boughner, Philip
   Private, New Jersey Volunteers
Boulser, John
   Private, Militia
   Private, Continental Army
Bower, John
   Private, Militia
   Signer, Association to Oppose the Return of Tories, 1783
Bower, John
   Private, New Jersey Volunteers
Bower, Joseph   Upper Freehold
Bower, William   Upper Freehold
Bowman, Coleman
   Private, Militia
Bowman, John   Freehold
   Private, Militia
   Signer, Articles of Retaliation, 6/79
   Signer, Association to Oppose the Return of Tories, 1783
Bowman, Samuel   Upper Freehold
Bowne, Andrew
   Juror, Court of Oyer and Terminer, 11/82
Bowne, Andrew   Middletown
   Convicted of High Treason, 4/25/82
   estate confiscated
Bowne, Ann   Middletown
   household head
Bowne, Catherine   Middletown

household head
Bowne, Daniel
   Private, Militia, delinquent 10/9/80
Bowne, David						Freehold
   Private, Militia
   Signer, Petition Urging Compensation for Inflated Money, 5/22/83
Bowne, Elias						Middletown
   Private, Militia, serves as substitute 2/78
   Signer, Articles of Retaliation, 6/79
   present at the capture of the British ship, Britannia, 12/31/79
   Signer, Petition Supporting Retaliation, 9/17/80
   Signer, Petition Opposing the Return of Tories 6/10/83
Bowne, Elizabeth					Shrewsbury
   Delegate, Friends' Quarterly Meeting, 1778
Bowne, James						Middletown
   Signer, Petition Favoring Quick Division of Prize Money, 12/79
Bowne, John
   Coroner, 1778, fined L3 for not attending Court, 1/78
Bowne, John
   estate inquisitioned for Forfeiture, 7/4/77
   estate confiscated
Bowne, Jonathan					Freehold
   Refugee in New York, 1782
Bowne, Jonathan
   indicted for Misdemeanor and Seditious Words, 6/78
   sells produce to Continental Army, 5/80
   Juror, Court of Oyer and Terminer, 5/82
   Grand Juror, Court of Oyer and Terminer, 11/82
   Signer, Petition Urging Compensation for Inflated Money, 5/22/83
Bowne, Joseph					Freehold
   Corporal of Militia, Prior to the First General Militia Muster, 6/76
   Signer, Articles of Retaliation, 6/79
   Juror, Court of Oyer and Terminer, 8/79
       fined L30 for missing all or some of jury duty
   sells produce to Continental Army, 5/80
   Juror, Court of Oyer and Terminer, 5/82
   Grand Juror, Court of Oyer and Terminer, 11/82
   Signer, Petition Urging Compensation for Inflated Money, 5/22/83
Bowne, Joseph
   Private, Militia
   sells produce to Continental Army, 5/80
Bowne, Nathaniel

Roster of the People of Revolutionary Monmouth County

Private, Continental Army
Bowne, Obadiah   Shrewsbury
   lost slaves during the war
Bowne, Obadiah
   Convicted of High Treason, 4/25/82
   Refugee in New York, 1782
Bowne, Peter
   Militia Volunteer, Prior to the First General Militia Muster, 6/76
   Private, Militia
Bowne, Phoebe   Middletown
   household head
Bowne, Robert   Shrewsbury
   Delegate, Friends' Quarterly Meeting, 1778-9
Bowne, Robert, Jr.   Shrewsbury
   Private, New Jersey Volunteers, enlisted for bounty 4/79
Bowne, Samuel   Middletown
Bowne, Samuel   Middletown
   Private, Militia
Bowne, Samuel, Jr.   Middletown
Bowne, Susannah   Middletown
   household head
Bowne, William   Middletown
   Private, Militia
Bowne, William   Middletown
   Baptist
   Commissioner of Appeals, 1774-7 and 1780-1
   Signer, Articles of Retaliation, 6/79
   present at the capture of the British ship, Britannia, 12/31/79
   Signer, Petition Supporting Retaliation, 1780
   Juror, Court of Oyer and Terminer, 5/82
   Juror, Court of Oyer and Terminer, 11/82
   Township Collector, 1782-3
   Overseer of the Poor, 1782-3
   donates to Charity Fund for Stevenson Family, 5/83
Boyce, *see* Boice
Boyer, Amos   Shrewsbury
   orphan child
   recipient of poor relief
Boyer, Eve   Shrewsbury
   listed on Militia return 6/29/80
Boyer, John
   arrested for Disaffection, 11/76

accused of being active in Tory Rebellions of 12/76
Boyles, Anthony
    Private, New Jersey Volunteers, captured
Boyles, Caleb
    Private, New Jersey Volunteers
Boyles, Martin
    Private, New Jersey Volunteers
Brack, Burbridge   Upper Freehold
Braden, Jospeh   Upper Freehold
Bradley, William
    Private, New Jersey Volunteers, enlists: 10/5/77 deserts: 12/16/77
Bradshaw, James   Freehold
Bradshaw, John
    convicted of Assault, 12/80
Braisted, *see* Brasted
Brand, James
    Private, New Jersey Volunteers
Brand, John   Dover
Brand, John   Shrewsbury
    Private, Militia
Brand, Thomas   Shrewsbury
    Private, Militia, delinquent 8/80
Brand, William   Shrewsbury
    helps keep the poor
Brand, William, Jr.   Shrewsbury
    Private, Militia, delinquent 8/80
Brannon, John
    Private, New Jersey Volunteers
Brasted, Isaac   Freehold
    Private, Militia
    Private, State Troops
Bray, Daniel
    indicted for Trespass, 1/20/78, convicted 6/78
    convicted of Misdemeanor, 1/81
    indicted for Misdemeanor, 5/82
Bray, Samuel   Freehold and Middletown
    Baptist
    Overseer of the Poor, 1770
    Signer, Petition Opposing Slave Manumission, 2/2/74
    sells clothing to Continental Army, 3/78
    Signer, Petition Against Confiscation Commissioners, 5/8/79
    Signer, Articles of Retaliation, 6/79

    Overseer of Highways, 1782
    Juror, Court of Oyer and Terminer, 5/82
       fined for missing jury duty
    Signer, Petition Opposing the Return of Tories 6/10/83
Bray, Samuel   Middletown
    Signer, Petition Opposing the Return of Tories 6/10/83
Brearley, David   Upper Freehold
    Lawyer
    Colonel, Militia
    Signer, Petition in Support of Richard Lloyd, 1/31/76
    Signer, Petition in Support of William Barton, 1/31/76
    Chief Justice, State of New Jersey, 1779
    Justice of the Court of Oyer and Terminer, 12/80
Brearley, John   Upper Freehold
    indicted for Misdemeanor, 1/78
    Private, Militia, drafted into Continental Army 5/78
    Private, State Troops
Breese, John   Shrewsbury
    Private, Militia
    Private, Continental Army
Breese, Samuel   Shrewsbury
    Colonel, Militia
    Member, Shrewsbury Committee of Observation
    lost slaves during the war
Brelone, Samuel   Shrewsbury
Brent, John   Upper Freehold
Brewer, Aaron   Shrewsbury
Brewer, Aaron, Jr.   Shrewsbury
    indicted for Murder, 8/79
Brewer, Abram
    Private, Militia
Brewer, Adam
    Private, New Jersey Volunteers
Brewer, Benjamin   Shrewsbury
    indicted for Misdemeanor, 1/81
    indicted for Misdemeanor, 11/81
Brewer, Elezares   Shrewsbury
Brewer, Elias   Shrewsbury
    Private, Militia
Brewer, Eleanor   Upper Freehold
    household head
Brewer, George   Shrewsbury

Brewer, Hannah Shrewsbury
  household head
Brewer, Harvey Middletown
  Overseer of Highways, 1771
Brewer, Hendrick
  Juror, Court of Oyer and Terminer, 1/78
    fined L5 for not attending all or part of Jury duty
  convicted of Misdemeanor, 12/80
Brewer, Isaac
  Private, New Jersey Volunteers
Brewer, Jacob Shrewsbury
  Private, Militia
  Signer, Petition from Victims of the Association for Retaliation 9/82
Brewer, James Upper Freehold
  Captain, Militia
  Signer, Petition Calling for Action Against the Disaffected, 2/21/77
  Signer, Petition Urging Action Against the Disaffected, 3/14/77
  Juror, Court of Oyer and Terminer, 12/80
    fined L3 for missing all or some of jury duty
  Signer, Petition Against Association for Retaliation 12/81
Brewer, John Freehold
  Private, Militia
Brewer, John Shrewsbury
  Private, Militia
Brewer, John Upper Freehold
Brewer, John
  Private, New Jersey Volunteers, enlisted: 1/4/77 dead: 3/1/77
Brewer, John, Jr. Shrewsbury
  indicted for Misdemeanor, 11/81
  Private, Militia, delinquent 4/82
  indicted for Misdemeanor, 5/82
Brewer, Joshua
  Captain, Militia
Brewer, Mary Shrewsbury
  household head
Brewer, Peter Shrewsbury
  Private, Militia, delinquent, 10/9/80
  indicted for Misdemeanor, 1/81
  indicted for Misdemeanor, 5/82
  indicted for Misdemeanor, 11/82
Brewer, Peter Shrewsbury
  Private, Militia

Roster of the People of Revolutionary Monmouth County

Brewer, Thomas
    takes Loyalty Oath to New Jersey Government, 2/19/77
    Signer, Association for Opposing the Return of Tories, 1783
Brewer, William   Shrewsbury
Briggs, John
    arrested for Disaffection, 1/77
Brightly, John   Upper Freehold
Brindley, Elizabeth   Shrewsbury
    listed on Militia return 6/29/80
Brindley, George   Shrewsbury
    Private, Militia
    Signer, Articles of Retaliation, 6/79
    Signer, Petition Supporting Retaliation, 9/17/80
Brindley, Jacob   Freehold
    Private, Militia
    Private, State Troops
Brindley, John   Freehold
    Lieutenant, Militia
    Signer, Petition Favoring Quick Division of Prize Money, 12/79
    sells produce to Continental Army, 5/80
    sells produce to Continental Army, 7/80
    indicted for Misdemeanor, 1/81
    Signer, Petition for Renewing Guard at Toms River, 12/10/81
    Juror, Court of Oyer and Terminer, 5/82
    Coroner, 1783
    Signer, Petition Supporting Quick Division of Militia Prizes, no date
Brindley, John   Shrewsbury
    Private, Militia
    Signer, Articles of Retaliation, 6/79
    sells produce to Continental Army, 5/80
    Signer, Petition Urging Action Against the Pine Robbers, 12/27/81
Brindley, Reap
    indicted for Misdemeanor, 1/81
Brindley, Rhea
    sells produce to Continental Army, 5/80
Brindley, Samuel   Dover
    indicted for Misdemeanor, 1/81
    indicted for Misdemeanor, 11/81
    estate confiscated
Brindley, Samuel   Shrewsbury
    Private, Militia
Brindley, William   Shrewsbury

Brine, John
  Private, Militia
Bringley, Margaret   Shrewsbury
  household head
Bringley, Samuel   Shrewsbury
Bringley, William   Shrewsbury
Brinley, *see* Brindley *and* Bringley
Brison, Ursula   Freehold
  household head
Britain, Briton, *see* Brittan
Brittan, Abraham   Middletown
  Private, Militia
Brittan, Abraham   Upper Freehold
Brittan, Benjamin   Middletown
Brittan, Israel
  Militia Volunteer, Prior to the First General Militia Muster, 6/76
  Private, Militia
Brittan, Israel   Freehold
  Private, Militia
  Ensign, New Jersey Volunteers
  estate inquisitioned for Forfeiture, 3/18/79
  estate confiscated
Brittan, John   Upper Freehold
Brittan, Richard   Shrewsbury
  Laborer, Pennsylvania Salt Works, intermittent 8/76-6/77
Brittan, Richard   Upper Freehold
  Militia Volunteer, Prior to the First General Militia Muster, 6/76
  Signer, Petition in Support of Richard Lloyd, 1/31/76
Brittan, William   Upper Freehold
  Private, New Jersey Volunteers
  Private, Continental Army
Britten, Britton, *see* Brittan
Brock, Mary   Upper Freehold
  household head
Broderick, Absalom
  Private, Militia
Broderick, Thomas   Upper Freehold
  Signer, Petition Against Association for Retaliation 12/81
Broderick, William
  Private, Militia
Brodgom, Samuel   Upper Freehold

Roster of the People of Revolutionary Monmouth County

Brooks, David   Freehold
  Signer, Articles of Retaliation, 6/79
  Signer, Association for Opposing the Return of Tories, 1783
  Signer, Petition Urging Compensation for Inflated Money, 5/22/83
Brooks, Jonathan   Freehold
  Private, Militia
  Private, State Troops, enlisted 6/80
Brooks, Jonathan   Middletown
  Private, Militia
  Signer, Petition Opposing the Return of Tories 6/10/83
Broom, Joseph
  Signer, Articles of Retaliation, 6/79
Brower, see Brewer
Brown, Abraham   Upper Freehold
  Laborer, Pennsylvania Salt Works, intermittent 8/76-6/77
Brown, Andrew   Dover
  Signer, Petition to Better Defend Toms River Area, 5/18/77
  Signer, Petition Urging Action Against the Pine Robbers, 12/27/81
Brown, Andrew   Middletown
  Captain, Militia
  Signer, Petition Against Loyalist Auction Commissioners, 3/24/79
  present at the capture of the British ship, Britannia, 12/31/79
Brown, Asher   Upper Freehold
  Private, Continental Army
Brown, Benjamin
  Laborer, Pennsylvania Salt Works, intermittent 8/76-6/77
Brown, Catherine   Shrewsbury
  orphan child
  recipient of poor relief
Brown, Daniel   Middletown
  indicted for Misdemeanor, 6/78
Brown, David
  Private, New Jersey Volunteers, enlisted 12/30/76 deserts 2/9/77
  Private, Militia
  sells clothing to Continental Army, 3/78
Brown, Dinah   Shrewsbury
  child "put out"
  recipient of poor relief
Brown, George   Shrewsbury
  Corporal, New Jersey Volunteers
Brown, George, Jr.   Shrewsbury
Brown, Hendrick   Middletown

Private, Militia, delinquent 11/29/78, delinquent 6/11/80
Brown, Jacob   Upper Freehold
Brown, Jacob   Upper Freehold
Brown, James
   Sergeant, New Jersey Volunteers
Brown, Jeremiah   Shrewsbury
   Grand Juror, Court of Oyer and Terminer, 5/82
   Signer, Association for Opposing the Return of Tories, 1783
   helps keep the poor
Brown, John   Middletown
   Private, New Jersey Volunteers, captured 8/22/77
   estate confiscated
Brown, John   Upper Freehold
   Signer, Articles of Retaliation, 6/79
   Signer, Petition Favoring Quick Division of Prize Money, 12/79
Brown, John   Upper Freehold
   Sergeant, Continental Army
   Private, Militia
Brown, Jonathan
   convicted on two counts of Seditious Words, 6/3/78
Brown, Joseph   Freehold and Middletown
   Private, State Troops, enlists 6/80
   sells produce to Continental Army, 5/80
   Signer, Petition Urging Action Against Disaffected
      & Favoring Retaliation, 5/12/81
   Signer, Petition Opposing the Return of Tories 6/10/83
Brown, Joseph   Stafford
   Private, New Jersey Volunteers, captured
   Private, Militia
   indicted for Misdemeanor, 7/83
Brown, Joseph   Stafford
   Private, Militia
Brown, Joshua
   Laborer, Pennsylvania Salt Works, intermittent 8/76-6/77
Brown, Nancy
   indicted for Misdemeanor, 7/83
Brown, Obadiah   Middletown
   estate confiscated
Brown, Patty
   indicted for Misdemeanor, 7/83
Brown, Peter
   Private, New Jersey Volunteers, enlisted 1/3/77 deserts 3/21/77

Brown, Phoebe
    indicted for Misdemeanor, 5/82
Brown, Samuel   Dover
    Privateer Captain
    Salt works owner at Forked River
    Signer, Petition Against Association for Retaliation 12/81
    Signer, Petition Urging Action Against the Pine Robbers, 12/27/81
    Signer, Association for Opposing the Return of Tories, 1783
Brown, Samuel   Freehold
    Private, State Troops
    indicted for Misdemeanor, 7/83
Brown, Sarah
    wife of Jonathan
    convicted of Seditious Words, 6/3/78
    indicted for Seditious Words, 8/79
Brown, Solomon   Upper Freehold
    accused of being active in Loyalist Rebellion of 12/76
    indicted for Misdemeanor, 1/78
Brown, Thomas   Dover
    Private, Continental Army
Brown, Thomas
    Private, New Jersey Volunteers, enlisted: 2/3/77   dead: 3/4/77
Brown, William   Freehold
    Private, New Jersey Volunteers, captured 8/22/77
    Private, Militia
    Private, State Troops
    Signer, Articles of Retaliation, 6/79
Bruce, John   Middletown
    donates to Charity Fund for Stevenson Family, 5/83
Bruce, John, Jr.   Middletown
    indicted for Misdemeanor, 5/82
Bruce, Mathias
    Corporal, Militia, captured 2/13/77
Bruere, *see* Brewer
Bruff, Thomas
    Private, New Jersey Volunteers, enlisted 5/19/77   deserts 7/15/77
Bryant, Christopher
    Private, New Jersey Volunteers
Bryant, James
    Private, Continental Army, Jonathan Forman's Company
        deserted prior to 10/77
Bryant, Patrick

Private, New Jersey Volunteers
Bryant, William
  Private, Militia
  Private, Continental Army, Jonathan Forman's Company
    dead 9/15/77
Bryde, Patrick
  Private, New Jersey Volunteers, enlisted 12/29/76 deserts 3/20/78
Buck, Aaron   Dover
  Militia Volunteer, Prior to the First General Militia Muster, 6/76
  sells goods to Pennsylvania Salt Works, 8/76-10/76
  Signer, Petition to Better Defend Toms River Area, 5/18/77
  Signer, Articles of Retaliation, 6/79
  leased horse team to Continental Quarter Master 12/81
  indicted for Misdemeanor, 11/82
Buck, Ephraim   Shrewsbury
  Lieutenant, Militia
  Signer, Petition to Better Provision Militia, 2/25/78
  Signer, Articles of Retaliation, 6/79
  Signer, Petition Favoring Quick Division of Prize Money, 12/79
  Signer, Petition for Renewing Guard at Toms River, 12/10/81
  Signer, Association for Opposing the Return of Tories, 1783
Buckalew, Abraham   Shrewsbury
Buckalew, Arthur
  Juror, Court of Oyer and Terminer, 11/82
Buckalew, George   Upper Freehold
Buckalew, George
  Private, New Jersey Volunteers, enlisted 4/2/77 deserts 7/19/77
  indicted for Assault, 6/3/78
Buckalew, Gilbert
  Private, New Jersey Volunteers, deserted 10/19/77
Buckalew, Isaac
  Signer, Articles for Opposing the Return of Tories, 1783
Buckalew, James   Upper Freehold
  indicted for Misdemeanor, 6/3/78
  indicted for Robbery, 8/79
Buckalew, John
  Ensign, Militia
  Signer, Petition to Better Provision Militia, 2/25/78
Buckalew, John   Upper Freehold
  Captain, Militia
  Constable, 1783
Buckalew, Richard   Upper Freehold

Buckalew, Richard
    Private, New Jersey Volunteers, enlisted 12/19/76 deserts 5/27/77
    indicted for Assault, 6/3/78
Buckalew, Samuel
    Private, Militia, hires substitute 2/10/78
    Private, State Troops, enlisted 6/80
    Signer, Association for Opposing the Return of Tories, 1783
Buckaloo, see Buckalew
Buddle, see Bedell
Bunting, Ramath
    Private, Militia
    Private, State Troops
    Private, Continental Army
Bunton, see Bunting
Burch, Elizabeth   Upper Freehold
    household head
Burch, Jeremiah   Upper Freehold
Burcham, Uriah   Upper Freehold
Burdge, Abel   Shrewsbury
Burdge, David   Middletown
    Overseer of Highways, 1776
    Signer, Petition from Victims of the Association for Retaliation 9/82
Burdge, Jacob   Dover
    indicted for Misdemeanor, 8/79
    indicted for Misdemeanor, 1/81
    Delegate, Friends' Quarterly Meeting, 1782
    arrested as "Tory freebooter"
Burdge, John   Dover
    Private, New Jersey Volunteers, captured 8/22/77
    indicted for Misdemeanor, 8/79
    imprisoned for "robbery"
Burdge, John   Middletown
    Baptist
    Private, Militia, delinquent 11/29/78
    indicted for Misdemeanor, 5/82
Burdge, John   Shrewsbury
    Refugee in New York, 1777
Burdge, Jonathan
    arrested for Disaffection, 11/76
    accused of being active in Tory Rebellions of 12/76
    Private, New Jersey Volunteers
    joins Continental Army in exchange for Pardon, 5/23/77

indicted for Murder, 8/79
convicted of Murder, 12/80
Burdge, Joseph   Shrewsbury
    Private, Militia
    Private, Continental Army
Burdge, Joseph
    Signer, Petition Supporting Issuing of New Jersey Currency, 1771
    Signer, Petition from Victims of the Association for Retaliation 9/82
Burdge, Mary   Shrewsbury
    household head
Burdge, Richard   Shrewsbury
    Private, Militia
    Private, Continental Army
    Signer, Petition Favoring Quick Division of Prize Money, 12/79
    helps keep the poor
Burdge, Uriah   Shrewsbury
    indicted for Misdemeanor, 1/81
Burdge, William
    Private, Militia, delinquent 10/9/80
Burham, Martin   Shrewsbury
    Private, Militia, delinquent 8/80
Burk, David   Shrewsbury
    of Rumson
    Private, Militia
    helps keep the poor
    indicted for Misdemeanor, 1/81
Burk, James   Upper Freehold
Burk, John
    Private, New Jersey Volunteers
Burk, Richard
    Corporal, New Jersey Volunteers
Burk, Samuel   Freehold
    Private, Militia, serves as substitute 2/10/78
Burke, *see* Burk
Burling, Samuel
    arrested for Disaffection, 1777
Burnes, John
    Private, New Jersey Volunteers, enlisted 12/25/76 dead 3/3/77
Burnes, Terence
    Private, New Jersey Volunteers
Burnes, Thomas
    Private, New Jersey Volunteers, enlisted 4/4/77 dead 8/15/77

Burnes, William   Shrewsbury
    deceased prior to 1779
Burnes, William   Shrewsbury
Burnes, William
    Private, New Jersey Volunteers, enlisted 12/27/76 dead 3/3/77
Burnett, Benjamin
    Private, New Jersey Volunteers, enlisted 2/12/77 dead 4/1/77
Burris, Sarah   Shrewsbury
    recipient of poor relief
Burroughs, *see* Burrowes
Burrowes, Eden
    Private, Militia, captured 2/13/77
Burrowes, Edward   Middletown
    Signer, Petition Opposing Slave Manumission, 2/2/74
Burrowes, John, Sr.   Middletown
    Committeeman
    Signer, Petition Opposing Slave Manumission, 2/2/74
    Signer, Petition Urging Compensation for Raid Victims, 5/25/79
    Signer, Petition for Stricter Militia Law, 5/31/79
    Mill Owner, Merchant
Burrowes, John, Jr.   Middletown
    Major, Continental Army
    indicted for Trespass, 1/78
    rented Confiscated Tory estate, prior to 5/79
    Sheriff, Monmouth County, 1782-4
    Signer, Association for Opposing the Return of Tories, 1783
    Signer, Petition Opposing the Return of Tories 6/10/83
Burrowes, Thomas
    Laborer, Pennsylvania Salt Works, intermittent 8/76-6/77
Burtis, William   Upper Freehold
    Signer, Petition Affirming Loyalty of Moses Ivens, 3/12/77
    sells produce to Continental Army, 5/80
    Signer, Petition Urging Action Against Disaffected
        & Favoring Retaliation, 5/12/81 -- opposes Retaliation clause
    Signer, Petition Against Association for Retaliation 12/81
Burton, Jesse   Middletown and Shrewsbury
    indicted for Misdemeanor, 8/79
    estate confiscated
Burton, John
    Private, Militia, delinquent 4/82
Busby, Samuel   Dover
    Militia Volunteer, Prior to the First General Militia Muster, 6/76

Butler, Daniel   Shrewsbury
    deceased prior to 1779
Butler, Obadiah
    Private, New Jersey Volunteers, enlisted 12/15/76 dead 11/9/77
Byrnes, *see* Burnes

C

Caesar, Abraham   Shrewsbury
    free black householder
Caesar, Free   Upper Freehold
    free black householder
Cafford, John
    Juror, Court of Oyer and Terminer, 5/82
       fined for missing jury duty
Cain, Jesse
    Private, New Jersey Volunteers
Cain, John   Shrewsbury
Cain, Thomas
    Private, New Jersey Volunteers, deserted 12/23/78
Cahill, Lawrence   Upper Freehold
    Private, Militia
    Signer, Petition in Favor of Daniel Longstreet, 11/21/80
Cairns, *see* Kearns
Calaghan, Daniel   Upper Freehold
Caldwell, Thomas   Middletown
    Private, Militia
Callahan, *see* Calaghan
Calvert, Samuel
    sells produce to Continental Army, 5/80
Camble, *see* Camel *and* Campbell
Camburn, Joseph   Stafford
    Private, Militia
Camburn, Nathaniel
    Private, Militia, drafted into Continental Army 5/78
    Private, State Troops
Camel, John
    Private, Militia
    sells produce to Continental Army, 5/80
Cameron, Duncan
    Private, New Jersey Volunteers
Campbell, Alexander

    Private, New Jersey Volunteers
Campbell, Colin   Upper Freehold
    schoolmaster
    arrested for Disaffection, 1777
Campbell, Duncan
    Signer, Petition for Stricter Militia Law, 5/31/79
    Signer, Association for Opposing the Return of Tories, 1783
Campbell, John   Freehold
    Signer, Petition Supporting Issuing of New Jersey Currency, 1771
    Quartermaster, Militia, resigns 10/9/77
    Signer, Petition for Stricter Militia Law, 5/31/79
    Signer, Articles of Retaliation, 6/79
    Signer, Petition Encouraging Free Trade, 5/12/81
    Juror, Court of Oyer and Terminer, 5/82
Campbell, John   Upper Freehold
    Sergeant, New Jersey Volunteers
    Private, Militia
    Private, State Troops, enlists 5/81
Campbell, Lewis
    Private, Continental Army, Jonathan Forman's Company, 10/77
Campbell, Neil
    Sergeant, New Jersey Volunteers
Campbell, Robert
    Private, New Jersey Volunteers
Canady, *see* Kennedy
Caner, Levi   Upper Freehold
Card, Andrew   Shrewsbury
    sells produce to Continental Army, 5/80
Carey, Bryant
    Private, New Jersey Volunteers
Carhart, John   Middletown
    Juror, Court of Oyer and Terminer, 5/82
    Juror, Court of Oyer and Terminer, 11/82
Carhart, John, Jr.   Middletown
    Baptist
    Private, Militia
    present at the capture of the British ship, Britannia, 12/31/79
Carhart, Matthew
    Private, State Troops
Carhart, Robert
    Private, Militia
Carhart, Samuel

Captain, Militia, captured 10/18/76
Signer, Petition to Better Provision Militia, 2/25/78
Signer, Petition Against Loyalist Auction Commissioners, 3/24/79
Signer, Articles of Retaliation, 6/79
present at the capture of the British ship, Britannia, 12/31/79
Signer, Association for Opposing the Return of Tories, 1783
Signer, Petition Opposing the Return of Tories 6/10/83
Carhart, Thomas   Middletown
   Private, Militia
   present at the capture of the British ship, Britannia, 12/31/79
Carl, *see* Carle
Carle, Adrian   Middletown
   Private, Militia
   present at the capture of the British ship, Britannia, 12/31/79
   Private, State Troops, enlists 6/80
   Signer, Petition Opposing the Return of Tories 6/10/83
Carle, John   Freehold
Carle, Uriah
   Private, Militia
Carle, William   Freehold
Carlton, Francis   Freehold
   Corporal, Militia
Carlton, Lewis
   Signer, Articles of Retaliation, 6/79
Carman, Benjamin   Middletown
Carman, Elijah   Middletown
Carman, Samuel   Middletown
   Overseer of Highways, 1771 and 1780
   Signer, Petition Opposing Slave Manumission, 2/2/74
   Commissioner of Appeals, 1783
Carman, Samuel, Jr.   Middletown
   Private, New Jersey Volunteers, enlisted 12/25/76 deserts 1/28/77
   Signer, Petition Opposing Slave Manumission, 2/2/74
Carney, Alexander
   Corporal, New Jersey Volunteers
Carney, James
   Private, New Jersey Volunteers
Carr, Andrew   Shrewsbury
   Private, Militia, delinquent 8/80
   Laborer, Pennsylvania Salt Works, intermittent 8/76-6/77
Carr, Ebenezer
   Private, State Troops, enlisted 6/80

Roster of the People of Revolutionary Monmouth County

    sells produce to Continental Army, 7/80
Carr, James
    Laborer, Pennsylvania Salt Works, intermittent 8/76-6/77
Carr, Thomas   Dover
    Signer, Petition Urging Action Against the Pine Robbers, 12/27/81
Carr, William
    Private, Militia, serves as substitute 2/10/78, delinquent 3/11/78
Carrow, *see* Conrow
Carson, William
    accused of being active in Tory Rebellions of 12/76
Carter, John
    Private, New Jersey Volunteers, enlisted 11/1/76 dead 4/26/77
Carter, Jonathan
    Private, New Jersey Volunteers
Carter, Moses   Dover
    Signer, Petition Urging Action Against the Pine Robbers, 12/27/81
Carter, Richard
    Private, Continental Army, Jonathan Forman's Company, 10/77
Carter, Thomas   Upper Freehold
    Private, New Jersey Volunteers
Cartwright, Henry
    Private, New Jersey Volunteers
Case, William
    Private, Militia
    Private, State Troops
Casler, George
    Signer, Articles of Retaliation, 6/79
    Signer, Petition Encouraging Free Trade, 5/12/81
Casler, Robert   Freehold
Casley, Samuel   Upper Freehold
Cassleman, William   Stafford
    Private, Militia
Cate, Wardell
    estate confiscated
Caterlone, Ebenezer
    Private, Continental Army, Jonathan Forman's Company,
        deserted prior to 10/77
Cavana, John   Upper Freehold
    Militia Volunteer, Prior to the First General Militia Muster, 6/76
    Private, Militia
    Private, Continental Army
Cavana, Patrick

Private, New Jersey Volunteers
Caviner, *see* Cavana
Cawtrill, *see* Cottrell
Celes, David
    Private, Militia
    Private, Continental Army
Chacey, *see* Chasey
Chadwick, Elihu (Elisha)   Shrewsbury
    Signer, Articles of Retaliation, 6/79
    Signer, Petition Favoring Quick Division of Prize Money, 12/79
    Vestryman, Anglican Christ Church, 1780-2
    Signer, Petition for Renewing Guard at Toms River, 12/10/81
    Signer, Petition Supporting Quick Division of Militia Prizes, no date
Chadwick, Francis   Shrewsbury
    holds tavern license, 1775
    Vestryman, Anglican Christ Church, 1783
Chadwick, Jeremiah   Shrewsbury
    Lieutenant, Militia
    Sideman, Anglican Christ Church, 1779
Chadwick, John   Dover
    Signer, Articles of Retaliation, 6/79
    Vestryman, Anglican Christ Church, 1780
    Signer, Petition Against Association for Retaliation 12/81
Chadwick, Thomas   Shrewsbury
    Captain, Militia
    Signer, Petition to Better Provision Militia, 2/25/78
    Signer, Petition Urging Action Against the Disaffected, 3/14/77
    Vestryman, Anglican Christ Church, 1778-9 and 1783,
        Church Warden, 1779
    Signer, Articles of Retaliation, 6/79
    rented Confiscated Tory estate, prior to 5/79
    Signer, Petition Favoring Quick Division of Prize Money, 12/79
    Signer, Petition Supporting Retaliation, 9/17/80
    Grand Juror, Court of Oyer and Terminer, 12/80
    Signer, Petition for Renewing Guard at Toms River, 12/10/81
    leased horse team to Continental Quarter Master 12/81
    Grand Juror, Court of Oyer and Terminer, 7/83
    Signer, Petition Supporting Quick Division of Militia Prizes, no date
Chadwick, William   Shrewsbury
    Sideman, Anglican Christ Church, 1782
Chamberlain, Aaron   Dover
    Private, Militia

Chamberlain, Henry
   Private, Militia
Chamberlain, Job   Dover
   indicted for Misdemeanor, 11/81
Chamberlain, James   Upper Freehold
   Signer, Petition for Stricter Militia Law, 5/31/79
   sells produce to Continental Army, 5/80
Chamberlain, John   Dover
Chamberlain, John, Esq.   Upper Freehold
   Juror, Court of Oyer and Terminer, 1/78
      fined L5 for not attending all or part of Jury duty
   Signer, Petition Against Association for Retaliation 12/81
Chamberlain, Richard   Shrewsbury
   Private, Militia, deserts 6/79
Chamberlain, Richard   Upper Freehold
   Militia Volunteer, Prior to the First General Militia Muster, 6/76
   sells produce to Continental Army, 7/80
Chamberlain, Samuel   Dover
Chamberlain, Thomas   Stafford
   Private, Militia
Chamberlain, William   Shrewsbury
   Private, New Jersey Volunteers
   Private, Militia
Chambers, Abijah
   Private, New Jersey Volunteers
Chambers, David
   witness at Monmouth Court, 1778
Chambers, James   Freehold
   Private, New Jersey Volunteers
   Private, Militia
Chambers, John   Freehold
   Private, Militia
   Private, State Troops, enlisted 6/80
   Signer, Petition Urging Compensation for Inflated Money, 5/22/83
Chambers, Jonathan
   Private, New Jersey Volunteers
Chambers, Joseph   Shrewsbury
Chambers, Robert
   Private, Militia
Chambers, Thomas   Shrewsbury
Chambers, William   Freehold
   Private, Militia, captured 2/13/77

Signer, Association for Opposing the Return of Tories, 1783
Chambers, William
　　Private, New Jersey Volunteers, enlisted 12/20/76 deserts 8/17/77
　　Private, Militia
Chandler, Azail (Assid)　　Shrewsbury
　　estate inquisitioned for Forfeiture, 7/4/77
　　estate confiscated
Chandler, Benjamin
　　arrested for Disaffection, 11/76
　　accused of being active in Tory Rebellions of 12/76
　　Private, New Jersey Volunteers, dead 10/6/77
Chandler, Pontius　　Shrewsbury
　　Private, Militia
　　indicted on two counts of Seditious Words, 1/81
　　indicted for Contraband Trading and Seditious Words, 11/81
Chandler, William
　　Private, New Jersey Volunteers, enlisted 11/2/76 deserts 3/26/77
Chap, *see* Chapman
Chapman, Abraham
　　sells produce to Continental Army, 5/80
Chapman, John　　Middletown
　　Private, Militia, captured 2/13/77
Chapman, Joseph　　Upper Freehold
　　sells produce to Continental Army, 5/80
Charlton, John　　Upper Freehold
　　Private, Militia
Chasey, Ann　　Middletown
　　household head
Chasey, John　　Middletown
　　Sergeant, Militia
　　Sergeant, Continental Army, Jonathan Forman's Company, 10/77
　　Private, State Troops
　　Signer, Articles of Retaliation, 6/79
　　Signer, Petition Opposing the Return of Tories 6/10/83
Chasey, Pearce　　Middletown
Chasey, Thomas
　　Private Militia
Chasey, William
　　Private, State Troops
Cheeseman, Joseph　　Upper Freehold
　　Juror, Court of Oyer and Terminer, 5/82
　　Juror, Court of Oyer and Terminer, 11/82

Cheeseman, Joseph   Upper Freehold
Cheeseman, Joseph, Jr.   Upper Freehold
   Private, Militia
Cheeseman, William   Upper Freehold
   Signer, Articles of Retaliation, 6/79
   Juror, Court of Oyer and Terminer, 8/79
      fined L30 for missing all or some of jury duty
Cheeseman, William, Jr.   Upper Freehold
   Private, Militia
   Signer, Articles of Retaliation, 6/79
Chew, Richard   Freehold
   Private, Continental Army
   Signer, Articles of Retaliation, 6/79
   Signer, Petition Urging Compensation for Inflated Money, 5/22/83
Childerhouse, John
   Private, Militia
   Private, Continental Army
Childs, Isaac
   Private, New Jersey Volunteers, enlisted 12/21/76 dead 4/7/77
Childs, Isaac   Dover
   Private, State Troops
Chiles, William   Dover
   Militia Volunteer, Prior to the First General Militia Muster, 6/76
Christy, James   Dover
Clark, Alexander   Freehold
   Private, Militia
   Signer, Articles of Retaliation, 6/79
Clark, Alexander
   Private, Militia
   estate inquisitioned for Forfeiture, 7/5/77
   estate confiscated
Clark, Andrew   Freehold
   Signer, Articles of Retaliation, 6/79
   Juror, Court of Oyer and Terminer, 11/82
   Signer, Association for Opposing the Return of Tories, 1783
Clark, Asa
   wife of Samuel
   indicted for Misdemeanor, 1/81
Clark, Cornelius   Freehold and Shrewsbury
   Signer, Petition Opposing Slave Manumission, 2/2/74
   Signer, Petition Urging Compensation for Raid Victims, 5/25/79
   Signer, Articles of Retaliation, 6/79

Clark, Elijah
    Laborer, Pennsylvania Salt Works, intermittent 8/76-6/77
Clark, John   Freehold
    Private, Militia, hires substitute, 2/10/78
    Signer, Articles of Retaliation, 6/79
    Signer, Petition Urging Compensation for Inflated Money, 5/22/83
Clark, John   Middletown
    son of Richard
    Laborer, Pennsylvania Salt Works, intermittent 8/76-6/77
    indicted for Misdemeanor, 8/79
Clark, Nicholas   Freehold
    Signer, Articles of Retaliation, 6/79
    Constable, 1780
    Signer, Petition Encouraging Free Trade, 5/12/81
    Signer, Petition Urging Compensation for Inflated Money, 5/22/83
Clark, Daniel   Middletown
Clark, Daniel   Shrewsbury
Clark, John   Middletown
    Juror, Court of Oyer and Terminer, 5/82
    Signer, Association for Opposing the Return of Tories, 1783
Clark, Mary
    indicted for Misdemeanor, 1/81
Clark, Nicholas
    Private, Militia
    Juror, Court of Oyer and Terminer, 5/82
Clark, Richard   Middletown
Clark, Samuel
    Private, New Jersey Volunteers
    indicted for Misdemeanor, 1/81
Clark, Thomas
    Laborer, Pennsylvania Salt Works, intermittent 8/76-6/77
    indicted for Misdemeanor, 1/78
Clark, William   Freehold
    Private, Militia, captured 2/13/77
Clark, William
    Doctor
Clark, William, Jr.   Dover
    indicted for High Treason, 1/20/78, convicted 6/78
    convicted horse thief
Clayton, Asher   Freehold
    Private, Militia
    Private, State Troops, enlisted 6/80

Clayton, Asher   Freehold
   Private, Militia
   Signer, Articles for Opposing the Return of Tories, 1783
Clayton, Cornelius   Shrewsbury
   Private, Militia, delinquent 8/80
   arrested for Disaffection, 11/76
   accused of being part of Samuel Wright's Tory Association 11/76
   accused of being active in Tory Rebellions of 12/76
   convicted of Misdemeanor, 1/81
Clayton, David   Freehold
   Signer, Petition for Stricter Militia Law, 5/31/79
   sells produce to Continental Army, 5/80
Clayton, David   Middletown
Clayton, David, Jr.   Middletown
Clayton, Edward   Freehold
   Private, Militia, hires substitute 2/10/78
   Juror, Court of Oyer and Terminer, 11/82
Clayton, Elisha   Middletown
   Private, Militia, captured 4/2/77
   Private, New Jersey Volunteers
Clayton, James   Upper Freehold
   Militia Volunteer, Prior to the First General Militia Muster, 6/76
   Signer, Petition Favoring Quick Division of Prize Money, 12/79
Clayton, Jehu
   Private, Militia, delinquent 10/9/80
   Private, New Jersey Volunteers, enlisted 9/5/77 deserts 11/20/78
   indicted for Misdemeanor, 1/81
Clayton, John   Freehold
   Signer, Petition for Stricter Militia Law, 5/31/79
   Signer, Association for Opposing the Return of Tories, 1783
Clayton, John   Upper Freehold
   Private, Militia
   Private, State Troops, enlisted 6/80
   Signer, Association for Opposing the Return of Tories, 1783
Clayton, John
   arrested for Disaffection, 11/76
   accused of being active in Tory Rebellions of 12/76
   indicted for Misdemeanor, 1/81
Clayton, Jonathan   Freehold
   Signer, Petition for Stricter Militia Law, 5/31/79
   Signer, Articles of Retaliation, 6/79
Clayton, Jonathan

Private, Militia
Private, State Troops, enlisted 6/80
Signer, Petition for Stricter Militia Law, 5/31/79
Signer, Articles of Retaliation, 6/79
Clayton, Joseph   Freehold
Private, Militia
Signer, Petition for Stricter Militia Law, 5/31/79
Signer, Articles of Retaliation, 6/79
sells produce to Continental Army, 5/80
Signer, Petition Supporting Retaliation, 9/17/80
Juror, Court of Oyer and Terminer, 11/82
Clayton, Joseph   Freehold
estate inquisitioned for Forfeiture, 3/23/79
estate confiscated
Clayton, Moses   Upper Freehold
witness at Monmouth Court, 1778
Clayton, Noah
Private, Militia
indicted for Assault, 11/82
Clayton, Robert   Freehold
Private, Militia
Private, State Troops, enlisted 6/80
Signer, Association for Opposing the Return of Tories, 1783
Clayton, Samuel
Signer, Articles of Retaliation, 6/79
Clayton, Theodore
arrested for Disaffection, 11/76
Clayton, Thomas   Shrewsbury
Clayton, Thomas, Jr.   Shrewsbury
Private, Militia, delinquent 8/80, delinquent 4/82
accused of being active in Tory Rebellions of 12/76
Clayton, William   Freehold
arrested for Disaffection, 11/76
Clayton, William   Upper Freehold
Clayton, Zebulon   Upper Freehold
Private, Militia
Signer, Petition in Favor of Daniel Longstreet, 11/21/80
Constable, 1782-3
Cleark, John
sells produce to Continental Army, 5/80
Cleark, Samuel
Private, New Jersey Volunteers

Cleavenger, Eleanor　　　　　Upper Freehold
　　household head
Cleavenger, Isaiah　　　　　　Middletown
　　indicted for Misdemeanor, 11/81
Cleavenger, Jesse　　　　　　Upper Freehold
Cleavenger, Job　　　　　　　Upper Freehold
Cleavenger, Samuel　　　　　Upper Freehold
Cleavenger, Thomas　　　　　Upper Freehold
　　Private, Continental Army
Clerk, *see* Cleark
Clevenger, *see* Cleavenger
Clifton, Delaney
　　Private, New Jersey Volunteers
Clinton, George　　　　　　　Freehold
　　Private, Militia
　　Private, State Troops, enlisted 6/80
　　Signer, Articles of Retaliation, 6/79
Clutch, Uriah　　　　　　　　Upper Freehold
Coals, *see also* Coles
Coals, Jacob　　　　　　　　Freehold
　　Private, Militia
　　Private, State Troops
Coals, William　　　　　　　Upper Freehold
Coalton, John
　　Captain, Militia
Coalton, Thomas
　　witness at Monmouth Court, 1778
Cock, David
　　Private, Militia
Cogill, George　　　　　　　Upper Freehold
Coin, Edward
　　Private, New Jersey Volunteers
Coin, Thomas
　　Sergeant, New Jersey Volunteers
Coles, *see also* Coals
Cole, David　　　　　　　　Upper Freehold
　　Private, Militia
Cole, Jacob
　　Private, State Troops, enlisted 6/80
Cole, Richard　　　　　　　Middletown
　　estate inquisitioned for Forfeiture, 7/4/77
　　estate confiscated

Roster of the People of Revolutionary Monmouth County

Cole, William
   Sergeant, Militia
Cole, William
   Private, Militia, captured 2/13/77, dies in prison 3/15/78
Coleman, Elizabeth
   indicted for Misdemeanor, 1/78
Collins, Edward
   Private, Militia
Collins, George
   Sergeant, Militia
Collins, James
   sells goods to Pennsylvania Salt Works, intermittent 8/76-6/77
Collins, John   Middletown
   Lieutenant, Militia
Collins, John   Middletown
   Private, New Jersey Volunteers
   Private, Militia
   present at the capture of the British ship, Britannia, 12/31/79
   indicted for Misdemeanor, 11/82
Collins, Patrick
   Private, New Jersey Volunteers
Collins, Peter
   Private, New Jersey Volunteers, enlisted 1/30/77 deserts 5/19/77
Collins, Thomas
   Private, New Jersey Volunteers, listed as dead 6/28/78
   indicted for Misdemeanor, 11/81
Collins, Zebadiah
   Private, New Jersey Volunteers, enlisted 1/30/77 dead 2/27/77
Colton, see Coalton
Colvin, James   Upper Freehold
   Private, Militia
Colvin, James   Upper Freehold
   Private, Militia
Combs, Campbell
   Corporal, Continental Army, Jonathan Forman's Company, 10/77
Combs, Gilbert   Freehold
Combs, Isaac   Upper Freehold
   Private, Militia
Combs, James   Upper Freehold
   Signer, Petition Supporting Retaliation, 1780
Combs, John, Esq.   Freehold
   Militia Volunteer, Prior to the First General Militia Muster, 6/76

Combs, John — Freehold
    Signer, Petition for Stricter Militia Law, 5/31/79
    sells produce to Continental Army, 5/80
    Signer, Petition Against Association for Retaliation 12/81
    Signer, Petition for Renewing Guard at Toms River, 12/10/81
    Signer, Association for Opposing the Return of Tories, 1783
Combs, John — Freehold
    Private, Militia
Combs, John — Upper Freehold
Combs, Joseph — Freehold
    Sergeant, Militia
    Signer, Articles of Retaliation, 6/79
    Private, State Troops, enlisted 6/80
    Signer, Petition Supporting Retaliation, 9/17/80
    sells produce to Continental Army, 5/80
Combs, Solomon — Freehold
    Signer, Petition for Stricter Militia Law, 5/31/79
    Signer, Articles of Retaliation, 6/79
    Signer, Petition Supporting Retaliation, 1780
    Signer, Petition Encouraging Free Trade, 5/12/81
Combs, Solomon
    substitute, Militia, 2/10/78
    indicted for Misdemeanor, 11/82
Combs, Thomas — Freehold
Combs, Thomas — Upper Freehold
    sells produce to Continental Army, 5/80
Combs, William — Freehold
    Signer, Petition for Stricter Militia Law, 5/31/79
    Signer, Association for Opposing the Return of Tories, 1783
    Signer, Petition Supporting Quick Division of Militia Prizes, no date
Common, William — Middletown
Compton, Aaron
    Private, New Jersey Volunteers
    arrested for Disaffection, 1/77
Compton, Cornelius — Freehold
    Signer, Petition Favoring Quick Division of Prize Money, 12/79
    Signer, Petition Opposing the Return of Tories 6/10/83
Compton, George — Middletown
    Private, State Troops, enlists 5/80
    Private, Continental Army
Compton, Ichabod — Upper Freehold
    Signer, Petition in Favor of Daniel Longstreet, 11/21/80
    Constable, 1782

Compton, Jacob　　　　　　　Upper Freehold
　Private, Militia
Compton, James　　　　　　　Upper Freehold
　Private, Militia
　Private, State Troops, enlists 5/80
Compton, James
　arrested for Disaffection, 1/77
　joins Continental Army in exchange for pardon, 5/23/77
Compton, James
　Private, New Jersey Militia, enlisted 12/26/76　dead 5/17/77
Compton, Job
　Ensign, Militia
　indicted for Misdemeanor, 1/81
Compton, John　　　　　　　Middletown
　Private, Militia
　Signer, Petition in Favor of Daniel Longstreet, 11/21/80
Compton, John　　　　　　　Upper Freehold
　Private, Militia
　Private, Continental Army
　Signer, Petition in Favor of Daniel Longstreet, 11/21/80
Compton, Joseph　　　　　　Middletown
　Private, Militia
　Overseer of Highways, 1775
　arrested for Disaffection, 1/77
Compton, Lewis
　Private, Militia
Compton, Richard　　　　　　Freehold
Compton, William　　　　　　Freehold
Compton, William　　　　　　Freehold
　Laborer, Pennsylvania Salt Works, intermittent 8/76-6/77
Compton, William　　　　　　Middletown
　Private, New Jersey Volunteers
Compton, William　　　　　　Upper Freehold
　Sergeant, Militia
Concas, John
　indicted for Seditious Words, 1/20/78
Condon, Michael
　Private, New Jersey Volunteers
Cone, Richard
　Juror, Court of Oyer and Terminer, 12/80
　　　fined L3 for missing all or some of jury duty
Conine, Cornelius

Private, New Jersey Volunteers, deserted 8/22/77
Conine, Derrick   Freehold
Private, Militia, hires substitute, 2/10/78
Conine, Joseph
Signer, Petition for Stricter Militia Law, 5/31/79
Conk, Anthony
Private, New Jersey Volunteers, enlisted 5/15/77 dead 7/15/77
Conk, Hendrick
Private, Militia
Conk, Henry   Freehold
Private, Militia, delinquent 6/79, delinquent 10/9/80
Conk, John   Freehold
Private, Militia
Conk, Thomas   Freehold
Conklin, Daniel   Dover
Signer, Petition Urging Action Against the Pine Robbers, 12/27/81
Conklin, John   Dover
Juror, Court of Oyer and Terminer, 1/78
   fined L5 for not attending all or part of Jury duty
indicted for Misdemeanor, 11/81
Signer, Petition Urging Action Against the Pine Robbers, 12/27/81
Conklin, John, Jr.   Dover
Signer, Petition Urging Action Against the Pine Robbers, 12/27/81
Conn, Peter   Middletown
Connelly, John
Private, New Jersey Volunteers, enlisted 4/15/77 deserts 3/16/78
Private, Militia
Private, State Troops
Private, Continental Army
Connett, Matthew   Freehold
Private, Militia
Private, State Troops
Connor, David
Private, New Jersey Volunteers, captured
Connor, Thomas
Private, New Jersey Volunteers, deserted 7/2/77
Conover, *see also* Covenhoven
Conover, Benjamin
Signer, Association for Opposing the Return of Tories, 1783
Conover, Elias
Militia Volunteer, Prior to the First General Militia Muster, 6/76
Private, Militia

Signer, Articles of Retaliation, 6/79
Conover, Elias
    Private, Militia
Conover, Hendrick
    Signer, Association for Opposing the Return of Tories, 1783
Conover, John
    Private, Militia
Conover, John
    Captain, State Troops
    Signer, Association for Opposing the Return of Tories, 1783
Conover, Mathias
    Signer, Articles of Retaliation, 6/79
Conover, Ruliff
    Ensign, Militia
Conover, William
    Militia Volunteer, Prior to the First General Militia Muster, 6/76
    Private, Militia
Conrow, Levi
    Private, Militia, delinquent 8/80, delinquent 4/82
    Private, New Jersey Volunteers, enlisted 12/23/76 deserts 3/3/77
    convicted of Misdemeanor and Harboring Prisoners of War, 1/81
Convey, Peter
    Lieutenant, Militia
    Signer, Petition Calling for Action Against the Disaffected, 2/21/77
    Signer, Petition Against Loyalist Auction Commissioners, 3/24/79
    Juror, Court of Oyer and Terminer, 5/82
        fined for missing jury duty
    Signer, Petition Opposing the Return of Tories 6/10/83
Convey, Thomas
    Private, Militia
    present at the capture of the British ship, Britannia, 12/31/79
Cook, *see also* Cooke
Cook, Abiel   Upper Freehold
    Signer, Petition Against Association for Retaliation 12/81
Cook, Bennett   Dover
    Signer, Petition Urging Action Against the Pine Robbers, 12/27/81
Cook, Catherine
    indicted for Misdemeanor, 7/83
Cook, David
    Private, State Troops, enlisted 6/80
    sells produce to Continental Army, 5/80
Cook, Ebenezer   Shrewsbury

Roster of the People of Revolutionary Monmouth County

Cook, Elihu Shrewsbury
Cook, George Freehold
   Private, Militia
   Private, State Troops
Cook, George Freehold
   Militia Volunteer, Prior to the First General Militia Muster, 6/76
   Adjutant, Militia
   Ensign, Militia
   Signer, Petition to Better Provision Militia, 2/25/78
   sells produce to Continental Army, 5/80
Cook, George Dover
   Signer, Petition to Better Defend Toms River Area, 5/18/77
   Signer, Petition for Renewing Guard at Toms River, 12/10/81
   Signer, Petition Urging Action Against the Pine Robbers, 12/27/81
Cook, Green Shrewsbury
   accused of being part of Samuel Wright's Tory Association 11/76
Cook, Hannah
   daughter of Michael
   indicted for Misdemeanor, 8/79
Cook, Jacob Shrewsbury
Cook, James Shrewsbury
   son of Jesse
   Private, Militia
   indicted for Misdemeanor, 8/79
   indicted for Misdemeanor, 11/81
   indicted for Misdemeanor, 5/82
Cook, Jasper Shrewsbury
Cook, Jesse Shrewsbury
   Private, Militia
Cook, Jesse, Jr. Shrewsbury
   indicted for Misdemeanor, 11/81
Cook, Job Shrewsbury
   Private, Militia
   helps keep the poor
Cook, John Dover
   Captain of Militia, Prior to the First General Militia Muster, 6/76
   Major, Militia killed March 24, 1782
   Signer, Petition to Better Defend Toms River Area, 5/18/77
   Signer, Articles of Retaliation, 6/79
   Signer, Petition for Renewing Guard at Toms River, 12/10/81
   Signer, Petition Urging Action Against the Pine Robbers, 12/27/81
Cook, John Freehold

sells goods to Pennsylvania Salt Works, 8/76-10/76
Signer, Petition Against Association for Retaliation 12/81
Cook, Joseph   Shrewsbury
　Private, Militia
Cook, Mary   Shrewsbury
　household head
Cook, Nicholas   Freehold
　sells produce to Continental Army, 5/80
Cook, Peter (Peterson)   Shrewsbury
　Private, Militia
Cook, Peter
　son of Peterson
　indicted for Misdemeanor, 5/82
　indicted for High Treason, 11/82
Cook, Renn
　arrested for Disaffection, 11/76
　accused of being active in Tory Rebellions of 12/76
Cook, Silas   Shrewsbury
　indicted for Misdemeanor, 8/79
　indicted for Misdemeanor, 11/81
　indicted for Misdemeanor, 5/82
　estate confiscated
Cook, Stephen   Shrewsbury
　Private, Militia
Cook, Stephen, Jr.   Shrewsbury
　Private, Militia
Cook, Sylvanus   Dover
　Signer, Petition Urging Action Against the Pine Robbers, 12/27/81
Cook, Thomas   Freehold
　Private, Continental Army
　　captured at Fort Washington 11/16/76, released
　Lieutenant, Militia, captured 2/13/77, paroled 8/78
　　captured again 1780
　Signer, Petition for Renewing Guard at Toms River, 12/10/81
　Grand Juror, Court of Oyer and Terminer, 11/82
　Signer, Association for Opposing the Return of Tories, 1783
　Juror, Court of Oyer and Terminer, 7/83
Cook, Thomas
　Private, Militia
　Private, New Jersey Volunteers, 2/78
　convicted of Misdemeanor 12/80
Cook, William   Shrewsbury

son of Jesse
Private, Militia
indicted for Misdemeanor, 6/3/78
Cooke, *see also* Cook
Cooke, Robert
  arrested for Disaffection, 1777
Cooke, Samuel   Shrewsbury
  Anglican Minister for Monmouth County
  Chaplain in British Army
  Signer, Petition Opposing Slave Manumission, 2/2/74
  holds tavern license, 1775
  estate inquisitioned for Forfeiture, 3/31/79
Coombs, *see* Combs
Coon, John   Upper Freehold
Cooper, *see also* Coupar
Cooper, Benjamin   Middletown
  Private, Militia, delinquent 3/11/78
Cooper, David   Shrewsbury
  Private, Militia
Cooper, David, Jr.   Shrewsbury
  Private, Militia, delinquent 3/11/78, deserts 6/79
Cooper, Deborah   Middletown
  household head
Cooper, Esther   Shrewsbury
  household head
Cooper, Ezekiel   Middletown
Cooper, Gosper   Shrewsbury
Cooper, Jacob   Shrewsbury
  arrested for Disaffection, 1/77
  Private, New Jersey Volunteers, 1777
Cooper, James   Middletown
  indicted for Misdemeanor, 8/79
  indicted for Misdemeanor, 1/81
  indicted for Misdemeanor, 11/81
  indicted for Misdemeanor, 5/82
  estate confiscated
Cooper, James
  Private, Militia
  present at the capture of the British ship, Britannia, 12/31/79
Cooper, John
  Private, New Jersey Volunteers, enlisted 5/1/77
    discharged 11/14/78

Cooper, Joseph　　　　　　　Freehold
  Private, State Troops
Cooper, Josiah
  Private, Militia, captured 2/13/77
Cooper, Philip　　　　　　　Shrewsbury
Cooper, Samuel　　　　　　Middletown
  Private, Militia, delinquent 11/29/78, delinquent 6/11/80
  sells goods to Pennsylvania Salt Works, intermittent 8/76-6/77
Cooper, Thomas　　　　　　Shrewsbury
  Private, Militia, delinquent 10/9/80
  Signer, Petition Supporting Issuing of New Jersey Currency, 1771
Cooper, William　　　　　　Shrewsbury
  arrested for Disaffection, 11/76
  accused of being part of Samuel Wright's Tory Association 11/76
  accused of being active in Tory Rebellions of 12/76
  indicted for Misdemeanor, 8/79
Cooper, William　　　　　　Shrewsbury
  Private, Militia
Copeland, Couperthwaite　　Shrewsbury
  Delegate, Friends' Quarterly Meeting, 1775
Copman, John
  Private, New Jersey Volunteers
Core, Thomas
  Private, New Jersey Volunteers
Corlies, *see also* Curtis
Corlies, Benjamin　　　　　Shrewsbury
  Delegate, Friends' Quarterly Meeting, 1775-83
Corlies, Britten　　　　　　Shrewsbury
  Private, Militia
  sells produce to Continental Army, 5/80
Corlies, George　　　　　　Shrewsbury
  Private, Militia, exempt from Militia service, 2/10/78
Corlies, Jacob　　　　　　　Shrewsbury
  exempt from Militia service, 2/10/78
Corlies, James　　　　　　 Shrewsbury
  Private, Militia
  estate inquisitioned for Forfeiture, 7/4/77
  estate confiscated
Corlies, John　　　　　　　Shrewsbury
  of Rumson
  indicted for Misdemeanor, 5/82
Corlies, Joseph　　　　　　Shrewsbury

Corlies, Lydia   Shrewsbury
    Private, New Jersey Volunteers
Corlies, Lydia   Shrewsbury
    indicted for Misdemeanor, 8/79
Corlies, Margaret   Shrewsbury
    Delegate, Friends' Quarterly Meeting, 1774-82
Corlies, Peter   Shrewsbury
    Delegate, Friends' Quarterly Meeting, 1778
    indicted for Misdemeanor, 11/82
Corlies, Samuel   Shrewsbury
    indicted for Misdemeanor, 1/81
Corlies, Sarah   Shrewsbury
    Delegate, Friends' Quarterly Meeting, 1774-5, 1782
    listed on Militia return 6/29/80
Corlies, Timothy   Shrewsbury
    Private, Militia
Corlies, Uriah   Shrewsbury
Corlies, William   Shrewsbury
Corlies, William   Upper Freehold
Corman, *see* Carman
Cornelius, James   Dover
Congrove, *see* Cosgrove
Cornish, Timothy   Middletown
    Private, Militia
Cornwall, John
    Private, State Troops
Cornwall, William   Dover
    indicted for Misdemeanor, 11/81
Cornwell, *see* Cornwall
Cosgrove, Joseph
    Private, New Jersey Volunteers, enlisted 1/3/77
        impressed into Royal Navy
Cosgrove, Joseph
    Lieutenant, Militia
    Signer, Petition to Better Provision Militia, 2/25/78
Cosgrove, Thomas
    Private, New Jersey Volunteers
Cosgrove, William   Shrewsbury
    Private, Militia
    Indicted for Riot, 11/82
    Signer, Association for Opposing the Return of Tories, 1783
Cosgrove, William
    Private, New Jersey Volunteers, enlisted 1/3/77   dead 3/4/77

Coslick, David
  Private, Militia
Cotteral, Cotterell, *see* Cottrell
Cottrell, Effy   Freehold
Cottrell, Elezar   Middletown
  Private, Militia
  Signer, Articles of Retaliation, 6/79
Cottrell, Gavin
  Private, New Jersey Volunteers, enlisted 12/15/76 dead 5/23/79
Cottrell, George   Dover
  Signer, Association for Opposing the Return of Tories, 1783
Cottrell, James
  Private, Militia
Cottrell, James
  Private, Militia, delinquent 8/9/80
Cottrell, John   Middletown and Shrewsbury
  estate inquisitioned for Forfeiture, 7/4/77
  estate confiscated
  Signer, Petition Opposing Slave Manumission, 2/2/74
Cottrell, John   Middletown
  Private, Militia
Cottrell, Nicholas   Middletown
  Private, Militia
  Signer, Articles of Retaliation, 6/79
  Signer, Petition Opposing the Return of Tories 6/10/83
Cottrell, Robert   Middletown
  indicted for Misdemeanor, 5/82
Cottrell, Samuel   Shrewsbury
  estate inquisitioned for Forfeiture, 7/4/77
  estate confiscated
Cottrell, Thomas   Middletown
  Private, Militia
  Private, State Troops, enlists 6/80
  Signer, Articles of Retaliation, 6/79
Cottrell, William
  Private, Militia
Coupar, *see also* Cooper
Coupar, Jonathan
  Private, New Jersey Volunteers, enlisted 2/6/77 dead 6/13/77
Coupar, Josiah
  Private, New Jersey Volunteers, enlisted 12/23/76 dead 11/14/77
Couperthwaite, John   Upper Freehold

Captain, Militia
   takes Loyalty Oath to New Jersey Government, 3/19/77
Couperthwaite, Joseph   Dover
   Signer, Petition Urging Action Against the Disaffected, 3/14/77
Courlies, *see* Corlies
Courtney, Luke   Stafford
   Private, Militia
Courtwright, *see* Cartwright
Couslin, James
   Sergeant, New Jersey Volunteers
Coutson, James
   Private, New Jersey Volunteers, enlisted 3/23/79 deserted 4/5/79
Couwenhoven, *see* Covenhoven
Covenhoven, *see also* Conover
Covenhoven, Albert   Freehold
   Private, Militia
   sells goods to Pennsylvania Salt Works, intermittent 8/76-6/77
   Signer, Articles of Retaliation, 6/79
   sells produce to Continental Army, 5/80
   Signer, Petition for Renewing Guard at Toms River, 12/10/81
   Juror, Court of Oyer and Terminer, 11/82
Covenhoven, Benjamin   Freehold
   Captain, Militia
   Signer, Petition Urging Action Against the Disaffected, 3/14/77
   Signer, Petition for Settlement of Quartermaster Debts, 9/6/77
   house burned by British Army, 6/28/78
   Signer, Articles of Retaliation, 6/79
   Juror, Court of Oyer and Terminer, 11/82
   Grand Juror, Court of Oyer and Terminer, 7/83
Covenhoven, Benjamin   Freehold
   Private, Militia discharged (presumably wounded)
   Signer, Petition Urging Action Against the Disaffected, 3/14/77
   Signer, Articles of Retaliation, 6/79
Covenhoven, Cornelius   Freehold
   house burned by British Army, 6/28/78
   Signer, Articles of Retaliation, 6/79
   sells produce to Continental Army, 5/80
   Signer, Petition Against Association for Retaliation 12/81
   Signer, Petition for Renewing Guard at Toms River, 12/10/81
Covenhoven, Cornelius   Freehold
   Private, Militia
   present at the capture of the British ship, Britannia, 12/31/79

Covenhoven, Cornelius Freehold
  Private, Militia
  present at the capture of the British ship, Britannia, 12/31/79
  Private, State Troops, enlists 6/80
Covenhoven, Cornelius Middletown
  Private, Militia
  Signer, Petition Opposing Slave Manumission, 2/2/74
  Overseer of Highways, 1775
  Highway Surveyor, 1779-83
  Signer, Petition Opposing the Return of Tories 6/10/83
Covenhoven, Cornelius Middletown
  Captain, Militia
  Overseer of Highways, 1775
  donates to Charity Fund for Stevenson Family, 5/83
  Signer, Petition Opposing Slave Manumission, 2/2/74
  Signer, Articles of Retaliation, 6/79
  Signer, Petition Against Loyalist Auction Commissioners, 3/24/79
  Township Assessor, 1780-2
  Grand Juror, Court of Oyer and Terminer, 11/81
  Grand Juror, Court of Oyer and Terminer, 11/82
  Signer, Petition Opposing the Return of Tories 6/10/83
  Grand Juror, Court of Oyer and Terminer, 7/83
Covenhoven, Daniel Freehold
  Signer, Petition in Favor of Daniel Longstreet, 11/21/80
  Juror, Court of Oyer and Terminer, 7/83
Covenhoven, Daniel Middletown
  Private, Militia
  Signer, Petition Opposing Slave Manumission, 2/2/74
  sells produce to Continental Army, 5/80
  Signer, Petition Encouraging Free Trade, 5/12/81
  indicted for Misdemeanor, 5/82
  Signer, Petition Opposing the Return of Tories 6/10/83
Covenhoven, David Freehold
  Private, Militia
  Signer, Petition for Settlement of Quartermaster Debts, 9/6/77
  house burned by British Army, 6/28/78
  Signer, Petition for Stricter Militia Law, 5/31/79
  Signer, Articles of Retaliation, 6/79
  sells produce to Continental Army, 5/80
  Signer, Petition Supporting Retaliation, 9/17/80
  Grand Juror, Court of Oyer and Terminer, 5/82
  Juror, Court of Oyer and Terminer, 11/82

Grand Juror, Court of Oyer and Terminer, 7/83
Covenhoven, Elias   Upper Freehold
   Private, Militia
   witness at Monmouth Court, 1778
   Signer, Petition in Favor of Daniel Longstreet, 11/21/80
Covenhoven, Garret   Freehold
   Signer, Petition for Settlement of Quartermaster Debts, 9/6/77
   Signer, Articles of Retaliation, 6/79
   sells clothing to Continental Army, 3/78
   Signer, Petition Against Loyalist Auction Commissioners, 3/24/79
   Signer, Petition Against Monmouth Loyalist Confiscation Commissioners, 5/8/79
   sells produce to Continental Army, 5/80
   Grand Juror, Court of Oyer and Terminer, 12/80
   Signer, Petition Encouraging Free Trade, 5/12/81
   Juror, Court of Oyer and Terminer, 5/82
   Grand Juror, Court of Oyer and Terminer, 11/82
Covenhoven, Garret   Freehold
Covenhoven, Garret   Middletown
   Baptist
   Private, Militia
   arrested for Disaffection, 11/76
   accused of being active in Tory Rebellions of 12/76
   Signer, Petition Opposing the Return of Tories 6/10/83
Covenhoven, Garret,   Middletown
   Private, Militia
   present at the capture of the British ship, Britannia, 12/31/79
   Signer, Petition Opposing the Return of Tories 6/10/83
Covenhoven, Hendrick   Freehold
   Signer, Articles of Retaliation, 6/79
   Grand Juror, Court of Oyer and Terminer, 5/82
Covenhoven, Isaac   Freehold
   Private, State Troops
   convicted of Riot & Trespass, 1/20/78
Covenhoven, Jacob   Freehold
   son of William
   Militia Volunteer, Prior to the First General Militia Muster, 6/76
   Private, Militia
   indicted for Riot, 1/78
Covenhoven, Jacob   Middletown
   Captain, Militia, Light Horse, captured 1777, paroled 8/78
     captured again 9/80

Roster of the People of Revolutionary Monmouth County

    Signer, Petition Opposing Slave Manumission, 2/2/74
    Signer, Articles of Retaliation, 6/79
    present at the capture of the British ship, Britannia, 12/31/79
    sells produce to Continental Army, 5/80
    sells produce to Continental Army, 7/80
    Signer, Petition for Renewing Guard at Toms River, 12/10/81
Covenhoven, Jacob   Middletown
    Signer, Petition Opposing Slave Manumission, 2/2/74
    Signer, Petition Opposing the Return of Tories 6/10/83
Covenhoven, Job
    Private, Militia
Covenhoven, John   Freehold
    Vice President, New Jersey Provincial Congress, 1776
    Delegate, New Jersey Legislature, Lower House, 1776
    Delegate, New Jersey Legislature, Upper House, 1781-2
    captured by Tories, 11/76
    Signer, Petition for Stricter Militia Law, 5/31/79
    Signer, Articles of Retaliation, 6/79
    Signer, Petition Favoring Quick Division of Prize Money, 12/79
    sells produce to Continental Army, 5/80
    Signer, Petition Supporting Retaliation, 9/17/80
    Signer, Petition in Favor of Daniel Longstreet, 11/21/80
    Signer, Petition Encouraging Free Trade, 5/12/81
    Signer, Association for Opposing the Return of Tories, 1783
    Signer, Petition Supporting Quick Division of Militia Prizes, no date
Covenhoven, John   Freehold
    sells goods to Pennsylvania Salt Works, 8/76-10/76
    Signer, Articles of Retaliation, 6/79
    sells produce to Continental Army, 5/80
    Signer, Petition in Favor of Daniel Longstreet, 11/21/80
    Signer, Petition Encouraging Free Trade, 5/12/81
    Grand Juror, Court of Oyer and Terminer, 5/82
    Juror, Court of Oyer and Terminer, 11/82
Covenhoven, John   Freehold
    Signer, Articles of Retaliation, 6/79
Covenhoven, John   Freehold
    son of Peter
    Private, Militia
    Private, Militia Dragoons, delinquent one tour
    Private, State Troops, enlisted 6/80
Covenhoven, John   Middletown
    Township Assessor, 1770

Overseer of the Poor, 1777
Signer, Petition for Stricter Militia Law, 5/31/79
Signer, Articles of Retaliation, 6/79
Signer, Petition Favoring Quick Division of Prize Money, 12/79
sells produce to Continental Army, 5/80
lost slaves during the war

Covenhoven, John   Upper Freehold
Private, Militia
Private, State Troops
sells produce to Continental Army, 5/80
Signer, Petition in Favor of Daniel Longstreet, 11/21/80
leased horse team to Continental Quarter Master 12/81

Covenhoven, John, Jr.   Middletown
Private, Militia, delinquent 6/11/80
present at the capture of the British ship, Britannia, 12/31/79

Covenhoven, Joseph   Middletown
Private, State Troops
indicted for Riot & Trespass, 1/20/78
sells produce to Continental Army, 5/80
Signer, Petition Opposing the Return of Tories 6/10/83

Covenhoven, Joseph   Shrewsbury
Private, Militia
Signer, Petition Opposing Slave Manumission, 2/2/74
Signer, Articles of Retaliation, 6/79
sells produce to Continental Army, 5/80
Juror, Court of Oyer and Terminer, 5/82

Covenhoven, Lewis   Freehold
Covenhoven, Lewis   Upper Freehold
Covenhoven, Mathias
Private, Militia
present at the capture of the British ship, Britannia, 12/31/79

Covenhoven, Peter, Esq.   Middletown
Township Collector, 1770-1
Signer, Petition Supporting Issuing of New Jersey Currency, 1771
Delegate, New Jersey Legislature, Upper House, 1783
Signer, Petition Opposing Slave Manumission, 2/2/74
Commissioner of Appeals, 1779
Signer, Petition Favoring Quick Division of Prize Money, 12/79
sells produce to Continental Army, 5/80
Justice of the Peace, 1780-2
Signer, Petition for Renewing Guard at Toms River, 12/10/81
lost slaves during the war

Signer, Petition Opposing the Return of Tories 6/10/83
Covenhoven, Peter   Upper Freehold and Shrewsbury
    Signer, Petition Opposing Slave Manumission, 2/2/74
Covenhoven, Peter   Upper Freehold
    Paymaster, Militia
    Signer, Petition in Support of Richard Lloyd, 1/31/76
    Signer, Petition in Support of William Barton, 1/31/76
    Signer, Petition for Stricter Militia Law, 5/31/79
    sells produce to Continental Army, 5/80
    sells sheep to Continental Commissary 7/80
    Grand Juror, Court of Oyer and Terminer, 12/80
    Signer, Petition Urging Action Against Disaffected
        & Favoring Retaliation, 5/12/81, opposes Retaliation clause
    Grand Juror, Court of Oyer and Terminer, 11/82
Covenhoven, Ruliff   Freehold
    Private, State Troops, enlisted 6/80
    Signer, Articles of Retaliation, 6/79
Covenhoven, Ruliff   Middletown
    Private, Militia
    Signer, Petition Opposing Slave Manumission, 2/2/74
    sells clothing to Continental Army, 3/78
    sells produce to Continental Army, 5/80
Covenhoven, Ruliff   Shrewsbury
    Lieutenant, Militia, discharged 7/5/79
    Signer, Petition Opposing Slave Manumission, 2/2/74
Covenhoven, Sarah   Middletown
    household head
Covenhoven, Theodorus   Freehold
    Sergeant, Militia
    Signer, Petition for Settlement of Quartermaster Debts, 9/6/77
    Grand Juror, Court of Oyer and Terminer, 8/79
    Private, State Troops, enlisted 6/80
    Signer, Petition Supporting Retaliation, 1780
    Signer, Petition Supporting Retaliation, 9/17/80
    Signer, Petition Encouraging Free Trade, 5/12/81
    Grand Juror, Court of Oyer and Terminer, 11/82
Covenhoven, Thomas   Freehold
    Signer, Association for Opposing the Return of Tories, 1783
Covenhoven, Thomas   Upper Freehold
    Signer, Association for Opposing the Return of Tories, 1783
Covenhoven, Tunis   Middletown
    Signer, Petition Opposing the Return of Tories 6/10/83

Roster of the People of Revolutionary Monmouth County

Covenhoven, William   Freehold
  Signer, Petition for Settlement of Quartermaster Debts, 9/6/77
  Signer, Petition Against Loyalist Auction Commissioners, 3/24/79
  Signer, Petition for Stricter Militia Law, 5/31/79
  Signer, Articles of Retaliation, 6/79
  sells produce to Continental Army, 5/80
  Signer, Petition Supporting Retaliation, 9/17/80
  Signer, Petition Encouraging Free Trade, 5/12/81
  Signer, Petition for Renewing Guard at Toms River, 12/10/81
Covenhoven, William   Freehold
  of Englishtown
  Juror, Court of Oyer and Terminer, 1/78
    fined L5 for not attending all or part of Jury duty
  sells produce to Continental Army, 5/80
Covenhoven, William   Middletown
  Private, Militia
  donates to Charity Fund for Stevenson Family, 5/83
  Signer, Petition for Stricter Militia Law, 5/31/79
  Signer, Articles of Retaliation, 6/79
  present at the capture of the British ship, Britannia, 12/31/79
  sells produce to Continental Army, 5/80
  Juror, Court of Oyer and Terminer, 5/82
    fined for missing jury duty
  Juror, Court of Oyer and Terminer, 11/82
  Signer, Petition Opposing the Return of Tories 6/10/83
Covenhoven, William   Middletown
  Signer, Petition Opposing the Return of Tories 6/10/83
Covenhoven, William, Jr.   Freehold
  Private, Militia
  present at the capture of the British ship, Britannia, 12/31/79
  Juror, Court of Oyer and Terminer, 5/82
    fined for missing jury duty
Covert, Adrian
  Private, Militia
Covert, Benjamin
  Private, State Troops, enlisted 6/80
  Signer, Petition Supporting Quick Division of Militia Prizes, no date
Covert, Berrian (Bunyan)
  Private, Militia
  Private, State Troops
  Signer, Articles of Retaliation, 6/79
Covert, John   Freehold

Signer, Petition for Renewing Guard at Toms River, 12/10/81
Signer, Association for Opposing the Return of Tories, 1783
Covert, Sarah   Freehold
 household head
Covert, William   Freehold and Middletown
 Private, Militia
 Signer, Articles of Retaliation, 6/79
 present at the capture of the British ship, Britannia, 12/31/79
 Signer, Petition Opposing the Return of Tories 6/10/83
Covert, William   Shrewsbury
 Private, Militia
Covet, *see* Covert
Coward, Alice   Upper Freehold
 household head
Coward, John
 Laborer, Pennsylvania Salt Works, intermittent 8/76-6/77
Coward, John   Upper Freehold
 Captain, Militia
 Signer, Petition for Renewing Guard at Toms River, 12/10/81
 Grand Juror, Court of Oyer and Terminer, 11/82
Coward, Jonathan   Upper Freehold
Coward, Joseph   Upper Freehold
 Private, Militia
 Private, Continental Army
 witness at Monmouth County, 1778
 Constable, 1778
 Juror, Court of Oyer and Terminer, 5/82
  fined for missing jury duty
Coward, Mary   Upper Freehold
 household head
Coward, Samuel
 Private, Militia
Cox, Ann   Upper Freehold
 household head
Cox, Asher   Upper Freehold
 Private, Militia
 Signer, Petition Against Association for Retaliation, 12/81
 Juror, Court of Oyer and Terminer, 11/82
Cox, Elizabeth   Upper Freehold
 household head
Cox, Esek   Upper Freehold
Cox, Fenwick   Upper Freehold

Cox, Isaac   Upper Freehold
    Private, Militia
    Signer, Petition Urging Action Against Disaffected
        & Favoring Retaliation, 5/12/81, opposes Retaliation clause
Cox, James   Upper Freehold
    Lieutenant, Militia
    Signer, Petition to Better Provision Militia, 2/25/78
    sells produce to Continental Army, 5/80
    Signer, Petition Against Association for Retaliation 12/81
Cox, James   Upper Freehold
    Private, Militia
Cox, John   Upper Freehold
    sells produce to Continental Army, 5/80
    indicted for Misdemeanor, 11/81
    Signer, Petition Against Association for Retaliation 12/81
Cox, John   Upper Freehold
    Private, Militia
Cox, Joseph   Upper Freehold
    Signer, Petition Against Association for Retaliation 12/81
Cox, Joseph   Upper Freehold
    Private, Militia, captured 2/13/77
Cox, Nathaniel   Upper Freehold
Cox, Richard   Upper Freehold
    Signer, Petition Urging Action Against Disaffected
        & Favoring Retaliation, 5/12/81, opposes Retaliation clause
    Juror, Court of Oyer and Terminer, 12/80
        fined L3 for missing all or some of jury duty
    Signer, Association for Opposing the Return of Tories, 1783
    Judge of the Court of Oyer and Terminer, 5/82 & 11/82
Cox, Samuel   Upper Freehold
Cox, Thomas   Upper Freehold
    sells produce to Continental Army, 5/80
    Signer, Petition in Favor of Daniel Longstreet, 11/21/80
    Signer, Petition Urging Action Against Disaffected
        & Favoring Retaliation, 5/12/81, opposes Retaliation clause
    Signer, Petition Against Association for Retaliation 12/81
    Coroner, 1782
Cox, Thomas, Jr.   Upper Freehold
    Private, Militia
    Signer, Petition in Favor of Daniel Longstreet, 11/21/80
    Signer, Petition Urging Action Against Disaffected
        & Favoring Retaliation, 5/12/81, opposes Retaliation clause

Juror, Court of Oyer and Terminer, 5/82
Cox, William				Upper Freehold
	Juror, Court of Oyer and Terminer, 11/82
Coyn, *see* Coin
Craddock, John			Shrewsbury
	Vestryman, Anglican Christ Church, 1778-3
Craft, David
	Signer, Association for Opposing the Return of Tories, 1783
	Signer, Petition Urging Compensation for Inflated Money, 5/22/83
Craft, Richard
	Signer, Association for Opposing the Return of Tories, 1783
Craig, David				Freehold
	Sergeant, Militia
	Private, State Troops, enlisted 6/80
	Signer, Articles of Retaliation, 6/79
	Signer, Petition Supporting Retaliation, 1780
	Grand Juror, Court of Oyer and Terminer, 5/82
Craig, David
	Private, State Troops, enlisted 6/80
	Signer, Articles of Retaliation, 6/79
Craig, James				Freehold
	Ensign, Militia
	Private, Militia Dragoons, delinquent one tour
	Private, State Troops, enlisted 6/80
	witness at Monmouth Court
	Signer, Articles of Retaliation, 6/79
	Signer, Petition Encouraging Free Trade, 5/12/81
	Signer, Association for Opposing the Return of Tories, 1783
Craig, John				Freehold
	Sergeant of Militia, Prior to the First General Militia Muster, 6/76
	Lieutenant, Militia, captured 2/13/77, paroled 8/78
	Deacon, Tennent Church
	Signer, Petition for Stricter Militia Law, 5/31/79
	Signer, Articles of Retaliation, 6/79
	sells produce to Continental Army, 5/80
	sells produce to Continental Army, 7/80
	Signer, Petition Supporting Retaliation, 9/17/80
	Grand Juror, Court of Oyer and Terminer, 12/80
	Signer, Petition for Renewing Guard at Toms River, 12/10/81
	Grand Juror, Court of Oyer and Terminer, 5/82
	Juror, Court of Oyer and Terminer, 11/82
	Juror, Court of Oyer and Terminer, 7/83

Craig, John Freehold
   Militia Volunteer, Prior to the First General Militia Muster, 6/76
   Private, Militia
   Private, Militia Dragoons, delinquent one tour
   Private, State Troops, enlisted 6/80
   sells produce to Continental Army, 5/80
Craig, John, Jr. Freehold
   Private, Militia
   Grand Juror, Court of Oyer and Terminer, 8/79
Craig, Samuel
   Private, Militia
   Signer, Articles of Retaliation, 6/79
   Signer, Petition Encouraging Free Trade, 5/12/81
Craig, William Freehold
   Signer, Articles of Retaliation, 6/79
   sells produce to Continental Army, 5/80
   sells produce to Continental Army, 7/80
   Signer, Petition Encouraging Free Trade, 5/12/81
   Grand Juror, Court of Oyer and Terminer, 5/82
   Grand Juror, Court of Oyer and Terminer, 11/82
Crammer, [?] Shrewsbury
   mulatto orphan child
   recipient of poor relief
Crammer, David
   Private, New Jersey Volunteers
Crammer, Josiah Stafford
   indicted for Misdemeanor, 1/81
   indicted for Misdemeanor, 5/82
Crammer, Samuel Stafford
   indicted for Misdemeanor, 1/81
Crammer, William Stafford
   indicted for Misdemeanor, 11/81
Crane, Nathan Dover
   Adjutant, Militia
   Juror, Court of Oyer and Terminer, 1/78
      fined L5 for not attending all or part of Jury duty
   Signer, Petition Urging Action Against the Pine Robbers, 12/27/81
Crane, Seth Dover
   Signer, Petition Urging Action Against the Pine Robbers, 12/27/81
Crane, Silas Dover
   Private, Militia, drafted into Continental Army 5/78
   Private, Continental Army

Signer, Petition Urging Action Against the Pine Robbers, 12/27/81
Cranmer, *see* Crammer
Craven, William   Freehold
    Private, Militia, drafted into Continental Army 5/78
    Private, State Troops, enlists 5/78
Crawford, Andrew   Middletown
    Private, Militia
Crawford, David   Shrewsbury
    Private, Militia
    Signer, Articles of Retaliation, 6/79
    Signer, Petition Favoring Quick Division of Prize Money, 12/79
    sells produce to Continental Army, 5/80
    Signer, Petition Supporting Retaliation, 9/17/80
    Signer, Petition for Renewing Guard at Toms River, 12/10/81
Crawford, George
    donates to Charity Fund for Stevenson Family, 5/83
Crawford, Gideon   Middletown
    Laborer, Pennsylvania Salt Works, intermittent 8/76-6/77
Crawford, James   Middletown
    Private, Militia, killed 2/13/77
Crawford, John   Middletown
    Private, Militia, delinquent 2/10/78
Crawford, Richard   Middletown
    Coroner, 1778
    Signer, Petition Against Loyalist Auction Commissioners, 3/24/79
    Signer, Petition Against Confiscation Commissioners, 5/8/79
    sells produce to Continental Army, 5/80
    Commissioner of Appeals, 1782
    Signer, Petition Opposing the Return of Tories 6/10/83
    lost slaves during the war
Crawford, Richard, Jr.   Middletown
    Baptist
Crawford, Stephen   Middletown
    Private, Militia
Crawford, William   Middletown
    Private, Militia
    Juror, Court of Oyer and Terminer, 8/79
       fined L30 for missing all or some of jury duty
    Township Assessor, 1780
    Juror, Court of Oyer and Terminer, 11/82
    Overseer of Highways, 1783
Creol, *see* Crowell

Crine, Vincent Essex County
  Monmouth County land holdings confiscated
Croell, see Crowell
Crookshank, George
  Signer, Articles of Retaliation, 6/79
Crosley, Abiel
  Laborer, Pennsylvania Salt Works, intermittent 8/76-6/77
Cross, Thomas Upper Freehold
Crossman, John
  sells produce to Continental Army, 5/80
Crossman, Thomas Upper Freehold
Crowell, Christian
  wife of Thomas
  convicted of Misdemeanor, 1/20/78
Crowell, John
  Private, New Jersey Volunteers
Crowell, Joseph Middletown
  Captain, New Jersey Volunteers
Crowell, Samuel
  Private, New Jersey Volunteers, captured 8/22/77
Crowell, Thomas Middletown
  Captain, New Jersey Volunteers
  estate inquisitioned for Forfeiture, 7/1/77
  estate confiscated
  Signer, Petition Opposing Slave Manumission, 2/2/74
Crowell, Thomas Shrewsbury
  recipient of poor relief
Crowell, William Shrewsbury
  orphan child
  recipient of poor relief
Croxen, John
  Signer, Petition for Renewing Guard at Toms River, 12/10/81
Croxen, Sarah Shrewsbury
  household head
  listed on Militia return 6/29/80
Cuffey, Amos Stafford
  Private, Militia
Cuffey, William Stafford
  American Indian
  Private, Militia, drafted into Continental Army 5/78
  Private, State Troops
  Private, Continental Army

Culbert, Charles
  Private, New Jersey Volunteers, enlisted 2/8/77 dead 4/12/77
Culver, Jones
  Private, New Jersey Volunteers
Cummings, see Cummins
Cummins, John
  Private, New Jersey Volunteers, captured
Cummins, Jonathan
  Private, New Jersey Volunteers, enlisted 11/2/76 dead 4/29/77
Cummins, Lawrence   Freehold
Cummins, Leah
  household head
  Signer, Petition for Stricter Militia Law, 5/31/79
Cummins, Richard
  Militia, Private
Cummins, Robert   Freehold
  Private, Militia
  Private, Militia
Cummins, Samuel
  Signer, Petition for Stricter Militia Law, 5/31/79
Curlis, see Curtis and Corlies
Curran, William
  Signer, Articles of Retaliation, 6/79
Curtis, see also Corlies
Curtis, Asher   Shrewsbury
  indicted for Misdemeanor, 1/81
Curtis, Benjamin   Shrewsbury
  Private, Militia, delinquent 9/80
Curtis, David   Shrewsbury
  indicted for Misdemeanor, 8/79
  indicted for Misdemeanor, 1/81
  Signer, Petition from Victims of the Association for Retaliation 9/82
Curtis, David, Jr.   Shrewsbury
  Private, Militia, delinquent 8/80
  exempt from Militia service, 2/10/78
Curtis, Elisha   Shrewsbury
  indicted for Misdemeanor, 1/81
  indicted for Misdemeanor, 5/82
Curtis, John   Shrewsbury
  Private, Militia, delinquent 9/80
  sells produce to Continental Army, 5/80
Curtis, Jonathan   Shrewsbury

Curtis, Joseph — Shrewsbury
  Private, New Jersey Volunteers
  exempt from Militia service, 2/10/78
Curtis, Thomas — Shrewsbury
  Private, Militia, delinquent 8/80, delinquent 4/82
  sells produce to Continental Army, 5/80
  indicted for Misdemeanor, 1/81
  indicted for Misdemeanor, 11/82
Curtis, Walter — Shrewsbury
  Private, Militia, delinquent 8/80
  Private, New Jersey Volunteers, enlisted 12/20/76 deserts 1/15/77
  indicted for Misdemeanor, 8/79
  indicted for Misdemeanor, 1/81
  indicted for Misdemeanor, 11/81
Curtis, Walter — Shrewsbury
  estate confiscated
Curtis, William — Shrewsbury
  Private, Militia, delinquent 9/80
  Convicted of High Treason, 4/25/82
  Refugee in New York, 1782
Cuyler, DeLancey — Upper Freehold

D

Dane, Joseph
  Private, Militia
  Private, State Troops
  Private, Continental Army
Danford, Samuel — Upper Freehold
Dangler, Valentine — Shrewsbury
  Private, New Jersey Volunteers
  indicted for Misdemeanor, 8/79
Darah, William
  Private, New Jersey Volunteers, deserted 7/2/77
David, Hannah — Shrewsbury
  household head
David, Jacob — Shrewsbury
David, James — Shrewsbury
David, Joseph — Shrewsbury
David, Josiah — Shrewsbury
David, Nathan — Shrewsbury
David, Thomas — Shrewsbury

David, William Shrewsbury
David, William, Jr. Shrewsbury
Davidson, *see* Davison
Davis, Aaron Freehold
   Signer, Articles of Retaliation, 6/79
   Signer, Petition Encouraging Free Trade, 5/12/81
   Juror, Court of Oyer and Terminer, 11/82
Davis, Charles
   Private, New Jersey Volunteers, enlisted 1/15/77 dead 9/5/77
Davis, Ebenezer
   Private, New Jersey Volunteers
Davis, Hannah
   indicted for Misdemeanor, 5/82
Davis, Isaac
   sells produce to Continental Army, 5/80
Davis, James
   Private, New Jersey Volunteers
   witness at Monmouth Court, 1778
   Coroner, 1778
   Signer, Association for Opposing the Return of Tories, 1783
Davis, John Shrewsbury
   Corporal, New Jersey Volunteers
   Private, Militia, serves as substitute 2/10/78, delinquent 8/80
   Laborer, Pennsylvania Salt Works, intermittent 8/76-6/77
Davis, Joseph
   Private, Militia captured 2/13/77 dies in prison 3/11/77
Davis, Joseph
   indicted for Misdemeanor, 8/79
   Signer, Petition Favoring Quick Division of Prize Money, 12/79
Davis, Moses
   Lieutenant, Militia
   Signer, Petition Calling for Action Against the Disaffected, 2/21/77
Davis, Nathan Shrewsbury
   Private, Militia, delinquent 8/80
   Constable, 1779, fined L150 for not attending court
   sells produce to Continental Army, 5/80
Davis, Penelope
   indicted for Misdemeanor, 11/81
Davis, Samuel
   Private, New Jersey Volunteers
Davis, Thomas Middletown
   Private, New Jersey Volunteers, enlisted 12/19/76 deserts 1/15/77

  Signer, Petition Favoring Quick Division of Prize Money, 12/79
  Signer, Petition Opposing the Return of Tories 6/10/83
Davis, Travis   Shrewsbury
  Private, Militia, deserts 6/79
Davis, William   Shrewsbury
  Sergeant, New Jersey Volunteers
  Private, Militia, delinquent 9/80
Davis, William, Jr.   Shrewsbury
  Private, Militia, delinquent 8/80
  Private, New Jersey Volunteers, enlisted 4/18/77 deserts 3/18/79
Davison, James
  Private, Militia
  Private, State Troops, enlisted 6/80
  Signer, Association for Opposing the Return of Tories, 1783
Davison, James
  Private, New Jersey Volunteers, enlisted for bounty 4/79
Davison, John
  arrested for Disaffection, 11/76
  accused of being active in Tory Rebellions of 12/76
Davison, John
  Private, Militia
  Signer, Petition for Stricter Militia Law, 5/31/79
  Signer, Articles of Retaliation, 6/79
  Signer, Petition for Renewing Guard at Toms River, 12/10/81
Davison, Nathaniel   Upper Freehold
  Ensign, Militia
  Signer, Petition Urging Action Against the Disaffected, 3/14/77
Davison, William
  Private, Militia
Day, *see* Dey
Dean, John   Upper Freehold
  Signer, Petition Urging Action Against Disaffected
    & Favoring Retaliation, 5/12/81, opposes Retaliation clause
Dean, Joseph   Middletown
  Private, State Troops, enlists 5/78
Dean, Matthew   Middletown
  Private, Militia
  present at the capture of the British ship, Britannia, 12/31/79
Debough, *see* DeBow
DeBow, Elizabeth
  indicted for Misdemeanor, 8/79
DeBow, James

Private, New Jersey Volunteers, at Sandy Hook, 4/78
    indicted for Robbery, 6/3/78
DeBow, John   Middletown and Upper Freehold
    convicted of Misdemeanor, 12/80
DeBow, William
    sells produce to Continental Army, 5/80
DeCamp, David   Middletown
DeCoo, DeCou, *see* DeCow
DeCow, Eber   Upper Freehold
DeCow, Isaac
    Private, New Jersey Volunteers
DeGraff, John   Freehold
    Signer, Articles of Retaliation, 6/79
DeGraff, Jacob
    Signer, Articles of Retaliation, 6/79
DeHart, Maurice   Shrewsbury
    Vestryman, Anglican Christ Church, 1777-83
Delaney, Michael
    Private, New Jersey Volunteers
DeLong, John   Upper Freehold
Delonson, Cuyler   Dover
Deloplane, Joseph   Shrewsbury
    Delegate, Friends' Quarterly Meeting, 1776
Deloplane, Samuel   Shrewsbury
Denice, *see also* Dennis
Denice, Britten
    witness at Monmouth Court, 1778
Denice, Daniel   Freehold
    Militia Volunteer, Prior to the First General Militia Muster, 6/76
    Signer, Petition Supporting Retaliation, 1780
    sells produce to Continental Army, 5/80
Denice, Dennis (Denice)   Shrewsbury
    Major, Militia
    Signer, Articles of Retaliation, 6/79
    Judge of the Court of Oyer and Terminer, 8/79
    Judge of the Court of Oyer and Terminer, 12/80
    Signer, Petition Encouraging Free Trade, 5/12/81
    Signer, Petition for Renewing Guard at Toms River, 12/10/81
    Judge of the Court of Oyer and Terminer, 5/82
    Signer, Association for Opposing the Return of Tories, 1783
    Justice of the Peace, 1783
Denice, Jacques

Captain-Lieutenant, State Troops
Signer, Articles of Retaliation, 6/79
present at the capture of the British ship, Britannia, 12/31/79
Denice, Tunis   Freehold
Denice, Tunis   Dover
  lost slaves during the war
Denyse, *see* Denice *and* Dennis
DeNight, James
  Private, Militia
  Private, Continental Army
DeNight, John
  Private, Militia
  Private, Continental Army
Dennis, *see also* Denice
Dennis, Anthony   Shrewsbury
  indicted for Misdemeanor, 8/79
  estate inquisitioned for Forfeiture, 6/10/79
  estate confiscated
Dennis, Benjamin   Shrewsbury
  Member, Shrewsbury Committee of Observation
  Captain, Militia
  Signer, Petition Urging Action Against the Disaffected, 3/14/77
  Sideman, Anglican Christ Church, 1778,
    Vestryman, 1779
  Signer, Petition to Better Provision Militia, 2/25/78
Dennis, Jacob   Shrewsbury
  Vestryman, Anglican Christ Church, 1770-5
Dennis, John   Shrewsbury
  Captain, Militia, captured 6/77, dies in prison 1/15/78
  Signer, Petition Urging Action Against the Disaffected, 3/14/77
Dennis, John
  Signer, Petition Against Loyalist Auction Commissioners, 3/24/79
Dennis, Joseph   Shrewsbury and Middletown
  Private, Militia
  Signer, Petition Against Slave Manumission, 2/2/74
  Signer, Petition Opposing the Return of Tories 6/10/83
Dennis, Philip
  Private, Militia
Dennis, Rebecca   Shrewsbury
  listed on Militia return 6/29/80
Dennis, Samuel   Shrewsbury and Middletown
  Captain, Militia

Signer, Petition Opposing Slave Manumission, 2/2/74
Signer, Petition Calling for Action Against the Disaffected, 2/21/77
Signer, Petition Urging Action Against the Disaffected, 3/14/77
Signer, Articles of Retaliation, 6/79
present at the capture of the British ship, Britannia, 12/31/79
Signer, Petition Encouraging Free Trade, 5/12/81
Signer, Petition Opposing the Return of Tories 6/10/83
Dennis, Samuel   Shrewsbury
    indicted for Misdemeanor, 8/79
    indicted for Misdemeanor, 1/81
Dennis, Sarah
    indicted for Misdemeanor, 8/79
Dennison, William
    accused of being active in Tory Rebellions of 12/76
    Private, New Jersey Volunteers, enlisted 7/14/77 deserts 2/26/78
Devinney, William   Freehold
    Private, Militia
    Signer, Articles of Retaliation, 6/79
    Signer, Petition Supporting Retaliation, 9/17/80
    Signer, Petition Urging Compensation for Inflated Money, 5/22/83
Dewinney, *see* Devinney
DeWitt, John
    Private, New Jersey Volunteers
DeWitt, Luke
    Grand Juror, Court of Oyer and Terminer, 8/79
    sells produce to Continental Army, 5/80
    sells sheep to Continental Commissary 7/80
    Juror, Court of Oyer and Terminer, 5/82
    Juror, Court of Oyer and Terminer, 11/82
Dey, Amos   Upper Freehold
    Private, Militia
Dey, Cyrus
    Private, Militia
Dey, Daniel   Upper Freehold
Dey, Ezekiel   Upper Freehold
Dey, John
    Private, Militia
    Signer, Petition Encouraging Free Trade, 5/12/81
Dey, Josiah   Upper Freehold
    Private, Militia
Dey, William   Freehold
Dey, William   Upper Freehold

Dey, William
   Signer, Association for Opposing the Return of Tories, 1783
   Private, New Jersey Volunteers, enlisted 12/19/76 dead 5/5/77
Dibbins, see Dobbins
Dick, James   Upper Freehold
Dicknick, Jarred   Middletown
Diffidoff, Henry   Middletown
Dill, Abraham
   Private, New Jersey Volunteers
Dill, Henry
   Private, New Jersey Volunteers
Dillon, John   Dover
   Militia Volunteer, Prior to the First General Militia Muster, 6/76
   sells goods to Pennsylvania Salt Works, 8/76-10/76
   Signer, Petition for Renewing Guard at Toms River, 12/10/81
Dillon, Margaret   Dover
   household head
   sells goods to Pennsylvania Salt Works, 8/76-10/76
Dillon, Mathias   Upper Freehold
Dillon, William   Dover
   convicted of Robbery, 6/3/78, sentenced to death, pardoned
   indicted for Robbery and Misdemeanor, 5/82
   indicted for Misdemeanor, 11/82
   Tory partisan/boat captain
Dineen, John
   Private, New Jersey Volunteers
Disbrough, see Disbrow
Disbrow, Henry   Upper Freehold
   Private, Militia
Disbrow, James
   indicted for Robbery, 6/78
Disbrow, John   Upper Freehold
   Private, Militia
   Private, State Troops
Disbrow, William   Upper Freehold
   sells produce to Continental Army, 7/80
   Signer, Petition Urging Action Against Disaffected
      & Favoring Retaliation, 5/12/81
   Juror, Court of Oyer and Terminer, 5/82
   Juror, Court of Oyer and Terminer, 11/82
Dobbins, Barney
   Private, New Jersey Volunteers

Dobbins, William   Freehold
    Signer, Petition Favoring Quick Division of Prize Money, 12/79
Dobbs, Adam   Shrewsbury
Dodd, Alexander
    Sergeant, Militia
Dodd, Daniel
    indicted for Misdemeanor, 5/82
    indicted for Misdemeanor, 11/81
Dodge, David
    Private, Militia
    Private, State Troops
    Signer, Petition Favoring Quick Division of Prize Money, 12/79
Donald, Joseph   Upper Freehold
Donley, Edward
    Private, New Jersey Volunteers
Donnelson, Arthur   Upper Freehold
Doren, see Dorn and Van Doren
Dorn, Cornelius   Middletown
    Private, Militia
    present at the capture of the British ship, Britannia, 12/31/79
Dorn, Nicholas   Middletown
    Private, Militia, hires substitute 2/10/78
Dorsett, Andrew   Middletown
Dorsett, Benjamin
    Private, Militia
Dorsett, Catherine   Middletown
    household head
Dorsett, James   Middletown
    Private, Militia
    Signer, Articles of Retaliation, 6/79
Dorsett, John   Middletown
    Private, Militia
    Overseer of Highways, 1776
    present at the capture of the British ship, Britannia, 12/31/79
Dorsett, Joseph   Middletown
    Private, Militia
    Signer, Petition Opposing Slave Manumission, 2/2/74
    present at the capture of the British ship, Britannia, 12/31/79
    Overseer of Highways, 1780-1
Dorsett, Samuel   Middletown
    Private, Militia
    Signer, Petition Opposing Slave Manumission, 2/2/74

Signer, Articles of Retaliation, 6/79
present at the capture of the British ship, Britannia, 12/31/79
indicted for Misdemeanor, 11/81
indicted for Misdemeanor, 5/82
Dorsey, Timothy
Signer, Articles of Retaliation, 6/79
Doty, Dougherty, *see* Doughty
Doughty, Edward
convicted of Misdemeanor, 1/81
Doughty, Henry   Middletown
Doughty, Jacob   Middletown
Esquire
Doughty, Jeremiah
Private, New Jersey Volunteers
Doughty, Linton   Middletown
Private, Militia, captured 2/13/77
Doughty, Samuel   Middletown
Doughty, William   Dover
Militia Volunteer, Prior to the First General Militia Muster, 6/76
Douglas, James
Private, New Jersey Volunteers, enlisted for bounty 4/79
Douglas, Joseph   Upper Freehold
plundered by Tories, 12/76
sells produce to Continental Army, 5/80
Douglas, Thomas
witness at Monmouth Court, 1778
Dove, Samuel   Freehold
Down, George   Upper Freehold
Juror, Court of Oyer and Terminer, 11/82
Down, James   Upper Freehold
Downie, John
Captain, Militia
Downs, *see* Down
Doyle, Francis
arrested for Disaffection, 11/76
accused of being active in Tory Rebellions of 12/76
Doyle, Hugh
Private, New Jersey Volunteers
Doyle, John
Private, New Jersey Volunteers
Doyle, Joseph
Private, New Jersey Volunteers, enlisted 12/13/76 dead 1/1/79

Drake, Henry
    Signer, Articles of Retaliation, 6/79
    Signer, Petition Encouraging Free Trade, 5/12/81
    Signer, Petition for Renewing Guard at Toms River, 12/10/81
    Signer, Association for Opposing the Return of Tories, 1783
    Signer, Petition Supporting Quick Division of Militia Prizes, no date
Drake, Silas
    Private, New Jersey Volunteers
Drake, Thomas   Middletown
    runaway slave
    Private, Black Brigade
Driskell, Cornelius   Upper Freehold
    Private, Militia
Driskell, Hannah   Shrewsbury
    blind child
    recipient of poor relief
Driskell, John
    Private, State Troops, enlisted 6/80
    Signer, Association for Opposing the Return of Tories, 1783
Driskell, Peggy
    indicted for Misdemeanor, 1/78
Driskey, *see* Driskell
Drumm, Andrew   Shrewsbury
    Private, Militia
Drumm, Christian   Shrewsbury
    Private, Militia
    Private, Continental Army
Drumm, Christopher   Shrewsbury
    Private, Militia, drafted into Continental Army 5/78
Drumm, David
    Private, Militia, captured 2/13/77
Drumm, George   Shrewsbury
    Private, Militia
Drumm, Martin   Shrewsbury
Drumill, Cornelius   Freehold
Drummond, Gavin   Shrewsbury
    sells produce to Continental Army, 5/80
Drummond, William   Shrewsbury
    Lieutenant, New Jersey Volunteers
DuBois, Benjamin   Freehold
    Minister, Dutch Reformed or Presbyterian Congregations
    sells produce to Continental Army, 5/80

Signer, Petition Encouraging Free Trade, 5/12/81
Duggan, Henry
   Private, New Jersey Volunteers
Duggan, Michael
   Corporal, New Jersey Volunteers
Dulavan, John
   Fifer, New Jersey Volunteers
Duline, Barnett   Upper Freehold
Dumfrey, Thomas   Upper Freehold
Dumpler, Frederick
   Drummer, New Jersey Volunteers
Dunigan, Alexander   Shrewsbury
   indicted for Murder and Receiving Stolen Goods, 1/81
Dunigan, Barnes
   indicted for Robbery, 1/81
   indicted for Horse Stealing, 11/82
Dunham, Benjamin   Shrewsbury
   convicted of Misdemeanor, 1/20/78
   indicted for Misdemeanor, 1/81
Dunham, Manasseh
   Private, Militia
   Signer, Articles of Retaliation, 6/79
   present at the capture of the British ship, Britannia, 12/31/79
Dunham, Phineas
   Private, New Jersey Volunteers
Dunite, James   Dover
Dunlop, Samuel
   Private, Militia
Dunn, Barnes
   Private, New Jersey Volunteers
Dunn, George   Shrewsbury
   Private, Militia
Dunnigan, *see* Dunigan
Dye, William
   sells produce to Continental Army, 5/80
   Signer, Petition Against Association for Retaliation 12/81

E

Eakman, Peter   Middletown
   Private, Militia
   Signer, Petition Opposing the Return of Tories 6/10/83

Earle, Charles
   Surgeon, New Jersey Volunteers
Eastlick, Alexander   Freehold
   Private, State Troops, enlists 5/78, deserts
   Signer, Petition Urging Compensation for Inflated Money, 5/22/83
Eastlick, Stephen
   Private, Continental Army, Jonathan Forman's Company, 10/77
Eaton, John   Shrewsbury
   Lieutenant, Militia
   Signer, Petition Supporting Retaliation, 9/17/80
   indicted for Misdemeanor, 1/81
Eaton, Peter
   indicted on two counts of Horse Stealing, 11/82
Eaton, Thomas
   Signer, Petition Supporting Issuing of New Jersey Currency, 1771
Eckman, see Eakman
Edsal, James
   Private, Militia
   Private, State Troops
Edwards, John   Middletown
   Private, Militia, delinquent 11/29/78, delinquent 6/11/80
Edwards, Joseph
   Private, New Jersey Volunteers, enlisted 7/22/77 deserts 10/19/77
   Private, New Jersey Volunteers, 2/78
Edwards, Josiah
   Private, New Jersey Volunteers, enlisted 1/15/77 dead 9/5/77
Edwards, Margaret   Shrewsbury
   household head
Edwards, Philip   Shrewsbury
   Private, Militia
   sells produce to Continental Army, 7/80
   Signer, Petition Supporting Retaliation, 9/17/80
Edwards, Samuel   Middletown
   witness at Monmouth Court, 1778
   deceased, 1779
Edwards, Stephen   Shrewsbury
   Private, New Jersey Volunteers, hanged 1777
Edwards, Thomas   Upper Freehold
   Lieutenant, Militia
   Signer, Petition Urging Action Against the Disaffected, 3/14/77
   Signer, Articles of Retaliation, 6/79
   Juror, Court of Oyer and Terminer, 11/82

Egbert, James
    sells produce to Continental Army, 5/80
Egbert, Lewis   Freehold
    substitute, Militia, 2/10/78
    Private, State Troops, enlists 5/78
Eldridge, David
    Private, New Jersey Volunteers, enlisted 12/15/76 dead 7/24/77
Eldridge, John
    Private, New Jersey Volunteers, captured 7/1/78
    Private, Militia
    Private, State Troops
    indicted for Assault, 5/82
Eldridge, Jonathan   Shrewsbury
    Private, Militia, captured 2/13/77
    Signer, Petition Opposing Slave Manumission, 2/2/74
Eldridge, Joseph
    Private, New Jersey Volunteers, enlisted 12/17/76 dead 11/19/77
Elliot, John
    Private, New Jersey Volunteers
Elliot, Morris
    arrested, estate confiscated
Elliot, Samuel   Freehold
    Signer, Articles of Retaliation, 6/79
Ellis, Charles
    Private, New Jersey Volunteers
Ellis, John   Upper Freehold
Ellison, Benjamin   Dover
Ellison, Catherine
    indicted for Misdemeanor, 7/83
Ellison, Daniel   Shrewsbury
Ellison, Jarvis
    arrested for Disaffection, 11/76
Ellison, John   Shrewsbury
    mulatto child orphan
    recipient of poor relief
Ellison, Lewis   Shrewsbury
    accused of being active in Tory Rebellions of 12/76
    Signer, Petition from Victims of the Association for Retaliation 9/82
Ellison, Sarah
    indicted for Misdemeanor, 7/83
Elston, Samuel   Shrewsbury
    Delegate, Friends' Quarterly Meeting, 1775

Ely, Allison   Upper Freehold
    household head
Ely, Isaac
    sells goods to Pennsylvania Salt Works, 8/76-10/76
Ely, John   Upper Freehold
    sells produce to Continental Army, 5/80
Ely, Matthew
    indicted for Misdemeanor, 11/82
Ely, Richard   Upper Freehold
Ely, William   Upper Freehold
Emans, see Emmons
Embry, Lawrence   Shrewsbury
Emley, Ezekiel   Upper Freehold
    Ensign, Militia
Emley, Jonathan
    Private, Militia
    Signer, Association for Opposing the Return of Tories, 1783
Emley, Jonathan
    Private, Militia
    Private, State Troops, enlisted 6/80
Emley, Joseph   Upper Freehold
    Private, Militia
    Private, State Troops, enlisted 6/80
    Signer, Articles of Retaliation, 6/79
Emley, Robert
    sells produce to Continental Army, 5/80
Emley, Samuel   Upper Freehold
    Private, State Troops, enlists 5/81
Emley, William   Upper Freehold
    sells produce to Continental Army, 5/80
Emley, William, Jr.   Upper Freehold
    Signer, Petition Affirming Loyalty of Moses Ivens, 3/12/77
    sells sheep to Continental Commissary 7/80
Emmerick, George   Shrewsbury
    recipient of poor relief
Emmons, Able   Shrewsbury
Emmons, Abraham   Freehold
    Private, Militia
    Private, State Troops, enlists 5/80
    Private, Continental Army
    Signer, Articles of Retaliation, 6/79
    listed as "lame" in 1781

recipient of poor relief in Shrewsbury Township
Emmons, Amos
   Private, Militia
Emmons, Charity   Shrewsbury
   household head
Emmons, Daniel   Freehold
   Private, Militia, hires substitute 2/10/78
   Signer, Articles of Retaliation, 6/79
Emmons, Daniel, Jr.   Freehold
   Private, New Jersey Volunteers, enlisted 7/26/77 deserts 1/19/78
Emmons, Ezekiel   Shrewsbury
   Private, Militia
Emmons, Hendrick   Shrewsbury
   blind
   recipient of poor relief
Emmons, Isaac
   Private, Militia, delinquent 2/10/78
Emmons, Jacob   Shrewsbury
   estate inquisitioned for Forfeiture, 6/1/78
   estate confiscated
Emmons, Jacob
   Private, New Jersey Volunteers, enlisted 4/5/77 dead 8/30/77
Emmons, Jedediah   Shrewsbury
   Private, Militia
Emmons, Jesse
   Private, Militia
   helps keep the poor
   Signer, Petition Supporting Retaliation, 9/17/80
Emmons, Jesse, Jr.   Shrewsbury
   Private, Militia, deserts 6/79
Emmons, John   Freehold
   Sergeant, Militia
   indicted for Gaming, 12/80
Emmons, John, Jr.   Freehold
   house burned by British Army, 6/28/78
   Signer, Articles of Retaliation, 6/79
   indicted for Misdemeanor, 1/81
Emmons, John   Shrewsbury
   Signer, Articles of Retaliation, 6/79
Emmons, John
   Private, New Jersey Volunteers, enlisted 4/6/77 dead 6/16/77
Emmons, Lewis

Emmons, Mary   Shrewsbury
  Private, Militia
  household head
Emmons, Peter   Freehold
  Signer, Articles of Retaliation, 6/79
Emmons, Peter   Freehold
  Private, Militia, captured 2/13/77
Emmons, Pontius   Shrewsbury
  Private, Militia
Emmons, Stephen   Dover
  Pine Robber, a.k.a. "Burke", killed
Emmons, Thomas   Dover
  Private, New Jersey Volunteers, enlisted 4/15/77 deserts 8/23/77
  indicted for Robbery, 6/78
  Pine Robber
Emmons, Thomas   Shrewsbury
  witness at Monmouth Court
English, David
  Signer, Association for Opposing the Return of Tories, 1783
English, Ezekiel   Freehold
  household head
English, James   Freehold
  Signer, Articles of Retaliation, 6/79
  Signer, Petition Supporting Retaliation, 9/17/80
  Signer, Petition Encouraging Free Trade, 5/12/81
English, James   Freehold
  Private, Militia
  Signer, Articles of Retaliation, 6/79
English, William   Upper Freehold
Enobly, Jonathan
  Signer, Articles of Retaliation, 6/79
Ensley, Jacob
  Corporal, New Jersey Volunteers
Ensley, Randall
  Private, New Jersey Volunteers
Erickson, Erik
  Private, Militia
Erickson, John   Freehold
  Ensign, Militia
  Signer, Articles of Retaliation, 6/79
Erickson, John, Jr.   Freehold
  Laborer, Pennsylvania Salt Works, intermittent 8/76-6/77

Erickson, Michael				Freehold
  Signer, Articles of Retaliation, 6/79
Erickson, Michael, Jr.			Freehold
  Private, Militia
  Sergeant, Continental Army
  Signer, Petition Urging Compensation for Inflated Money, 5/22/83
Erickson, Susannah			Middletown
  household head
Erickson, Thomas
  Private, Militia
  Signer, Articles of Retaliation, 6/79
Ervin, see Irvin
Erwin, John
  Private, Militia
Essick, Stephen
  Private, Militia
  Private, Continental Army
Estell, Jacob				Shrewsbury
Estell, Jonathan			Upper Freehold
Estell, John				Shrewsbury
Estell, Joseph				Upper Freehold
Evans, Emanuel
  Private, New Jersey Volunteers, enlisted for bounty 4/79
Evengen, William
  Private, Militia
Everingham, Dinah			Upper Freehold
Everingham, James			Upper Freehold
Everingham, John			Upper Freehold
  Private, Militia
Everingham, Nathaniel			Upper Freehold
  Private, Militia
  Signer, Petition Against Association for Retaliation 12/81
Everingham, Thomas			Upper Freehold
  Private, Militia
  Signer, Petition Against Association for Retaliation 12/81
Everingham, William			Upper Freehold
  indicted for Misdemeanor, 1/81
  Signer, Petition Against Association for Retaliation 12/81
Evilman, John				Upper Freehold
  Signer, Petition Against Association for Retaliation 12/81
Evilman, Robert				Upper Freehold
  sells produce to Continental Army, 5/80

Signer, Petition Against Association for Retaliation 12/81
Eyre, Hannah
  indicted for Misdemeanor, 11/81

F

Faddle, George
  Private, New Jersey Volunteers
Fagan, Jacob   Shrewsbury
  Private, New Jersey Volunteers, captured or deserts 6/26/78
  Pine Robber, killed
Fagan, Patrick   Upper Freehold
  Militia Volunteer, Prior to the First General Militia Muster, 6/76
Fagan, Philip   Upper Freehold
Fagan, Philip
  Private, New Jersey Volunteers, enlisted 5/14/77 deserts 12/4/78
Fagan, Pomphilus   Freehold
Fagan, William   Upper Freehold
Fall, Terence
  Private, New Jersey Volunteers, deserted 7/2/77
Falsey, Annaniah
  indicted for Misdemeanor, 5/82
Farmer, Dennis
  Private, Militia
  present at the capture of the British ship, Britannia, 12/31/79
Farnham, John
  indicted for Robbery, 6/3/78
  indicted for Murder, 1/81
  Pine Robber
Farr, John
  Private, Militia
  Private, State Troops killed 3/24/82
Farr, Thomas   Upper Freehold
  Signer, Petition for Stricter Militia Law, 5/31/79
Farr, William
  Private, Continental Army, Jonathan Forman's Company, 10/77
Farrah, see Farrow
Farrow, Catherine
  wife of David
  convicted of Misdemeanor, 1778
Farrow, David
Farrow, Elizabeth   Middletown

wife of Peter
  indicted for Misdemeanor, 1/78
  indicted for Misdemeanor, 6/78
Farrow, Peter				Middletown
  indicted for Misdemeanor, 6/78
Fary, William
  Private, Militia
  Private, Continental Army
Farveaux, Henry
  Private, State Troops, enlists 5/81
Feel, Nathaniel			Freehold
Felton, Joseph
  Private, Militia, delinquent 4/82
Fennimore, see Finamore
Fenton, George			Upper Freehold
  Private, Militia
Fenton, George, Jr.		Upper Freehold
Fenton, James			Upper Freehold
  Private, Militia
Fenton, John			Upper Freehold
Fenton, Lewis			Freehold
  witness at Monmouth Court, 1778
  Pine Robber, killed
Fenton, Thomas			Shrewsbury
  Private, Militia
Fenton, Thomas			Upper Freehold
  Private, Militia
Fenton, William			Upper Freehold
  delinquent, hires Substitute 2/10/78
Ferguson, William			Upper Freehold
  accused of being active in Loyalist Rebellion of 12/76
  Signer, Petition Favoring Quick Division of Prize Money, 12/79
Ferrel, Absalom
  Private, Militia
Ferrel, James
  Private, New Jersey Volunteers, enlisted 12/23/76 dead 3/24/77
Ferrel, William
  Private, New Jersey Volunteers
  estate inquisitioned for Forfeiture, 4/1/80
Ferris, Nathaniel
  Private, Militia
  Private, State Troops, enlisted 6/80

Roster of the People of Revolutionary Monmouth County

Ferris, William
   Private, Militia
   Private, State Troops, enlisted 6/80
Fetters, William   Upper Freehold
Field, Elijah   Upper Freehold
Field, Elnathan   Middletown
   indicted for Misdemeanor, 6/78
Field, John
   Private, New Jersey Volunteers
Field, Thomas
   substitute, Militia 2/10/78
   convicted of Misdemeanor, 1/81
Fielder, Rice   Shrewsbury
Fields, *see* Field
Finamore, John
   Private, New Jersey Volunteers, enlisted 12/17/76 deserts 9/5/78
   indicted for Misdemeanor, 1/81
Finnen, Jesse
   indicted for High Treason, 6/3/78
Finney, George
   Private, New Jersey Volunteers, captured 8/22/77
   witness at Monmouth Court, 1778
Fischer, *see* Fisher
Fish, Benjamin
   Private, New Jersey Volunteers, 2/78
   Private, Militia, delinquent 4/82
Fish, David
   Private, Militia, delinquent, 8/9/80
Fish, John   Shrewsbury
   Private, New Jersey Volunteers, dead 8/15/77
Fisher, Bartholomew
   Private, New Jersey Volunteers, enlisted 2/5/77 deserted 6/7/77
Fisher, Charles   Upper Freehold
   Private, Militia
Fisher, Elizabeth   Shrewsbury
   household head
   indicted for Misdemeanor, 8/79
   listed on Militia return 6/29/80
Fisher, George
   Private, New Jersey Volunteers, enlisted 2/5/77 dead 9/3/77
Fisher, Henry   Upper Freehold
   Private, Militia

Signer, Association for Opposing the Return of Tories, 1783
Fisher, John   Freehold
    Private, Continental Army
Fisher, Rebecca   Upper Freehold
    household head
Fisher, Ruliff   Freehold
Fisher, Thomas
    Private, New Jersey Volunteers, enlisted 12/2/76 dead 1/5/77
Fitch, William
    Sergeant, New Jersey Volunteers
Fitzgerald, Ambrose
    Private, New Jersey Volunteers
Fitzrandolph, *see also* Randolph
Fitzrandolph, Joseph
    indicted for Felony, 6/3/78
Fitzsimmon, James   Freehold
    Private, Militia
Fitzsimmon, Robert   Freehold
    Private, State Troops
Fleet, Thomas   Middletown
Fleming, Christian   Shrewsbury
Fleming, Jacob   Shrewsbury
    Lieutenant, Militia
    Signer, Petition Opposing Slave Manumission, 2/2/74
    holds tavern license, 1775
    Signer, Petition to Better Provision Militia, 2/25/78
    Signer, Petition Favoring Quick Division of Prize Money, 12/79
Fleming, James   Shrewsbury
    helps keep the poor
    indicted for Misdemeanor, 5/82
    indicted for two counts of Misdemeanor, 11/82
Fleming, John   Upper Freehold
    sells produce to Continental Army, 5/80
Fleming, Joseph   Shrewsbury
    Signer, Petition to Better Provision Militia, 2/25/78
    Signer, Articles of Retaliation, 6/79
Fleming, Stephen   Shrewsbury and Middletown
    Captain, Militia captured 1780
    Signer, Articles of Retaliation, 6/79
    Grand Juror, Court of Oyer and Terminer, 8/79
    Signer, Petition Favoring Quick Division of Prize Money, 12/79
    sells produce to Continental Army, 7/80

Signer, Petition Supporting Retaliation, 9/17/80
Signer, Petition for Renewing Guard at Toms River, 12/10/81
indicted for Misdemeanor, 5/82
Grand Juror, Court of Oyer and Terminer, 11/82
Signer, Petition Opposing the Return of Tories 6/10/83

Flin, Alexander
   Private, New Jersey Volunteers

Flin, Edward   Dover
   Militia Volunteer, Prior to the First General Militia Muster, 6/76

Flin, Walter
   Private, New Jersey Volunteers

Fling, Flynn, see Flin

Forman, Aaron
   Drummer, Militia

Forman, Andrew

Forman, Caty   Upper Freehold

Forman, David   Freehold
   Lieutenant of Militia, Prior to the First General Militia Muster, 6/76
   Brigadier General, Militia, 1777
   Colonel, Continental Army
   Signer, Petition for Settlement of Quartermaster Debts, 9/6/77
   rented Confiscated Tory estate, prior to 5/79
   Signer, Petition for Stricter Militia Law, 5/31/79
   Signer, Articles of Retaliation, 6/79
   sells produce to Continental Army, 5/80
   Grand Juror, Court of Oyer and Terminer, 12/80
   Signer, Petition Encouraging Free Trade, 5/12/81
   Signer, Petition for Renewing Guard at Toms River, 12/10/81
   leased horse team to Continental Quarter Master 12/81
   Judge of the Court of Oyer and Terminer, 5/82 & 7/83
   Signer, Association for Opposing the Return of Tories, 1783
   lost slaves during the war

Forman, David   Upper Freehold
   Lieutenant, Militia
   Paymaster, Militia
   Sheriff, 1779-81
   Signer, Petition Urging Action Against the Disaffected, 3/14/77
   Grand Juror, Court of Oyer and Terminer, 8/79
   Signer, Articles of Retaliation, 6/79
   sells produce to Continental Army, 5/80
   leased horse team to Continental Quarter Master 12/81
   Grand Juror, Court of Oyer and Terminer, 5/82

Coroner, 1783
Forman, David   Upper Freehold
   sells produce to Continental Army, 5/80
   leased horse team to Continental Quarter Master 12/81
   Juror, Court of Oyer and Terminer, 7/83
Forman, Dennis (Denice)
   Private, Militia
Forman, Ezekiel   Upper Freehold
   Signer, Petition in Support of William Barton, 1/31/76
   convicted of High Treason, 6/78
Forman, Jane   Upper Freehold
   household head
   sells produce to Continental Army, 5/80
Forman, John
   Lieutenant of Militia, Prior to the First General Militia Muster, 6/76
   Ensign, Militia
   Signer, Petition Supporting Issuing of New Jersey Currency, 1771
Forman, Jonathan   Freehold
   Cornet, State Troops
   Signer, Articles of Retaliation, 6/79
   present at the capture of the British ship, Britannia, 12/31/79
   sells produce to Continental Army, 5/80
   sells produce to Continental Army, 7/80
   Signer, Petition for Renewing Guard at Toms River, 12/10/81
   Grand Juror, Court of Oyer and Terminer, 11/82
   Signer, Association for Opposing the Return of Tories, 1783
   Juror, Court of Oyer and Terminer, 7/83
Forman, Jonathan   Freehold and Middletown
   Militia Volunteer, Prior to the First General Militia Muster, 6/76
   Captain, Militia
   Lt. Colonel, Continental Army
   Signer, Articles of Retaliation, 6/79
   Signer, Petition Supporting Retaliation, 9/17/80
   Signer, Petition Encouraging Free Trade, 5/12/81
   Signer, Association for Opposing the Return of Tories, 1783
Forman, Jonathan
   Private, Militia
   indicted for Misdemeanor, 1/78
   Private, State Troops, enlisted 6/80
Forman, Lewis   Middletown
   Signer, Petition to Better Provision Militia, 2/25/78
   Signer, Petition Against Loyalist Auction Commissioners, 3/24/79

Roster of the People of Revolutionary Monmouth County

    Signer, Petition for Stricter Militia Law, 5/31/79
    Signer, Petition Against Association for Retaliation 12/81
Forman, Peter, Esq.   Freehold and Middletown
    Justice of the Court
    Signer, Petition Opposing Slave Manumission, 2/2/74
    Coroner, 1779
    Signer, Petition for Stricter Militia Law, 5/31/79
    Signer, Articles of Retaliation, 6/79
    Signer, Petition Urging Compensation for Raid Victims, 5/25/79
    Signer, Petition Favoring Quick Division of Prize Money, 12/79
    sells produce to Continental Army, 5/80
    Signer, Petition Supporting Retaliation, 9/17/80
    Signer, Petition Encouraging Free Trade, 5/12/81
    Judge of the Court of Oyer and Terminer, 12/80
    Juror, Court of Oyer and Terminer, 11/82
    Judge of the Court of Oyer and Terminer, 5/82 & 11/82 & 7/83
    Signer, Association for Opposing the Return of Tories, 1783
Forman, Samuel   Freehold
    Signer, Petition Urging Compensation for Raid Victims, 5/25/79
    Signer, Articles of Retaliation, 6/79
    sells produce to Continental Army, 5/80
    Signer, Petition Supporting Retaliation, 9/17/80
Forman, Samuel, Jr.   Middletown
    Militia Volunteer, Prior to the First General Militia Muster, 6/76
    Private, Militia
    Signer, Petition for Stricter Militia Law, 5/31/79
    sells produce to Continental Army, 5/80
Forman, Samuel   Middletown
    merchant
    Signer, Petition Opposing Slave Manumission, 2/2/74
    Signer, Petition for Stricter Militia Law, 5/31/79
    sells produce to Continental Army, 5/80
    Juror, Court of Oyer and Terminer, 12/80
        fined L3 for missing all or some of jury duty
    Signer, Petition Opposing the Return of Tories 6/10/83
Forman, Samuel   Upper Freehold
    Colonel, Militia
    Signer, Petition Calling for Action Against the Disaffected, 2/21/77
    Signer, Petition Urging Action Against the Disaffected, 3/14/77
    Signer, Petition for Stricter Militia Law, 5/31/79
    Signer, Articles of Retaliation, 6/79
    sells produce to Continental Army, 5/80

sells sheep to Continental Commissary 7/80
Signer, Petition in Favor of Daniel Longstreet, 11/21/80
Signer, Petition Encouraging Free Trade, 5/12/81
Signer, Petition Urging Action Against Disaffected
& Favoring Retaliation, 5/12/81
Signer, Petition for Renewing Guard at Toms River, 12/10/81
Signer, Association for Opposing the Return of Tories, 1783
Signer, Petition Supporting Quick Division of Militia Prizes, no date

Forman, Sarah   Upper Freehold
   household head

Forman, Thomas   Upper Freehold
   witness at Monmouth Court, 1778
   Signer, Petition for Stricter Militia Law, 5/31/79
   Judge of the Court of Oyer and Terminer, 8/79
   Signer, Association for Opposing the Return of Tories, 1783

Forman, Tunis
   Sergeant, Militia
   Signer, Articles of Retaliation, 6/79

Forman, William   Freehold
   Sergeant, Militia
   Private, State Troops, enlisted 6/80
   Signer, Articles of Retaliation, 6/79
   Signer, Petition Favoring Quick Division of Prize Money, 12/79
   Signer, Association for Opposing the Return of Tories, 1783

Forrill, Absalom   Upper Freehold

Forster, *see* Foster

Foster, Ephraim
   Ensign, Militia

Foster, Jacob   Upper Freehold
   indicted for Misdemeanor, 6/3/78
   convicted of Misdemeanor, 12/80

Foster, Jacob   Dover
   Militia Volunteer, Prior to the First General Militia Muster, 6/76
   indicted for Misdemeanor, 8/79
   indicted for Misdemeanor, 1/81
   Township Overseer of the Highways, 1783

Foster, Lawrence
   Tory, flees to New York

Foster, Nathaniel   Dover

Foster, Samuel   Shrewsbury

Fowe, Moses
   Private, New Jersey Volunteers, enlisted 3/18/77   dead 5/23/77

Fowler, Barton
   Private, New Jersey Volunteers, dead 8/12/77
Fowler, Josiah
   Private, Continental Army
Fowler, Moses   Middletown
   Signer, Petition Opposing Slave Manumission, 2/2/74
Fowler, Purdy
   household head
   sells goods to Pennsylvania Salt Works, 8/76-10/76
Fowler, William   Upper Freehold
   Militia Volunteer, Prior to the First General Militia Muster, 6/76
   Private, New Jersey Volunteers
   Accused of Being Active in Tory Uprising of 12/76
Fowness, Henry   Middletown
   lost slaves during the war
Fox, Jonathan
   Private, New Jersey Volunteers, enlisted 12/2/76 deserted 3/4/77
Francis, Richard   Upper Freehold
   witness at Monmouth Court, 1778
   Signer, Petition Against Association for Retaliation 12/81
Frease, Henry   Upper Freehold
   Corporal, Militia
Frease, Jesse
   Sergeant, Continental Army
Freeman, Israel (Asael)   Shrewsbury
   indicted for Misdemeanor, 11/82
Freeman, Israel, Jr.   Shrewsbury
   indicted for Misdemeanor, 11/82
Freeman, James
   Signer, Petition Supporting Retaliation, 9/17/80
Freeman, John   Freehold
   Signer, Articles of Retaliation, 6/79
   Signer, Petition Supporting Retaliation, 1780
   sells produce to Continental Army, 5/80
   Signer, Petition Supporting Retaliation, 9/17/80
   Signer, Petition Encouraging Free Trade, 5/12/81
   Signer, Petition Supporting Quick Division of Militia Prizes, no date
Freeman, John   Freehold
   Private, Militia
   Private, State Troops, enlisted 6/80
   Signer, Articles of Retaliation, 6/79
Freeman, Morris

Private, New Jersey Volunteers, dead prior to 1779
Freeman, Philip
    Private, Militia
Freeze, see Frease
French, William   Upper Freehold
Friend, Deborah   Middletown
    household head
Friend, Hendrick
    Private, Militia
Frisalear, James
    Private, Militia
Frisnaw, Dennis
    Private, State Troops
    present at the capture of the British ship, Britannia, 12/31/79
Fritzeller, John   Shrewsbury
    convicted of Misdemeanor, 1/20/78
Frost, Garret   Middletown
    Signer, Petition Opposing the Return of Tories 6/10/83
Frost, Hester (Esther)   Middletown
    household head
    indicted for Misdemeanor, 1/78
    indicted for Misdemeanor, 6/78
Frost, James   Middletown
    Signer, Petition Opposing Slave Manumission, 2/2/74
Furgeson, see Ferguson
Furtier, David   Shrewsbury
    Private, Militia
    Private, State Troops

G

Gainer, Abraham
    indicted for Misdemeanor, 1/81
Gale, Alexander   Stafford
    Private, Continental Army
Galledat, see Giledat
Gallahan, Hardy   Shrewsbury
    recipient of poor relief
Gammage, Agnes
    widow of John
    indicted for Misdemeanor, 8/79
Gamberton, Charles

Sergeant, Continental Army, Jonathan Forman's Company, 10/77
Gant, *see* Gount, Grant
Gardner, Edward
    Private, New Jersey Volunteers, enlisted 12/16/76 dead 3/17/77
Gardner, Peter
    Private, New Jersey Volunteers, enlisted 12/2/76 dead 2/3/77
Garn, George
    Private, New Jersey Volunteers, captured 8/22/77
Garret, *see* Garrot
Garrison, Christopher   Shrewsbury
    helps keep the poor
Garrison, Garret   Middletown
    Private, Militia
    present at the capture of the British ship, Britannia, 12/31/79
Garrison, Hannah   Middletown
    household head
Garrison, Jason
    Private, New Jersey Volunteers
Garrison, John
    indicted for Misdemeanor, 1/81
    indicted for Horse Stealing, 11/82
Garrot, Richard   Upper Freehold
Garvey, Alexander
    Private, New Jersey Volunteers, captured 8/22/77
Garvey, Ann
    wife of Alexander
    indicted for Misdemeanor, 8/79
Garvey, Catherine   Shrewsbury
    household head
    indicted for Misdemeanor, 8/79
Garvey, John
    Drummer, New Jersey Volunteers, captured prior to 1779
Garvey, Patrick
    Private, New Jersey Volunteers
    indicted for Misdemeanor, 11/81
    indicted for Contraband Trading, 5/82
Garwood, Andrew   Upper Freehold
Gaston, Daniel   Upper Freehold
    Private, Militia
    Signer, Petition Urging Action Against Disaffected
        & Favoring Retaliation, 5/12/81
    Juror, Court of Oyer and Terminer, 5/82

Gaston, Hugh Upper Freehold
  Signer, Petition Urging Action Against Disaffected
    & Favoring Retaliation, 5/12/81
Gaston, John Upper Freehold
Gaston, John, Jr. Upper Freehold
  Sergeant, Militia
  Signer, Petition Urging Action Against Disaffected
    & Favoring Retaliation, 5/12/81
Gaston, William Upper Freehold
  Sergeant, Militia
  Signer, Association for Opposing the Return of Tories, 1783
Gaunt, see Grant, Gount
Genkins, see Jenkins
George, Thomas Shrewsbury
Geron, Abraham
  indicted for Misdemeanor, 5/82
Geron, Thomas Middletown
  Private, Militia
  Private, State Troops
  present at the capture of the British ship, Britannia, 12/31/79
Gerricks, Aaron
  Private, New Jersey Volunteers
Gettings, Edward
  Private, New Jersey Volunteers, captured 2/18/77
Gibbs, Daniel Freehold
Gibbs, Joshua Upper Freehold
Gibbons, Benjamin
  Signer, Petition Supporting Issuing of New Jersey Currency, 1771
Gibbons, Jacob Upper Freehold
Gibbons, Safety Upper Freehold
  household head
Giberson, Benjamin Dover
  Militia Volunteer, Prior to the First General Militia Muster, 6/76
Giberson, Benjamin Upper Freehold
  estate inquisitioned for Forfeiture, 4/5/79
  estate confiscated
Giberson, Guisebert Upper Freehold
  Private, New Jersey Volunteers, enlisted 1/19/77 deserts 6/17/77
Giberson, Guisebert Upper Freehold
  Captain, Militia, resigns 8/8/76
  Captain, New Jersey Volunteers
  indicted for Misdemeanor, 1/78

Roster of the People of Revolutionary Monmouth County

    estate inquisitioned for Forfeiture, 7/4/77
    estate confiscated, settles in PA. after the war
Giberson, Guisebert   Upper Freehold
    Private, Militia
Giberson, Harmon   Upper Freehold
Giberson, Harmon, Jr.   Upper Freehold
Giberson, Hezekiah
    Private, New Jersey Volunteers, enlisted 4/12/77 deserts 6/17/77
Giberson, Israel (Isaiah)   Upper Freehold
    Private, Militia
Giberson, James   Upper Freehold
    Private, Militia
Giberson, John   Dover
    Private, New Jersey Volunteers, enlisted 4/2/77 deserted 8/21/77
Giberson, John   Upper Freehold
Giberson, Joseph   Dover
    Private, Militia
Giberson, Joseph   Upper Freehold
    Private, Militia
    indicted on two counts of Riot, 6/3/78
Giberson, Josiah   Upper Freehold
    indicted for Misdemeanor, 1/78
Giberson, Malachi   Upper Freehold
    estate confiscated
Giberson, Meribah   Upper Freehold
Giberson, Reuben   Upper Freehold
    Private, Militia
Giberson, William   Upper Freehold
Giberson, William, Jr.   Upper Freehold
   arrested for Disaffection, 1777
   indicted for Misdemeanor, 6/3/78
   estate inquisitioned for Forfeiture, 4/5/79
   estate confiscated
   indicted for Misdemeanor, 1/81
   indicted for Horse Stealing, 5/82
Gifford, Abraham   Shrewsbury
Gifford, Abram
    Private, New Jersey Volunteers, enlisted 12/16/76 dead 4/1/77
Gifford, Annaniah   Shrewsbury
    Private, Militia, delinquent 8/9/80
    Laborer, Pennsylvania Salt Works, intermittent 8/76-6/77
Gifford, Elisha   Middletown

Gifford, Joshua Shrewsbury
Gifford, Joshua, Jr. Shrewsbury
Gifford, Joseph Shrewsbury
   Private, Militia, delinquent 8/80
Gifford, Joseph Shrewsbury
Gifford, William Dover
   Militia Volunteer, Prior to the First General Militia Muster, 6/76
Gilchrist, John
   Private, New Jersey Volunteers, captured prior to 1779
Giledat, Ebenezer Shrewsbury
   Private, Militia
Giledat, Naomi Freehold
   household head
Giledat, Peter Freehold
   Private, Militia
   Private, State Troops, enlists 5/78
   Private, Continental Army
Gill, John Shrewsbury
   Private, Militia
   Private, State Troops, enlists 5/78
   Private, Continental Army
Gill, Thomas
   Juror, Court of Oyer and Terminer, 8/79
      fined L30 for missing all or some of jury duty
   Juror, Court of Oyer and Terminer, 11/82
Gillian, William
   Tory partisan, killed 1780
Gilman, see Gilmore
Gilmore, Charles Middletown
   Private, Militia, hires substitute 2/78
   witness at Monmouth Court, 1778
   Signer, Petition Against Loyalist Auction Commissioners, 3/24/79
   Signer, Articles of Retaliation, 6/79
   Signer, Petition Favoring Quick Division of Prize Money, 12/79
Gilmore, Charles, Jr. Middletown
   Private, Militia, serves as substitute 3/78
   Signer, Petition Favoring Quick Division of Prize Money, 12/79
   indicted for Misdemeanor, 1/81
Ginkins, see Jenkins
Gittings, see Gettings
Golahar, Ebenezer Freehold
   Private, Militia

Golahar, Lewis   Freehold
    Private, Militia
Golahar, William   Freehold
Gold, Edward
    estate inquisitioned for Forfeiture, 7/5/77
Gold, James
    indicted for Misdemeanor, 1/81
    indicted for Misdemeanor, 5/82
    indicted for Misdemeanor, 11/82
Golden, Abraham   Middletown
Golden, Joseph   Middletown
    Overseer of Highways, 1775
    donates to Charity Fund for Stevenson Family, 5/83
Golder, *see* Golden
Goodenough, Joseph
    Corporal, Militia, captured 2/13/77
Google, Hendrick   Middletown
    Sergeant, Militia
Gordon, Benjamin
    Private, New Jersey Volunteers, dead 6/28/78
Gordon, Charles
    Justice of the Peace, 1782-3
    Juror, Court of Oyer and Terminer, 5/82
        fined for missing jury duty
    Signer, Petition Urging Compensation for Inflated Money, 5/22/83
Gordon, David   Freehold
    sells produce to Continental Army, 5/80
Gordon, David, Jr.   Freehold
    Captain, Militia
    plundered by Tories, 12/76
    Signer, Petition Calling for Action Against the Disaffected, 2/21/77
    Signer, Petition Urging Action Against the Disaffected, 3/14/77
    Signer, Petition to Better Provision Militia, 2/25/78
    Signer, Petition for Stricter Militia Law, 5/31/79
    Signer, Articles of Retaliation, 6/79
    Signer, Petition Favoring Quick Division of Prize Money, 12/79
    Signer, Petition Supporting Retaliation, 1780
    sells produce to Continental Army, 5/80
    Signer, Petition Encouraging Free Trade, 5/12/81
    Juror, Court of Oyer and Terminer, 5/82
        fined for missing jury duty
    Grand Juror, Court of Oyer and Terminer, 11/82

Signer, Petition Urging Compensation for Inflated Money, 5/22/83
Gordon, James					Freehold
   sells goods to Pennsylvania Salt Works, 8/76-10/76
   sells sheep to Continental Commissary 7/80
Gordon, John
   Private, New Jersey Volunteers, captured 8/22/77
Gordon, Lewis					Freehold
   Signer, Articles of Retaliation, 6/79
   Signer, Petition Against Loyalist Auction Commissioners, 3/24/79
   Signer, Petition Supporting Retaliation, 9/17/80
   Signer, Petition Urging Compensation for Inflated Money, 5/22/83
Gordon, Peter					Freehold
   Private, Militia
   Signer, Articles of Retaliation, 6/79
   Signer, Petition Supporting Retaliation, 1780
   Signer, Petition Encouraging Free Trade, 5/12/81
   Signer, Association for Opposing the Return of Tories, 1783
Gordon, Timothy					Freehold
   Signer, Articles of Retaliation, 6/79
   Signer, Petition Supporting Retaliation, 1780
   Signer, Petition Encouraging Free Trade, 5/12/81
   Signer, Petition Urging Compensation for Inflated Money, 5/22/83
Gordon, William					Freehold
   Private, Militia
   Private, Continental Army
   Signer, Articles of Retaliation, 6/79
   sells produce to Continental Army, 5/80
   Signer, Petition Urging Compensation for Inflated Money, 5/22/83
Gore, James
   Private, Militia
Gorman, John
   Private, New Jersey Volunteers, captured 8/22/77
Gorman, Thomas
   Drummer, New Jersey Volunteers
Gorton, *see* Gordon
Gount, *see also* Grant
Gount, Israel					Dover
Gount, John					Dover
   Militia Volunteer, Prior to the First General Militia Muster, 6/76
Gount, Zachariah				Dover
Grandin, Daniel					Freehold
   Signer, Petition Supporting Issuing of New Jersey Currency, 1771

sells Produce to Continental Army 5/80
Grandin, Daniel   Shrewsbury
    Ensign, New Jersey Volunteers
    accused of being part of Samuel Wright's Tory Association 11/76
    accused of being active in Tory Rebellions of 12/76
    arrested for Disaffection, 1/77
    indicted for Misdemeanor, 5/82
Grandin, Thomas
    Ensign, New Jersey Volunteers, court martialed 1778
    Indicted for Riot & Assault, 1/20/78
Grandin, William   Freehold
    Militia Volunteer, Prior to the First General Militia Muster, 6/76
    Private, New Jersey Volunteers, deserts
Grandin, William   Shrewsbury
    accused of being part of Samuel Wright's Tory Association 11/76
    arrested for Disaffection, 1/77
    indicted on four counts of Riot, and one count of Assault, 1/20/78
Grant, *see also* Gount
Grant, James   Dover
Grant, John   Dover
    Private, New Jersey Volunteers, enlisted 12/5/76 deserts 3/19/77
    Juror, Court of Oyer and Terminer, 1/78
        fined L5 for not attending all or part of Jury duty
Grant, John
    Private, New Jersey Volunteers, enlisted 12/24/76 dead 1/18/78
Grant, Zachariah
    Militia Volunteer, Prior to the First General Militia Muster, 6/76
    Private, New Jersey Volunteers, enlisted 12/5/76 dead 2/11/77
Grass, Jacob
    Private, New Jersey Volunteers
Gravat, John   Upper Freehold
    Private, Militia
Gravat, Johnson   Upper Freehold
    Private, Militia
Gravat, Joseph   Upper Freehold
    Private, Militia
Gravat, Peter   Freehold
Gravat, Peter   Upper Freehold
Garvat, Robert   Upper Freehold
    Signer, Petition Favoring Quick Division of Prize Money, 12/79
Gravat, William   Upper Freehold
    Private, Militia

Gray, James
    Drummer, New Jersey Volunteers
Gregley, James
    sells produce to Continental Army, 5/80
Green, Henry   Shrewsbury
    Baptist
Green, James   Shrewsbury and Freehold
    Captain, Militia
    Signer, Petition Urging Action Against the Disaffected, 3/14/77
    Signer, Petition for Stricter Militia Law, 5/31/79
    Signer, Articles of Retaliation, 6/79
    Signer, Petition Favoring Quick Division of Prize Money, 12/79
    Signer, Petition Supporting Retaliation, 9/17/80
    Signer, Petition in Favor of Daniel Longstreet, 11/21/80
    Signer, Petition Encouraging Free Trade, 5/12/81
    Signer, Petition for Renewing Guard at Toms River, 12/10/81
    Signer, Petition Urging Action Against the Pine Robbers, 12/27/81
    Juror, Court of Oyer and Terminer, 5/82
    Grand Juror, Court of Oyer and Terminer, 11/82
    Signer, Association for Opposing the Return of Tories, 1783
Green, James   Upper Freehold
    free black householder
Green, John   Shrewsbury
Green, Reuben
    Sergeant, New Jersey Volunteers
Green, William   Shrewsbury
    Private, New Jersey Volunteers
    indicted for Misdemeanor, 1/81
    indicted for Misdemeanor, 11/81
Greenwood, Daniel
    Private, New Jersey Volunteers, captured 8/22/77
    Private, Militia
    Private, Continental Army
Gregory, Hannah   Upper Freehold
    household head
Gregory, John
    Private, Militia
Grevat, see Gravat
Griffey, Edward
    Private, Continental Army
Griffey, Joseph
    Private, Continental Army

Griffins, James
   Private, New Jersey Volunteers
Griffins, Richard
   Private, New Jersey Volunteers
Griggs, Daniel   Dover
   Militia Volunteer, Prior to the First General Militia Muster, 6/76
   Merchant, sells goods to Pennsylvania Salt Works, 8/76-10/76
   Signer, Petition to Better Defend Toms River Area, 5/18/77
   Signer, Articles of Retaliation, 6/79
   Signer, Petition Urging Action Against the Pine Robbers, 12/27/81
   Grand Juror, Court of Oyer and Terminer, 11/82
Griggs, James
   indicted for Misdemeanor, 5/82
Griggs, Joseph   Upper Freehold and Dover
   Militia Volunteer, Prior to the First General Militia Muster, 6/76
   sells goods to Pennsylvania Salt Works, 8/76-10/76
Griggs, Matthew
   Private, Militia
Griggs, Thomas
   Private, Militia
Grimes, George
   Private, Militia
   Private, Continental Army
Grimes, James
   Sergeant, New Jersey Volunteers
Grogen, Ezekiel   Freehold
Grooms, Elijah (Elisha)
   Sergeant, New Jersey Volunteers, 1776-82
   indicted for Robbery and Murder, 8/79
   indicted for Robbery, 1/81
Grooms, Ezekiel   Freehold
Grooms, Joseph
   Private, New Jersey Volunteers, captured 6/26/78
Grooms, Thomas   Upper Freehold
Grooms, Thomas
   Private, New Jersey Volunteers, enlisted 5/3/77 dead 7/9/77
Grover, Barzilla   Upper Freehold
   Captain of Militia, Prior to the First General Militia Muster, 6/76
   estate confiscated
Grover, James, Esq.   Middletown
   Baptist, converts to Quaker
   Chosen Freeholder, 1770-6

Signer, Petition Supporting Issuing of New Jersey Currency, 1771
Signer, Petition Opposing Slave Manumission, 2/2/74
convicted of Misdemeanor, 6/3/78
Signer, Petition from Victims of the Association for Retaliation 9/82
Delegate, Friends' Quarterly Meeting, 1782

Grover, James, Jr.　　　　　Middletown
　Baptist
　Commissioner of Appeals, 1771

Grover, John　　　　　　　Middletown
　indicted for Misdemeanor, 1/78

Grover, Joseph　　　　　　Middletown
　Signer, Petition Opposing Slave Manumission, 2/2/74

Grover, Joseph　　　　　　Upper Freehold
　Militia Volunteer, Prior to the First General Militia Muster, 6/76
　estate confiscated

Grover, Samuel　　　　　　Upper Freehold
　estate confiscated

Grover, Sarah　　　　　　　Middletown
　wife of James
　household head
　indicted for Misdemeanor, 1/20/78

Grover, Sylvanus　　　　　 Middletown
　Overseer of Highways, 1780-2

Grover, Theodorus
　indicted for Misdemeanor, 1/20/78

Grover, Thomas　　　　　　Upper Freehold
　Militia Volunteer, Prior to the First General Militia Muster, 6/76
　accused of being active in Loyalist Rebellion of 12/76
　indicted for Misdemeanor, 1/20/78
　estate confiscated

Grover, William　　　　　　Upper Freehold
　Militia Volunteer, Prior to the First General Militia Muster, 6/76
　arrested for Disaffection, 11/76
　convicted of High Treason, 6/3/78
　estate confiscated

Guisebertson, *see* Giberson

Gunnup, Benjamin
　Private, State Troops, enlists 5/81

H

Hager, Andrew

Private, New Jersey Volunteers, captured 8/22/77
Hagerman, Cornelius   Freehold
    Signer, Petition Favoring Quick Division of Prize Money, 12/79
Hagerman, Dollance   Freehold
    Private, Militia
    Signer, Articles of Retaliation, 6/79
    sells produce to Continental Army, 5/80
    Signer, Petition Supporting Quick Division of Militia Prizes, no date
Hagerman, James   Shrewsbury
    Private, Militia, delinquent 8/17/80
Hagerty, John
    Private, Militia
    Signer, Petition Encouraging Free Trade, 5/12/81
Hagerty, Patrick
    Lieutenant, New Jersey Volunteers
Hagerty, Thomas
    Private, New Jersey Volunteers, discharged 12/17/77
Haight, Joseph   Upper Freehold
    Grand Juror, Court of Oyer and Terminer, 12/80
    sells produce to Continental Army, 5/80
Hale, William
    witness at Monmouth Court, 1778
Haley, George
    Private, Militia
Haley, Thomas   Freehold
    Private, State Troops
Hall, David
    Private, Militia
Hall, Edward
    Private, New Jersey Volunteers, enlisted 3/3/77 dead 8/19/77
Hall, Isaac
    Private, New Jersey Volunteers
Hall, Jacob
    Private, New Jersey Volunteers
    Private, Militia
    Private, State Troops
Hall, John   Shrewsbury
    Private, Militia
    convicted of Assault, 1/20/78
Hall, Levi
    Private, New Jersey Volunteers
Hall, William   Middletown

Private, Militia, drafted into Continental Army 5/78
Private, Continental Army
Private, State Troops, wounded 6/22/81 at Middletown
Signer, Petition Encouraging Free Trade, 5/12/81
Signer, Petition for Renewing Guard at Toms River, 12/10/81
Hall, William, Jr.   Middletown
Hallet, Josiah
Private, New Jersey Volunteers, enlisted 2/3/77 dead 5/17/77
Halsey, see Hilsey
Halstead, Christopher
Laborer, Pennsylvania Salt Works, intermittent 8/76-6/77
Halstead, Daniel   Shrewsbury
Vestryman, Anglican Christ Church, 1770 and 1775
holds tavern license, 1775
Halstead, Josiah   Shrewsbury
Vestryman, Anglican Christ Church, 1770
Signer, Petition Opposing Slave Manumission, 2/2/74
Corporal, New Jersey Volunteers
Private, Militia, drafted into Continental Army 5/78
Private, Continental Army
Private, State Troops
Halstead, Sarah
indicted for Misdemeanor, 1/81
Halstead, Timothy
Private, New Jersey Volunteers, enlisted 12/21/76 dead 2/14/77
Hamilton, Richard
Private, New Jersey Volunteers
Hamilton, Robert
Sergeant, New Jersey Volunteers
Hampton, Daniel   Shrewsbury
Signer, Articles of Retaliation, 6/79
Hampton, Forest
Signer, Petition Supporting Retaliation, 9/17/80
Hampton, James   Freehold
Private, Militia
Signer, Articles of Retaliation, 6/79
Hampton, John   Freehold
Private, Militia, drafted into Continental Army 5/78
Private, State Troops, enlists 5/78
helps keep the poor
Signer, Articles of Retaliation, 6/79
Signer, Petition Urging Compensation for Inflated Money, 5/22/83

Hampton, John Shrewsbury
   Private, Militia
   estate confiscated
Hamton, see Hampton
Hance, Benjamin Shrewsbury
   Private, Militia, delinquent 8/80
Hance, Catherine Shrewsbury
   household head
Hance, Cornelius Freehold
   Signer, Petition Against Loyalist Auction Commissioners, 3/24/79
   Signer, Articles of Retaliation, 6/79
Hance, David Middletown
   Private, Militia
Hance, David Shrewsbury
   Private, Militia
   helps keep the poor
   Delegate, Friends' Quarterly Meeting, 1778
   Signer, Articles of Retaliation, 6/79
   leased horse team to Continental Quarter Master 12/81
Hance, David, Jr. Shrewsbury
   indicted for Misdemeanor, 8/79
   indicted for Misdemeanor, 1/81
Hance, Elizabeth Shrewsbury
   Delegate, Friends' Quarterly Meeting, 1775
Hance, Francis
   Private, Militia, delinquent 4/82
Hance, Jacob Shrewsbury
   Delegate, Friends' Quarterly Meeting, 1775-83
Hance, Jeremiah Shrewsbury
Hance, Molly Shrewsbury
   helps keep the poor
Hance, Thomas Shrewsbury and Middletown
   mill owner
   holds tavern license, 1775
   indicted for Misdemeanor, 8/79
   indicted for Misdemeanor, 1/81
Hance, William
   Private, Militia, hires substitute 2/10/78, delinquent 3/11/78
Hand, Abraham Middletown
Handlin, Andrew Upper Freehold
Haney, see Hanzey and Heigney
Hankins, Albert Freehold

Hankins, Ann	Militia Volunteer, Prior to the First General Militia Muster, 6/76
Laborer, Pennsylvania Salt Works, , intermittent 8/76-6/77
Hankins, Daniel	Upper Freehold
Private, New Jersey Volunteers
Private, Militia
Private, Continental Army
Private, State Troops, enlists 5/80
arrested for Disaffection, 1/77
Hankins, Gilbert
Signer, Association for Opposing the Return of Tories
Hankins, John	Upper Freehold
Private, New Jersey Volunteers, enlisted 12/1/76 deserts 3/31/78
Hankins, Jonathan	Upper Freehold
convicted of Assault, 1/20/78
Hankins, Joseph
Private, Militia
Private, State Troops
Hankins, Richard	Freehold
Signer, Association for Opposing the Return of Tories, 1783
Hankins, Thomas
Private, Militia
Hankins, William	Upper Freehold
Private, New Jersey Volunteers, enlisted 1/4/77 dead 4/13/77
Hankins, William
son of Jonathan
Private, Militia
indicted for Assault, 6/3/78
indicted for Robbery, 8/79
Hankins, Zachariah	Upper Freehold
Militia Volunteer, Prior to the First General Militia Muster, 6/76
Hankinson, Daniel
Signer, Petition Urging Action Against Disaffected
& Favoring Retaliation, 5/12/81
Hankinson, James	Shrewsbury
Private, Militia
Private, State Troops, enlisted 6/80
Signer, Association for Opposing the Return of Tories, 1783
Hankinson, John	Shrewsbury
Militia Volunteer, Prior to the First General Militia Muster, 6/76
estate confiscated
Hankinson, John

Hankinson, Joseph
Private, Militia
Hankinson, Kenneth   Freehold
Captain, Militia
Signer, Petition for Settlement of Quartermaster Debts, 9/6/77
rented Confiscated Tory estate, prior to 5/79
Signer, Articles of Retaliation, 6/79
sells produce to Continental Army, 5/80
Signer, Petition Supporting Retaliation, 9/17/80
Signer, Petition in Favor of Daniel Longstreet, 11/21/80
Signer, Petition Encouraging Free Trade, 5/12/81
Signer, Petition for Renewing Guard at Toms River, 12/10/81
Juror, Court of Oyer and Terminer, 11/82
Chairman, Association for Retaliation, 1783
Hankinson, Reuben
Militia Volunteer, Prior to the First General Militia Muster, 6/76
Private, New Jersey Volunteers, 8/76
Ensign, New Jersey Volunteers, 8/81
Hankinson, Thomas   Shrewsbury
Signer, Petition Opposing Slave Manumission, 2/2/74
sells produce to Continental Army, 5/80
Signer, Association for Opposing the Return of Tories, 1783
Hankinson, William   Freehold
Private, Militia
Hankinson, William, Jr.   Freehold
Corporal, Militia
Private, State Troops, enlisted 6/80
Hanna, Robert   Shrewsbury
helps keep the poor
Private, New Jersey Volunteers, enlisted 12/19/76 dead 3/8/77
Hanner, see Hanzey
Hanson, Thomas
convicted of Misdemeanor, 6/3/78
Hanzey, John   Upper Freehold
Private, Militia
Hanzey, Samuel
Sergeant, Militia, captured 2/13/77
Harbert, see also Herbert
Harbert, Abraham
Private, New Jersey Volunteers
Harbert, Daniel

    Private, Militia
    Private, State Troops, enlisted 6/80
    sells produce to Continental Army, 5/80
    Signer, Petition Supporting Retaliation, 9/17/80
    Grand Juror, Court of Oyer and Terminer, 11/82
    Signer, Petition Supporting Quick Division of Militia Prizes, no date
Harbert, David
    Private, New Jersey Militia, enlisted 12/31/76 deserted 3/15/77
Harbert, Edward
    Private, New Jersey Volunteers, enlisted 1/13/77 dead 4/5/77
Harbert, Isaac   Shrewsbury
    Private, Militia, delinquent 9/80
Harbert, Jacob   Shrewsbury
    Private, New Jersey Volunteers, dead 9/12/77
    estate confiscated
Harbert, James
    Sergeant, Militia
    Private, State Troops, enlisted 6/80
    Constable, 1780
Harbert, John
    Private, New Jersey Volunteers
    Private, Militia
    Signer, Petition Against Association for Retaliation 12/81
    leased horse team to Continental Quarter Master 12/81
Harbert, Samuel   Shrewsbury
    Private, Militia, deserts 6/79
Harbert, Thomas   Shrewsbury
    Private, Militia
Harbert, William
    Private, Militia, captured 2/13/77
Harcourt, Richard   Upper Freehold
Harcourt, William
    Private, Militia
Harker, John   Upper Freehold
    Private, Militia
Harker, Rhoda   Upper Freehold
    household head
Harper, Henry   Upper Freehold
    Militia Volunteer, Prior to the First General Militia Muster, 6/76
    sells produce to Continental Army, 5/80
Harper, John
    Private, New Jersey Volunteers, enlisted for bounty 4/79

Harper, William   Upper Freehold
    Private, New Jersey Volunteers, enlisted for bounty 4/79
Harison, *see* Harrison
Harrington, James
    Private, New Jersey Volunteers
Harrington, John
    Private, New Jersey Volunteers
Harris, Edmund   Freehold
    Militia Volunteer, Prior to the First General Militia Muster, 6/76
    arrested for Disaffection, 1/77
    pleads guilty on four counts of Riot, 1/20/78
    Signer, Petition Supporting Retaliation, 1780
    sells produce to Continental Army, 5/80
Harris, Henry
    Private, New Jersey Volunteers, captured 8/22/77
Harrison, George   Shrewsbury
    Private, Militia
    Signer, Petition Opposing Slave Manumission, 2/2/74
Harrison, Job
    Private, Militia
Harrison, John   Upper Feehold
    Militia Volunteer, Prior to the First General Militia Muster, 6/76
    plundered by Tories, 12/76
    Signer, Petition Affirming Loyalty of Moses Ivens, 3/12/77
    Juror, Court of Oyer and Terminer, 8/79
        fined L30 for missing all or some of jury duty
    sells sheep to Continental Commissary 7/80
    Juror, Court of Oyer and Terminer, 11/82
    Juror, Court of Oyer and Terminer, 7/83
Hart, Ebenezer   Middletown
    Private, Militia
    Private, State Troops
    Signer, Articles of Retaliation, 6/79
    Signer, Petition Favoring Quick Division of Prize Money, 12/79
    present at the capture of the British ship, Britannia, 12/31/79
    indicted for Misdemeanor, 5/82
    Signer, Petition Opposing the Return of Tories 6/10/83
Hart, Elizabeth   Shrewsbury
    recipient of poor relief
Hart, Jacob   Shrewsbury
    Sergeant, Militia
    Signer, Petition Favoring Quick Division of Prize Money, 12/79

indicted for Riot, 11/82
   Signer, Association for Opposing the Return of Tories, 1783
Hart, William
   Private, New Jersey Volunteers, enlisted 2/16/77 deserts 4/11/77
Hartshorn, see Hartshorne
Hartshorne, Esek   Middletown
   Township Assessor, 1771
   arrest warrant issued for his capture, 1777
   indicted for Misdemeanor, 8/79
   indicted for Misdemeanor, 1/81
   Signer, Petition from Victims of the Association for Retaliation 9/82
   donates to Charity Fund for Stevenson Family, 5/83
Hartshorne, Ezekiel   Shrewsbury
   refuses militia service
Hartshorne, James
   indicted for High Treason, 8/79
Hartshorne, John   Shrewsbury
   Delegate, Friends' Quarterly Meeting, 1778-80, 1783
   Signer, Petition from Victims of the Association for Retaliation 9/82
Hartshorne, Richard   Middletown
   Quartermaster, Militia
   Overseer of Highways, 1772 and 1779
   Signer, Petition Against Loyalist Auction Commissioners, 3/24/79
   present at the capture of the British ship, Britannia, 12/31/79
   Signer, Petition Against Association for Retaliation 12/81
   Refugee in New York, 1782
Hartshorne, Robert   Shrewsbury and Middletown
   Quartermaster, Militia
   Signer, Petition to Better Provision Militia, 2/25/78
Hartshorne, Robert   Shrewsbury
   refuses militia service
   arrested for Disaffection, 1777
   indicted for Misdemeanor, 8/79
   Delegate, Friends' Quarterly Meeting, 1779-83
   Signer, Petition from Victims of the Association for Retaliation 9/82
Hartshorne, Sarah   Shrewsbury
   Delegate, Friends' Quarterly Meeting, 1778, 1781
   helps keep the poor
Hartshorne, Thomas   Middletown
Hartshorne, Thomas, Jr.   Middletown
Hartshorne, William   Shrewsbury
   Delegate, Friends' Quarterly Meeting, 1782-3

Harvey, Daniel — Upper Freehold
Harvey, Hannah — Freehold
   household head
Harvey, Jacob — Shrewsbury
   accused of being active in Tory Rebellions of 12/76
Harvey, Peter — Shrewsbury
Harvey, Samuel — Shrewsbury
Harvey, Stephen — Shrewsbury
   Private, Militia, delinquent 4/82
   arrested for Disaffection, 11/76
   accused of being part of Samuel Wright's Tory Association 11/76
   accused of being active in Tory Rebellions of 12/76
Harvey, Thomas — Shrewsbury
Harvey, Thomas
   Private, New Jersey Volunteers, enlisted 1/12/77 dead 4/13/77
Harwood, John
   Private, New Jersey Volunteers, enlisted 3/13/79 deserts 3/18/79
Haslep, *see* Heslip
Hathaway, Simeon
   Private, New Jersey Volunteers, captured 8/22/77
Hatten, Peter
   indicted for Robbery, 1/81
Havens, Jesse — Shrewsbury
   Private, Militia, delinquent 8/80
   indicted for Misdemeanor and Harboring Prisoners of War, 1/81
Havens, John — Shrewsbury
   Private, Militia, delinquent 8/80
   Laborer, Pennsylvania Salt Works, intermittent 8/76-6/77
Havens, Moses — Shrewsbury
   Private, Militia, delinquent 8/80
Havens, Sarah
   witness at Monmouth Court, 1778
Havens, Stout
   arrested for Disaffection, 1/77
Haviland, *see* Heavilon
Hawn, Peter
   Private, New Jersey Volunteers
Hay, Hayes, *see* Hays
Hays, Charles — Upper Freehold
Hays, Daniel
   Private, Militia
Hays, David — Upper Freehold

Ensign, Militia
Signer, Petition in Support of Richard Lloyd, 1/31/76
Grand Juror, Court of Oyer and Terminer, 8/79
Juror, Court of Oyer and Terminer, 12/80
    fined L3 for missing all or some of jury duty
Signer, Petition Urging Action Against Disaffected
    & Favoring Retaliation, 5/12/81
Juror, Court of Oyer and Terminer, 5/82
    fined for missing jury duty
indicted for Perjury, 11/82
indicted for Perjury, 7/83

Hays, John
    Ensign, Continental Army, Jonathan Forman's Company, 10/77
    Private, Militia, hires substitute 2/10/78

Hays, Joseph
    Private, Continental Army

Hays, Samuel   Shrewsbury
    Signer, Petition Opposing Slave Manumission, 2/2/74
    Signer, Articles of Retaliation, 6/79

Hays, Thomas
    indicted for Misdemeanor, 5/82

Hays, William
    Private, Militia
    Signer, Association for Opposing the Return of Tories, 1783

Hazen, Daniel
    Private, New Jersey Volunteers

Headon, Marcus   Middletown
    indicted for Misdemeanor, 1/81
    indicted for Misdemeanor, 5/82
    indicted for Misdemeanor, 11/81

Hedger, Ann   Middletown

Heagerman, *see* Hagerman

Heaviland, *see* Heavilon

Heavilon, Benjamin   Shrewsbury
    sells produce to Continental Army, 5/80

Heavilon, Job   Freehold
    Private, Militia
    Private, Continental Army
    Private, State Troops, enlists 5/80

Heavilon, John
    Juror, Court of Oyer and Terminer, 5/82
    indicted for Misdemeanor, 5/82

Heavilon, Joseph   Freehold
   Private, Militia
   Private, State Troops, enlists 5/80
   Private, Continental Army
   indicted for Misdemeanor, 1/81
   Juror, Court of Oyer and Terminer, 5/82
Heavilon, Stephen
   sells produce to Continental Army, 5/80
Hedden, *see* Headon
Hedges, Stephen
   Convicted of High Treason, 4/25/82
   Refugee in New York, 1782
Heigney, Jacob
   arrested for Disaffection, 11/76
Heigney, Samuel
   Private, Militia
   present at the capture of the British ship, Britannia, 12/31/79
Helmes, Frederick   Shrewsbury
Heldrick, David   Shrewsbury
Heldrick, Jonathan   Middletown
Heldrick, Jonathan   Shrewsbury
Heldrick, Jonathan, Jr.   Middletown
Hen, Michael
   Private, New Jersey Volunteers
Henderson, David
   Private, Militia
   Signer, Petition for Stricter Militia Law, 5/31/79
Henderson, David
   Signer, Petition for Stricter Militia Law, 5/31/79
Henderson, John   Freehold
   Captain, Militia
   Signer, Petition for Settlement of Quartermaster Debts, 9/6/77
   Signer, Petition for Stricter Militia Law, 5/31/79
   Signer, Petition Favoring Quick Division of Prize Money, 12/79
   sells produce to Continental Army, 5/80
   Signer, Petition for Renewing Guard at Toms River, 12/10/81
   Signer, Petition Supporting Quick Division of Militia Prizes, no date
Henderson, John
   Private, State Troops, enlisted 6/80
Henderson, Samuel   Freehold
   Signer, Petition for Stricter Militia Law, 5/31/79
   Signer, Articles of Retaliation, 6/79

Henderson, Thomas   Freehold
- Signer, Association for Opposing the Return of Tories, 1783
- Lt. Colonel, Militia
- Delegate, New Jersey Legislature, Lower House, 1780-5
- rented Confiscated Tory estate, prior to 5/79
- Signer, Petition Urging Compensation for Raid Victims, 5/25/79
- Signer, Petition for Stricter Militia Law, 5/31/79
- Signer, Articles of Retaliation, 6/79
- Signer, Petition Favoring Quick Division of Prize Money, 12/79
- sells produce to Continental Army, 5/80
- Signer, Petition Supporting Quick Division of Militia Prizes, no date

Hendricks, Abraham   Upper Freehold
- Militia Volunteer, Prior to the First General Militia Muster, 6/76
- Signer, Petition in Support of Richard Lloyd, 1/31/76
- Signer, Petition in Support of William Barton, 1/31/76
- indicted for Misdemeanor, 1/78
- Signer, Association for Opposing the Return of Tories, 1783

Hendricks, Conradt   Middletown
- Captain, New Jersey Volunteers
- estate inquisitioned for Forfeiture, 7/4/77
- estate confiscated

Hendricks, John   Middletown
- Militia Volunteer, Prior to the First General Militia Muster, 6/76
- Private, Militia

Hendricks, Joseph
- Sergeant, New Jersey Volunteers

Hendricks, Stephen
- witness at Monmouth Court, 1778

Hendrickson, Abraham   Freehold
- Private, Militia
- Signer, Articles of Retaliation, 6/79

Hendrickson, Abram (Abraham) Upper Freehold
- Private, Militia
- Signer, Articles of Retaliation, 6/79
- present at the capture of the British ship, Britannia, 12/31/79
- Private, State Troops, enlists 6/80
- Signer, Petition Supporting Retaliation, 1780
- Grand Juror, Court of Oyer and Terminer, 12/80
- Grand Juror, Court of Oyer and Terminer, 7/83

Hendrickson, Albert   Freehold
- Signer, Articles of Retaliation, 6/79

Hendrickson, Ann

convicted of Misdemeanor, 1/20/78
Hendrickson, Auke (Oakey)   Upper Freehold
   Lieutenant, Militia
   Signer, Petition Affirming Loyalty of Moses Ivens, 3/12/77
Hendrickson, Conradt
   indicted for Burglary, 11/82
Hendrickson, Cornelius
   Private, Militia
Hendrickson, Daniel   Shrewsbury and Upper Freehold
   Colonel, Militia
   Delegate, New Jersey Legislature, Lower House, 1782-5
   Signer, Petition Opposing Slave Manumission, 2/2/74
   Signer, Petition Calling for Action Against the Disaffected, 2/21/77
   Signer, Petition Urging Action Against the Disaffected, 3/14/77
   Signer, Petition to Better Provision Militia, 2/25/78
   Signer, Articles of Retaliation, 6/79
   sells produce to Continental Army, 5/80
   leased horse team to Continental Quarter Master 12/81
Hendrickson, Daniel, Jr.   Middletown
   Captain, Militia
   Signer, Petition Opposing Slave Manumission, 2/2/74
   indicted for Misdemeanor, 1/81
   indicted for Misdemeanor, 5/82
   indicted for Misdemeanor, 11/81
   Signer, Petition Opposing the Return of Tories 6/10/83
Hendrickson, Daniel   Middletown
   Commissioner of Appeals, 1771 and 1779-81
   Signer, Petition Supporting Issuing of New Jersey Currency, 1771
   Signer, Petition Opposing Slave Manumission, 2/2/74
   Township Collector, 1775-6
   Overseer of the Poor, 1775-6
   arrested for Disaffection, 1777
   Tory, refuses oath of loyalty, 1777
   Overseer of Highways, 1778
   indicted for Perjury, 1/81
   indicted for Perjury, 5/82
   Signer, Petition from Victims of the Association for Retaliation 9/82
Hendrickson, Daniel   Upper Freehold
   Private, Militia
   sells produce to Continental Army, 5/80
   Juror, Court of Oyer and Terminer, 12/80
      fined L3 for missing all or some of jury duty

Hendrickson, Daniel, Jr.   Middletown
   Signer, Petition Opposing the Return of Tories 6/10/83
Hendrickson, David   Middletown
   Ensign, Militia
Hendrickson, Denice   Middletown
   Signer, Petition Opposing the Return of Tories 6/10/83
Hendrickson, Elias   Middletown
   Private, Militia
   Private, State Troops
Hendrickson, Elias   Middletown
   Private, Militia
   present at the capture of the British ship, Britannia, 12/31/79
   Signer, Petition Opposing the Return of Tories 6/10/83
Hendrickson, Frederick
   Ensign, New Jersey Volunteers, 3 years
Hendrickson, Garret   Middletown
   Lieutenant, Militia, shot in the ear, 7/17/80
   Signer, Petition Opposing Slave Manumission, 2/2/74
   Signer, Petition Urging Action Against the Disaffected, 3/14/77
   Signer, Petition to Better Provision Militia, 2/25/78
   sells clothing to Continental Army, 3/78
   Signer, Petition Favoring Quick Division of Prize Money, 12/79
   Signer, Petition Opposing the Return of Tories 6/10/83
Hendrickson, Gilbert
   indicted for Misdemeanor, 8/79
Hendrickson, Hendrick   Middletown
   Private, Militia
   present at the capture of the British ship, Britannia, 12/31/79
Hendrickson, Hendrick   Middletown
   Commissioner of Appeals, 1770
   Signer, Petition Supporting Issuing of New Jersey Currency, 1771
   Corporal, Militia, captured 2/13/77
   sells clothing to Continental Army, 3/78
   Township Collector, 1779-81
   Overseer of the Poor, 1779-81
   Signer, Petition Against Confiscation Commissioners, 5/8/79
   sells produce to Continental Army, 5/80
   Assistant to the Tax Assessor, 1782
   Juror, Court of Oyer and Terminer, 5/82
   donates to Charity Fund for Stevenson Family, 5/83
   Signer, Petition Opposing the Return of Tories 6/10/83
Hendrickson, Jacob   Upper Freehold

Roster of the People of Revolutionary Monmouth County

    Militia Volunteer, Prior to the First General Militia Muster, 6/76
    plundered by Tories, 12/76
    Juror, Court of Oyer and Terminer, 1/78
        fined L5 for not attending all or part of Jury duty
    Signer, Petition Urging Action Against Disaffected
        & Favoring Retaliation, 5/12/81, opposes Retaliation clause
    Juror, Court of Oyer and Terminer, 11/82
    Juror, Court of Oyer and Terminer, 7/83
Hendrickson, James   Freehold
    Private, Militia
Hendrickson, John   Upper Freehold
    Private, Militia
    present at the capture of the British ship, Britannia, 12/31/79
    Signer, Petition Supporting Retaliation, 1780
Hendrickson, Tobias   Upper Freehold
    Signer, Petition Affirming Loyalty of Moses Ivens, 3/12/77
    indicted for Misdemeanor, 1/78
Hendrickson, William   Upper Freehold
    Militia Volunteer, Prior to the First General Militia Muster, 6/76
    Private, Militia
    Signer, Petition Affirming Loyalty of Moses Ivens, 3/12/77
    Juror, Court of Oyer and Terminer, 7/83
Hendrickson, William, Esq.   Middletown
    Signer, Petition Opposing Slave Manumission, 2/2/74
    Signer, Articles of Retaliation, 6/79
    Signer, Petition for Renewing Guard at Toms River, 12/10/81
    Grand Juror, Court of Oyer and Terminer, 11/82
    Assistant to the Tax Assessor, 1783
    Grand Juror, Court of Oyer and Terminer, 7/83
Hendrix, *see* Hendricks
Henry, John
    Private, Militia, captured 2/13/77
Hensey, Samuel   Freehold
Herbert, *see also* Harbert
Herbert, David   Freehold
    Signer, Articles of Retaliation, 6/79
Herbert, Francis   Freehold
    Signer, Articles of Retaliation, 6/79
Herbert, Francis   Shrewsbury
Herbert, Henry   Shrewsbury
Herbert, Isaac   Shrewsbury
Herbert, Jacob   Middletown

    Signer, Petition Opposing Slave Manumission, 2/2/74
    helps keep the poor
Herbert, James   Freehold and Middletown
    Private, Militia
    Signer, Petition Opposing Slave Manumission, 2/2/74
    Signer, Articles of Retaliation, 6/79
Herbert, James   Upper Freehold
Herbert, John   Middletown
    Private, Militia
    leased horse team to Continental Quarter Master 12/81
    Signer, Petition Opposing the Return of Tories 6/10/83
Herbert, Samuel   Upper Freehold
Herbert, Thomas   Upper Freehold
    Private, Militia
    Signer, Petition Urging Action Against Disaffected & Favoring
Retaliation, 5/12/81
Herbert, Timothy   Upper Freehold
Herbert, William   Freehold
    sells produce to Continental Army, 5/80
    indicted for High Treason, 5/82
Heron, John
    Private, New Jersey Volunteers, dead prior to 1779
Herot, David   Shrewsbury
Herot, John   Shrewsbury
Hesenger, James   Upper Freehold
Heslip, David
    arrested for Disaffection, 1/77
    indicted for High Treason, 6/3/78
Hewlet, *see also* Hullett
Hewlet, Joseph
    indicted for Misdemeanor, 6/78
Hewlet, Peter
    Private, New Jersey Volunteers, enlisted 1/4/77 dead 3/14/77
Hewlet, Samuel
    Signer, Petition Encouraging Free Trade, 5/12/81
Hewlet, Thomas
    arrested for Disaffection, 1777
Hewlet, Timothy   Upper Freehold
Hewling, *see* Hewlet
Hibbetts, James
    Private, Militia, captured 2/13/77, dies in prison 6/1/80
Hibler, Cornelius

Corporal, New Jersey Volunteers
Hibler, Christopher
 Private, New Jersey Volunteers
Hibler, Samuel
 Corporal, New Jersey Volunteers, captured 8/22/77
Hickey, James
 Private, New Jersey Volunteers
Hicks, Jacob
 Private, New Jersey Volunteers, enlisted 12/23/76 dead 7/9/77
Hicks, Oliver   Shrewsbury
 estate inquisitioned for Forfeiture, 3/23/79
 estate confiscated
Hicks, Thomas   Middletown
Hier, see Hyer
Hill, Alexander
 Private, New Jersey Volunteers
Hill, Daniel   Freehold
 Signer, Articles of Retaliation, 6/79
Hill, James   Freehold
 Private, Militia
 Private, State Troops
 schoolmaster
 Signer, Petition Encouraging Free Trade, 5/12/81
Hill, John
 Private, Militia
Hill, Thomas   Freehold
Hill, Thomas   Freehold
 Signer, Petition Opposing the Return of Tories 6/10/83
Hill, William   Middletown
Hillier, see Hilyer
Hillow, Jonathan
 Private, Militia
 Private, Continental Army
Hilsey, James
 indicted for Misdemeanor, 1/81
Hilsey, Jesse, Esq.   Dover
 Justice of the Peace, 1780-2
 Signer, Petition Urging Action Against the Pine Robbers, 12/27/81
Hilsey, Joseph
 Private, Continental Army, Jonathan Forman's Company, 10/77
Hilsey, Mary   Middletown
 household head

Hilsey, Mathias
   Signer, Petition Supporting Retaliation, 9/17/80
Hilsey, William   Freehold
   Private, Militia
   Signer, Petition for Stricter Militia Law, 5/31/79
   Signer, Articles of Retaliation, 6/79
   Signer, Petition Supporting Quick Division of Militia Prizes, no date
Hilyer, Henry   Upper Freehold
   Militia Volunteer, Prior to the First General Militia Muster, 6/76
Hilyer, John   Freehold
   Private, Militia
Hilyer, Simon   Freehold
   Private, Militia
   sells produce to Continental Army, 5/80
Hilyer, William   Freehold
   Ensign, Militia
   Signer, Petition to Better Provision Militia, 2/25/78
Himes, George   Freehold and Middletown
   Signer, Petition Against Loyalist Auction Commissioners, 3/24/79
   Signer, Petition Against Association for Retaliation 12/81
   Signer, Petition Opposing the Return of Tories 6/10/83
Himes, John
   substitute, Militia, 2/10/78
Hingry, Samuel
   Signer, Articles of Retaliation, 6/79
Hinckson, Benezar   Freehold
   estate confiscated
Hinxson, *see* Hinckson
Hoagland, James
   Private, Militia
   Signer, Articles of Retaliation, 6/79
   present at the capture of the British ship, Britannia, 12/31/79
Hoagland, Obadiah
   Private, New Jersey Volunteers
Hodgson, Joseph   Upper Freehold
Hoff, see Huff
Hoffmier, Hoffmire, *see* Hophmire
Hoffman, Christian
   Private, New Jersey Volunteers
Hoffman, George
   Private, New Jersey Volunteers
Holdman, Ezekiel   Upper Freehold

Holdman, Joseph   Upper Freehold
    Private, Militia
Holland, Henry
    Private, New Jersey Volunteers
Hollingsworth, Levi
    Laborer, Pennsylvania Salt Works, intermittent 8/76-6/77
Holloway, John   Shrewsbury
    Private, Militia, delinquent 8/80
    indicted for Riot & Trespass, 6/3/78
Holloway, Joseph
    indicted for Misdemeanor, 5/82
Holman, Aaron
    sells produce to Continental Army, 7/80
Holman, John
    Signer, Petition Encouraging Free Trade, 5/12/81
Holman, Joseph   Upper Freehold
Holman, William   Freehold
Holman, William   Upper Freehold
Holmes, Anthony   Freehold
    Private, Militia
    Signer, Articles of Retaliation, 6/79
    Signer, Petition Supporting Retaliation, 1780
    Signer, Petition Urging Action Against Disaffected
       & Favoring Retaliation, 5/12/81
    Signer, Petition for Renewing Guard at Toms River, 12/10/81
    Signer, Association for Opposing the Return of Tories, 1783
Holmes, Asher   Freehold
    Colonel, Militia
    Colonel, State Troops
    Sheriff, 1776
    Signer, Petition Calling for Action Against the Disaffected, 2/21/77
    Signer, Petition Urging Action Against the Disaffected, 3/14/77
    Signer, Petition to Better Provision Militia, 2/25/78
    Signer, Petition Against Loyalist Auction Commissioners, 3/24/79
    Signer, Petition Against Confiscation Commissioners, 5/8/79
    Signer, Petition Urging Compensation for Raid Victims, 5/25/79
    Signer, Petition for Stricter Militia Law, 5/31/79
    Signer, Articles of Retaliation, 6/79
    present at the capture of the British ship, Britannia, 12/31/79
    sells produce to Continental Army, 7/80
    Signer, Petition Opposing the Return of Tories 6/10/83

Holmes, Daniel
Holmes, Elisha   Freehold
    Signer, Petition Supporting Retaliation, 1780
Holmes, Jacob   Shrewsbury
    Laborer, Pennsylvania Salt Works, intermittent 8/76-6/77
    Vestryman, Anglican Christ Church, 1777-83,
        Sideman, 1780
Holmes, James
    Private, Militia
    Signer, Articles of Retaliation, 6/79
    Signer, Association for Opposing the Return of Tories, 1783
Holmes, John   Dover
Holmes, John   Middletown
    Captain, Militia
    Overseer of the Poor, 1772-3
    Chosen Freeholder, 1778-9
    Signer, Articles of Retaliation, 6/79
    sells produce to Continental Army, 5/80
    Grand Juror, Court of Oyer and Terminer, 5/82
    Overseer of Highways, 1783
    Signer, Association for Opposing the Return of Tories, 1783
    Signer, Petition Opposing the Return of Tories 6/10/83
Holmes, John   Upper Freehold
    Militia Volunteer, Prior to the First General Militia Muster, 6/76
    Private, Militia
    plundered by Tories, 12/76
    Signer, Petition in Support of William Barton, 1/31/76
    sells clothing to Continental Army, 3/78
    Juror, Court of Oyer and Terminer, 8/79
        fined L30 for missing all or some of jury duty
    sells produce to Continental Army, 5/80
    Judge of the Court of Oyer and Terminer, 12/80
    Signer, Petition Against Association for Retaliation 12/81
Holmes, John, Jr.   Middletown
    Juror, Court of Oyer and Terminer, 12/80
        fined L3 for missing all or some of jury duty
    indicted for Misdemeanor, 11/82
Holmes, Jonathan   Freehold
    Lieutenant, Militia
    plundered by Tories
    Signer, Petition Favoring Quick Division of Prize Money, 12/79
Holmes, Jonathan   Upper Freehold

Roster of the People of Revolutionary Monmouth County

Holmes, Joseph   Middletown
    Militia Volunteer, Prior to the First General Militia Muster, 6/76
    substitute, Militia, 2/10/78
Holmes, Joseph   Middletown
    Delegate, New Jersey Legislature, Lower House, 1776
    Signer, Articles of Retaliation, 6/79
Holmes, Joseph   Upper Freehold
    Private, Militia
    plundered by Tories, 12/76
    sells produce to Continental Army, 5/80
    Signer, Petition Against Association for Retaliation 12/81
Holmes, Joseph   Upper Freehold
    accused of being active in Loyalist Rebellion of 12/76
    indicted for Trespass, 1/78
    Private, Militia, delinquent 6/11/80
Holmes, Joseph
    Private, Militia
    Private, Militia Dragoons, delinquent one tour
    present at the capture of the British ship, Britannia, 12/31/79
    Signer, Petition Opposing the Return of Tories 6/10/83
Holmes, Josiah   Upper Freehold
    Militia Volunteer, Prior to the First General Militia Muster, 6/76
    Signer, Petition Urging Action Against Disaffected
        & Favoring Retaliation, 5/12/81
Holmes, Josiah   Shrewsbury
    Member, Shrewsbury Committee of Observation
    Vestryman, Anglican Christ Church, 1770-83
    sells goods to Pennsylvania Salt Works, 8/76-10/76
    Signer, Articles of Retaliation, 6/79
Holmes, Josiah, Jr.   Shrewsbury
    Vestryman, Anglican Christ Church, 1778-82,
        Sideman, 1783
Holmes, Leah
    donates to Charity Fund for Stevenson Family, 5/83
Holmes, Lydia   Upper Freehold
    household head
Holmes, Margaret
    plaintiff at Monmouth Court, 1778
Holmes, Obadiah   Freehold
    Colonel (?)
Holmes, Obadiah   Middletown
    Signer, Petition Opposing Slave Manumission, 2/2/74
Holmes, Samuel   Upper Freehold and Shrewsbury

Signer, Petition Supporting Issuing of New Jersey Currency, 1771
Private, Militia
Laborer, Pennsylvania Salt Works, intermittent 8/76-6/77
Signer, Petition Urging Action Against Disaffected
    & Favoring Retaliation, 5/12/81
Vestryman, Anglican Christ Church, 1782
Holmes, Stout
    Private, New Jersey Volunteers, deserted 2/22/78
    Private, Militia, substitute Militia, 2/10/78
    Signer, Articles of Retaliation, 6/79
Holmes, Thomas   Freehold
    Vestryman, Anglican Christ Church, 1778-82
Holmes, William   Upper Freehold
    Private, Militia
    Signer, Petition Supporting Issuing of New Jersey Currency, 1771
    Signer, Petition Urging Action Against Disaffected
        & Favoring Retaliation, 5/12/81
    Signer, Petition for Renewing Guard at Toms River, 12/10/81
Holmes, William   Upper Freehold
    indicted for Misdemeanor, 7/83
Holsart, *see* Hulsart *and* Hulse
Holt, Thomas
    Private, New Jersey Volunteers, captured 8/22/77
Homer, Fuller   Upper Freehold
    estate confiscated
Hommett, John
    Private, New Jersey Volunteers, enlisted 5/11/77 dead 6/26/77
Honce, *see* Hance
Hooker, John
    Signer, Association for Opposing the Return of Tories, 1783
Hooper, Jacob   Upper Freehold
Hooper, James
    indicted for Misdemeanor, 1/81
Hophmire, Isaac   Middletown
    Overseer of Highways, 1779
Hophmire, William   Shrewsbury
    holds tavern license, 1775
    Private, Militia, delinquent 8/17/80
    indicted for Misdemeanor, 8/79
    indicted for Misdemeanor, 1/81
    indicted for Misdemeanor, 5/82
Hopkins, Edward   Upper Freehold

Private, Militia
Signer, Petition Against Association for Retaliation 12/81
Hopkins, Isaiah   Upper Freehold
    accused of being active in Loyalist Rebellion of 12/76
Hopkins, Joseph   Upper Freehold
    sells produce to Continental Army, 5/80
Hopkins, Moses   Upper Freehold
    accused of being active in Loyalist Rebellion of 12/76
Hopkins, Sarah   Upper Freehold
    household head
Horace, Henry
    Private, New Jersey Volunteers, captured 8/22/77
Horn, Henry
    Private, New Jersey Volunteers
Horn, Peter
    Private, New Jersey Volunteers
Horner, Content   Dover
Horner, Elisha   Upper Freehold
Horner, Fuller   Upper Freehold
    accused of being active in Loyalist Rebellion of 12/76
    indicted for Misdemeanor, 11/82
    estate inquisitioned for Forfeiture, 4/5/79
    estate confiscated
Horner, Hugh   Dover
    Militia Volunteer, Prior to the First General Militia Muster, 6/76
Horner, Isaac   Upper Freehold
    indicted for Misdemeanor, 1/78
Horner, John   Upper Freehold
    Militia Volunteer, Prior to the First General Militia Muster, 6/76
    Accused of Being Active in Tory Uprising of 12/76
    Ensign, King's Militia Volunteers
    estate inquisitioned for Forfeiture, 4/5/79
    estate confiscated
Horner, Joshua   Upper Freehold
Horner, Joshua, Jr.   Upper Freehold
Horner, Samuel   Upper Freehold
    Private, Militia
Horner, William   Upper Freehold
    accused of being active in Loyalist Rebellion of 12/76
    Signer, Petition Against Association for Retaliation 12/81
    indicted for Misdemeanor, 7/83
Hornor, *see* Horner

Horsefield, Richard — Upper Freehold
  plundered by Tories, 12/76
  Juror, Court of Oyer and Terminer, 8/79
    fined L30 for missing all or some of jury duty
  sells produce to Continental Army, 5/80
  Juror, Court of Oyer and Terminer, 12/80
    fined L3 for missing all or some of jury duty
Horton, Benjamin
  Private, Militia
  Signer, Petition Encouraging Free Trade, 5/12/81
Horton, Thomas — Shrewsbury
Houghland, Henry
  sells produce to Continental Army, 5/80
House, David
House, David, Jr.
  convicted of Misdemeanor, 1/81
Houston, see Huston
Hout, Peter — Middletown
  estate confiscated
Hout, Robert — Shrewsbury
  estate confiscated
Howard, Alexander — Upper Freehold
Howard, Mathias — Middletown
Howell, David — Stafford
  Private, Militia
Howell, Frederick
  Private, New Jersey Volunteers
Howell, Robert
  indicted for Misdemeanor, 1/81
Howell, William — Dover
  Militia Volunteer, Prior to the First General Militia Muster, 6/76
Howland, George — Shrewsbury
  Private, Militia
Howland, James — Shrewsbury
  Private, Militia
  convicted of Misdemeanor, 6/3/78
  indicted for Misdemeanor, 11/81
Howland, Michael
  indicted for Misdemeanor, 1/81
  indicted for Misdemeanor, 5/82
Howler, James
  indicted for Misdemeanor, 8/79

Hubbard, Jacob   Middletown
   doctor
   Private, Militia
   Signer, Petition Opposing Slave Manumission, 2/2/74
   donates to Charity Fund for Stevenson Family, 5/83
Hubbard, Thomas
   Surgeon, Militia
Hubbert, *see* Hubbard
Hubbs, David
   Private, Militia
   Private, Continental Army
Huddy, Catherine   Shrewsbury
   helps keep the poor
Huddy, Joshua   Shrewsbury
   tavernkeeper at Colts Neck
   Captain, Militia
   Captain, State Troops
   indicted for Assault, 1/78
   Signer, Articles of Retaliation, 6/79
   sells produce to Continental Army, 5/80
Huff, Christian
   sells produce to Continental Army, 7/80
Huff, Henry
   Private, New Jersey Volunteers
Huff, John   Middletown
   Sergeant, Militia
   Signer, Petition Opposing Slave Manumission, 2/2/74
   present at the capture of the British ship, Britannia, 12/31/79
Huggins, John
   Private, Militia
Huggins, Mary   Freehold
   household head
   sells produce to Continental Army, 5/80
Huggins, William
   sells produce to Continental Army, 5/80
Hughes, Samuel
   Private, New Jersey Volunteers
Hughes, Timothy
   Signer, Articles of Retaliation, 6/79
   Signer, Petition Urging Compensation for Inflated Money, 5/22/83
Hulce, *see* Hulsart *and* Hulse
Hulcehart, *see* Hulsart *and* Hulse

Hulebart, Mathias
   Private, Militia
Hull, Benjamin
   Private, New Jersey Volunteers
Hull, Jeremiah   Upper Freehold
   Private, Militia
Hull, John
   Private, State Troops
   indicted for Misdemeanor, 5/82
Hull, Rague (?)   Upper Freehold
Hull, Randolph
   Laborer, Pennsylvania Salt Works, intermittent 8/76-6/77
Hull, Richard   Upper Freehold
   Militia Volunteer, Prior to the First General Militia Muster, 6/76
Hullett, Hullate, see Hulletts and Hewlet
Hulletts, see also Hewlet
Hulletts, Constant   Shrewsbury
Hulletts, Daniel
   Signer, Petition Favoring Quick Division of Prize Money, 12/79
   indicted for Misdemeanor, 8/79
   indicted for High Treason, 1/81
   indicted for Misdemeanor, 5/82
   indicted for High Treason, 11/82
Hulletts, George   Shrewsbury
   holds tavern license, 1775
Hulletts, John
   Private, Militia, delinquent 8/9/80
Hulletts, Joseph   Shrewsbury
   arrested for Disaffection, 11/76
   accused of being active in Tory Rebellions of 12/76
   sells produce to Continental Army, 5/80
   helps keep the poor
   indicted for Murder, 5/82
Hulletts, Michael   Shrewsbury
   indicted for Misdemeanor, 8/79
   estate confiscated, 1780
   indicted for Misdemeanor, 1/81
Hulletts, Patience   Shrewsbury
   sick with pleurisy
   recipient of poor relief
Hulletts, Samuel   Dover
Hulletts, Thomas   Shrewsbury

Hulletts, William   Middletown
    Laborer, Pennsylvania Salt Works, intermittent 8/76-6/77
    Private, State Troops, enlists 6/80
Hulletts, William   Shrewsbury
Hulit, see Hewlet *and* Hulletts
Huln, Matthew
    Private, Militia
Huln, William
    Private, Militia
Hulsart, Anthony   Middletown
Hulsart, Benjamin   Freehold
    Private, Militia
Hulsart, Cornelius   Freehold
    Private, Militia
Hulsart, Cornelius
    Private, Militia
Hulsart, David
    Private, New Jersey Volunteers
Hulsart, Gaston
    Signer, Petition Against Loyalist Auction Commissioners, 3/24/79
Hulsart, Hannah   Freehold
    household head
Hulsart, James
    Private, Militia, captured 2/13/77
Hulsart, John   Freehold
    Private, Militia
    rented Confiscated Tory estate, prior to 5/79
    Signer, Articles of Retaliation, 6/79
Hulsart, Matthew
    Private, Militia
Hulsart, Mathias   Middletown
    Private, Militia
    present at the capture of the British ship, Britannia, 12/31/79
Hulsart, Peter   Middletown
    rented Confiscated Tory estate, prior to 5/79
    Signer, Petition Opposing the Return of Tories 6/10/83
Hulsart, Tice
    Private, Militia, captured 2/13/77
Hulsart, William   Freehold
    Private, State Troops
    Signer, Articles of Retaliation, 6/79
    present at the capture of the British ship, Britannia, 12/31/79

Hulse, Anthony				Dover
Hulse, John				Middletown
   Signer, Petition Opposing the Return of Tories 6/10/83
Hulse, Mathias
   Private, Militia, captured 2/13/77
Hulse, Sylvanus				Shrewsbury
Hulse, Thomas				Shrewsbury
Hulse, Timothy
   Private, Militia
   present at the capture of the British ship, Britannia, 12/31/79
Hulse, William
   sells produce to Continental Army, 5/80
   Signer, Petition Supporting Retaliation, 1780
   Signer, Petition Urging Compensation for Inflated Money, 5/22/83
Hulsehart, *see* Hulsart
Hume, Elijah
   Private, New Jersey Volunteers
Humphrey, Thomas
   Private, New Jersey Volunteers, enlisted 12/5/76 deserts 3/16/78
Hunn, John Smith
   Private, Militia
   Signer, Articles of Retaliation, 6/79
   indicted for Misdemeanor, 1/81
Hunn, Thomas				Middletown
   Major, Militia, cashiered from service 5/27/78
   Overseer of Highways, 1770 and 1778
   Signer, Petition Calling for Action Against the Disaffected, 2/21/77
   Signer, Petition Against Loyalist Auction Commissioners, 3/24/79
   present at the capture of the British ship, Britannia, 12/31/79
   sells produce to Continental Army, 5/80
   donates to Charity Fund for Stevenson Family, 5/83
   Signer, Petition Opposing the Return of Tories 6/10/83
Hunt, Richard				Upper Freehold
Hunter, John
   Private, Continental Army, Jonathan Forman's Company, 10/77
Hunter, William				Middletown
   Private, Militia, delinquent 2/10/78
   Constable, 1780-2
Huntley, Richard			Upper Freehold
   takes Loyalty Oath to New Jersey Government, 3/19/77
Hurlehoy, Dennis
   indicted for Murder, 8/79

Hurley, Denice   Shrewsbury
Hurley, John
    Private, New Jersey Volunteers
Hurley, William   Shrewsbury
    Private, Militia
Husten, Christary
    Private, Militia
Hustiss, John
    Corporal, New Jersey Volunteers
Hutch, see Hutchin
Hutchin, Amos
    sells goods to Pennsylvania Salt Works, intermittent 8/76-6/77
Hutchin, Hugh   Upper Freehold
    Signer, Petition Against Association for Retaliation 12/81
Hutchin, John   Dover
    Ensign of Militia, Prior to the First General Militia Muster, 6/76
    Juror, Court of Oyer and Terminer, 1/78
        fined L5 for not attending all or part of Jury duty
Hutchin, Thomas   Dover
    sells goods to Pennsylvania Salt Works, 8/76-10/76
    frees two slaves, 1777
Hutchin, William   Dover
    Militia Volunteer, Prior to the First General Militia Muster, 6/76
    Signer, Petition Urging Action Against the Pine Robbers, 12/27/81
Hutchinson, Joseph
    sells goods to Pennsylvania Salt Works, 8/76-10/76
Hutchinson, William   Upper Freehold and Dover
    Lieutenant, New Jersey Volunteers
    Signer, Petition to Better Defend Toms River Area, 5/18/77
    Juror, Court of Oyer and Terminer, 11/82
        fined L8 for missing jury duty
Hutson, Joshua   Dover
    Signer, Petition to Better Defend Toms River Area, 5/18/77
Hyer, Garret   Shrewsbury
Hyer, Hannah
    indicted for Misdemeanor, 1/81
    indicted for Misdemeanor, 11/81
Hyer, Hendrick   Freehold
    Private, Militia
    Private, Continental Army
    Signer, Articles of Retaliation, 6/79
    present at the capture of the British ship, Britannia, 12/31/79

Hyer, John　　　　　　　　　Middletown
Hyer, John　　　　　　　　　Shrewsbury
　　Private, Militia, serves as substitute, 2/10/78
Hyer, Peter　　　　　　　　Middletown
　　Signer, Petition Opposing the Return of Tories 6/10/83
Hyer, Walter　　　　　　　　Freehold
　　Private, Militia
　　Private, Continental Army
　　Private, State Troops, wounded at Middletown 6/21/81
　　Signer, Petition Opposing the Return of Tories 6/10/83
Hyer, Walter　　　　　　　　Middletown
　　haymaker
　　indicted for Misdemeanor, 11/81
　　indicted for Misdemeanor, 11/82
Hyer, William　　　　　　　　Middletown
　　Private, Militia
　　Signer, Petition Opposing the Return of Tories 6/10/83
Hymes, *see* Himes

I

Imlay, David　　　　　　　　Upper Freehold
　　Captain, Militia
Imlay, Ezekiel　　　　　　　Upper Freehold
　　Ensign, Militia
Imlay, Gilbert　　　　　　　Upper Freehold
　　Lieutenant, Continental Army
Imlay, Isaac　　　　　　　　Upper Freehold
　　Lieutenant, Militia
　　Signer, Petition Calling for Action Against the Disaffected, 2/21/77
　　Signer, Petition Urging Action Against the Disaffected, 3/14/77
　　indicted for Misdemeanor, 1/78
Imlay, James　　　　　　　　Upper Freehold
　　Major, Militia
Imlay, John　　　　　　　　　Upper Freehold
　　Justice of the Court
　　Signer, Petition Urging Action Against Disaffected
　　　　& Favoring Retaliation, 5/12/81
Imlay, Jonathan　　　　　　　Upper Freehold
　　Private, Militia
Imlay, Joseph
　　Juror, Court of Oyer and Terminer, 11/82

Roster of the People of Revolutionary Monmouth County

Imlay, Nathaniel   Upper Freehold
Imlay, Peter   Upper Freehold
    mill owner
    Signer, Petition in Support of Richard Lloyd, 1/31/76
    Signer, Petition in Support of William Barton, 1/31/76
    Signer, Petition for Stricter Militia Law, 5/31/79
    sells produce to Continental Army, 5/80
    Signer, Petition Against Association for Retaliation 12/81
    Juror, Court of Oyer and Terminer, 11/82
Imlay, Robert
    Private, Militia
    witness at Monmouth Court, 1778
Imlay, Samuel   Upper Freehold
    takes Oath to New Jersey Government, 3/19/77
    Juror, Court of Oyer and Terminer, 11/82
       fined L8 for missing jury duty
Imlay, William   Upper Freehold
    Signer, Petition Calling for Action Against the Disaffected, 2/21/77
    Signer, Petition Urging Action Against the Disaffected, 3/14/77
    Juror, Court of Oyer and Terminer, 11/82
       fined L8 for missing jury duty
Imlay, William, Jr.   Upper Freehold
    takes Oath to New Jersey Government, 3/19/77
    indicted for Misdemeanor, 1/78
    Ensign, Militia
    Lieutenant, State Troops
Indian, David   Shrewsbury
    blind orphan child
    recipient of poor relief
Irons, Garret   Dover
    Militia Volunteer, Prior to the First General Militia Muster, 6/76
Irons, Gilbert
    Private, New Jersey Volunteers, enlisted 1/11/77   dead 7/26/77
Irons, James   Upper Freehold
    Private, Militia
Irons, John   Dover
    estate inquisitioned for Forfeiture, 7/3/77
    estate confiscated
Irvin, John
    Private, Militia
    sells produce to Continental Army, 5/80
Isaac, William

witness at Monmouth Court
Iscoe, George
   Private, Militia, hires substitute
Isleton, Jonathan
   Private, Militia
   Private, State Troops
   Private, Continental Army
Ivens, see Ivins
Ivins, Aaron   Upper Freehold
Ivins, Abel
   Private, Militia
Ivins, Caleb   Upper Freehold
   Juror, Court of Oyer and Terminer, 11/82
      fined L8 for missing jury duty
Ivins, Isaac   Freehold
Ivins, Moses   Upper Freehold
   accused of being active in Loyalist Rebellion of 12/76
   takes Oath to New Jersey Government, 3/19/77
   sells produce to Continental Army, 5/80
Ivins, Solomon   Upper Freehold
   Private, Militia
   Private, State Troops, enlists 5/80
   sells sheep to Continental Commissary 7/80

J

Jacob, Negro
   indicted for Murder, 5/82
Jacaway, Robert   Upper Freehold
Jackson, Benjamin   Shrewsbury
   Delegate, Friends' Quarterly Meeting, 1775-83
Jackson, Benjamin, Jr.   Shrewsbury
Jackson, Hannah   Shrewsbury
   Delegate, Friends' Quarterly Meeting, 1774, 1780, 1782
Jackson, Hugh   Shrewsbury
Jackson, James   Upper Freehold
   Militia Volunteer, Prior to the First General Militia Muster, 6/76
   plundered by Tories, 12/76
   sells produce to Continental Army, 5/80
Jackson, John   Shrewsbury
   exempt from Militia service, 2/10/78
Jackson, Joseph   Shrewsbury

Delegate, Friends' Quarterly Meeting, 1774-5, 1778
Jackson, Joseph, Jr.   Upper Freehold
   plundered by Tories, 12/76
Jackson, Mary   Shrewsbury
   household head
   Delegate, Friends' Quarterly Meeting, 1782
Jackson, Nathan
   indicted for Misdemeanor, 11/81
   indicted for Misdemeanor, 7/83
Jackson, Peter
   indicted on two counts of Contraband Trading, 11/81
Jackson, Prudence   Shrewsbury
   Delegate, Friends' Quarterly Meeting, 1774-5, 1780, 1782
Jackson, Rebecca   Shrewsbury
   Delegate, Friends' Quarterly Meeting, 1775, 1779, 1781-82
Jackson, Richard   Upper Freehold
   indicted for Petty Larceny
   sells produce to Continental Army, 5/80
Jackson, Robert
   Corporal, New Jersey Volunteers
Jackson, Samuel
   Private, New Jersey Volunteers, enlisted 1/13/77 dead 2/26/77
Jackson, William   Shrewsbury
Jackson, William, Jr.   Shrewsbury
   exempt from Militia service, 2/10/78
Jacobs, Thomas   Upper Freehold
James, John
   Signer, Association for Opposing the Return of Tories, 1783
James, Richard   Freehold
James, Richard   Upper Freehold
   Militia Volunteer, Prior to the First General Militia Muster, 6/76
   sells produce to Continental Army, 5/80
   Signer, Petition Against Association for Retaliation 12/81
   Juror, Court of Oyer and Terminer, 5/82
      fined for missing jury duty
James, Robert   Freehold
   Militia Volunteer, Prior to the First General Militia Muster, 6/76
   arrested for Disaffection, 11/76
   accused of being active in Tory Rebellions of 12/76
   estate inquisitioned for Forfeiture, 7/5/77
   sells produce to Continental Army, 5/80
   indicted for Misdemeanor and High Treason, 1/81

hanged at Freehold, 1781
estate confiscated
James, William
   Private, Militia
Jamison, David
   Private, State Troops, enlists 4/81
Jamison, John   Freehold
   Private, Militia
   Private, State Troops, enlisted 6/80
   Signer, Petition for Stricter Militia Law, 5/31/79
   Signer, Articles of Retaliation, 6/79
   Signer, Petition Encouraging Free Trade, 5/12/81
Jarvis, George
   Private, New Jersey Volunteers, enlisted 11/15/76
      discharged 7/12/78
Jeffers, *see* Jeffrey
Jeffery, Jeffries, *see* Jeffrey
Jeffrey, Daniel   Shrewsbury
Jeffrey, Daniel   Shrewsbury
Jeffrey, Francis
   Private, Militia
   Private, State Troops, wounded at Shrewsbury, 5/24/81
Jeffrey, Humphrey
   Private, Militia
   Private, State Troops, enlisted 6/80
   Private, Continental Army
   Signer, Petition Supporting Retaliation, 9/17/80
   Signer, Petition Supporting Quick Division of Militia Prizes, no date
Jeffrey, John   Dover
Jeffrey, John   Shrewsbury
Jeffrey, Joseph   Shrewsbury
   Private, Militia, delinquent 9/80
Jeffrey, Lewis   Shrewsbury
Jeffrey, Richard   Shrewsbury
   accused of being part of Samuel Wright's Tory Association 11/76
   accused of being active in Tory Rebellions of 12/76
   Signer, Articles of Retaliation, 6/79
Jeffrey, Ruhaw
   arrested for Disaffection, 11/76
Jeffrey, Thomas   Shrewsbury
   helps keep the poor
Jeffrey, William   Shrewsbury

Private, Militia
    indicted for Misdemeanor, 1/81
Jemison, *see* Jamison
Jennings, James   Upper Freehold
Jennings, James   Upper Freehold
Jenkins, Aaron
    Private, New Jersey Volunteers
Jenkins, Daniel
    Private, New Jersey Volunteers
Jenkins, David
    Private, State Troops, enlist 5/81
Jenkins, Ephraim   Dover
    Militia Volunteer, Prior to the First General Militia Muster, 6/76
    Captain, Militia
    Signer, Petition Urging Action Against the Pine Robbers, 12/27/81
Jenkins, Nathaniel
    Private, New Jersey Volunteers
Jenkins, William   Dover
    Signer, Petition to Better Defend Toms River Area, 5/18/77
    Signer, Articles of Retaliation, 6/79
Jervis, *see* Jarvis
Jessup, John   Upper Freehold
    Militia Volunteer, Prior to the First General Militia Muster, 6/76
Jewell, John (James)   Freehold
    Private, Militia
    Private, State Troops, enlisted 6/80
    Signer, Articles of Retaliation, 6/79
    sells produce to Continental Army, 5/80
    sells produce to Continental Army, 7/80
Jinkins, *see* Jenkins
Jo   Freehold
    free black householder
Jobs, *see* Jobes
Jobes, Joel
    indicted for Misdemeanor, 5/82
Jobes, Robert
    Private, Militia
Jobes, Samuel
    Private, New Jersey Volunteers
Johnson, *see also* Johnston
Johnson, Abraham   Freehold
    Signer, Petition Urging Compensation for Inflated Money, 5/22/83

Roster of the People of Revolutionary Monmouth County

Johnson, Amos   Upper Freehold
    Private, Militia
Johnson, Barnes
Johnson, Benjamin   Dover
    Signer, Petition Against Association for Retaliation 12/81
Johnson, Cornelia
    indicted for Misdemeanor, 5/82
Johnson, David   Shrewsbury and Stafford
    Private, Militia
    Private, State Troops
Johnson, Elisha   Shrewsbury
Johnson, Ezekiel   Dover
Johnson, George   Dover
    Militia Volunteer, Prior to the First General Militia Muster, 6/76
    convicted of Assault, 1/20/78
    indicted for Assault, 6/78
Johnson, George   Shrewsbury
    Signer, Petition Favoring Quick Division of Prize Money, 12/79
    Signer, Petition Supporting Retaliation, 9/17/80
    helps keep the poor
Johnson, George
    Private, New Jersey Volunteers, enlisted 12/20/76 dead 5/13/77
Johnson, Gilbert   Dover
    Militia Volunteer, Prior to the First General Militia Muster, 6/76
Johnson, Harmon
    Indicted for Robbery, 6/78
    indicted for Burglary, 11/82
Johnson, Hendrick (Henry)   Shrewsbury
    Signer, Petition Favoring Quick Division of Prize Money, 12/79
    Signer, Petition Encouraging Free Trade, 5/12/81
    Signer, Association for Opposing the Return of Tories, 1783
Johnson, Henry
    Private, Militia
    Private, Continental Army
Johnson, Henry
    Sergeant, Militia
Johnson, Ichabod   Dover
    Pine Robber, killed 1783
Johnson, Isaac
    indicted for Misdemeanor, 7/83
Johnson, Jacobus
    indicted for Misdemeanor, 11/82

Johnson, James   Shrewsbury
    Militia Volunteer, Prior to the First General Militia Muster, 6/76
    Signer, Association for Opposing the Return of Tories, 1783
Johnson, James, Jr.   Shrewsbury
    Private, Militia, delinquent 8/9/80
Johnson, John   Dover
    Militia Volunteer, Prior to the First General Militia Muster, 6/76
    Private, Militia, captured 2/13/77, dies in prison
Johnson, John   Shrewsbury
    Doctor
    Grand Juror, Court of Oyer and Terminer, 8/79
    Juror, Court of Oyer and Terminer, 12/80
        fined L3 for missing all or some of jury duty
    Juror, Court of Oyer and Terminer, 5/82
Johnson, John
    son of Barnes
    Private, New Jersey Volunteers
    indicted for Misdemeanor, 1/78
    indicted for Misdemeanor, 6/78
    Private, Militia, delinquent 8/9/80
    Signer, Petition Favoring Quick Division of Prize Money, 12/79
Johnson, Jonas
    Private, New Jersey Volunteers
Johnson, Joseph   Middletown
    Signer, Petition Opposing Slave Manumission, 2/2/74
    Private, Militia
     present at the capture of the British ship, Britannia, 12/31/79
    leased horse team to Continental Quarter Master 12/81
    Signer, Petition Opposing the Return of Tories 6/10/83
Johnson, Lambert   Middletown
    Ensign, Militia
    Signer, Articles of Retaliation, 6/79
    present at the capture of the British ship, Britannia, 12/31/79
    Signer, Petition Opposing the Return of Tories 6/10/83
Johnson, Lambert, Jr.   Middletown
    Private, Militia, captured 2/13/77, dies in prison 4/15/77
    Signer, Petition Opposing the Return of Tories 6/10/83
Johnson, Levi
    Private, New Jersey Volunteers, enlisted 1/13/77 dead 7/26/77
Johnson, Luke   Dover
Johnson, Luke, Jr.   Dover
Johnson, Michael

Juror, Court of Oyer and Terminer, 11/82
Johnson, Minard   Shrewsbury
Johnson, Peter   Middletown and Freehold
    Sergeant, Militia
    Constable, 1778, misses Court due to illness
    Signer, Petition Against Loyalist Auction Commissioners, 3/24/79
    Constable, 1779-80
    Sergeant, State Troops, enlisted 6/80
    Overseer of Highways, 1783
Johnson, Phoebe
    convicted of Misdemeanor, 1/20/78
Johnson, Ruliff   Shrewsbury
Johnson, Samuel   Dover and Stafford
    Militia Volunteer, Prior to the First General Militia Muster, 6/76
    indicted for Misdemeanor, 5/82
Johnson, Stephen   Shrewsbury
    Private, Militia
Johnson, Thomas   Stafford
    Private, Militia
Johnson, William   Dover
    Militia Volunteer, Prior to the First General Militia Muster, 6/76
    Private, New Jersey Volunteers
    Signer, Petition Against Association for Retaliation 12/81
Johnson, William   Freehold
    Private, Militia
    Private, State Troops, enlisted 6/80
    blacksmith
Johnson, William   Freehold
    Private, Militia
    Private, State Troops, enlisted 6/80
    witness at Monmouth Court, 1778
    Signer, Petition Urging Compensation for Raid Victims, 5/25/79
    Signer, Petition Favoring Quick Division of Prize Money, 12/79
    Grand Juror, Court of Oyer and Terminer, 5/82
Johnson, William
    Sergeant, Militia, captured
Johnston, *see also* Johnson
Johnston, Abraham
    Private, Militia
    Signer, Petition Supporting Retaliation, 1780
    sells produce to Continental Army, 5/80
Johnston, Amos   Upper Freehold

Johnston, Cornelius
   sells produce to Continental Army, 5/80
Johnston, David   Upper Freehold
   Signer, Petition Urging Action Against the Pine Robbers, 12/27/81
Johnston, Hendrick (Henry)
   Private, Militia
   sells produce to Continental Army, 5/80
Johnston, Isaac   Freehold
   Signer, Articles of Retaliation, 6/79
Johnston, John   Freehold
   Private, Militia
   Signer, Articles of Retaliation, 6/79
Johnston, Joseph   Shrewsbury
   Private, Militia
   Signer, Articles of Retaliation, 6/79
   sells produce to Continental Army, 5/80
Johnston, Joseph
   Signer, Articles of Retaliation, 6/79
Johnston, Michael   Freehold
   Signer, Articles of Retaliation, 6/79
   Signer, Petition Encouraging Free Trade, 5/12/81
Johnston, Peter   Freehold
   Signer, Articles of Retaliation, 6/79
   Signer, Petition Encouraging Free Trade, 5/12/81
   donates to Charity Fund for Stevenson Family, 5/83
Johnston, Stephen
   sells produce to Continental Army, 5/80
Johnston, William   Upper Freehold
   Signer, Articles of Retaliation, 6/79
   sells produce to Continental Army, 5/80
   Signer, Association for Opposing the Return of Tories, 1783
Johnston, William   Upper Freehold
   Private, Militia
   sells produce to Continental Army, 5/80
Johnstone, Benjamin
   sells goods to Pennsylvania Salt Works, 8/76-10/76
Johnstone, John
   Laborer, Pennsylvania Salt Works, intermittent 8/76-6/77
Jones, Aaron
   runaway slave
   Private, Black Brigade
Jones, Benjamin

Jones, Caleb   Upper Freehold
    accused of being active in Tory Rebellions of 12/76
Jones, Caleb   Upper Freehold
    accused of being active in Loyalist Rebellion of 12/76
Jones, Charity   Shrewsbury
    household head
    sells produce to Continental Army, 5/80
Jones, Christopher   Shrewsbury
Jones, David   Stafford
    Private, Militia
    indicted for Misdemeanor, 1/81
Jones, Henry
    Private, Militia
    Private, Continental Army
    Private, State Troops
Jones, Hugh
    Private, New Jersey Volunteers
Jones, Isaac   Middletown
    runaway slave
    Private, Black Brigade
Jones, James
    Private, Militia
    Signer, Association for Opposing the Return of Tories, 1783
Jones, John
    arrested for Disaffection, 11/76
    Private, New Jersey Volunteers, 2nd. Batt., enlisted 2/16/77
        listed as dead 8/19/77
    Private, Continental Army, Jonathan Forman's Company, 10/77
    Private, New Jersey Volunteers, 1st Batt., enlisted for bounty 4/79
    indicted for Misdemeanor, 5/82
Jones, Jonathan   Freehold
    Private, Militia
    Private, State Troops, enlists 5/80
Jones, Thomas
    Private, New Jersey Volunteers
Jones, William
    accused of being active in Tory Rebellions of 12/76
Jordan, Michael
    Private, Militia
    Private, State Troops
Journee, James   Shrewsbury
Journee, John   Upper Freehold
Journee, Joseph   Upper Freehold

Journey, *see* Journee
Jube, Negro
   indicted for Murder, 5/82

K

Kane, John   Shrewsbury
   Private, Militia, delinquent 8/80
Kearney, Gilbert   Freehold
Kearney, Revaud   Shrewsbury
Kearney, Michael   Shrewsbury
   holds tavern license, 1775
Kearney, Thomas   Middletown
   jailed for disaffection, 1777
   indicted for Misdemeanor, 1/78
Kearns, Edward
   Private, New Jersey Volunteers, enlisted 12/27/76 dead 4/19/77
Kearns, Richard
   Private, New Jersey Volunteers, enlisted 12/19/76 deserts 2/29/77
Kelley, David
   Private, New Jersey Volunteers
Kels, John   Middletown
   indicted for Misdemeanor, 11/81
Kelsey, James
   indicted for Misdemeanor, 1/81
   indicted for Misdemeanor, 11/82
Kelsey, John   Middletown
   Private, Militia
   indicted for Misdemeanor, 11/82
Kelson, Thomas   Stafford
   Private, Militia
Kemble, William
   indicted for Misdemeanor, 6/78
Kennedy, George   Upper Freehold
Kennedy, George   Upper Freehold
Kennedy, Hugh   Upper Freehold
Kerby, *see also* Kirby
Kerby, Emson   Upper Freehold
Kerby, Thomas   Upper Freehold
Kerby, Thomas   Dover
Kerr, Andrew   Upper Freehold
Kerr, Ebenezer   Freehold

    Private, Militia
    Signer, Petition Urging Compensation for Raid Victims, 5/25/79
    Signer, Articles of Retaliation, 6/79
    sells produce to Continental Army, 5/80
    Signer, Petition for Renewing Guard at Toms River, 12/10/81
    Grand Juror, Court of Oyer and Terminer, 5/82
    Juror, Court of Oyer and Terminer, 11/82
Kerr, James   Upper Freehold
Kerr, James, Jr.   Upper Freehold
Kerr, John   Upper Freehold
    Militia Volunteer, Prior to the First General Militia Muster, 6/76
Kerr, Joseph   Upper Freehold
Kerr, Walter   Upper Freehold
    Private, Militia
    Private, Continental Army
Kerr, Walter   Upper Freehold
Kerr, Watson   Freehold
    Private, Militia
    Private, State Troops
    Signer, Petition in Favor of Daniel Longstreet, 11/21/80
Kerr, William   Freehold
    Private, Militia
Kerrel, Judah   Middletown
Kerrel, William
    Private, Militia
Ketcham, Daniel   Freehold
    Private, Militia, delinquent 2/10/78
    Signer, Articles of Retaliation, 6/79
    Juror, Court of Oyer and Terminer, 8/79
        fined L30 for missing all or some of jury duty
    sells produce to Continental Army, 5/80
    sells produce to Continental Army, 7/80
    Juror, Court of Oyer and Terminer, 5/82
        fined for missing jury duty
    Juror, Court of Oyer and Terminer, 11/82
Ketcham, David
    Juror, Court of Oyer and Terminer, 5/82
Ketcham, David, Jr.
    Signer, Petition Urging Compensation for Inflated Money, 5/22/83
    indicted for Misdemeanor, 7/83
Ketcham, Margaret   Middletown
    household head

Ketcham, Micajah   Freehold
Ketcham, Micajah   Shrewsbury
Kiker, Tobias   Shrewsbury
   estate inquisitioned for Forfeiture, 3/31/79
   estate confiscated
Kilborn, Elijah
   Private, New Jersey Volunteers, captured 8/22/77
Kiley, David
   Signer, Petition Supporting Issuing of New Jersey Currency, 1771
Kiley, James   Middletown
Kiley, Thomas
   Private, New Jersey Volunteers, deserted 7/2/77
Kilpatrick, Elizabeth   Upper Freehold
   household head
Kilpatrick, James   Upper Freehold
   Private, Militia, drafted into Continental Army 5/78
   Drummer, State Troops
Kilpatrick, Thomas   Upper Freehold
Kimmings, Alexander   Upper Freehold
Kincard, George
   Private, Militia
King, Andrew
   indicted for Misdemeanor, 1/81
   indicted for High Treason, 11/82
King, Benjamin
   convicted of Misdemeanor, 12/80
King, Daniel   Upper Freehold
   Laborer, Pennsylvania Salt Works, intermittent 8/76-6/77
   indicted for Misdemeanor, 11/81
King, James   Shrewsbury
   estate confiscated
King, James
   Private, New Jersey Volunteers, enlisted 2/6/77 deserted 2/28/77
King, John
   Private, New Jersey Volunteers, enlisted 5/15/77 dead 7/13/77
King, John
   Private, New Jersey Volunteers, enlisted 3/23/79 deserted 4/5/79
   Signer, Petition Favoring Quick Division of Prize Money, 12/79
   indicted for Misdemeanor, 1/81
King, Joseph   Shrewsbury
   Private, Militia, delinquent 8/9/80
King, William

Private, New Jersey Volunteers, enlisted 1/2/77 deserted 1/16/77
Kinnan, John   Upper Freehold
Kinnan, Richard   Upper Freehold
Kinsey, James, Jr.   Shrewsbury
   Private, Militia
   Private, State Troops, killed at Toms River 3/24/82
   Signer, Petition for Stricter Militia Law, 5/31/79
Kinsey, James   Shrewsbury
   Signer, Petition for Stricter Militia Law, 5/31/79
   Signer, Articles of Retaliation, 6/79
Kirby, *see also* Kerby
Kirby, John
   convicted of Misdemeanor, 6/3/78, went to Phila. without a pass
Kirby, Thomas
   Juror, Court of Oyer and Terminer, 8/79
      fined L30 for missing all or some of jury duty
Kirby, William   Upper Freehold
   Sergeant, Militia
   Signer, Petition in Favor of Daniel Longstreet, 11/21/80
Kitchen, Andrew
   Private, New Jersey Volunteers
Kitchen, John
   Corporal, New Jersey Volunteers
Kite, James
   Private, New Jersey Volunteers, enlisted 1/4/77 deserted 7/13/78
Kite, John
   arrested for Disaffection, 11/76
   joins Continental Army in exchange for pardon, 5/23/77
Kithcart, Joseph   Upper Freehold
   Private, Militia
Kithcart, Robert
   Private, New Jersey Volunteers, deserted 1/8/78
Knoll, Henry   Upper Freehold
Knott, David   Shrewsbury
   Member, Shrewsbury Committee of Observation
   Signer, Petition Favoring Quick Division of Prize Money, 12/79
   convicted of Misdemeanor, 1/81
Knott, Peter   Shrewsbury
   Signer, Petition Favoring Quick Division of Prize Money, 12/79
Knott, Samuel   Shrewsbury
Knox, Joseph   Freehold
   Private, Militia

Signer, Articles of Retaliation, 6/79
Private, State Troops, enlisted 6/80
Konine, see Conine

L

Lacey, Daniel
   Private, State Troops, enlists 4/81
Lacey, Isaac
   Private, Continental Army, Jonathan Forman's Company, 10/77
Lacey, Joseph
   Private, Continental Army, Jonathan Forman's Company, 10/77
Lafeter, Laffeter, Lafetra. see Lefetra
Laird, David   Freehold
   Private, State Troops, enlisted 6/80
Laird, Lydia   Freehold
   household head
Laird, Moses   Freehold
   Signer, Petition for Stricter Militia Law, 5/31/79
   Signer, Articles of Retaliation, 6/79
   Grand Juror, Court of Oyer and Terminer, 8/79
   Signer, Petition Supporting Retaliation, 9/17/80
   Signer, Petition Encouraging Free Trade, 5/12/81
   Juror, Court of Oyer and Terminer, 5/82
   Signer, Petition Supporting Quick Division of Militia Prizes, no date
Laird, Richard   Freehold
   Sergeant, Militia
   Signer, Articles of Retaliation, 6/79
   Sergeant, State Troops, enlisted 6/80
   Signer, Petition Supporting Retaliation, 9/17/80
   Signer, Petition Supporting Quick Division of Militia Prizes, no date
Laird, Robert   Freehold
   Private, Militia
   Signer, Articles of Retaliation, 6/79
   Signer, Petition Favoring Quick Division of Prize Money, 12/79
   present at the capture of the British ship, Britannia, 12/31/79
   sells produce to Continental Army, 5/80
   Signer, Petition for Renewing Guard at Toms River, 12/10/81
   Juror, Court of Oyer and Terminer, 5/82
   Juror, Court of Oyer and Terminer, 11/82
Laird, Sarah   Freehold

Laird, William   household head
Freehold
    Militia Volunteer, Prior to the First General Militia Muster, 6/76
    Private, Militia
    Signer, Articles of Retaliation, 6/79
    Grand Juror, Court of Oyer and Terminer, 8/79
    Signer, Petition Supporting Retaliation, 1780
    Signer, Petition Encouraging Free Trade, 5/12/81
    Signer, Petition for Renewing Guard at Toms River, 12/10/81
    Signer, Association for Opposing the Return of Tories, 1783

Laird, William   Freehold
    Private, Militia
    Private, State Troops, enlisted 6/80
    carpenter

Lairey, Daniel
    Private, New Jersey Volunteers, dead 6/24/78

Lairey, Daniel
    Private, State Troops

Lake, John   Shrewsbury
    Private, Militia
    Signer, Articles of Retaliation, 6/79
    Signer, Petition Supporting Retaliation, 9/17/80

Laland, James   Freehold

Laland, Thomas   Upper Freehold

Lambert, Abraham
    Signer, Petition Supporting Retaliation, 9/17/80

Lambert, John
    Private, New Jersey Volunteers

Lambert, Josiah   Upper Freehold

Landon, David
    Sergeant, Militia
    Sergeant, State Troops

Lane, Aaron
    Private, Militia, wounded 7/78

Lane, Abraham   Shrewsbury
    Ensign, Militia

Lane, Alexander
    Signer, Petition Encouraging Free Trade, 5/12/81

Lane, Cornelius   Shrewsbury
    Private, Militia
    Member, Shrewsbury Committee of Observation
    Signer, Articles of Retaliation, 6/79

witness at Monmouth Court, 1778
Lane, Cornelius, Jr.   Shrewsbury
  Private, Militia
Lane, Daniel   Freehold
  Signer, Articles of Retaliation, 6/79
Lane, Jacob   Dover
  Signer, Articles of Retaliation, 6/79
  Signer, Petition Encouraging Free Trade, 5/12/81
  Signer, Petition Against Association for Retaliation 12/81
  Signer, Petition Urging Compensation for Inflated Money, 5/22/83
Lane, Jacob   Freehold
  Private, Militia
  Signer, Articles of Retaliation, 6/79
  Signer, Petition Urging Compensation for Inflated Money, 5/22/83
  indicted for Misdemeanor, 7/83
Lane, James
  Private, New Jersey Volunteers, captured prior to 1779
Lane, John
  Signer, Articles of Retaliation, 6/79
  Signer, Petition Urging Compensation for Inflated Money, 5/22/83
Lane, Mathias   Freehold
  Signer, Petition Supporting Issuing of New Jersey Currency, 1771
  house burned by British Army, 6/28/78
  Signer, Petition Urging Compensation for Inflated Money, 5/22/83
Lane, Mathias, Jr.   Freehold
  Signer, Petition Urging Compensation for Inflated Money, 5/22/83
Lane, Ruth   Shrewsbury
  household head
  listed on Militia return 6/29/80
Lane, Thomas
  Private, New Jersey Volunteers, enlisted 12/21/76 dead 3/13/77
Lane, William   Freehold
  Signer, Articles of Retaliation, 6/79
  Signer, Petition Urging Compensation for Inflated Money, 5/22/83
Lane, William   Freehold
  Private, Militia
Lang, Annabel   Shrewsbury
  Delegate, Friends' Quarterly Meeting, 1775, 1777
Lang, Elizabeth   Shrewsbury
  Delegate, Friends' Quarterly Meeting, 1775
Lang, Jacob   Shrewsbury
  Delegate, Friends' Quarterly Meeting, 1782

Roster of the People of Revolutionary Monmouth County

Lang, John   Shrewsbury
    Delegate, Friends' Quarterly Meeting, 1775, 1779-80
Lang, Mary   Shrewsbury
    Delegate, Friends' Quarterly Meeting, 1774-6
Lang, Susannah   Shrewsbury
    Delegate, Friends' Quarterly Meeting, 1780
Lard, Robert   Shrewsbury
Lard, William
    Private, Militia
Larkin, John
    Private, New Jersey Volunteers
Lashels, Ann   Middletown
    household head
Laurence, see Lawrence
Lawrence, Alice   Shrewsbury
    Delegate, Friends' Quarterly Meeting, 1776-82
Lawrence, Benjamin   Shrewsbury
Lawrence, Benjamin   Upper Freehold
Lawrence, Daniel   Middletown
    Militia Volunteer, Prior to the First General Militia Muster, 6/76
    arrested for Disaffection, 1/77
Lawrence, Elisha   Upper Freehold
    Lt. Colonel, New Jersey Volunteers
    Signer, Petition in Support of Richard Lloyd, 1/31/76
    Signer, Petition in Support of William Barton, 1/31/76
    estate confiscated
Lawrence, Elisha   Upper Freehold
    Quartermaster, Lt. Colonel, Militia
    Signer, Petition in Support of Richard Lloyd, 1/31/76
    Signer, Petition in Support of William Barton, 1/31/76
    plundered by Tories, 12/76
    Signer, Petition Urging Action Against the Disaffected, 3/14/77
    sells produce to Continental Army 5/80
    Signer, Petition Against Association for Retaliation 12/81
Lawrence, Elisha, Jr.   Upper Freehold
    sells produce to Continental Army, 5/80
Lawrence, George   Upper Freehold
    Militia Volunteer, Prior to the First General Militia Muster, 6/76
Lawrence, Jacob   Middletown
    Signer, Petition Opposing Slave Manumission, 2/2/74
Lawrence, Jacob   Upper Freehold
    Constable, 1783

Lawrence, James, Esq.   Upper Freehold
   Militia Volunteer, Prior to the First General Militia Muster, 6/76
   plundered by Tories, 12/76
   sells sheep to Continental Commissary 7/80
   Signer, Petition from Victims of the Association for Retaliation 9/82
Lawrence, John   Freehold
   lawyer
   jailed for disaffection
Lawrence, John   Shrewsbury
   Private, Militia, delinquent 8/80
Lawrence, John, Dr.   Upper Freehold
   arrested for disaffection, 1776 and 1777
   Accused of Being Active in Tory Uprising of 12/76
   Surgeon, New Jersey Volunteers
   estate inquisitioned for Forfeiture, 4/5/79
Lawrence, John, Esq.   Upper Freehold
   Militia Volunteer, Prior to the First General Militia Muster, 6/76
   Signer, Petition in Support of Richard Lloyd, 1/31/76
   Signer, Petition in Support of William Barton, 1/31/76
   Signer, Petition Affirming Loyalty of Moses Ivens, 3/12/77
Lawrence, John
   Lieutenant, New Jersey Volunteers, 7 years service
   estate confiscated
Lawrence, Jonathan
   Ensign, New Jersey Volunteers
Lawrence, Joseph, Esq.   Upper Freehold
   Signer, Petition in Support of Richard Lloyd, 1/31/76
   Signer, Petition in Support of William Barton, 1/31/76
   Signer, Petition Affirming Loyalty of Moses Ivens, 3/12/77
   Signer, Petition for Stricter Militia Law, 5/31/79
   Judge of the Court of Oyer and Terminer, 12/80
   Signer, Petition from Victims of the Association for Retaliation 9/82
   Judge of the Court of Oyer and Terminer, 5/82 & 11/82
   Justice of the Peace, 1783
Lawrence, Joseph   Shrewsbury
   of Squan
   accused of being part of Samuel Wright's Tory Association 11/76
   Private, Militia, delinquent 8/80
Lawrence, Nathaniel   Upper Freehold
Lawrence, Richard   Shrewsbury
   Private, Militia
   Delegate, Friends' Quarterly Meeting, 1781-82

Lawrence, Richard   Upper Freehold
Lawrence, Robert   Upper Freehold
Lawrence, Robert, Jr.   Upper Freehold
Lawrence, William   Middletown
   Overseer of Highways, 1780-1
Lawrence, William   Shrewsbury
   estate confiscated
   Private, Militia
   Lieutenant, New Jersey Volunteers
Lawrence, William   Upper Freehold
Lawrie, see Lawry
Lawry, Jacob   Upper Freehold
Lawry, James   Upper Freehold
   sells sheep to Continental Commissary 7/80
Lawry, John   Upper Freehold
Lawry, Michael   Upper Freehold
   sells produce to Continental Army, 5/80
   Signer, Petition Against Association for Retaliation 12/81
Lawry, Thomas   Dover
   Militia Volunteer, Prior to the First General Militia Muster, 6/76
Lawry, William   Dover
   Militia Volunteer, Prior to the First General Militia Muster, 6/76
Lawyer, see Lawry
Layton, Andrew   Middletown
   Overseer of Highways, 1781-2
Layton, Andrew
   Private, New Jersey Volunteers, enlisted 4/6/77 dead 7/9/77
Layton, Anthony   Middletown
Layton, Asher   Shrewsbury
   Signer, Petition Opposing Slave Manumission, 2/2/74
Layton, Catherine   Shrewsbury
   household head
Layton, Daniel   Middletown
Layton, Hannah   Shrewsbury
   household head
Layton, James
   Private, New Jersey Volunteers, enlisted 1/3/77 deserted 3/13/77
Layton, Job   Middletown
Layton, John   Middletown
   Private, Militia, hires substitute, 2/10/78
Layton, John   Shrewsbury
Layton, John

Roster of the People of Revolutionary Monmouth County

    Private, New Jersey Volunteers, enlisted 12/29/76 dead 4/6/77
Layton, Lemuel
    Private, New Jersey Volunteers
Layton, Mary   Shrewsbury
    household head
Layton, Peter   Middletown
    Captain (?)
Layton, Rebecca   Middletown
    household head
Layton, Safety   Shrewsbury
    household head
Layton, Samuel   Shrewsbury
    Private, New Jersey Volunteers, captured 8/22/77
    estate confiscated
Layton, Sarah   Shrewsbury
    household head
Layton, Thomas
    Private, New Jersey Volunteers, enlisted 4/5/77 dead 10/19/77
Layton, William   Shrewsbury
Layton, William, Jr.   Shrewsbury
    Private, New Jersey Volunteers
Leaming, *see also* Liming
Leaming, Ephraim   Upper Freehold
    Private, Militia
Leaming, John   Upper Freehold
    Private, Militia
    indicted for Misdemeanor, 11/82
Leaming, Josiah   Upper Freehold
    Private, Militia
Leaming, Thomas   Freehold
    Private, Militia
    accused of being active in Loyalist Rebellion of 12/76
    witness at Monmouth Court, 1778
    present at the capture of the British ship, Britannia, 12/31/79
LeConte, John   Freehold and Middletown
    Signer, Petition Supporting Issuing of New Jersey Currency, 1771
    Signer, Articles of Retaliation, 6/79
    Signer, Petition Encouraging Free Trade, 5/12/81
    Justice of the Peace, 1782
    Judge of the Court of Oyer and Terminer, 11/82
    Signer, Petition Opposing the Return of Tories 6/10/83
    Judge of the Court of Oyer and Terminer, 7/83

LeCount, *see* LeConte
Lee, Benjamin
   convicted of Rape, 12/80
Lee, John   Shrewsbury
   Private, Militia, enlists 5/80
   Private, State Troops
   Private, Continental Army
Lee, Sarah   Upper Freehold
   household head
Lefeter, *see* Lafetra
Lefetra, Admond
   Private, Militia, delinquent 4/82
Lefetra, Daniel   Shrewsbury
   estate inquisitioned for Forfeiture, 3/23/80
   estate confiscated
Lefetra, Edmund   Shrewsbury
Lefetra, Elihu   Shrewsbury
   Delegate, Friends' Quarterly Meeting, 1775
Lefetra, Hannah   Shrewsbury
   household head
Lefetra, James   Shrewsbury
   Private, Militia
   Delegate, Friends' Quarterly Meeting, 1780
Lefetra, Joseph   Shrewsbury
Lefferts, Benjamin   Middletown
   Signer, Petition Opposing the Return of Tories 6/10/83
Leffertson, Arthur   Upper Freehold
   Militia Volunteer, Prior to the First General Militia Muster, 6/76
   Juror, Court of Oyer and Terminer, 1/78
      fined L5 for not attending all or part of Jury duty
   Juror, Court of Oyer and Terminer, 8/79
      fined L30 for missing all or some of jury duty
   Grand Juror, Court of Oyer and Terminer, 12/80
   Signer, Petition Urging Action Against Disaffected
      & Favoring Retaliation, 5/12/81
   Juror, Court of Oyer and Terminer, 11/82
   Grand Juror, Court of Oyer and Terminer, 7/83
Leffertson, Aucke (Oakey)   Upper Freehold
   Signer, Articles of Retaliation, 6/79
   Juror, Court of Oyer and Terminer, 11/82
Leffertson, Benjamin   Upper Freehold
   witness at Monmouth Court, 1778

Leffertson, Peter   Dover
Lefferty, Daniel   Shrewsbury
   estate confiscated
Lefferty, Joseph
   Private, Militia, delinquent 8/17/80
Leirey, *see* Lairey
Leister, *see* Leyster
Leland, *see* Laland
Lemming, *see* Leaming, Lemmon, *and* Liming
Lemmon, Isaiah
   Private, Militia
Lemmon, Michael
   Private, New Jersey Volunteers
Lemmon, Thomas
   Private, Militia
Leonard, Deborah   Middletown
   household head
   wife of Samuel
   indicted for Misdemeanor, 8/79
Leonard, Deliverance   Middletown
   household head
Leonard, John   Upper Freehold
   arrested "for slanderous charges against the Congress", 6/76
   Accused of Being Active in Tory Uprising of 12/76
   flees to British Army 12/76
   estate inquisitioned for Forfeiture, 5/10/78
Leonard, John   Middletown
   Ensign, New Jersey Volunteers
   estate inquisitioned for Forfeiture, 7/29/77
   estate confiscated
Leonard, John   Upper Freehold
Leonard, Joseph   Middletown
   arrested for Disaffection, 1777
   estate inquisitioned for Forfeiture, 7/2/77
   estate confiscated
Leonard, Joseph   Shrewsbury
   Vestryman, Anglican Christ Church, 1770-8
   indicted for Misdemeanor, 5/82
Leonard, Margaret   Shrewsbury
   listed on Militia return 6/29/80
Leonard, Mary
   wife of Thomas Leonard

indicted for Seditious Words, 6/3/78
Leonard, Nancy   Upper Freehold
   household head
Leonard, Samuel   Shrewsbury
Leonard, Samuel   Freehold
   Militia Volunteer, Prior to the First General Militia Muster, 6/76
   Lieutenant, New Jersey Volunteers (promoted to Captain 8/14/81)
   estate inquisitioned for Forfeiture, 7/29/77
Leonard, Thomas   Freehold
   Vestryman, Anglican Christ Church, 1770
   Signer, Petition Supporting Issuing of New Jersey Currency, 1771
   arrested for Disaffection, 11/76
   Major, New Jersey Volunteers
   estate inquisitioned for Forfeiture, 7/5/77
   estate confiscated
Leonard, Thomas, Jr.   Upper Freehold
   Accused of Being Active in Tory Uprising of 12/76
   indicted for Misdemeanor, 8/79
   indicted for Misdemeanor, 5/82
LeQueer, John   Middletown
   Signer, Petition Opposing Slave Manumission, 2/2/74
   Signer, Petition Opposing the Return of Tories 6/10/83
LeQueer, William   Middletown
   Corporal, Militia
   Overseer of Highways, 1779
   Signer, Petition Opposing the Return of Tories 6/10/83
Leseter, Daniel   Shrewsbury
   estate confiscated
Leston, Thomas   Middletown
   indicted for Misdemeanor, 5/82
Leston, Thomas, Jr.   Middletown
   Private, Militia
Letson, *see* Leston
Lett, Francis   Dover
   Township, Overseer of Highways, 1783
Lett, John
   Private, Militia
   Private, State Troops
   indicted for Misdemeanor, 7/83
Lett, Nehemiah
   Private, Militia
Lett, Thomas

Laborer, Pennsylvania Salt Works, intermittent 8/76-6/77
Letts, *see* Lett
Levi, Joshua   Upper Freehold
Levins, Richard   Freehold
    Private, Militia
Leviston, Peter   Upper Freehold
Lewis, Amasiah   Shrewsbury
    Private, Militia
Lewis, Barber   Dover
    Militia Volunteer, Prior to the First General Militia Muster, 6/76
Lewis, David   Shrewsbury
    Private, New Jersey Volunteers
Lewis, Ezekiel   Freehold
    Signer, Articles of Retaliation, 6/79
Lewis, Ezekiel   Middletown
    Private, Militia
    present at the capture of the British ship, Britannia, 12/31/79
Lewis, George
    Private, New Jersey Volunteers
Lewis, John
    Private, New Jersey Volunteers, enlisted 1/19/77 dead 3/17/77
Lewis, Nathaniel   Upper Freehold
Lewis, Philip   Shrewsbury
    holds tavern license, 1775
    helps keep the poor
Lewis, Philip, Jr.   Shrewsbury
Lewis, Thomas   Shrewsbury
    indicted for Misdemeanor, 6/78
Lewis, William   Freehold
    Signer, Articles of Retaliation, 6/79
Lewis, William   Shrewsbury
    Private, Militia
Lewis, William   Shrewsbury
Leyster, Cornelius   Middletown
    Signer, Petition Opposing Slave Manumission, 2/2/74
Leyster, John
    Private, Militia
Leyster, Peter   Middletown
    Signer, Petition Opposing Slave Manumission, 2/2/74
    Juror, Court of Oyer and Terminer, 12/80
       fined L3 for missing all or some of jury duty
Leyton, *see* Layton *and* Leyster

Liming, *see also* Leaming *and* Lemmon
Liming, Ephraim   Upper Freehold
Liming, Isaac   Upper Freehold
Liming, Isaiah   Upper Freehold
Liming, John   Upper Freehold
Liming, Thomas   Upper Freehold
Liming, Thomas   Upper Freehold
Liming, William   Upper Freehold
Limus, Trader   Freehold
Lindsey, *see* Linsey
Linsey, James
    Private, New Jersey Volunteers, enlisted for bounty 4/79
Linsey, Thomas
    Private, Militia, serves as substitute 2/10/78
Lippencott, Lippincutt, *see* Lippincott
Lippincott, David   Shrewsbury
Lippincott, Elisha
    Private, New Jersey Volunteers, enlisted 3/10/77 dead 8/11/77
Lippincott, Jacob   Freehold
    Private, Militia
    Private, State Troops
    Private, Continental Army
    Signer, Petition Supporting Quick Division of Militia Prizes, no date
Lippincott, James   Dover
    leased horse team to Continental Quarter Master 12/81
Lippincott, Jedediah
    arrested for Disaffection, 11/76
    accused of being active in Tory Rebellions of 12/76
Lippincott, John   Shrewsbury
    Private, Militia
    Private, New Jersey Volunteers, captured 7/1/78
    holds tavern license, 1775
Lippincott, Jonathan   Upper Freehold
    Signer, Petition Affirming Loyalty of Moses Ivens, 3/12/77
    sells produce to Continental Army, 5/80
Lippincott, Judiah
    Private, Militia, delinquent 8/17/80
    indicted for Murder, 1/81
    indicted for Murder, 11/82
Lippincott, Lydia   Shrewsbury
    household head
Lippincott, Mary   Shrewsbury

household head
Lippincott, Obadiah
   Laborer, Pennsylvania Salt Works, intermittent 8/76-6/77
Lippincott, Patience   Shrewsbury
   household head
   Delegate, Friends' Quarterly Meeting, 1775-82
Lippincott, Preston
   Private, Militia, hires substitute, 2/10/78
Lippincott, Rebecca   Shrewsbury
   helps keep the poor
Lippincott, Remembrance   Shrewsbury
   accused of being part of Samuel Wright's Tory Association 11/76
   helps keep the poor
Lippincott, Richard   Shrewsbury
   Ensign, New Jersey Volunteers, 4/77
   Captain, Associated Loyalists, 2/17/81
   sells goods to Pennsylvania Salt Works, 8/76-10/76
   estate confiscated
Lippincott, Robert   Shrewsbury
   helps keep the poor
Lippincott, Robert
   Private, New Jersey Volunteers, enlisted 12/27/76 dead 7/28/78
Lippincott, Samuel   Shrewsbury
   Private, Militia
   accused of being part of Samuel Wright's Tory Association 11/76
   arrested for Disaffection, 11/76
   accused of being active in Tory Rebellions of 12/76
   convicted of Riot & Trespass, 6/3/78
Lippincott, Samuel   Upper Freehold
   sells produce to Continental Army, 5/80
Lippincott, Sarah   Shrewsbury
   listed on Militia return 6/29/80
Lippincott, William   Dover
Lippincott, William   Shrewsbury
   Private, Militia
   sells produce to Continental Army, 5/80
   Vestryman, Anglican Christ Church, 1779 and 1783
   Signer, Association for Opposing the Return of Tories, 1783
Lippincott, William   Shrewsbury
   arrested for Disaffection, 11/76
   accused of being part of Samuel Wright's Tory Association 11/76
   accused of being active in Tory Rebellions of 12/76

Private, Militia, delinquent 6/79
helps keep the poor
Lippincott, Zebulon
Signer, Petition Supporting Quick Division of Militia Prizes, no date
Lippincutt, see Lippincott
Lippitt, John   Middletown
Lister, Cornelius   Middletown
Signer, Petition Opposing the Return of Tories 6/10/83
Little, Christopher
Captain, Militia, captured, 1780
Little, John, Esq.   Shrewsbury
Member, Shrewsbury Committee of Observation
Little, John
Private, Militia
Little, Stophel   Middletown
Chosen Freeholder, 1777-8
Little, Theophilus   Middletown
Captain, Militia
Signer, Petition Opposing Slave Manumission, 2/2/74
Signer, Petition Calling for Action Against the Disaffected, 2/21/77
Signer, Petition Urging Action Against the Disaffected, 3/14/77
Signer, Petition Favoring Quick Division of Prize Money, 12/79
sells produce to Continental Army, 5/80
Little, Thomas
Captain, Militia
Signer, Petition Encouraging Free Trade, 5/12/81
Little, William   Shrewsbury
Doctor
Vestryman, Anglican Christ Church, 1779 and 1783,
    Warden, 1779
Signer, Petition Favoring Quick Division of Prize Money, 12/79
sells produce to Continental Army, 5/80
Lloyd, David
Militia Volunteer, Prior to the First General Militia Muster, 6/76
Ensign, Militia
Signer, Petition Calling for Action Against the Disaffected, 2/21/77
Signer, Petition Urging Action Against the Disaffected, 3/14/77
Signer, Articles of Retaliation, 6/79
sells produce to Continental Army, 5/80
Juror, Court of Oyer and Terminer, 12/80
    fined L3 for missing all or some of jury duty
Juror, Court of Oyer and Terminer, 5/82

Grand Juror, Court of Oyer and Terminer, 11/82
lost slaves during the war

Lloyd, James　　　　　　　　Upper Freehold
Private, Militia
Private, Militia Dragoons, delinquent one tour
present at the capture of the British ship, Britannia, 12/31/79

Lloyd, James　　　　　　　　Freehold
indicted for Misdemeanor, 5/82
indicted for Misdemeanor, 11/82
donates to Charity Fund for Stevenson Family, 5/83

Lloyd, John　　　　　　　　Upper Freehold
Militia Volunteer, Prior to the First General Militia Muster, 6/76
Assistant Commissary for Monmouth County
Signer, Petition to Better Provision Militia, 2/25/78
indicted for two Misdemeanors, 6/3/78, acquitted
indicted for Assault, 8/79
Signer, Petition Favoring Quick Division of Prize Money, 12/79
sells produce to Continental Army, 5/80
leased horse team to Continental Quarter Master 12/81
Signer, Petition for Renewing Guard at Toms River, 12/10/81
donates to Charity Fund for Stevenson Family, 5/83

Lloyd, John
Private, Militia
leased horse team to Continental Quarter Master 12/81

Lloyd, Levi　　　　　　　　Upper Freehold
Lloyd, Richard　　　　　　　Upper Freehold
Lloyd, Thomas　　　　　　　Middletown
Corporal, Militia
Private, Militia Dragoons, delinquent one tour
indicted for Misdemeanor, 6/3/78, acquitted
Overseer of the Poor, 1779-82
present at the capture of the British ship, Britannia, 12/31/79
sells produce to Continental Army, 7/80
Chosen Freeholder, 1783

Lloyd, Timothy
Sideman, Anglican Christ Church, 1780
Signer, Petition Encouraging Free Trade, 5/12/81

Lloyd, William　　　　　　　Upper Freehold
Sergeant, Militia

Logan, Patrick
Private, New Jersey Volunteers

Logan, Stomphel　　　　　　Middletown

Township Assessor, 1778-9
Signer, Petition Urging Compensation for Raid Victims, 5/25/79
Signer, Petition Favoring Quick Division of Prize Money, 12/79
Signer, Petition for Renewing Guard at Toms River, 12/10/81
Signer, Petition Opposing the Return of Tories 6/10/83
London, David
  Private, State Troops
Longstreet, Aaron   Freehold
  Militia Volunteer, Prior to the First General Militia Muster, 6/76
  Captain, Militia
  leased horse team to Continental Quarter Master 12/81
  indicted for Misdemeanor, 5/82
  indicted for Misdemeanor, 11/82
Longstreet, Aaron
  Private, Militia
  Private, Militia Dragoons, delinquent one tour
Longstreet, Derrick
  convicted of Riot & Trespass, 6/3/78
Longstreet, Elias   Freehold and Middletown
  Captain, Continental Army, 1775-6
  Signer, Articles of Retaliation, 6/79
  indicted for Assault, 8/79
  Signer, Petition Supporting Retaliation, 9/17/80
  Signer, Petition for Renewing Guard at Toms River, 12/10/81
  indicted for Assault, 5/82
  indicted for Riot, 11/82
  Signer, Petition Opposing the Return of Tories 6/10/83
  Signer, Petition Supporting Quick Division of Militia Prizes, no date
Longstreet, Garret, Esq.   Shrewsbury
  Member, Shrewsbury Committee of Observation
  witness at Monmouth Court, 1778
  Signer, Petition for Stricter Militia Law, 5/31/79
  Justice of the Peace, 1780-2
  Signer, Petition for Renewing Guard at Toms River, 12/10/81
  lost slaves during the war
Longstreet, Gilbert   Upper Freehold
  Militia Volunteer, Prior to the First General Militia Muster, 6/76
  sells produce to Continental Army, 5/80
  Signer, Petition Urging Action Against Disaffected
    & Favoring Retaliation, 5/12/81
  Signer, Petition for Renewing Guard at Toms River, 12/10/81
  Grand Juror, Court of Oyer and Terminer, 11/82

Longstreet, Guisebert (Gilbert)   Shrewsbury
   Private, Militia, delinquent 8/80
   indicted for Riot & Trespass, 6/3/78
   convicted of Riot, 12/80
Longstreet, Helena   Freehold
   witness at Monmouth Court, 1778
   indicted for Misdemeanor, 11/81
Longstreet, James
   Laborer, Pennsylvania Salt Works, intermittent 8/76-6/77
Longstreet, John, Esq.   Shrewsbury
   Signer, Petition Urging Compensation for Raid Victims, 5/25/79
   Signer, Articles of Retaliation, 6/79
   Judge of the Court of Oyer and Terminer, 8/79
   sells produce to Continental Army, 5/80
Longstreet, John   Freehold
   Private, Militia
Longstreet, John   Freehold
   Private, Militia
Longstreet, John, Jr.   Freehold
   Militia Volunteer, Prior to the First General Militia Muster, 6/76
   founder of "Loyalists of Freehold", 4/76
   Captain, New Jersey Volunteers, captured 8/22/77
   Captain, Roger's Kings Rangers
   estate inquisitioned for Forfeiture, 3/23/79
   estate confiscated
Longstreet, Peter   Shrewsbury
   Signer, Articles of Retaliation, 6/79
   Signer, Petition Encouraging Free Trade, 5/12/81
Longstreet, Richard   Shrewsbury
   Private, Militia, delinquent 8/80, delinquent 4/82
   Signer, Petition from Victims of the Association for Retaliation 9/82
Longstreet, Richard   Shrewsbury
   Private, Militia, delinquent 8/80
Longstreet, Samuel   Shrewsbury
   Member, Shrewsbury Committee of Observation
   indicted for two counts of Riot, 6/78
   Private, Militia, delinquent 8/80
Longstreet, Stomphel (Stoffel)   Upper Freehold and Shrewsbury
   Private, Militia
Loop, Christopher
   Private, New Jersey Volunteers
   indicted for Misdemeanor, 6/78

Lord, David
    Private, Militia
Lord, John
    Private, New Jersey Volunteers
Louton, John
    Private, New Jersey Volunteers
Low, Alexander
    Sergeant, Militia
    Signer, Petition for Stricter Militia Law, 5/31/79
    Signer, Articles of Retaliation, 6/79
    Juror, Court of Oyer and Terminer, 5/82
        fined for missing jury duty
Low, Edward
    Private, New Jersey Volunteers
Lowry, see Lawry
Loyd, see Lloyd
Lucas, Charles
    arrested for Disaffection, 11/76
    accused of being active in Tory Rebellions of 12/76
Lucas, Miles
    Signer, Association for Opposing the Return of Tories, 1783
Lucre, William
    sells goods to Pennsylvania Salt Works, 8/76-10/76
Ludlow, John
    Signer, Articles of Retaliation, 6/79
Luffburrow, George   Middletown
    estate confiscated, 1782
Luffburrow, John   Middletown
    Laborer, Pennsylvania Salt Works, intermittent 8/76-6/77
    Refugee in New York, 1782
Luffburrow, William   Middletown
    arrested for spying
    Convicted of High Treason, 4/25/82
    estate confiscated, 1782
Luif, John
    Private, Militia
    Private, State Troops, enlisted 6/80
Luip, see Loop
Luker, Thomas
    Private, Militia
Lumes, Elijah
    Private, New Jersey Volunteers

Lyall, Helena
    wife of Phoenix
    indicted for Misdemeanor, 8/79
Lyon, Nathan
    Corporal, New Jersey Volunteers
    indicted for Misdemeanor, 5/82
Lyster, *see* Leyster

Mc

McAffee, [?]   Shrewsbury
    recipient of poor relief
McAffee, James
    Private, New Jersey Volunteers, deserted 11/20/77
McAllister, Charles
    indicted for Misdemeanor, 1/81
McBride, John   Upper Freehold
    Private, Militia
    Private, Continental Army
McCabe, Elisha
    Private, New Jersey Volunteers
McCafferty, John   Shrewsbury
    recipient of poor relief
McCafferty, Thomas   Shrewsbury
    recipient of poor relief
McCall, John
    Private, New Jersey Volunteers
McCall, Thomas
    Private, New Jersey Volunteers, 7/2/77
McCarter, Henry
    Private, State Troops
McCarter, John
    Private, State Troops, enlists 4/81
McCarty, Florence
    listed on rolls of New Jersey Volunteers
McCarty, Matthew   Freehold
McChesney, James
    Private, Militia
    Signer, Articles of Retaliation, 6/79
    Signer, Petition Supporting Retaliation, 1780
    Signer, Petition Supporting Retaliation, 9/17/80

Roster of the People of Revolutionary Monmouth County

McChesney, Robert
   Private, Militia
McClarkin, James
   indicted for Misdemeanor, 1/81
   indicted for Misdemeanor, 5/82
McClease, Cornelius   Middletown
   Captain, New Jersey Volunteers
   estate confiscated
McClease, Cornelius, Jr.   Middletown
   Convicted of High Treason, 4/25/82
   Refugee in New York, 1782
McClease, John
   Private, Militia, captured 2/13/77
   rented Confiscated Tory estate, prior to 5/79
McClease, Peter   Middletown
   Signer, Petition Opposing the Return of Tories 6/10/83
McClening, John
   Private, New Jersey Volunteers, captured prior to 1779
McClure, Andrew
   Signer, Petition Encouraging Free Trade, 5/12/81
McConky, William   Freehold
McConnell, John
   Signer, Articles of Retaliation, 6/79
McConnor, John   Middletown
McConnor, John   Upper Freehold
McContier, Thomas   Upper Freehold
McConville, John
   Signer, Association for Opposing the Return of Tories, 1783
McCormick, Bernard   Upper Freehold
   Private, Militia
McCormick, Stephen   Freehold
   Private, Militia
   Private, State Troops
   Private, Continental Army
   Signer, Association for Opposing the Return of Tories, 1783
McCoy, Charles   Upper Freehold
   accused of being active in Loyalist Rebellion of 12/76
   indicted for High Treason, 6/78
McCullough, Robert   Upper Freehold
McDaniel, Cornelius
   Private, Militia
   Private, State Troops

Roster of the People of Revolutionary Monmouth County

McDaniel, Cornelius
   Private, Militia
   Private, State Troops
   Private, Continental Army
McDaniel, Daniel   Shrewsbury
   Private, Militia
McDaniel, John
   Private, New Jersey Volunteers, enlisted 1/15/77 dead 5/17/77
McDaniel, Thomas
   Private, New Jersey Volunteers, enlisted 8/13/77 deserts 11/9/78
McDermott, Matthew   Shrewsbury
   Private, Militia, deserts 6/79
McDonald, Abraham
   Signer, Petition Supporting Retaliation, 9/17/80
McDonald, Alexander
   Signer, Articles of Retaliation, 6/79
McDonald, Benjamin   Freehold
   Private, Militia
   Signer, Articles of Retaliation, 6/79
McDonald, Cornelius
   Private, State Troops
McDonald, Donald
   arrested for Disaffection, 11/76
   accused of being active in Tory Rebellions of 12/76
McDonald, James
   indicted for Petty Larceny
McDonald, Jane   Upper Freehold
   household head
McDonald, John
   Private, New Jersey Volunteers
McDormant, Morris   Shrewsbury
McDougall, William
   Private, Militia
McDowell, James   Shrewsbury
   Signer, Petition Favoring Quick Division of Prize Money, 12/79
McDuff, Ellen   Freehold
McDuffee, Daniel   Shrewsbury
   Private, Militia
McDuffee, James   Shrewsbury
   Private, Militia
   Signer, Articles of Retaliation, 6/79
   present at the capture of the British ship, Britannia, 12/31/79

McDuffee, Malcolm
   Corporal, New Jersey Volunteers
McDuffee, Robert   Shrewsbury
   Private, Militia
McDuffy, see McDuffee
McElvin, Robert
   convicted of High Treason, 6/3/78
McErkin, James   Middletown
McFadden, Henry
   Private, New Jersey Volunteers
McFadden, Cornell
   Private, New Jersey Volunteers, deserted 12/23/78
McFall, John
   Private, New Jersey Volunteers
McGallard, Robert   Freehold
   Militia Volunteer, Prior to the First General Militia Muster, 6/76
   sells produce to Continental Army, 5/80
McGalvey, see McGallard
McGee, James
   Private, Militia
   Private, State Troops
   Private, Continental Army
McGee, Thomas
   Signer, Petition Against Association for Retaliation 12/81
McGilkey, Thomas
   Private, New Jersey Volunteers, captured 8/22/77
McGowne, Alexander
   Private, New Jersey Volunteers, captured 8/22/77
McGuire, Daniel
   Private, New Jersey Volunteers
McGuire, Matthew   Freehold
McGuire, Thomas
   Private, New Jersey Volunteers
McKelvey, Robert
   Laborer, Pennsylvania Salt Works, intermittent 8/76-6/77
McKnight, James
   Private, Militia, captured 2/13/77
   Signer, Articles of Retaliation, 6/79
McKnight, Joseph   Freehold
   Private, Militia
   Signer, Association for Opposing the Return of Tories, 1783
McKnight, Lewis   Shrewsbury

Roster of the People of Revolutionary Monmouth County

    Private, Militia
    rented Confiscated Tory estate, prior to 5/79
    Signer, Petition for Stricter Militia Law, 5/31/79
    Signer, Articles of Retaliation, 6/79
    sells produce to Continental Army, 5/80
    Signer, Petition Encouraging Free Trade, 5/12/81
    Juror, Court of Oyer and Terminer, 5/82
        fined for missing jury duty
    Grand Juror, Court of Oyer and Terminer, 11/82
McKnight, Richard   Shrewsbury
    Captain, Militia, captured, paroled 8/78
    Signer, Petition to Better Provision Militia, 2/25/78
    sells produce to Continental Army, 5/80
McKnight, Robert   Freehold
    Juror, Court of Oyer and Terminer, 5/82
        fined for missing jury duty
McKnight, Robert   Upper Freehold
McKnight, Thomas
    arrested for disaffection
McKulvey, Robert   Dover
McLaughlin, Daniel
    Private, Militia
    Private, Continental Army
McLaughlin, John
    Private, New Jersey Volunteers
McLean, John   Upper Freehold
McLease, see McClease
McLeod, Cornelius
    Captain, New Jersey Volunteers
McMahon, John
    Private, New Jersey Volunteers
McManus, Miles
    Private, New Jersey Volunteers, deserted 2/22/78
McMullen, Cornelius
    Signer, Articles of Retaliation, 6/79
McMullen, James
    Private, New Jersey Volunteers, captured 8/22/77
        re-enlisted for bounty 4/79
McMullen, James
    Signer, Association for Opposing the Return of Tories, 1783
McMullen, John   Shrewsbury
    Private, Militia

Private, State Troops
Private, Continental Army
McMullen, John   Freehold
　Private, Militia
　Signer, Articles of Retaliation, 6/79
　Signer, Association for Opposing the Return of Tories, 1783
McMullen, Margaret   Shrewsbury
　orphan child
　recipient of poor relief
McMullen, Neal   Freehold
McMullen, Robert
　Private, New Jersey Volunteers, captured prior to 6/78
　arrested for disaffection, escapes from prison 1777
　convicted of Robbery, 6/3/78
　Pine Robber
McMurray, William   Freehold
　indicted for Assault, 8/79
McQuinn, John
　indicted for Misdemeanor, 1/81
　indicted for Misdemeanor, 11/81
McTeer, Thomas   Upper Freehold

M

Madden, Patrick   Middletown
　indicted for Misdemeanor, 8/79
　indicted for Misdemeanor, 5/82
Madlock, William
　Signer, Petition Supporting Issuing of New Jersey Currency, 1771
Magee, *see also* McGee
Magee, James   Shrewsbury
　Private, Militia
Magee, John
　Private, Militia
Magee, Thomas   Upper Freehold
Mains, Andrew   Freehold
　Signer, Petition Against Loyalist Auction Commissioners, 3/24/79
　Signer, Articles of Retaliation, 6/79
　Signer, Petition Favoring Quick Division of Prize Money, 12/79
　Signer, Petition Supporting Retaliation, 1780
　Signer, Petition Encouraging Free Trade, 5/12/81
　Signer, Association for Opposing the Return of Tories, 1783

Mains, Andrew, Jr.   Freehold
   Private, Militia, wounded at Battle of Germantown
Mains, Charles   Freehold
   Signer, Petition Favoring Quick Division of Prize Money, 12/79
   sells produce to Continental Army, 5/80
Mains, John   Shrewsbury
   Private, State Troops
Mains, William
   Private, Militia
Malet, John   Freehold
Mann, Henry
   Private, State Troops
Maps, Frederick
   Sergeant, Continental Army
Maps, Michael   Shrewsbury
   Private, Militia
Margison, Richard
   arrested for Disaffection, 11/76
   Private, New Jersey Volunteers, captured 6/28/78
Margison, Robert
   Private, New Jersey Volunteers
Marks, Philip   Shrewsbury
   Private, Militia, delinquent 8/9/80
Marlot, Abraham
   Private, Militia, captured 2/13/77
Marlot, Richard
   Signer, Articles of Retaliation, 6/79
Marr, Lawrence
   Private, New Jersey Volunteers
Marsh, Henry   Shrewsbury
   Private, Militia
   holds tavern license, 1775
Marsh, James   Middletown
   Private, Militia
   Private, State Troops, enlists 6/80
   Signer, Articles of Retaliation, 6/79
   present at the capture of the British ship, Britannia, 12/31/79
   Signer, Association for Opposing the Return of Tories, 1783
Marsh, Jesse   Stafford
   Ensign, Militia
Marshal, Robert
   Private, New Jersey Volunteers, enlisted 10/17/77

impressed into Royal Navy 1/16/79
Martin, Mathias
  Constable
Martin, Thomas
  Private, New Jersey Volunteers
Martin, William   Upper Freehold
  Private, Militia
  Private, Continental Army
Martizone, Charles   Shrewsbury
Masangail, Anthony
  German immigrant, 1770
  Private, Queens American Volunteers, 9/76, serves entire war
Mason, Albert   Upper Freehold
Mason, Joseph   Upper Freehold
  Private, Militia
  Private, State Troops
  Signer, Association for Opposing the Return of Tories, 1783
Mason, Robert   Upper Freehold
  Private, Militia
Mathias, Joseph   Freehold
Matthews, Charles   Shrewsbury
Matthews, David
  Private, Militia, hires substitute 2/10/78, delinquent 8/9/80
Matthews, James
  Private, New Jersey Volunteers
Matthews, John
  Private, New Jersey Volunteers
Matthews, Robert   Middletown
  Private, State Troops, enlists 6/80
Matthews, Thomas   Shrewsbury
Matthews, William
  Private, Militia, delinquent 8/9/80
Matthews, William
  Private, Militia, delinquent 8/9/80
  Private, New Jersey Volunteers, enlisted 12/12/76 deserts 1/2/77
Maxson, David
  Private, New Jersey Volunteers, enlisted 12/12/76 dead 1/2/77
Maxson, Ephraim   Shrewsbury
  Private, Militia, delinquent 8/80
Maxson, George
  Signer, Association for Opposing the Return of Tories, 1783
Maxson, James

Maxson, Jonathan
    Private, New Jersey Volunteers, enlisted 3/6/77 dead 12/20/77
Maxson, Joseph
    Private, Militia, delinquent 8/9/80
    Private, New Jersey Volunteers
    Signer, Petition Favoring Quick Division of Prize Money, 12/79
Maxson, Mazier   Shrewsbury
Maxson, Nathan   Shrewsbury
    Corporal, New Jersey Volunteers
    Private, Militia
Maxson, Nathan
    Sergeant, Militia, captured 2/13/77
Maxson, Simeon   Shrewsbury
Maxson, William   Shrewsbury
    Private, Militia, delinquent 8/80
    Private, New Jersey Volunteers, enlisted 2/1/77 deserted 6/13/77
Maxson, Zebulon   Shrewsbury
May, Ann   Shrewsbury
    recipient of poor relief
May, Moses
    Private, Militia
Melat, Derrick   Freehold
Melat, Gideon   Freehold
    Private, Militia
    Private, Continental Army
Merigold, Thomas
    runaway slave
    Paymaster's Assistant, New Jersey Volunteers
Metall, Peter   Shrewsbury
    helps keep the poor
Meyer, Meyers, *see* Miers
Middleton, Abel   Upper Freehold
Middleton, Amos   Upper Freehold
Middleton, Thomas   Freehold
    Private, Militia
    Private, State Troops
Middleton, Thomas   Upper Freehold
    Private, Militia
Miers, David   Upper Freehold
    Militia Volunteer, Prior to the First General Militia Muster, 6/76
Miers, George
    Private, New Jersey Volunteers

Roster of the People of Revolutionary Monmouth County

Miers, Hannah   Middletown
    household head
Miers, John   Shrewsbury
    Private, Militia, delinquent 8/9/80
    Private, State Troops
Miers, Joseph   Upper Freehold
    Militia Volunteer, Prior to the First General Militia Muster, 6/76
    Accused of Being Active in Tory Uprising of 12/76
    Private, New Jersey Volunteers, captured 8/22/77
    indicted for Riot, 1/78
    sells produce to Continental Army, 5/80
Miers, Joshua
    indicted for Indicted for Riot & Trespass, 1/78
Miers, Martin
    Private, Continental Army
Miers, Samuel   Middletown
    Signer, Petition Opposing Slave Manumission, 2/2/74
    arrested for Trespass, 1/20/78
Miers, William
    Private, New Jersey Volunteers, captured prior to 1779
Miligan, Jane
    wife of Philip
    convicted of Misdemeanor, 1/81
Miligan, Philip   Freehold
    indicted for Assault, 8/79
    indicted for Horse Stealing, 1/81
Miller, Benjamin
    Private, New Jersey Volunteers
Miller, David   Dover
Miller, Frederick   Upper Freehold
    Private, Militia
Miller, Jacob
    Private, New Jersey Volunteers, captured 3/15/77
Miller, Joseph   Shrewsbury
    Private, Militia
Miller, Joseph   Upper Freehold
Miller, Peter
    indicted for Horse Stealing, 11/82
Miller, William
    Signer, Petition Favoring Quick Division of Prize Money, 12/79
Millery, Michael
    convicted of Robbery, 6/3/78

Milligan, see Miligan
Mills, Henry
   Private, New Jersey Volunteers
Mills, Israel
   Private, New Jersey Volunteers, enlisted 4/13/77 deserts 5/29/77
Mills, William   Shrewsbury
Milton, Ann   Shrewsbury
   recipient of poor relief
Minchinton, Sylvanus
   Private, New Jersey Volunteers, enlisted 4/29/77 dead 8/20/77
Mingen, Joseph   Upper Freehold
Minks, Andrew
   Private, New Jersey Volunteers
Minks, Henry
   arrested for Disaffection, 1/77
Minks, Peter
   Private, New Jersey Volunteers, deserted 7/10/78
Mins, see Minks
Minny, James   Upper Freehold
   free black householder
Mitchell, Abram
   Private, New Jersey Volunteers, enlisted 12/27/76 dead 3/11/77
Mitchell, George
   Private, New Jersey Volunteers
Mithcell, James   Shrewsbury
   Private, Militia, delinquent 8/9/80
   Private, State Troops
Mitchell, John
   Private, Militia
   Private, State Troops
Mitchell, John
   Private, New Jersey Volunteers, enlisted 3/6/77 dead 12/13/77
Mitchell, Richard
   Private, Militia
   Private, Continental Army
Molat, see Melot
Montgomery, Alexander   Upper Freehold
   Signer, Petition in Support of William Barton, 1/31/76
   Militia Volunteer, Prior to the First General Militia Muster, 6/76
   plundered by Tories, 12/76
   indicted for Misdemeanor, 1/78
   witness at Monmouth Court, 1778

    Juror, Court of Oyer and Terminer, 8/79
        fined L30 for missing all or some of jury duty
    sells produce to Continental Army, 5/80
Montgomery, Burnett   Upper Freehold
Montgomery, Esther   Upper Freehold
    household head
Montgomery, James   Upper Freehold
    sells produce to Continental Army, 5/80
Montgomery, Robert   Upper Freehold
    Signer, Petition in Support of Richard Lloyd, 1/31/76
    Signer, Petition in Support of William Barton, 1/31/76
    Juror, Court of Oyer and Terminer, 12/80
        fined L3 for missing all or some of jury duty
    sells produce to Continental Army, 5/80
    sells sheep to Continental Commissary 7/80
    Signer, Petition Against Association for Retaliation 12/81
    Juror, Court of Oyer and Terminer, 11/82
Montgomery, William   Upper Freehold
Montgomery, William   Upper Freehold
    Militia Volunteer, Prior to the First General Militia Muster, 6/76
    Major, Militia
    Signer, Petition in Support of Richard Lloyd, 1/31/76
    plundered by Tories, 12/76
    Signer, Petition Urging Action Against the Disaffected, 3/14/77
    Juror, Court of Oyer and Terminer, 8/79
        fined L30 for missing all or some of jury duty
    sells produce to Continental Army, 5/80
Montjoy, James   Shrewsbury
Moon, Jacob   Upper Freehold
    Constable, 1779-80
Moore, Andrew   Upper Freehold
Moore, Bezcarrick
    sells produce to Continental Army, 5/80
Moore, Caleb
    Private, Militia
    Private, Continental Army
Moore, David   Shrewsbury
    Private, Militia, delinquent 8/80
Moore, Edward   Freehold
    Private, Militia
    Signer, Articles of Retaliation, 6/79
    present at the capture of the British ship, Britannia, 12/31/79

Moore, Henry
    Private, State Troops, enlists 4/81
Moore, John   Middletown
    Private, Militia
    Private, State Troops, enlists 6/80
    Signer, Articles of Retaliation, 6/79
Moore, Jonathan   Upper Freehold
    Private, State Troops, enlists 5/80
Moore, Joseph   Upper Freehold
    Private, Militia
Moore, Mathias
    Private, Militia
    Private, State Troops
    Private, Continental Army
Moore, Peter   Upper Freehold
Moore, Robert
    Drummer, New Jersey Volunteers
Moore, Thomas
    Private, Militia
    Private, State Troops
    Private, Continental Army
Morford, Garret   Shrewsbury
Morford, John   Freehold
    Militia Volunteer, Prior to the First General Militia Muster, 6/76
    Private, Militia, captured 2/13/77
    Private, State Troops, enlisted 6/80
    Signer, Petition for Stricter Militia Law, 5/31/79
    Signer, Articles of Retaliation, 6/79
    sells produce to Continental Army, 5/80
    Juror, Court of Oyer and Terminer, 5/82
    Juror, Court of Oyer and Terminer, 7/83
    Signer, Association for Opposing the Return of Tories, 1783
Morford, John   Middletown
    Private, Militia, delinquent 11/29/78, delinquent 6/11/80
    indicted for Misdemeanor, 6/78
    Signer, Petition for Stricter Militia Law, 5/31/79
    Signer, Articles of Retaliation, 6/79
Morford, Joseph   Freehold
    Private, Militia
    Signer, Petition for Stricter Militia Law, 5/31/79
    Signer, Petition Urging Compensation for Holders of Inflationary Money, 5/22/83

Morford, Rebecca — Shrewsbury
    household head
Morford, Thomas — Shrewsbury
    Member, Shrewsbury Committee of Observation
    Vestryman, Anglican Christ Church, 1770 and 1777,
        Warden, 1778, 1780, and 1783
    Private, Militia, delinquent 8/17/80
Morford, William — Middletown
    Signer, Petition Opposing the Return of Tories 6/10/83
Morford, William — Upper Freehold
    Militia Volunteer, Prior to the First General Militia Muster, 6/76
Morgan, Abel — Middletown
    Baptist Minister
    Chaplain, Militia
Morgan, Enoch
    Private, Militia
    present at the capture of the British ship, Britannia, 12/31/79
Morgan, James — Freehold
    Private, Militia
    Private, State Troops
Morgan, John — Middletown
    Baptist
Morgan, Samuel
    donates to Charity Fund for Stevenson Family, 5/83
Morgan, Thomas — Shrewsbury
    listed as "lame"
    recipient of poor relief
Morlatt, Gideon
    Private, Continental Army, Jonathan Forman's Company, 10/77
Morlat, John
    Signer, Articles of Retaliation, 6/79
    Constable, 1779
Morison, Daniel
    Private, Militia
Morison, William — Freehold
    Private, Militia
    Signer, Articles of Retaliation, 6/79
    Constable, 1779-83
    sells produce to Continental Army, 5/80
    Signer, Petition in Favor of Daniel Longstreet, 11/21/80
    Signer, Petition for Renewing Guard at Toms River, 12/10/81
Morris, Adam

Roster of the People of Revolutionary Monmouth County

    Private, Militia, delinquent 8/9/80
Morris, Annaniah (Amariah)   Shrewsbury
    sells produce to Continental Army, 5/80
    helps keep the poor
Morris, Amos   Shrewsbury
    indicted for Misdemeanor, 5/82
    indicted for Misdemeanor, 7/83
Morris, Benjamin   Dover
    Militia Volunteer, Prior to the First General Militia Muster, 6/76
    Laborer, Pennsylvania Salt Works, intermittent 8/76-6/77
    indicted for Misdemeanor, 7/83
Morris, Benjamin   Middletown
    Overseer of Highways, 1777
Morris, Benjamin   Upper Freehold
    sells produce to Continental Army, 5/80
Morris, Burrowes
    Private, Militia
Morris, Christopher   Upper Freehold
Morris, Elisha   Middletown
    indicted for Misdemeanor, 11/82
Morris, Elizabeth   Middletown
    household head
Morris, Elizabeth   Shrewsbury
    household head
Morris, Hannah   Middletown
    household head
Morris, Isaac   Middletown
Morris, Jacob   Upper Freehold
    indicted for Misdemeanor, 1/78
    indicted for Misdemeanor, 11/81
Morris, Jacob, Jr.   Upper Freehold
    indicted for Misdemeanor, 11/81
Morris, James   Middletown
    Private, Militia, captured 2/13/77
Morris, James   Middletown
Morris, Jane
    witness at Monmouth Court, 1778
Morris, Job   Shrewsbury
Morris, John   Middletown
    mill owner
    Signer, Petition Favoring Quick Division of Prize Money, 12/79
    indicted for Misdemeanor, 1/81

indicted for Misdemeanor, 11/81
  indicted for Misdemeanor, 5/82
Morris, John   Shrewsbury
  Colonel, New Jersey Volunteers
  Signer, Petition Opposing Slave Manumission, 2/2/74
  Vestryman, Anglican Christ Church, 1776
  estate inquisitioned for Forfeiture, 7/4/77
  estate confiscated
Morris, John
  Ensign, Militia
  Sideman, Anglican Christ Church, 1779
  Signer, Petition Favoring Quick Division of Prize Money, 12/79
  Signer, Petition Supporting Retaliation, 9/17/80
  Signer, Petition Encouraging Free Trade, 5/12/81
  Signer, Petition for Renewing Guard at Toms River, 12/10/81
Morris, John, Jr.   Middletown
  indicted for Misdemeanor, 11/81
Morris, John, Jr.   Shrewsbury
Morris, Jonah   Shrewsbury
Morris, Joseph
  convicted of Riot & Trespass, 1/20/78
Morris, Josiah   Upper Freehold
  Private, Militia
  indicted for Misdemeanor, 5/82
Morris, Lewis   Shrewsbury
  helps keep the poor
  convicted of Misdemeanor, 12/80
Morris, Major
  Private, New Jersey Volunteers, enlisted 3/29/77 dead 5/1/77
Morris, Richard   Middletown
Morris, Robert   Freehold
  Private, Militia
  Private, Continental Army
Morris, Robert   Shrewsbury
  Militia Volunteer, Prior to the First General Militia Muster, 6/76
  Captain, New Jersey Volunteers
  indicted on two counts of Riot & Trespass, 1/20/78
  estate inquisitioned for Forfeiture, 3/20/79
  estate confiscated
Morris, Robert
  Private, New Jersey Volunteers, captured 8/22/77
Morris, Samuel   Middletown

Morris, Thomas   Middletown
    Signer, Articles of Retaliation, 6/79
Morris, William   Middletown
    Private, Militia, delinquent 8/9/80
    convicted of Misdemeanor, 1/81
    indicted for Misdemeanor, 5/82
Morris, Zephaniah   Middletown and Shrewsbury
    Constable, 1778-9, 1783
    Grand Juror, Court of Oyer and Terminer, 7/83
Morrison, see Morison
Morton, William   Shrewsbury
    indicted for Misdemeanor, 1/81
    Signer, Petition from Victims of the Association for Retaliation 9/82
    donates to Charity Fund for Stevenson Family, 5/83
Mott, James, Esq.   Dover and Middletown
    Baptist
    Signer, Petition Opposing Slave Manumission, 2/2/74
    Major, Militia, resigns 6/18/76
    Sells land & goods to Pennsylvania Salt Works, 8/76-10/76
    Delegate, New Jersey Legislature, Upper House, 1776-8
    Signer, Petition Against Association for Retaliation 12/81
Mott, John   Dover
    Captain, (?)
    present at the capture of the British ship, Britannia, 12/31/79
    Signer, Petition Against Association for Retaliation 12/81
    Signer, Petition Urging Action Against the Pine Robbers, 12/27/81
Mount, Britten   Shrewsbury
Mount, Cornelius
    Signer, Association for Opposing the Return of Tories, 1783
Mount, Elizabeth   Upper Freehold
    household head
Mount, Else   Middletown
    household head
Mount, Evot
    Corporal, New Jersey Volunteers
Mount, Ezekiel
    sells produce to Continental Army, 5/80
Mount, Forman   Upper Freehold
    Militia Volunteer, Prior to the First General Militia Muster, 6/76
    Ensign, Militia
    Signer, Petition Calling for Action Against the Disaffected, 2/21/77
    Signer, Petition in Favor of Daniel Longstreet, 11/21/80

Signer, Petition Urging Action Against Disaffected
 & Favoring Retaliation, 5/12/81
Mount, George   Middletown
 "savagely murdered by the Rebels", 9/27/79
Mount, George
 Corporal, Militia, "died of fatigue at Burnt Tavern"
 Private, Continental Army
Mount, George, Jr.   Middletown
 Laborer, Pennsylvania Salt Works, intermittent 8/76-6/77
 arrested for conspiracy, 1781
Mount, James   Shrewsbury
 Vestryman, Anglican Christ Church, 1776 and 1783
 indicted for Misdemeanor, 1/81
 indicted for Misdemeanor, 11/81
 indicted for Misdemeanor, 5/82
 estate inquisitioned for Forfeiture, 3/31/79
 estate confiscated
Mount, James   Upper Freehold
 Private, Militia
 sells produce to Continental Army, 5/80
 Juror, Court of Oyer and Terminer, 11/82
Mount, Jesse   Upper Freehold
 Private, Militia
 sells produce to Continental Army, 5/80
 Juror, Court of Oyer and Terminer, 5/82
  fined for missing jury duty
 Juror, Court of Oyer and Terminer, 11/82
Mount, John   Middletown
Mount, John   Middletown
 refuses militia service, placed under house arrest
 flees to New York
 estate inquisitioned for Forfeiture, 7/2/77
 estate confiscated
Mount, Margaret
 indicted for Misdemeanor, 8/79
Mount, Mathias   Freehold and Middletown
 Private, Militia, captured 2/13/77
 Signer, Articles of Retaliation, 6/79
 Signer, Petition Opposing the Return of Tories 6/10/83
Mount, Michael   Upper Freehold
 Signer, Petition in Support of Richard Lloyd, 1/31/76
 Signer, Petition in Support of William Barton, 1/31/76

plundered by Tories, 12/76
Signer, Petition for Settlement of Quartermaster Debts, 9/6/77
witness at Monmouth Court, 1778
Grand Juror, Court of Oyer and Terminer, 8/79
sells sheep to Continental Commissary 7/80
Signer, Petition Urging Action Against Disaffected
  & Favoring Retaliation, 5/12/81
Grand Juror, Court of Oyer and Terminer, 7/83
Mount, Moses   Freehold
  Private, Militia
  Private, State Troops
  Signer, Petition for Stricter Militia Law, 5/31/79
  Signer, Articles of Retaliation, 6/79
  Signer, Association for Opposing the Return of Tories, 1783
Mount, Moses
  arrested for Disaffection, 1/77
Mount, Nathaniel
  Private, Militia
Mount, Samuel   Upper Freehold
  Signer, Petition Urging Action Against Disaffected
  & Favoring Retaliation, 5/12/81
Mount, Samuel   Upper Freehold
Mount, Rebecca   Upper Freehold
  household head
Mount, Thomas
  Private, Militia, captured 2/13/77
  Private, New Jersey Volunteers
Mount, Timothy   Middletown
  Sergeant, New Jersey Volunteers
Mount, Valerie
  daughter of John
  indicted for Misdemeanor, 8/79
Mount, William   Middletown
  Juror, Court of Oyer and Terminer, 5/82
Mount, William   Shrewsbury
  Juror, Court of Oyer and Terminer, 5/82
    fined for missing jury duty
  indicted for Misdemeanor, 5/82
Mount, William   Upper Freehold
  Private, Militia
Mountjoy, *see* Montjoy
Mullin, *see* McMullen

Munn, James — Upper Freehold
Munnion, Richard — Upper Freehold
Murdock, William
    Signer, Association for Opposing the Return of Tories, 1783
Murphy, Timothy — Middletown
Murphy, William
    Private, New Jersey Volunteers
Murray, John
    Private, New Jersey Volunteers
Murray, Joseph — Middletown
    Private, Militia, murdered while tending his fields, 6/9/80
Myer, Myers, *see* Miers

N

Naberling, Christian
    Private, Militia
    Private, Continental Army
Nance, John
    Private, Militia
    Private, Continental Army
Nancy — Shrewsbury
    mulatto child
    recipient of poor relief
Napier, Thomas — Freehold
Negro, Henry — Shrewsbury
    recipient of poor relief
Negro, Paris — Upper Freehold
    free black householder
Nelson, Andrew — Upper Freehold
Nelson, James
    sells produce to Continental Army, 5/80
Nestor, John
    Private, Militia
Neverson, *see* Nivison
Newberry, Daniel
    Private, New Jersey Volunteers, enlisted 12/19/76 dead ½/77
Newberry, Jacob — Shrewsbury
    Private, Militia, delinquent 8/80
Newberry, Jeremiah
    Private, Militia, delinquent 4/82
Newberry, John

Private, New Jersey Volunteers
Newberry, Seth   Shrewsbury
   Private, Militia, delinquent 8/80
Newberry, Stephen   Shrewsbury
   helps keep the poor
Newberry, William   Shrewsbury
Newberry, William, Jr.   Shrewsbury
   Private, New Jersey Volunteers, enlisted 3/14/77 deserted 7/3/77
   Private, Militia, delinquent 8/80
Newbold, Joseph
   indicted for Misdemeanor, 11/81
Newbury, see Newberry
Newell, Elisha   Upper Freehold
Newell, Hugh   Freehold and Middletown
   Private, Militia
   Signer, Petition Against Loyalist Auction Commissioners, 3/24/79
   Signer, Articles of Retaliation, 6/79
   Signer, Petition Supporting Retaliation, 1780
   leased horse team to Continental Quarter Master 12/81
   donates to Charity Fund for Stevenson Family, 5/83
   Signer, Petition Opposing the Return of Tories 6/10/83
Newell, James   Shrewsbury
   Sergeant, Militia
Newell, James   Upper Freehold
   doctor
   Signer, Petition in Support of Richard Lloyd, 1/31/76
   Signer, Petition in Support of William Barton, 1/31/76
   Signer, Petition Favoring Quick Division of Prize Money, 12/79
   Signer, Association for Opposing the Return of Tories, 1783
Newell, Mary
   sells clothing to Continental Army, 3/78
Newell, Robert
   sells produce to Continental Army, 5/80
Newland, Jonah
   arrested for Disaffection, 1/77
Newland, Jonathan
   Private, New Jersey Volunteers, enlisted 1/20/77 dead 7/20/77
Newland, Trevor   Stafford
Newland, William
   arrested for Disaffection, 1/77
Newlin, see Newland
Newman, Alexander   Shrewsbury

Private, Militia, delinquent 8/80
Newman, James
  Private, New Jersey Volunteers, enlisted 5/16/77 dead 8/20/77
Newman, Jeremiah
  Private, New Jersey Volunteers
Newman, John   Middletown
Newman, John   Shrewsbury
  Private, New Jersey Volunteers
  helps keep the poor
Newman, John, Jr.   Shrewsbury
  Private, Militia, delinquent 8/80
Newman, Joseph   Shrewsbury
  Private, Militia, delinquent 8/80
Newman, Joseph, Jr.   Shrewsbury
  indicted for Misdemeanor, 11/82
Newman, Joseph
  Private, New Jersey Volunteers, enlisted 12/24/76 dead 6/5/77
Newman, Joseph
  Private, New Jersey Volunteers, enlisted 12/19/76 dead 1/14/77
Newman, Peter   Shrewsbury
  Private, Militia, delinquent 8/80
Newman, Samuel   Shrewsbury
  Private, New Jersey Volunteers, deserted 10/19/77
Newman, Samuel, Jr.   Shrewsbury
  Private, Militia, delinquent 8/80, delinquent 4/82
  Private, New Jersey Volunteers, enlisted 1/1/77 deserted 3/13/77
  Private, Militia
Newman, Thomas   Shrewsbury
  Private, Militia, delinquent 8/80
Newman, William
  arrested for Disaffection
  Laborer, Pennsylvania Salt Works, intermittent 8/76-6/77
  Private, Militia
  Private, State Troops, enlisted 5/80
Nicholson, Joseph Stockton
  indicted for High Treason, 8/79
Nightingale, Isaac   Middletown
  Signer, Petition Against Loyalist Auction Commissioners, 3/24/79
Nivin, Patrick
  sells produce to Continental Army, 5/80
Nivison, John   Middletown
  Signer, Articles of Retaliation, 6/79

    Signer, Petition Against Loyalist Auction Commissioners, 3/24/79
Nivison, John, Jr.   Middletown
    Private, Militia
    Private, State Troops
    Signer, Articles of Retaliation, 6/79
Nivison, Nathan
    Private, Militia
    Signer, Articles of Retaliation, 6/79
Nivison, William   Middletown
    Private, State Troops, enlists 6/80
    Signer, Articles of Retaliation, 6/79
Norris, Burns
    Corporal, Militia
Norris, Burrowes   Middletown
    Private, Militia
    Private, State Troops, enlists 6/80
    Signer, Articles of Retaliation, 6/79
Norris, Eaton (Eden)   Shrewsbury
    Signer, Petition Opposing Slave Manumission, 2/2/74
    Private, New Jersey Volunteers, enlisted 4/5/77 dead 1/28/78
Norris, Mary   Freehold
    household head
Norris, Richard   Middletown
    substitute, Militia, 2/10/78
Norris, Robert   Middletown
Norris, Thomas
    Private, Continental Army
Norris, William
    Private, Militia, captured 2/13/77
North, James
    Private, New Jersey Volunteers, enlisted 5/16/77 dead 11/22/78
North, Jeremiah
    Private, New Jersey Volunteers, enlisted 12/17/76 dead 1/26/77
North, John
    arrested for Disaffection, 1/77
    Private, New Jersey Volunteers
    Private, Militia
    Private, Continental Army
    indicted for Riot, 11/82
North, Thomas   Shrewsbury
    Private, New Jersey Volunteers, enlisted 12/8/76 deserted 1/4/77
North, William

    arrested for Disaffection, 1/77
    Private, New Jersey Volunteers
North, Zara
    Private, New Jersey Volunteers, enlisted 12/24/76 deserts 1/1/77
    Laborer, Pennsylvania Salt Works, intermittent 8/76-12/76
North, Zerobable   Shrewsbury
Norton, John   Upper Freehold
Norton, Joshua   Upper Freehold
Norton, Michael
    Private, New Jersey Volunteers
Norton, William   Upper Freehold
Nubary, *see* Newberry
Numan, *see* Newman
Nurse, John   Middletown
    Private, Militia

O

Obadiah   Middletown
    free black householder
O'Bryan, Charles
    Private, New Jersey Volunteers
O'Bryan, Dennis
    Private, New Jersey Volunteers
O'Bryan, John
    Private, New Jersey Volunteers, enlisted 5/15/77
        discharged 11/14/78
Odle, Samuel   Shrewsbury
    accused of being active in Tory Rebellions of 12/76
    arrested for Disaffection 1/77
Odell, *see* Odle
Ogburn, *see* Osborn
Ogden, Charles
    Private, Militia
Ogle, Peter   Upper Freehold
Oglesbie, Robert   Shrewsbury
    Private, Militia, delinquent 8/80
Ogly, Robert   Shrewsbury
Okeson, *see* Okerson
Okerson, John   Freehold and Upper Freehold
    indicted for Murder, 11/82
    estate inquisitioned for Forfeiture, 7/4/77

estate confiscated
Okerson, Samuel				Freehold
	estate confiscated
Okerson, Thomas
	arrested for Disaffection, 1776
	Lieutenant, New Jersey Volunteers, 12/76
	Lieutenant, Roger's Kings Rangers, 1781
Okeson, see Okerson
Oliver, Ichabod
	Private, New Jersey Volunteers
Oliver, William
	Private, New Jersey Volunteers
Olson, John				Freehold
	Private, State Troops, enlists 5/80
Ommonck, John
	Private, New Jersey Volunteers, enlisted 12/20/76 deserts 1/20/77
O'Neal, Henry
	Private, Militia
	Private, Continental Army, Jonathan Forman's Company, 10/77
O'Neal, John
	Corporal, Militia
O'Neill, George				Upper Freehold
O'Neill, John
	Private, Continental Army
O'Neill, Thomas
	Private, New Jersey Volunteers
Orr, Edmund
	Private, New Jersey Volunteers
Osborn, Abraham			Shrewsbury
	Ensign, Militia, delinquent 8/80
Osborn, Caleb				Upper Freehold
Osborn, Caleb, Jr.			Upper Freehold
Osborn, James
	Private, New Jersey Volunteers, enlisted 1/15/77 dead 8/12/77
Osborn, Joseph				Upper Freehold
Osborn, Samuel				Middletown
	Baptist
	Juror, Court of Oyer and Terminer, 12/80
		fined L3 for missing all or some of jury duty
	indicted for Misdemeanor, 1/81
Osborn, Samuel				Shrewsbury
	last Royal Tax Collector for Monmouth County

Signer, Petition Opposing Slave Manumission, 2/2/74
flees to New York, 4/76
estate inquisitioned for Forfeiture, 3/19/79
estate confiscated
Osborn, Samuel   Middletown
    Overseer of Highways, 1772
    Corporal of Militia, Prior to the First General Militia Muster, 6/76
    Highway Surveyor, 1782-3
Osborn, Thomas
    Private, New Jersey Volunteers, enlisted 1/15/77 dead 9/14/77
Osborn, William   Middletown
    Private, New Jersey Volunteers, enlisted 12/8/76 deserts 1/20/77
    Private, Militia
    Private, Militia Dragoons, delinquent one tour
    rented Confiscated Tory estate, prior to 5/79
    Signer, Petition Favoring Quick Division of Prize Money, 12/79
    present at the capture of the British ship, Britannia, 12/31/79
    Signer, Association for Opposing the Return of Tories, 1783
Osburn, *see* Osborn
Otson, John
    Private, Militia
    Private, Continental Army
    Private, State Troops
Overfelt, Conrad   Middletown
    Militia Volunteer, Prior to the First General Militia Muster, 6/76
    Private, Militia
Overtuer, Henry
    Private, Militia
Owings, Michael
    Private, New Jersey Volunteers

P

Page, Abner   Upper Freehold
Page, Francis   Upper Freehold
Page, Joseph
    Laborer, Pennsylvania Salt Works, intermittent 8/76-6/77
    sells sheep to Continental Commissary 7/80
    Juror, Court of Oyer and Terminer, 12/80
        fined L3 for missing all or some of jury duty
    Juror, Court of Oyer and Terminer, 11/82
Page, Timothy   Upper Freehold

Pairs, see also Pearce
Pairs, John
    Private, Militia
    present at the capture of the British ship, Britannia, 12/31/79
Pairs, Jonathan   Middletown
    Private, Militia
    present at the capture of the British ship, Britannia, 12/31/79
Pairs, Samuel   Middletown
    Private, Militia
    Signer, Petition Opposing the Return of Tories 6/10/83
Pairs, William
    arrested for Disaffection, 11/76
Palmer, Isaac   Shrewsbury
Palmer, John   Shrewsbury
Palmer, Philip   Shrewsbury
    Private, Militia
    Private, Continental Army
Palmer, Philip, Jr.   Stafford
    Private, Militia
Pancast, John   Upper Freehold
Pangborn, Jonathan   Stafford
    Private, Militia
    Private, State Troops, discharged 3/1/77
Pangborn, Joseph   Stafford
    Private, Militia
    Private, State Troops, discharged 1/1/77
Pangborn, Linus (Lyons)   Stafford
    Laborer, Pennsylvania Salt Works, intermittent 8/76-6/77
    Private, Militia, killed 12/30/81 at Manahawkin
Pangborn, Nathaniel   Stafford
    Private, Militia
Pangburn, see Pangborn
Panton, William   Shrewsbury
Parent, Daniel   Freehold
    Private, New Jersey Volunteers, enlisted 4/20/77 deserts 5/25/77
Parent, James
    Signer, Association for Opposing the Return of Tories, 1783
Parent, John   Freehold
    Private, Militia, delinquent 2/10/78
    Signer, Articles of Retaliation, 6/79
    Private, State Troops, enlisted 6/80

Signer, Association for Opposing the Return of Tories, 1783
Parent, Robert   Upper Freehold
    Militia Volunteer, Prior to the First General Militia Muster, 6/76
    Private, Militia
Parent, Samuel   Freehold
    Juror, Court of Oyer and Terminer, 11/82
    Signer, Association for Opposing the Return of Tories, 1783
Parent, Samuel, Jr.   Freehold
Parent, Thomas   Upper Freehold
    arrested for Disaffection, 1/77
Parent, William   Freehold
Parent, William   Upper Freehold
Park, John
    Private, New Jersey Volunteers
Park, Ozias
    Private, New Jersey Volunteers
Parker, Abigail   Shrewsbury
    widow
    household head
    helps keep the poor
    indicted for Misdemeanor, 5/82
Parker, Abraham   Shrewsbury
Parker, Ann
    daughter of Thomas
    indicted for Seditious Words, 6/3/78
Parker, Benjamin   Upper Freehold
Parker, Benjamin, Jr.   Upper Freehold
Parker, David   Upper Freehold
Parker, Deborah   Shrewsbury
    Delegate, Friends' Quarterly Meeting, 1774
Parker, Ebenezer   Dover
Parker, Edward
    indicted for Misdemeanor, 1/78
Parker, Elisha
    Private, Militia
Parker, Elizabeth
    daughter of James
    indicted for Misdemeanor, 8/79
Parker, Ephraim   Shrewsbury
    holds tavern license, 1775
Parker, George   Shrewsbury
    Private, Militia, delinquent 8/9/80

Private, State Troops
Delegate, Friends' Quarterly Meeting, 1775-83
Parker, Hannah   Shrewsbury
   household head
Parker, Jerusha   Freehold
Parker, John   Freehold
Parker, John   Shrewsbury
   son of Peter
   Private, Militia, exempt from Militia service, 2/10/78
   Private, State Troops
   indicted for Misdemeanor, 1/81
   indicted for Robbery, 5/82
Parker, John   Shrewsbury
   indicted for Misdemeanor, 1/78
   estate inquisitioned for Forfeiture, 3/31/79
   convicted of Horse Stealing, 1/81
Parker, Jonathan
   indicted for Misdemeanor, 1/78
Parker, Joseph   Shrewsbury
   helps keep the poor
   Delegate, Friends' Quarterly Meeting, 1774
Parker, Joseph, Jr.   Shrewsbury
   Private, Militia, exempt from Militia service, 2/10/78
   Private, State Troops
Parker, Joshua   Shrewsbury
Parker, Josiah   Shrewsbury
   Lieutenant, New Jersey Volunteers
Parker, Mariboe
   indicted for Misdemeanor, 11/82
Parker, Mark
   Private, Militia
Parker, Nathaniel   Shrewsbury
   convicted of Misdemeanor, 6/3/78
   estate confiscated
Parker, Nathaniel   Shrewsbury
   Private, Militia, delinquent 8/17/80
   recipient of poor relief
Parker, Peter   Shrewsbury
   of Snag Swamp
   indicted for Misdemeanor, 6/78
   convicted of Seditious Words, 12/80
Parker, Peter   Shrewsbury

of Long Branch
Parker, Peter, Jr.   Shrewsbury
   convicted of Misdemeanor, 12/80
Parker, Robert
   exempt from Militia service, 2/10/78
   convicted of High Treason, 1/81
Parker, Samuel
   son of Ephraim
   indicted for Misdemeanor, 1/81
   indicted for Misdemeanor, 11/82
Parker, Thomas   Freehold
   Sergeant, New Jersey Volunteers
   indicted for Trespass, 1/20/78
   leased horse team to Continental Quarter Master 12/81
Parker, Thomas
   leased horse team to Continental Quarter Master 12/81
Parker, William   Shrewsbury
   arrested for Disaffection, 1/77
   convicted of Misdemeanor, 6/3/78
   rented Confiscated Tory estate, prior to 5/79
   convicted of Misdemeanor, 12/80
   Signer, Petition from Victims of the Association for Retaliation 9/82
Parker, William   Shrewsbury
   of Red Bank
   indicted for Misdemeanor, 1/81
Parks, William
   Private, New Jersey Volunteers, enlisted 4/7/77 dead 6/4/78
Parnell, John   Upper Freehold
Parse, *see* Pairs *and* Pearce
Parson, John   Upper Freehold
   Private, New Jersey Volunteers, captured 8/22/77
   Private, Militia, drafted into Continental Army 5/78
   Private, Continental Army
Paterson, Asa   Shrewsbury
Paterson, Esek   Shrewsbury
Paterson, James   Shrewsbury
Paterson, James   Middletown
   Overseer of Highways, 1770 and 1778
   Constable, 1779
Paterson, John   Freehold
Paterson, John   Middletown
   witness at Monmouth Court, 1778

Paterson, John — Shrewsbury
    Private, Militia, delinquent 8/80
Paterson, John
    Private, New Jersey Volunteers, enlisted 12/19/76 dead 3/5/77
Paterson, Joseph — Freehold
    Private, Militia, deserts 6/79
    convicted of Misdemeanor, 1/20/78
Paterson, Joseph
    Private, New Jersey Volunteers, enlisted 12/11/76 dead 5/27/77
Paterson, Josiah — Shrewsbury
    Signer, Petition Opposing Slave Manumission, 2/2/74
Paterson, Peter — Shrewsbury
    convicted of Misdemeanor, 1/81
Paterson, Robert — Middletown
    Signer, Petition Supporting Issuing of New Jersey Currency, 1771
Paterson, Robert, Jr.
    convicted of Horse Stealing, 12/80
Patrick, William — Shrewsbury
Patten, John
    Juror, Court of Oyer and Terminer, 11/82
Patten, James — Dover
    Laborer, Pennsylvania Salt Works, intermittent 8/76-6/77
Patten, John — Freehold
    Private, Militia
    Signer, Association for Opposing the Return of Tories, 1783
Patten, Thomas
    Private, New Jersey Volunteers
Patterson, see Paterson
Paul, Benjamin — Stafford
    Private, Militia
    Sergeant, Continental Army
Paxson, William
    Private, Militia
Peace, see Pease
Pearce, Edward
    Private, New Jersey Volunteers
Pearce, James
    Laborer, Pennsylvania Salt Works, intermittent 8/76-12/76
    arrested for Disaffection, 1/77
    enlists in Continental Army in exchange for pardon, 5/23/77
Pearce, Jeremiah — Shrewsbury
Pearce, Job — Shrewsbury

Pearce, Job   Shrewsbury
Pearce, John   Shrewsbury
   Militia Volunteer, Prior to the First General Militia Muster, 6/76
Pearce, John   Shrewsbury
Pearce, John   Shrewsbury
   Captain, Militia
Pearce, John   Shrewsbury
   Private, New Jersey Volunteers, enlisted 12/20/76 deserts 2/4/77
Pearce, Jonathan   Shrewsbury
   Private, Militia
   present at the capture of the British ship, Britannia, 12/31/79
Pearce, Jonathan   Middletown
   Captain, Militia
   Signer, Petition Opposing Slave Manumission, 2/2/74
   Signer, Petition Urging Action Against the Disaffected, 3/14/77
Pearce, Joseph   Shrewsbury
   Private, New Jersey Volunteers, enlisted 12/20/76 dead 8/6/77
Pearce, Joseph   Shrewsbury
   arrested for Disaffection, 1/77
   indicted for Misdemeanor, 11/82
Pearce, Joshua
   indicted for Felony, 11/81
Pearce, Lewis
   Private, New Jersey Volunteers
Pearce, Mary   Shrewsbury
   household head
   Delegate, Friends' Quarterly Meeting, 1782
Pearce, Richard
   Private, New Jersey Volunteers, enlisted 12/15/76 dead 4/19/77
Pearce, Samuel   Middletown
   Private, Militia
   Private, Militia Dragoons, delinquent one tour
   Private, State Troops
   Signer, Articles of Retaliation, 6/79
   present at the capture of the British ship, Britannia, 12/31/79
   leased horse team to Continental Quarter Master 12/81
Pearce, Samuel   Stafford
   indicted for Misdemeanor, 1/81
   indicted for Misdemeanor, 5/82
   indicted for Misdemeanor, 11/82
Pearce, Thomas   Shrewsbury
Pearce, William

Private, New Jersey Volunteers
Pearce, William   Shrewsbury
    Militia Volunteer, Prior to the First General Militia Muster, 6/76
    Private, Militia, drafted into Continental Army 5/78, delinquent 8/80
    Signer, Petition Supporting Retaliation, 9/17/80
Pears, Pearsall, *see* Pearce, Pairs *and* Sears
Pearson, Benjamin   Stafford
    Private, Militia
Pearson, Daniel
    Lieutenant, Cont. Army, Jonathan Forman's Company, 10/77
Peas, *see* Pease
Pease, Adam   Freehold
    sells produce to Continental Army, 5/80
Pease, Cornelius   Freehold
Pease, Jonathan   Freehold
    Private, State Troops, enlists 5/78
Pease, Samuel   Freehold
    Private, Militia
    Signer, Petition for Stricter Militia Law, 5/31/79
    Signer, Articles of Retaliation, 6/79
    Juror, Court of Oyer and Terminer, 11/82
    Signer, Petition Supporting Quick Division of Militia Prizes, no date
Pease, William
    Private, Militia, captured 2/13/77
Peep, Samuel
    Private, Militia
Peer, Jonathan
    Private, Militia
    Private, Continental Army
Peet, Herman
    Private, Militia
Pell, Samuel
    Signer, Association for Opposing the Return of Tories, 1783
Pellimore, John
    Private, State Troops
Pemberton, Robert   Freehold
    Lieutenant, Continental Army
Pen, James   Middletown
    estate confiscated
Pennington, Israel
    convicted of Misdemeanor, 1/81
Perine, *see* Perrine

Perkin, Nathaniel
    estate confiscated, 1780
Perkin, William   Dover
    Laborer, Pennsylvania Salt Works, intermittent 8/76-6/77
Perrine, Henry   Freehold
    Private, Militia
    Private, State Troops, enlisted 6/80
    rented Confiscated Tory estate, prior to 5/79
    Signer, Articles of Retaliation, 6/79
    sells produce to Continental Army, 5/80
    sells produce to Continental Army, 7/80
    Signer, Petition Encouraging Free Trade, 5/12/81
    Juror, Court of Oyer and Terminer, 5/82
Perrine, Isaac   Upper Freehold
Perrine, James   Freehold
    Private, Militia
    indicted for Misdemeanor, 5/82
Perrine, Job   Upper Freehold
    Private, Militia
Perrine, John   Upper Freehold
    Private, Militia
    Signer, Articles of Retaliation, 6/79
Perrine, John   Upper Freehold
    estate inquisitioned for Forfeiture, 6/1/78
    estate confiscated
Perrine, Kenneth   Freehold
    Signer, Petition for Renewing Guard at Toms River, 12/10/81
Perrine, Kenneth   Upper Freehold
    Private, Militia
Perrine, Lewis   Freehold
    Private, Militia
    Signer, Articles of Retaliation, 6/79
Perrine, Mary   Upper Freehold
    household head
Perrine, Silas
    Private, Militia
Perrine, William   Upper Freehold
    flees to New York
    estate inquisitioned for Forfeiture, 7/4/77
    estate confiscated
Perry, Joseph   Shrewsbury
    helps keep the poor

Peterson, Deborah   Shrewsbury
    household head
Peterson, James
    Private, New Jersey Volunteers, enlisted 12/19/76 dead 8/30/77
Peterson, Peter   Stafford
    Private, Continental Army
Peterson, Robert
    Lieutenant, New Jersey Volunteers, captured 8/22/77
Peterson, William
    Private, New Jersey Volunteers
Pette, Robert
    Private, Militia
    Private, State Troops
Pettemore, Jonathan
    Private, Militia
    Private, State Troops
Pettenger, *see* Pittenger
Pettit, George
    Private, New Jersey Volunteers, enlisted 12/19/76 dead 3/8/77
Pettit, Gideon   Upper Freehold
Pettit, Henry
    Private, New Jersey Volunteers
Pettit, John
    Private, New Jersey Volunteers
Pettit, William   Middletown
Pettit, William   Shrewsbury
    Private, Militia, delinquent 8/80
Pettit, William, Jr.
    Private, New Jersey Volunteers, enlisted 12/19/76 dead 4/30/77
Pew, Benoni
    Private, Continental Army
Pew, Deborah   Middletown
    household head
Pew, James   Middletown
    Signer, Petition Opposing Slave Manumission, 2/2/74
    flees to New York, 1778
    estate inquisitioned for Forfeiture, 6/1/78
    estate confiscated
    indicted for Misdemeanor, 5/82
Pew, John   Middletown
Pew, Jonathan   Middletown
    Signer, Articles of Retaliation, 6/79

Pew, Joseph
    Private, Militia
Pew, Rhoda
    wife of James Pew, Jr.
    convicted of Misdemeanor, 1/20/78
Pew, William   Middletown
    Private, Militia
    present at the capture of the British ship, Britannia, 12/31/79
Phegan, Phegans, *see* Fagan
Phoenix, Abigail   Middletown
    household head
Phillips, John
    Laborer, Pennsylvania Salt Works, intermittent 8/76-6/77
    Private, Militia
    Private, Continental Army
Phillips, John   Dover
    Private, New Jersey Volunteers, enlisted 11/1/77   deserts 9/17/78
Phillips, Joseph   Dover
    Militia Volunteer, Prior to the First General Militia Muster, 6/76
    Private, Militia
Phillips, Nicholas   Shrewsbury
Phillips, Obadiah   Dover
    Militia Volunteer, Prior to the First General Militia Muster, 6/76
Phillips, Peter   Shrewsbury
    Signer, Petition Supporting Retaliation, 9/17/80
Phillips, Richard   Dover
    Militia Volunteer, Prior to the First General Militia Muster, 6/76
    witness at Monmouth Court, 1778
    indicted for Murder, 5/82
Phillips, Sarah
    indicted for Misdemeanor, 1/81
Phillips, Thomas   Dover
    Militia Volunteer, Prior to the First General Militia Muster, 6/76
Phillwell, David
    Private, Militia
Philmele, David
    witness at Monmouth Court, 1778
    Private, Militia
    present at the capture of the British ship, Britannia, 12/31/79
Pierce, *see* Pearce
Pigeon, Isaac
    Private, Militia

Pike, Thomas
  Private, Militia
Piniset, Asa
  sells produce to Continental Army, 5/80
Pintard, John   Shrewsbury
  Refugee in New York, 1782
  estate inquisitioned for Forfeiture, 3/31/79
  estate confiscated
Pintard, John L.
  Laborer, Pennsylvania Salt Works, intermittent 8/76-6/77
Pintard, Samuel   Shrewsbury
  Sideman, Anglican Christ Church, 1781-2
Pintard, William   Shrewsbury
  Vestryman, Anglican Christ Church, 1778 and 1783
  indicted for Misdemeanor, 11/81
  indicted for Misdemeanor, 5/82
Pitcher, William
  Drummer, New Jersey Volunteers
Pitman, Jonathan   Upper Freehold
  Captain (?)
  Signer, Petition Urging Action Against Disaffected
    & Favoring Retaliation, 5/12/81
Pitman, John   Upper Freehold
Pitney, Benjamin   Middletown
Pitney, Elizabeth   Shrewsbury
  household head
Pittenger, Jacob   Freehold
  Signer, Petition for Stricter Militia Law, 5/31/79
  Signer, Articles of Retaliation, 6/79
  Signer, Association for Opposing the Return of Tories, 1783
Pittenger, John   Freehold
  Signer, Petition Urging Compensation for Inflated Money, 5/22/83
Pittenger, Richard   Freehold
  Sergeant, Militia
  Signer, Articles of Retaliation, 6/79
  Signer, Petition Urging Compensation for Inflated Money, 5/22/83
Pittenger, Samuel   Freehold
  Militia Volunteer, Prior to the First General Militia Muster, 6/76
  Private, Militia
Plant, William
  Private, New Jersey Volunteers, enlisted 12/20/76 dead 7/4/77
Platt, Abraham   Dover

Platt, Francis   Dover
    Private, Militia
Platt, John   Dover
    Signer, Petition for Renewing Guard at Toms River, 12/10/81
    Constable, 1782
Platt, Joseph
    Signer, Petition Against Association for Retaliation 12/81
Platt, Levi
    Signer, Petition Against Association for Retaliation 12/81
Platt, Richard   Upper Freehold
Platt, Tobias
    Signer, Petition Against Association for Retaliation 12/81
Plumb, Samuel   Upper Freehold
Poland, John   Dover
    Private, Continental Army
Polhemus, Daniel
    Private, Militia
    Signer, Petition Supporting Issuing of New Jersey Currency, 1771
    present at the capture of the British ship, Britannia, 12/31/79
Polhemus, James
    Private, Militia
Polhemus, John   Freehold
    arrested 1777
    estate confiscated
Polhemus, John   Shrewsbury
    Signer, Petition Opposing Slave Manumission, 2/2/74
Polhemus, John   Upper Freehold
    sells produce to Continental Army, 5/80
    sells sheep to Continental Commissary 7/80
Polhemus, John, Jr.   Freehold
    convicted of High Treason, 6/3/78
Polhemus, Leford
    Private, Militia
Polhemus, Mary   Upper Freehold
    household head
    sells sheep to Continental Commissary 7/80
Polhemus, Nathan
    Private, Militia
Polhemus, Nathaniel   Upper Freehold
    Militia Volunteer, Prior to the First General Militia Muster, 6/76
    Captain, Militia
    Signer, Petition Calling for Action Against the Disaffected, 2/21/77

Roster of the People of Revolutionary Monmouth County

   Signer, Petition Urging Action Against the Disaffected, 3/14/77
   Signer, Petition in Favor of Daniel Longstreet, 11/21/80
   Signer, Petition for Renewing Guard at Toms River, 12/10/81
   Juror, Court of Oyer and Terminer, 11/82
   Juror, Court of Oyer and Terminer, 7/83
Polhemus, Rebecca   Upper Freehold
   household head
Polhemus, Tobias   Middletown and Upper Freehold
   Captain, Militia, captured 2/13/77, paroled 8/78, captured 1780
   Signer, Petition Opposing Slave Manumission, 2/2/74
   sells produce to Continental Army, 5/80
Polling, Mary   Middletown
   household head
Polling, Richard   Middletown
   Private, Militia
   Signer, Articles of Retaliation, 6/79
   present at the capture of the British ship, Britannia, 12/31/79
Polling, Samuel   Middletown
   Private, Militia
   present at the capture of the British ship, Britannia, 12/31/79
   Signer, Petition Opposing the Return of Tories 6/10/83
Poole, George   Middletown
   substitute, Militia
   present at the capture of the British ship, Britannia, 12/31/79
   Signer, Petition Opposing the Return of Tories 6/10/83
Poole, Lewis   Middletown
   Private, Continental Army
Poole, Richard   Middletown
   Vestryman, Anglican Christ Church, 1772-7
   Signer, Articles of Retaliation, 6/79
   present at the capture of the British ship, Britannia, 12/31/79
   Signer, Petition Opposing the Return of Tories 6/10/83
Poole, Richard, Jr.   Middletown
   Drummer, Militia
Porter, John
   Private, New Jersey Volunteers, captured prior to 1779
   Private, Militia
Post, Elias
   Laborer, Pennsylvania Salt Works, intermittent 8/76-6/77
Post, George
   Private, Militia
Postens, Charles   Freehold

    Private, Militia
    Private, State Troops
    Signer, Articles of Retaliation, 6/79
    Signer, Petition Supporting Quick Division of Militia Prizes, no date
Postens, Jacob
    Private, Militia
    Private, State Troops
Postens, Richard   Freehold
    Private, State Troops, enlisted 6/80
    Signer, Articles of Retaliation, 6/79
Postens, William   Freehold
    Signer, Articles of Retaliation, 6/79
Potter, Daniel   Shrewsbury
    sells produce to Continental Army, 5/80
Potter, David   Shrewsbury
Potter, Ephraim   Shrewsbury
    recipient of poor relief
Potter, Isaac   Dover
    indicted for Misdemeanor, 1/78
    Juror, Court of Oyer and Terminer, 1/78
        fined L5 for not attending all or part of Jury duty
    Signer, Petition Against Association for Retaliation 12/81
    Township Freeholder of Appeals, 1783
    Grand Juror, Court of Oyer and Terminer, 7/83
Potter, Mary   Shrewsbury
    recipient of poor relief
Potter, Paul   Dover
    Private, Militia
    Signer, Petition Against Association for Retaliation 12/81
Potter, Phineas   Dover
    sells goods to Pennsylvania Salt Works, intermittent 8/76-6/77
Potter, Reuben   Dover
    Private, Militia
    Laborer, Pennsylvania Salt Works, intermittent 8/76-6/77
    Signer, Articles of Retaliation, 6/79
Potter, Robert
    Sergeant, New Jersey Volunteers, captured 8/22/77
Potter, Thomas   Dover
    Signer, Petition Against Association for Retaliation 12/81
Potts, Richard   Upper Freehold
Potts, Thomas   Freehold
    Private, New Jersey Volunteers, enlisted 1/1/77 deserted 3/15/77

arrested for Disaffection, 11/76
Signer, Petition Against Association for Retaliation 12/81
Potts, William
   Private, Militia
   Private, Continental Army
Powell, Richard   Upper Freehold
   indicted for Misdemeanor, 11/82
Powers, John
   Corporal, Militia, captured 2/13/77
Pratt, Isaac
   Private, New Jersey Volunteers
Pratt, James
   Drummer, New Jersey Volunteers
Prest, Richard   Freehold
   sells produce to Continental Army, 7/80
   Signer, Association for Opposing the Return of Tories, 1783
Prest, Richard, Jr.   Freehold
   Signer, Association for Opposing the Return of Tories, 1783
Preston, Jacob
   Signer, Association for Opposing the Return of Tories, 1783
Preston, John
   Private, Militia
   Signer, Association for Opposing the Return of Tories, 1783
Preston, Joseph
   Private, Militia
   Private, Continental Army
   Signer, Petition for Stricter Militia Law, 5/31/79
   Juror, Court of Oyer and Terminer, 11/82
   Signer, Association for Opposing the Return of Tories, 1783
Preston, Samuel   Dover
Preston, William   Shrewsbury
Price, Ann   Shrewsbury
   household head
Price, Benjamin
   Private, New Jersey Volunteers, enlisted 5/14/77 deserted 2/4/78
Price, Edward
   witness at Monmouth Court, 1778
   indicted for High Treason, 5/82
Price, James   Shrewsbury
   Private, Militia, delinquent 8/80
   estate inquisitioned for Forfeiture, 3/23/79
   indicted for Misdemeanor, 8/79

Price, John   Dover
    indicted for Misdemeanor and Receiving Stolen Goods, 1/81
    indicted for Misdemeanor, 11/82
    estate confiscated
Price, John   Dover
    Captain, Militia
    Signer, Petition Against Association for Retaliation 12/81
    Signer, Petition Urging Action Against the Pine Robbers, 12/27/81
Price, John   Dover
    Private, New Jersey Volunteers, enlisted 12/16/76 deserts 4/19/78
    Private, Militia
Price, Joseph   Shrewsbury
    of Red Bank
    Sergeant, New Jersey Volunteers
    indicted for Misdemeanor, 8/79
    convicted of Misdemeanor, 1/81
    estate confiscated
    Vestryman, Anglican Christ Church, 1783
Price, Lewis
    Private, New Jersey Volunteers, enlisted 12/19/76 dead 4/10/78
Price, Mary   Shrewsbury
    household head
    holds tavern license, 1775
Price, Michael   Shrewsbury
    Surgeon, New Jersey Volunteers
    estate inquisitioned for Forfeiture, 3/31/79
    estate confiscated
Price, Thomas
    Private, Continental Army
Price, William   Shrewsbury
    Corporal, New Jersey Volunteers
    estate confiscated
Prigmore, John   Upper Freehold
    Private, Militia
Primer, Adam   Upper Freehold
    Private, Militia
Probasco, Abraham   Middletown and Upper Freehold
Probasco, Abraham   Shrewsbury
    Sergeant, Militia
    Signer, Petition Opposing Slave Manumission, 2/2/74
    witness at Monmouth Court, 1778
Proctor, Nathan   Shrewsbury
    estate confiscated 1784

Provost, John
 convicted of Misdemeanor, 1/20/78
Prue, Michael					Shrewsbury
 estate confiscated
Purdy, Richard
 Private, Militia
Purtle, John					Shrewsbury

Q

Quackenbush, David				Freehold
 Private, Militia
Quackenbush, Jacob				Freehold
 Private, Militia, captured 2/13/77
 Signer, Articles of Retaliation, 6/79
 Signer, Association for Opposing the Return of Tories, 1783
Quackenbush, Peter				Freehold
 Private, Militia
 Signer, Articles of Retaliation, 6/79
Quay, John					Upper Freehold
Quay, Samuel					Upper Freehold
Queen, David
 Private, Militia
 Private, State Troops, enlisted 6/80
Queen, Patrick
 Private, New Jersey Volunteers
Quick, Elisha
 Private, New Jersey Volunteers
Quicksell, *see* Quixall
Quinlan, James
 Private, New Jersey Volunteers, captured 8/22/77
Quixall, John
 sells produce to Continental Army, 5/80
Quixall, Samuel				Upper Freehold

R

Radford, Samuel
 sells produce to Continental Army, 5/80
Raftsnider, Thomas
 Private, State Troops
Randolph, *see also* Fitzrandolph

Randolph, Annaniah Shrewsbury
  Private, Militia, delinquent 9/80
Randolph, Amos
  son of Joseph
  indicted for two Misdemeanors, 1/81
Randolph, Daniel Dover
  Signer, Petition to Better Defend Toms River Area, 5/18/77
Randolph, Daniel Freehold
  rented Confiscated Tory estate, prior to 5/79
  Signer, Articles of Retaliation, 6/79
  sells produce to Continental Army, 5/80
  Signer, Petition for Renewing Guard at Toms River, 12/10/81
  Justice of the Peace, 1782-3
  Signer, Association for Opposing the Return of Tories, 1783
Randolph, James Dover
  Militia Volunteer, Prior to the First General Militia Muster, 6/76
  sells goods to Pennsylvania Salt Works, intermittent 8/76-6/77
  Grand Juror, Court of Oyer and Terminer, 8/79
  Signer, Petition Urging Compensation for Raid Victims, 5/25/79
Randolph, James Middletown
  Private, Militia
Randolph, Job Dover
  Signer, Petition Urging Action Against the Pine Robbers, 12/27/81
Randolph, Joseph, Sr. Shrewsbury
  Private, Militia, delinquent 8/80
  convicted of Misdemeanor, 1/81
Randolph, Joseph Freehold and Dover
  Captain, Militia
  Juror, Court of Oyer and Terminer, 1/78
    fined L5 for not attending all or part of Jury duty
  Signer, Petition Urging Action Against the Pine Robbers, 12/27/81
Randolph, Moses Dover
  Signer, Petition Urging Action Against the Pine Robbers, 12/27/81
Randolph, Reuben Stafford
  leases shallop to Pennsylvania Salt Works, 8/76-6/77
  Captain, Militia
  Juror, Court of Oyer and Terminer, 1/78
    fined L5 for not attending all or part of Jury duty
  Signer, Petition Urging Action Against the Pine Robbers, 12/27/81
  Grand Juror, Court of Oyer and Terminer, 7/83
Randolph, Samuel
  Private, Militia

Randolph, William
    Signer, Petition for Renewing Guard at Toms River, 12/10/81
Rapalje, George   Middletown
    Overseer of Highways, 1774
    arrested for disaffection 1777
    estate confiscated
Ray, David
    Private, Militia
    Signer, Articles of Retaliation, 6/79
Ray, George
    Private, New Jersey Volunteers
Raymond, Isaac
    indicted for Misdemeanor, 1/81
Read, *see* Reid
Reading, Catherine   Middletown
    household head
Reading, Ferdinand   Middletown
Reder, *see* Reter
Reckless, Isaac
    indicted for Misdemeanor, 5/82
Reece, Henry
    Private, Militia, captured 2/13/77
Reed, *see* Reid
Reeves, Josiah (Hosea)
    Private, Militia
Reid, Aaron   Freehold
    Private, Militia
    Private, State Troops, enlisted 6/80
    Signer, Petition for Stricter Militia Law, 5/31/79
    Signer, Articles of Retaliation, 6/79
Reid, Aaron
    Private, Militia
Reid, Amy
    indicted for Misdemeanor, 11/82
Reid, Andrew   Upper Freehold
Reid, Enoch   Stafford
    Private, Militia
Reid, George   Freehold
Reid, Hamilton   Upper Freehold
    Private, Militia
Reid, Henry   Stafford
    Private, New Jersey Volunteers

    Corporal, Continental Army
Reid, Henry
    Private, New Jersey Volunteers, enlisted 3/1/78 deserts 11/20/78
Reid, James   Freehold
    Signer, Articles of Retaliation, 6/79
    sells produce to Continental Army, 5/80
    sells produce to Continental Army, 7/80
    Signer, Petition Encouraging Free Trade, 5/12/81
    Juror, Court of Oyer and Terminer, 5/82
    Juror, Court of Oyer and Terminer, 11/82
    Juror, Court of Oyer and Terminer, 7/83
Reid, James   Upper Freehold
    Private, Militia
Reid, Job
    Private, Militia
Reid, John   Freehold
    Private, Militia
    Signer, Petition for Settlement of Quartermaster Debts, 9/6/77
    Singer, Petition for Stricter Militia Law, 5/31/79
    Signer, Articles of Retaliation, 6/79
    Signer, Petition Urging Compensation for Inflated Money, 5/22/83
Reid, John   Freehold
    Private, Militia
    Signer, Articles of Retaliation, 6/79
    present at the capture of the British ship, Britannia, 12/31/79
Reid, John   Upper Freehold
    Signer, Petition for Stricter Militia Law, 5/31/79
    sells clothing to Continental Army, 3/78
    Signer, Articles of Retaliation, 6/79
    Grand Juror, Court of Oyer and Terminer, 8/79
    sells produce to Continental Army, 5/80
    Signer, Petition Encouraging Free Trade, 5/12/81
    Signer, Petition Urging Action Against Disaffected
        & Favoring Retaliation, 5/12/81, opposes Retaliation clause
    Signer, Petition Urging Compensation for Inflated Money, 5/22/83
Reid, John   Upper Freehold
    Ensign, New Jersey Volunteers
    Sergeant, Militia
Reid, Jonathan   Freehold
    Private, Militia, captured 2/13/77
    Signer, Articles of Retaliation, 6/79
Reid, Jonathan   Middletown

Private, Militia
Signer, Petition Favoring Quick Division of Prize Money, 12/79
present at the capture of the British ship, Britannia, 12/31/79
Signer, Petition Opposing the Return of Tories 6/10/83
Reid, Lewis
    Private, New Jersey Volunteers
Reid, Samuel   Freehold
    donates to Charity Fund for Stevenson Family, 5/83
Reid, William   Upper Freehold
    Signer, Petition Urging Compensation for Inflated Money, 5/22/83
Reidey, Andrew   Shrewsbury
    Private, Militia
Reiter, *see* Reter
Remind, John
    Private, Militia, delinquent 4/82
Remington, Amy   Shrewsbury
    household head
    listed on Militia return 6/29/80
Remson, Jacob   Middletown
Remson, William   Freehold
    Captain, Militia
    sells produce to Continental Army, 5/80
Reter, Henry   Middletown
    estate inquisitioned for Forfeiture, 6/8/79
    estate confiscated
Reter, Jacob   Upper Freehold
Reter, Nicholas
    Private, New Jersey Volunteers
Reter, Weir   Middletown
    estate confiscated
Reter, William   Upper Freehold
Rever, *see* Reter
Reynolds, Broughton
    estate inquisitioned for Forfeiture, 6/8/79
Reynolds, James   Freehold
    Private, Militia
Reynolds, John   Freehold
    Private, Militia
Reynolds, John   Freehold
Reynolds, Martha   Freehold
    household head
Reynolds, Peter

Reynolds, Samuel   Freehold
Private, New Jersey Volunteers, enlisted 12/6/76 dead 2/19/77

Reynolds, William
Private, New Jersey Volunteers, enlisted 2/10/77 dead 4/3/77

Reynolds, William, Sr.   Freehold
Private, New Jersey Volunteers, enlisted 12/16/76 deserts 2/5/77
convicted of Misdemeanor, 12/80
Refugee in New York, 1782
indicted for Horse Stealing, 5/82

Reynolds, William, Jr.
Private, New Jersey Volunteers, enlisted 4/20/77 dead 6/4/77

Rhea, David   Freehold
Adjutant, Quartermaster, Militia
Signer, Petition in Support of Richard Lloyd, 1/31/76
Signer, Articles of Retaliation, 6/79
sells produce to Continental Army, 5/80
Signer, Petition in Favor of Daniel Longstreet, 11/21/80
Grand Juror, Court of Oyer and Terminer, 12/80
Juror, Court of Oyer and Terminer, 5/82

Rhea, David, Jr.   Upper Freehold
Militia Volunteer, Prior to the First General Militia Muster, 6/76
Ensign, Militia (Monmouth and Middlesex Counties)
Signer, Petition Favoring Quick Division of Prize Money, 12/79
sells produce to Continental Army, 5/80
indicted for Assault, 8/79
indicted for Assault, 11/82
Signer, Association for Opposing the Return of Tories, 1783

Rhea, James   Freehold
Signer, Petition Favoring Quick Division of Prize Money, 12/79
Signer, Petition for Renewing Guard at Toms River, 12/10/81
Signer, Petition Urging Action Against the Pine Robbers, 12/27/81

Rhea, John   Freehold
Sergeant, Militia
Private, State Troops
Signer, Petition Urging Action Against the Pine Robbers, 12/27/81

Rhea, Lydia   Freehold
household head

Rhea, Rebecca   Upper Freehold
Signer, Petition in Support of Richard Lloyd, 1/31/76

Rhea, Robert   Freehold
Private, State Troops

Rhea, Robert   Freehold

Captain, Militia
Signer, Petition in Favor of William Barton, 1/31/76
Ribeth, William
Private, Militia
Private, Continental Army, Jonathan Forman's Company, 10/77
Ribbetts, *see* Ribeth
Rice, James   Shrewsbury
Richam, Hans
Private, New Jersey Volunteers, enlisted 12/26/76 deserts 6/5/77
Richardson, James   Upper Freehold
Private, State Troops, enlists 4/81
Richardson, John
Private, Militia
Signer, Petition Supporting Retaliation, 9/17/80
Constable, 1783
Richardson, Samuel   Shrewsbury
free black householder
Richardson, Thomas
Private, New Jersey Volunteers
Richmond, John   Freehold
Private, Militia, hires substitute, 2/10/78
Riding, Samuel   Freehold
Sergeant, Continental Army
Riddle, John   Shrewsbury
accused of being part of Samuel Wright's Tory Association 11/76
arrested for Disaffection, 11/76
Riddock, Joel
Private, Militia, delinquent 8/9/80
Ridgeway, Job   Dover
Ridgeway, Samuel   Dover
indicted for Misdemeanor, 1/81
Ridgeway, Solomon   Dover
Ridgeway, Thomas   Dover
indicted for Misdemeanor, 1/81
Riding, Richard   Middletown
estate confiscated
Riker, Tobias   Shrewsbury
estate confiscated
Ritter, Elizabeth   Middletown
household head
indicted for Misdemeanor, 11/81
Ritticus, Jacob   Shrewsbury

Rively, Andrew
   indicted for Misdemeanor, 11/82
River, Nicholas
   Private, New Jersey Volunteers
Rivets, George
   Private, Militia
Rivets, Thomas   Shrewsbury
   Private, Militia
Rivets, Widow   Shrewsbury
   listed on Militia return 6/29/80
Robbins, *see* Robins
Roberts, James   Middletown
   Private, Militia
   Signer, Petition Opposing Slave Manumission, 2/2/74
   present at the capture of the British ship, Britannia, 12/31/79
   Constable, 1782
Roberts, John   Middletown
   Signer, Petition Opposing Slave Manumission, 2/2/74
   Constable, 1781
Roberts, John   Freehold
   Private, Continental Army
Roberts, Joseph
   Private, Militia
   present at the capture of the British ship, Britannia, 12/31/79
Roberts, Matthew
   estate inquisitioned for Forfeiture, 7/4/77
Roberts, Mathias
   Private, Militia
   Private, State Troops
   Signer, Articles of Retaliation, 6/79
   present at the capture of the British ship, Britannia, 12/31/79
   Signer, Association for Opposing the Return of Tories, 1783
Roberts, Sarah
   wife of John
   convicted of Misdemeanor, 1/20/78
Roberts, Thomas   Middletown
   Private, Militia
   Private, State Troops, enlists 6/80
   Signer, Petition Opposing Slave Manumission, 2/2/74
   indicted for Riot & Trespass, 1/20/78, acquitted
   present at the capture of the British ship, Britannia, 12/31/79
   Signer, Petition Against Association for Retaliation 12/81

donates to Charity Fund for the Stevenson Family, 5/83
Signer, Petition Opposing the Return of Tories 6/10/83
Roberts, William
　Private, Militia
　present at the capture of the British ship, Britannia, 12/31/79
Robertson, Daniel
　Private, New Jersey Volunteers
Robertson, Edmund　　　　Middletown
　Private, Militia
Robertson, Ephraim
　Private, Militia, delinquent 8/9/80
Robertson, Robert
　indicted for Misdemeanor, 11/81
Robertson, William
　witness at Monmouth Court, 1778
Robing, John
　Private, State Troops
Robins, Daniel
　Private, State Troops, enlists 5/81
Robins, Jesse
　Laborer, Pennsylvania Salt Works, intermittent 8/76-6/77
Robins, John　　　　Upper Freehold
　Militia Volunteer, Prior to the First General Militia Muster, 6/76
　indicted for Misdemeanor, 1/81
　Private, State Troops, enlists 5/81
　indicted for Misdemeanor, 11/81
　indicted for Misdemeanor, 5/82
Robins, Joseph
　Private, Militia
Robins, Leonard　　　　Upper Freehold
　Private, Militia
　indicted for Misdemeanor, 11/81
　indicted for Misdemeanor, 5/82
　indicted for Misdemeanor, 11/82
Robins, Moses　　　　Dover
　Militia Volunteer, Prior to the First General Militia Muster, 6/76
　Signer, Petition to Better Defend Toms River Area, 5/18/77
　Signer, Petition Urging Action Against the Pine Robbers, 12/27/81
　Township Freeholder of Appeals, 1783
Robins, Moses　　　　Upper Freehold
　son of Joseph
　Private, Militia

Roster of the People of Revolutionary Monmouth County

    indicted for Misdemeanor, 1/78
    convicted of Felony & Misdemeanor, 6/3/78
Robins, Moses, Jr.   Dover
    Laborer, Pennsylvania Salt Works, intermittent 8/76-6/77
    Private, Militia
    Private, State Troops, wounded at Toms River, 3/24/82
    Signer, Articles of Retaliation, 6/79
Robins, Randle
    sells produce to Continental Army, 5/80
Robins, Richard   Upper Freehold
    Militia Volunteer, Prior to the First General Militia Muster, 6/76
    arrested for Disaffection, 1/77
    arrested for two counts of Riot and one count of
        Riot & Trespass, 1/20/78
    indicted for Misdemeanor, 1/81
    Lieutenant, Jessup's Rangers (Loyalists)
    Juror, Court of Oyer and Terminer, 7/83
Robins, Robert   Upper Freehold
    Militia Volunteer, Prior to the First General Militia Muster, 6/76
Robins, Thomas
    Private, Continental Army
Robins, Van Room
    sells produce to Continental Army, 5/80
Robins, William   Upper Freehold
    Private, Continental Army
    Private, Militia
Robins, Zebulon   Upper Freehold
    Private, Militia
    Laborer, Pennsylvania Salt Works, intermittent 8/76-6/77
Robinson, Catherine   Shrewsbury
    listed on Militia return 6/29/80
Robinson, Daniel
    Private, New Jersey Volunteers
Robinson, Edmund
    Private, Militia
    Private, Continental Army
    Signer, Articles of Retaliation, 6/79
    Signer, Petition Encouraging Free Trade, 5/12/81
Robinson, James
    Signer, Petition Supporting Issuing of New Jersey Currency, 1771
Robinson, John
    Signer, Petition Favoring Quick Division of Prize Money, 12/79

Robinson, Robert   Upper Freehold
    Private, Militia
Robinson, Thomas   Shrewsbury
    Private, Militia
    indicted for Misdemeanor, 1/81
Rock, Henry
    Private, New Jersey Volunteers, dead 6/27/78
Rockhill, Hannah   Shrewsbury
    blind
    recipient of poor relief
Rogers, Abner   Upper Freehold
    takes Loyalty Oath to New Jersey Government, 3/19/77
Rogers, Asa
    sells produce to Continental Army, 5/80
Rogers, David
    Private, New Jersey Volunteers, enlisted 12/6/76 dead 2/6/77
Rogers, David
    arrested for Disaffection, 1/77
Rogers, Henry
    Laborer, Pennsylvania Salt Works, intermittent 8/76-6/77
    Sergeant, New Jersey Volunteers
    Juror, Court of Oyer and Terminer, 8/79
        fined L30 for missing all or some of jury duty
Rogers, Isaac   Upper Freehold
    Signer, Petition in Favor of William Barton, 1/31/76
Rogers, James
    Private, Militia
    Private, Continental Army
Rogers, John
    arrested for Disaffection, 1/77
Rogers, John   Dover
    Township Chosen Freeholder, 1783
Rogers, Isaac   Upper Freehold
    Signer, Petition in Support of Richard Lloyd, 1/31/76
    takes Loyalty Oath to New Jersey Government, 3/19/77
Rogers, Michael
    sells produce to Continental Army, 5/80
Rogers, Richard
    Private, Militia
    indicted for Misdemeanor, 6/78
    sells produce to Continental Army, 5/80
    Juror, Court of Oyer and Terminer, 5/82

Juror, Court of Oyer and Terminer, 11/82
Rogers, Samuel   Shrewsbury
    Private, Militia
    Delegate, Friends' Quarterly Meeting, 1775
    Signer, Articles of Retaliation, 6/79
    sells produce to Continental Army, 5/80
    Signer, Petition Encouraging Free Trade, 5/12/81
    Juror, Court of Oyer and Terminer, 5/82
    Signer, Association for Opposing the Return of Tories, 1783
Rogers, Thomas
    Private, New Jersey Volunteers
Rogers, William
    Private, New Jersey Volunteers, enlisted 1/20/77
       deserted 6/23/78 or captured 6/28/78
Rogers, William   Upper Freehold
    Signer, Petition Affirming Loyalty of Moses Ivens, 3/12/77
    Signer, Association for Opposing the Return of Tories, 1783
Rohen, Philip   Shrewsbury
    Private, Militia
Roler, Philip   Shrewsbury
    Private, Militia
    Private, Continental Army
    Private, State Troops
Rolls, William
    Private, Militia
Rooler, William
    Private, Militia
Rooney, James
    Private, New Jersey Volunteers, captured prior to 1779
Rooney, Jason
    Private, New Jersey Volunteers
Rooney, John
    Private, New Jersey Volunteers, captured 8/22/77
Rope, *see* Rose
Rose, Christopher   Middletown
    donates to Charity Fund for the Stevenson Family, 5/83
Rose, Isaac   Middletown
    Private, Militia
Rose, Joseph   Freehold
    Private, Militia
    Private, State Troops
Rose, Mary   Middletown

Rose, Sarah
    household head   Middletown

Rose, Stephen
    household head   Middletown

Rose, William
    Convicted of High Treason, 4/25/82
    estate confiscated

Roter, Jacob   Upper Freehold
    Accused of Being Active in Tory Uprising of 12/76

Rouse, David
    Sergeant, New Jersey Volunteers

Rouse, John   Freehold
    Signer, Articles of Retaliation, 6/79
    Signer, Petition Encouraging Free Trade, 5/12/81

Rouse, Theodore   Upper Freehold

Rowland, John   Middletown

Rowler, Jacob   Middletown
    accused of being active in Loyalist Rebellion of 12/76

Rowler, William   Upper Freehold
    Signer, Articles of Retaliation, 6/79

Rowling, see Rowler

Rue, Henry   Freehold
    Private, Militia
    Private, State Troops, enlisted 6/80
    Signer, Articles of Retaliation, 6/79
    Signer, Association for Opposing the Return of Tories, 1783

Rue, Job
    Private, Militia

Rue, John   Freehold
    Private, Militia
    Private, State Troops, enlisted 6/80
    Signer, Articles of Retaliation, 6/79
    sells produce to Continental Army, 5/80

Rue, Matthew (Mathias)   Freehold
    Private, Militia, captured 2/13/77
    Private, State Troops, enlisted 6/80
    Signer, Articles of Retaliation, 6/79
    sells produce to Continental Army, 5/80

Rue, Matthew
    Private, Militia, captured, dies in prison in New York, 2/28/77

Rue, William   Freehold
    Private, Militia, serves as substitute 2/10/78

Private, State Troops, enlisted 6/80
Signer, Articles of Retaliation, 6/79
Signer, Petition Encouraging Free Trade, 5/12/81
Signer, Association for Opposing the Return of Tories, 1783
Ruff, John
   Private, Militia
Rulan, David
   sells produce to Continental Army, 5/80
Runnels, James
   Signer, Articles of Retaliation, 6/79
   Signer, Association for Opposing the Return of Tories, 1783
Russell, James   Shrewsbury
   Vestryman, Anglican Christ Church, 1778-82
   indicted for Petty Larceny and Assault, 5/82
Russell, John   Shrewsbury
   Vestryman, Anglican Christ Church, 1771 and 1778-82
   Signer, Petition Favoring Quick Division of Prize Money, 12/79
   Signer, Petition Supporting Quick Division of Militia Prizes, no date
Russell, John, Jr.   Shrewsbury and Freehold
   Sergeant, Militia
   Private, State Troops
   Signer, Association for Opposing the Return of Tories, 1783
Russell, Richard
   Signer, Articles of Retaliation, 6/79
   Signer, Association for Opposing the Return of Tories, 1783
Russell, Timothy   Shrewsbury
   Laborer, Pennsylvania Salt Works, intermittent 8/76-6/77
   Vestryman, Anglican Christ Church, 1778-9
   indicted for Misdemeanor, 1/81
Russell, William   Shrewsbury
   Sideman, Anglican Christ Church, 1780

S

Sackerson, John
   Private, New Jersey Volunteers, enlisted 1/15/77 deserts 6/11/77
Salmon, John
   Laborer, Pennsylvania Salt Works, intermittent 8/76-6/77
   Signer, Petition Supporting Quick Division of Militia Prizes, no date
Salter, Joseph   Shrewsbury and Dover
   Lt. Colonel, Militia
   sells land and goods to the Pennsylvania Salt Works, 8/76-10/76

indicted for Misdemeanor, 11/81
Signer, Petition from Victims of the Association for Retaliation 9/82
Salter, Thomas   Upper Freehold
Salter, William   Dover
   son of Joseph
   Militia Volunteer, Prior to the First General Militia Muster, 6/76
   indicted for Misdemeanor, 1/81
Sanford, William   Middletown
   Private, Militia
   present at the capture of the British ship, Britannia, 12/31/79
Sanford, William   Freehold
   Signer, Articles of Retaliation, 6/79
Sanderson, Joseph
   Signer, Petition Favoring Quick Division of Prize Money, 12/79
Sanderson, Joseph
   Signer, Petition Favoring Quick Division of Prize Money, 12/79
Sanderson, William   Dover
Sandy, Charles
   indicted for Misdemeanor, 1/81
Sargent, John
   rented Confiscated Tory estate, prior to 5/79
Savadge, Thomas   Dover
   Manager, Pennsylvania Salt Works at Toms River
Sayre, Ezekiel
   Ensign, Militia
Sayre, Jedediah
   Signer, Petition Favoring Quick Division of Prize Money, 12/79
Schanck, *see* Schenck
Schenck, Chrineyonce   Middletown
   Private, Militia
   Signer, Petition Against Loyalist Auction Commissioners, 3/24/79
   present at the capture of the British ship, Britannia, 12/31/79
   Signer, Petition Opposing the Return of Tories 6/10/83
Schenck, Cornelius   Freehold
   Private, Militia
   Signer, Articles of Retaliation, 6/79
   Signer, Petition Urging Compensation for Inflated Money, 5/22/83
Schenck, Cyrenus
   Private, Militia
Schenck, Garret   Middletown
   Private, Militia
   Private, Militia Dragoons, delinquent one tour

Overseer of Highways, 1773
Signer, Petition Opposing Slave Manumission, 2/2/74
sells clothing to Continental Army, 3/78
present at the capture of the British ship, Britannia, 12/31/79
sells produce to Continental Army, 5/80
Grand Juror, Court of Oyer and Terminer, 12/80
Chosen Freeholder, 1781-2
Signer, Petition Opposing the Return of Tories 6/10/83

Schenck, Hance
   Juror, Court of Oyer and Terminer, 5/82
   Juror, Court of Oyer and Terminer, 11/82

Schenck, James   Middletown
   Signer, Petition Opposing Slave Manumission, 2/2/74

Schenck, Jane   Middletown
   household head

Schenck, John   Freehold
   Captain, Militia
   Signer, Petition for Settlement of Quartermaster Debts, 9/6/77
   Signer, Petition Against Confiscation Commissioners, 5/8/79
   Signer, Articles of Retaliation, 6/79
   Signer, Petition Favoring Quick Division of Prize Money, 12/79
   present at the capture of the British ship, Britannia, 12/31/79
   sells produce to Continental Army, 5/80
   Signer, Petition Encouraging Free Trade, 5/12/81
   Grand Juror, Court of Oyer and Terminer, 5/82
   Juror, Court of Oyer and Terminer, 11/82
   Signer, Association for Opposing the Return of Tories, 1783

Schenck, John   Freehold
   Ensign, Militia
   Signer, Articles of Retaliation, 6/79
   Juror, Court of Oyer and Terminer, 5/82
   Juror, Court of Oyer and Terminer, 11/82
   Signer, Association for Opposing the Return of Tories, 1783

Schenck, John, Jr.   Freehold and Middletown
   Lieutenant, Militia
   Signer, Petition Urging Action Against the Disaffected, 3/14/77
   sells clothing to Continental Army, 3/78
   Signer, Petition Against Loyalist Auction Commissioners, 3/24/79
   Signer, Petition Against Confiscation Commissioners, 5/8/79
   Signer, Articles of Retaliation, 6/79
   Signer, Petition for Renewing Guard at Toms River, 12/10/81
   present at the capture of the British ship, Britannia, 12/31/79

Signer, Petition Opposing the Return of Tories 6/10/83
Schenck, John   Middletown
   Signer, Petition Opposing Slave Manumission, 2/2/74
   Overseer of the Poor, 1777-8
   Township Collector, 1777-8
   Signer, Articles of Retaliation, 6/79
   Signer, Petition Encouraging Free Trade, 5/12/81
   Signer, Petition Opposing the Return of Tories 6/10/83
Schenck, Koert   Freehold
   Signer, Articles of Retaliation, 6/79
   Signer, Petition Favoring Quick Division of Prize Money, 12/79
   Juror, Court of Oyer and Terminer, 5/82
      fined for missing jury duty
   Grand Juror, Court of Oyer and Terminer, 7/83
Schenck, Koert, Jr.   Freehold
Schenck, Martin
   sells produce to Continental Army, 5/80
Schenck, Parson   Upper Freehold
   plundered by Tories, 12/76
Schenck, Peter   Middletown
   Private, Militia
   Signer, Petition Opposing the Return of Tories 6/10/83
Schenck, Peter, Esq.   Middletown and Shrewsbury
   Delegate, New Jersey Legislature, Lower House, 1777-9
   Signer, Petition Supporting Issuing of New Jersey Currency, 1771
   Justice of the Peace, 1780
   Signer, Petition Against Association for Retaliation 12/81
   leased horse team to Continental Quarter Master 12/81
   Signer, Petition Opposing the Return of Tories 6/10/83
Schenck, Robert
   Signer, Petition Favoring Quick Division of Prize Money, 12/79
Schenck, Ruliff (Rudolph)   Freehold
   Private, Militia
   sells produce to Continental Army, 5/80
Schenck, Ruliff   Freehold and Shrewsbury
   Private, Militia
   Signer, Petition for Settlement of Quartermaster Debts, 9/6/77
   Juror, Court of Oyer and Terminer, 1/78
      fined L5 for not attending all or part of Jury duty
   sells clothing to Continental Army, 3/78
   Signer, Petition Against Loyalist Auction Commissioners, 3/24/79
   Signer, Articles of Retaliation, 6/79

    sells produce to Continental Army, 5/80
    Juror, Court of Oyer and Terminer, 5/82
       fined for missing jury duty
    donates to Charity Fund for the Stevenson Family, 5/83
Schenck, William   Freehold
    Captain, Militia
    Signer, Articles of Retaliation, 6/79
    Signer, Petition Urging Action Against the Disaffected, 3/14/77
    Signer, Petition Favoring Quick Division of Prize Money, 12/79
    present at the capture of the British ship, Britannia, 12/31/79
    Signer, Petition for Renewing Guard at Toms River, 12/10/81
    Signer, Association for Opposing the Return of Tories, 1783
Schenck, William   Middletown
    Private, Militia, delinquent 6/11/80
    Private, Militia Dragoons, delinquent one tour
    present at the capture of the British ship, Britannia, 12/31/79
Schenck, William   Middletown
    tavern keeper
    Private, Militia, delinquent 6/11/80
    Signer, Articles of Retaliation, 6/79
    Signer, Petition Against Association for Retaliation 12/81
    Signer, Petition Opposing the Return of Tories 6/10/83
Scoby, John
    Sergeant, Continental Army
Scoby, Timothy   Shrewsbury
    Militia Volunteer, Prior to the First General Militia Muster, 6/76
    Private, New Jersey Volunteers
    indicted for High Treason, 5/82
    estate confiscated
Scooly, Andrew
    Private, New Jersey Volunteers
Scooly, Azaliah   Upper Freehold
Scott, David   Upper Freehold
    Militia Volunteer, Prior to the First General Militia Muster, 6/76
Scott, Ebenezer   Shrewsbury
    Laborer, Pennsylvania Salt Works, intermittent 8/76-6/77
    Private, Militia, delinquent 8/17/80
Scott, James   Freehold
    sells produce to Continental Army, 7/80
    Signer, Petition Encouraging Free Trade, 5/12/81
Scott, John   Shrewsbury
Scott, John   Shrewsbury

Roster of the People of Revolutionary Monmouth County

    Private, Militia, delinquent 8/17/80
    indicted for Misdemeanor, 1/81
Scott, Samuel   Shrewsbury
Scudder, Job
    Private, Militia
    Private, State Troops, enlisted 6/80
Scudder, John Anderson   Freehold
    Surgeon's Mate, Militia
    Surgeon's Mate, Privateer vessels
    Clerk, War Department, United States Government
    Signer, Petition Supporting Retaliation, 9/17/80
    Signer, Petition Encouraging Free Trade, 5/12/81
Scudder, Kenneth
    Signer, Association for Opposing the Return of Tories
Scudder, Nathaniel   Freehold
    doctor
    Lt. Colonel, Militia
    Delegate, Continental Congress, 1778-9
    Delegate, New Jersey Legislature, Lower House, 1780-1
    Signer, Articles of Retaliation, 6/79
    Signer, Petition Supporting Retaliation, 9/17/80
Scudder, William
    Signer, Association for Opposing the Return of Tories, 1783
Seabrook, James   Middletown
    Private, Militia
    present at the capture of the British ship, Britannia, 12/31/79
    Signer, Petition Opposing the Return of Tories 6/10/83
Seabrook, Stephen   Middletown
    Private, Militia, delinquent 6/11/80
    Private, Militia Dragoons, delinquent one tour
    Signer, Articles of Retaliation, 6/79
    Signer, Petition Supporting Retaliation, 1780
    sells produce to Continental Army, 5/80
    Signer, Petition Opposing the Return of Tories 6/10/83
Seabrook, Thomas   Middletown and Shrewsbury
    Major, Militia
    Lt. Colonel, State Troops
    Delegate, New Jersey Legislature, Upper House, 1779-80
    Signer, Petition Opposing Slave Manumission, 2/2/74
    Signer, Articles of Retaliation, 6/79
    Grand Juror, Court of Oyer Terminer, 8/79
    Signer, Petition Opposing the Return of Tories 6/10/83

Seales, see Sears
Seaman, Isaiah					Upper Freehold
   accused of being active in Loyalist Rebellion of 12/76
Sears, David
   Private, Militia, drafted into Continental Army 5/78
   Private, Continental Army
Sears, Grizell					Shrewsbury
Sears, John
   arrested for Disaffection, 11/76
   Private, New Jersey Volunteers, enlisted 12/18/76 deserts 3/14/79
Sears, William
   arrested for Disaffection, 1/77
Seaton, see Sexton
Segollet, see Segulet
Segulet, Henry (Hendrick)			Middletown
   estate confiscated
   Signer, Petition Opposing Slave Manumission, 2/2/74
   indicted for Misdemeanor, 8/79
   donates to Charity Fund for the Stevenson Family, 5/83
Sellers, Henry
   Convicted of Robbery, 12/80
Sergeant, John					Middletown
Sexton, Daniel					Upper Freehold
   Private, Militia
   Signer, Petition Affirming Loyalty of Moses Ivens, 3/12/77
Sexton, James					Upper Freehold
   sells produce to Continental Army, 5/80
   Signer, Petition Supporting Retaliation, 9/17/80
   Signer, Petition Against Association for Retaliation 12/81
   Juror, Court of Oyer and Terminer, 5/82
      fined for missing jury duty
Sexton, Peter					Upper Freehold
   Signer, Petition Affirming Loyalty of Moses Ivens, 3/12/77
   Signer, Petition Against Association for Retaliation 12/81
Sexton, Samuel
   Ensign, Militia
   Signer, Petition Against Association for Retaliation 12/81
Sexton, William					Upper Freehold
   Private, Militia
Sexton, William					Upper Freehold
   Signer, Petition Affirming Loyalty of Moses Ivens, 3/12/77
   sells produce to Continental Army, 5/80

Signer, Petition Against Association for Retaliation 12/81
Seward, John
    Private, New Jersey Volunteers, enlisted 3/6/77 dead 6/1/78
Shaffey, William
    Private, Militia
    Private, Continental Army
Sharp, Cornelius
    Private, New Jersey Volunteers
Sharp, Robert
    Private, Militia
    Signer, Articles of Retaliation, 6/79
Shasabeer, Albertus   Dover
    Militia Volunteer, Prior to the First General Militia Muster, 6/76
Shaw, Adam   Shrewsbury
    holds tavern license, 1775
    arrested for Disaffection 11/76
Shaw, Alexander
    Private, New Jersey Volunteers
Shaw, George   Shrewsbury
Shaw, Thomas   Shrewsbury
    Militia Volunteer, Prior to the First General Militia Muster, 6/76
    Private, Militia
Shearman, Josiah   Shrewsbury
    Private, Militia, delinquent 8/80
Shearman, Oliver   Shrewsbury
    Private, Militia, delinquent 8/80
Shearman, Thomas   Shrewsbury
    Private, Militia, delinquent 4/82
    indicted for Misdemeanor, 11/82
Shearney, Gilbert
    Signer, Articles of Retaliation, 6/79
Sheldon, Joseph
    indicted for Robbery, 11/82
Shelft, William
    Signer, Articles of Retaliation, 6/79
Shemarr, Francis   Dover
Shemarr, William   Dover
Shephard, see Shepherd
Shepherd, Elisha   Shrewsbury and Middletown
    Sergeant, Militia
    Signer, Articles of Retaliation, 6/79
    sells produce to Continental Army, 7/80

Signer, Petition Opposing the Return of Tories 6/10/83
Shepherd, Englebert
    Private, New Jersey Volunteers, captured 8/22/77
Shepherd, Jacob
    Private, Militia
    present at the capture of the British ship, Britannia, 12/31/79
    Vestryman, Anglican Christ Church, 1780-3
Shepherd, James   Freehold
Shepherd, John   Freehold
    Private, Militia
Shepherd, Moses   Middletown
    Captain, Militia
    Signer, Articles of Retaliation, 6/79
    Signer, Petition Favoring Quick Division of Prize Money, 12/79
    Signer, Petition Encouraging Free Trade, 5/12/81
    Signer, Petition Opposing the Return of Tories 6/10/83
Shepherd, Moses, Jr.   Middletown
    Private, State Troops, enlists 5/78
Shepherd, Nathaniel
    Captain, State Troops
Shepherd, Samuel
    Fifer, Militia
Shepherd, Sarah   Middletown
    household head
Shepherd, Thomas
    Private, Militia
    Signer, Association for Opposing the Return of Tories, 1783
Sheppard, *see* Shepherd
Sherman, *see* Shearman
Shibly, Jacob   Shrewsbury
Shields, James
    Private, New Jersey Volunteers, captured prior to 1779
Shin, Francis   Upper Freehold
Shin, James   Upper Freehold
Shingleton, John   Upper Freehold
Shippen, Thomas
    witness at Monmouth Court, 1778
Shockalear, Albertus   Dover
    Private, Militia
    accused of being active in Tory Rebellions of 12/76
Shockelea, *see* Shockalear
Shoefelt, George

Shoemaker, Amos   Freehold
  Private, New Jersey Volunteers, 6/24/78
Shoemaker, Thomas
  Private, New Jersey Volunteers
Shorthem, Samuel
  Private, New Jersey Volunteers
Showber, Albertus
  Signer, Articles of Retaliation, 6/79
Shreave, see Shreve
Shreve, Joseph   Upper Freehold
Shuckey, Daniel
  arrested for Disaffection, 11/76
Sickles, Henry
  Private, New Jersey Volunteers
Sickles, James   Freehold
  Private, State Troops
  Signer, Articles of Retaliation, 6/79
  present at the capture of the British ship, Britannia, 12/31/79
Sickles, Tachanaty (?)
  accused of being active in Tory Rebellions of 12/76
Sickles, Thomas   Upper Freehold
Sickles, Zachariah
  arrested for Disaffection, 11/76
Sills, Thomas
  Juror, Court of Oyer and Terminer, 11/82
Simermore, John
  Signer, Articles of Retaliation, 6/79
Simons, Thomas
  Private, New Jersey Volunteers
Sippen, Derrick
  Corporal, Militia
Skidmore, Barnaby   Shrewsbury
Skidmore, John   Shrewsbury
  Private, Militia, delinquent 8/80
Slack, Benjamin   Upper Freehold
Slack, John   Upper Freehold
Sleet, Robert   Upper Freehold
Slocum, Asher
  indicted for Misdemeanor, 11/82
Slocum, Catherine   Shrewsbury
  household head
  listed on Militia return 6/29/80

helps keep the poor
Slocum, Daniel   Shrewsbury
   Laborer, Pennsylvania Salt Works, intermittent 8/76-6/77
Slocum, Hannah   Shrewsbury
   household head
   listed on Militia return 6/29/80
Slocum, John   Shrewsbury
   Private, New Jersey Volunteers, captured prior to 1779
   indicted for Misdemeanor, 11/81
   indicted for Misdemeanor, 5/82
Slocum, John, Jr.
   Private, Militia
   convicted of Felony and Misdemeanor, 6/3/78
   indicted for Misdemeanor and High Treason, 1/81
   indicted for Misdemeanor, 5/82
Slocum, Jonathan   Shrewsbury
   Private, Militia
   helps keep the poor
Slocum, Samuel   Shrewsbury
   Private, Militia
   indicted for Misdemeanor, 11/82
Slocum, Samuel, Jr.   Shrewsbury
   Private, Militia
   indicted for Misdemeanor, 11/81
   indicted for Misdemeanor, 5/82
Slocum, William   Shrewsbury
   Private, Militia
Smalley, James
   Private, Militia
   Private, State Troops, enlisted 6/80
   Signer, Articles of Retaliation, 6/79
Smart, Cornelius   Freehold
Smires, Joseph   Upper Freehold
Smith, Abraham   Upper Freehold and Middletown
   Overseer of Highways, 1774
   Signer, Petition Opposing Slave Manumission, 2/2/74
   indicted for Misdemeanor, 1/78
Smith, Adam
   indicted for Misdemeanor, 5/82
Smith, Alexander   Upper Freehold
   Private, Militia
   Signer, Petition in Favor of Daniel Longstreet, 11/21/80

Smith, Andrew   Freehold
   Signer, Association for Opposing the Return of Tories, 1783
Smith, Anthony   Shrewsbury
   Delegate, Friends' Quarterly Meeting, 1783
Smith, Benjamin   Dover
   Militia Volunteer, Prior to the First General Militia Muster, 6/76
   Private, Militia
Smith, Benjamin
   Private, Militia, delinquent 2/10/78
Smith, Christian   Middletown
Smith, David   Dover
   Private, New Jersey Volunteers
   estate inquisitioned for Forfeiture, 3/18/79
   estate confiscated
Smith, David   Freehold
   Signer, Articles of Retaliation, 6/79
   Signer, Petition for Renewing Guard at Toms River, 12/10/81
   Juror, Court of Oyer and Terminer, 5/82
   Constable, 1783
Smith, David   Middletown
   Signer, Petition Opposing the Return of Tories 6/10/83
Smith, David   Stafford
   Private, Militia
   indicted for Misdemeanor, 1/81
Smith, Deborah   Shrewsbury
   household head
   Delegate, Friends' Quarterly Meeting, 1777
Smith, Edward
   Drummer, New Jersey Volunteers
Smith, Elizabeth   Shrewsbury
   Delegate, Friends' Quarterly Meeting, 1777
Smith, Gilbert   Upper Freehold
Smith, George   Upper Freehold
   Private, Militia
Smith, George N.   Freehold
   Private, State Troops, enlists 6/81
Smith, Gideon
   Private, Militia
Smith, Gilbert
   Juror, Court of Oyer and Terminer, 8/79
     fined L30 for missing all or some of jury duty
   Juror, Court of Oyer and Terminer, 11/82

fined L8 for missing all or some of jury duty
Smith, Hart
   Private, New Jersey Volunteers
Smith, Hendrick
   slave runs away and joins Black Brigade
Smith, Isaac
   Private, New Jersey Volunteers
   indicted for Robbery, 8/79
Smith, Jacob   Freehold
   Private, State Troops, enlisted 6/80
   Signer, Articles of Retaliation, 6/79
   Signer, Association for Opposing the Return of Tories, 1783
Smith, Jacob   Shrewsbury
   Private, Militia
Smith, James   Shrewsbury
   Private, Militia
   Private, Continental Army
   helps keep the poor
   indicted for Misdemeanor, 8/79
Smith, Jesse
   Private, New Jersey Volunteers
   indicted for Misdemeanor, 1/81
Smith, John   Freehold
   sells produce to Continental Army, 5/80
Smith, John   Middletown
   son of Samuel
   Private, Militia, captured 2/13/77
   indicted for Misdemeanor, 5/82
Smith, John   Middletown
   Signer, Petition Opposing Slave Manumission, 2/2/74
   estate inquisitioned for Forfeiture, 7/4/77
   estate confiscated
Smith, John   Shrewsbury
   son of Richard
   Private, Militia
   convicted of Misdemeanor, 12/80
   indicted for Misdemeanor, 11/81
Smith, John   Upper Freehold
   Private, Militia
   arrested for Misdemeanor, 1/20/78
Smith, John   Upper Freehold
   Private, New Jersey Volunteers, captured prior to 1779

indicted for Misdemeanor and Horse Stealing, 1/81
Smith, Joseph   Middletown
    cooper
    Private, Militia
    Private, Continental Army
Smith, Joseph   Middletown
    blacksmith
    Private, Militia
    Private, New Jersey Volunteers, captured 8/22/77
    present at the capture of the British ship, Britannia, 12/31/79
    donates to Charity Fund for the Stevenson Family, 5/83
Smith, Joseph   Middletown
    millwright
    arrested for Misdemeanor, 1/20/78
Smith, Joseph   Upper Freehold
    Militia Volunteer, Prior to the First General Militia Muster, 6/76
Smith, Lewis
    Private, New Jersey Volunteers, dead prior to 1779
    estate inquisitioned for Forfeiture, 7/4/77
Smith, Lippincott
    indicted for Misdemeanor, 5/82
Smith, Margaret   Middletown
    household head
Smith, Mary   Middletown
    household head
Smith, Matthew
    Private, Continental Army
Smith, Noah   Shrewsbury
    Private, Militia
Smith, Peter   Freehold
    Private, Militia
    witness at Monmouth Court
    Signer, Petition Urging Compensation for Raid Victims, 5/25/79
    Signer, Articles of Retaliation, 6/79
    Signer, Petition Supporting Retaliation, 9/17/80
    Signer, Petition Urging Compensation for Inflated Money, 5/22/83
    Constable, 1782
Smith, Peter   Shrewsbury
    Private, Militia
    Signer, Petition Supporting Retaliation, 1780
    Signer, Petition Urging Compensation for Inflated Money, 5/22/83
Smith, Rachel   Freehold

Roster of the People of Revolutionary Monmouth County

    household head
Smith, Richard   Middletown
    Signer, Petition Opposing Slave Manumission, 2/2/74
Smith, Samuel   Freehold
    Drummer, State Troops
    Private, Continental Army
    present at the capture of the British ship, Britannia, 12/31/79
Smith, Samuel   Middletown
    Private, Militia
    Signer, Petition Opposing the Return of Tories 6/10/83
Smith, Samuel   Middletown
    Signer, Petition Opposing Slave Manumission, 2/2/74
    estate inquisitioned for Forfeiture, 7/4/77
    estate confiscated
Smith, Sophia
    indicted for Misdemeanor, 8/79
Smith, Thomas   Freehold
    Private, Militia
    Private, State Troops, enlists 5/80
    Private, Continental Army
    Signer, Articles of Retaliation, 6/79
Smith, Thomas   Middletown
Smith, Thomas   Upper Freehold
    Signer, Articles of Retaliation, 6/79
Smith, Timothy   Shrewsbury
    Private, New Jersey Volunteers, enlisted 12/8/76 deserts 2/28/77
Smith, William   Middletown
    arrested for Disaffection, 11/76
    accused of being active in Tory Rebellions of 12/76
    indicted for Misdemeanor, 11/81
    estate confiscated
Smith, William   Shrewsbury
    Delegate, Friends' Quarterly Meeting, 1775
    accused of being part of Samuel Wright's Tory Association 11/76
    Private, New Jersey Volunteers
Smith, William   Upper Freehold
    Militia Volunteer, Prior to the First General Militia Muster, 6/76
    Signer, Association to Oppose the Return of Tories, 1783
Smith, William, Jr.   Middletown
    Private, Militia
    Private, State Troops, enlists 5/80
    Private, Continental Army

indicted for Misdemeanor, 5/82
Smith, Zebulon   Shrewsbury
   Private, Militia, delinquent 8/80
Smock, Barnes   Middletown and Shrewsbury
   Overseer of Highways, 1770
   Captain, Militia, captured 2/13/77
   Captain, State Troops, captured 1780
   Signer, Petition Opposing Slave Manumission, 2/2/74
   Signer, Petition Against Loyalist Auction Commissioners, 3/24/79
   Signer, Petition Against Confiscation Commissioners, 5/8/79
   Signer, Articles of Retaliation, 6/79
   present at the capture of the British ship, Britannia, 12/31/79
   sells produce to Continental Army, 5/80
   Chosen Freeholder, 1783
   donates to Charity Fund for the Stevenson Family, 5/83
   Signer, Petition Opposing the Return of Tories 6/10/83
Smock, Barnes, Jr.   Middletown
   Private, Militia
   Private, Militia Dragoons, delinquent one tour
   present at the capture of the British ship, Britannia, 12/31/79
Smock, Cornelius   Middletown
   Private, Militia
   Signer, Petition Opposing Slave Manumission, 2/2/74
   present at the capture of the British ship, Britannia, 12/31/79
Smock, George   Middletown
   Private, Militia
   sells produce to Continental Army, 5/80
Smock, Hendrick   Middletown and Freehold
   Captain, Militia
   Delegate, New Jersey Legislature, Lower House, 1777-9
   Signer, Petition Urging Action Against the Disaffected, 3/14/77
   Signer, Petition for Settlement of Quartermaster Debts, 9/6/77
   Signer, Articles of Retaliation, 6/79
   sells produce to Continental Army, 5/80
Smock, Henry   Freehold
   Ensign, Militia, captured 9/80
   Signer, Articles of Retaliation, 6/79
   Juror, Court of Oyer and Terminer, 11/82
   Juror, Court of Oyer and Terminer, 7/83
Smock, John   Middletown
   Lt. Colonel, Militia
   Signer, Petition Opposing Slave Manumission, 2/2/74

Overseer of Highways, 1777-8
Township Assessor, 1777-8 and 1783
Signer, Petition Calling for Action Against the Disaffected, 2/21/77
Signer, Petition Urging Action Against the Disaffected, 3/14/77
Signer, Petition for Settlement of Quartermaster Debts, 9/6/77
Signer, Petition to Better Provision Militia, 2/25/78
captured and paroled, 8/78
Assistant to the Tax Assessor, 1779-81
present at the capture of the British ship, Britannia, 12/31/79
sells produce to Continental Army, 5/80
Signer, Petition Opposing the Return of Tories 6/10/83

Smock, John, Jr.   Middletown
     sells produce to Continental Army, 5/80
     Juror, Court of Oyer and Terminer, 11/82
     Signer, Petition Opposing the Return of Tories 6/10/83

Smock, Robert
     sells produce to Continental Army, 5/80

Smyth, Smythe, *see* Smith

Snider, Christopher   Middletown
     Private, Militia

Snider, Gasper   Freehold
     Signer, Association for Opposing the Return of Tories, 1783

Snider, Harmon (Herman)   Middletown
     Sergeant, Militia
     Signer, Articles of Retaliation, 6/79
     Signer, Petition Opposing the Return of Tories 6/10/83

Snider, Hendrick
     Signer, Articles of Retaliation, 6/79

Snider, John   Middletown
     Private, Militia
     Signer, Petition Opposing Slave Manumission, 2/2/74
     indicted for Misdemeanor, 1/81

Snider, William   Freehold and Middletown
     Overseer of Highways, 1774
     Signer, Petition Favoring Quick Division of Prize Money, 12/79
     sells produce to Continental Army, 5/80

Snowden, Thomas   Freehold

Snowden, William   Upper Freehold
     Private, Militia

Snyder, *see* Snider

Solomon, Hannah   Freehold
     household head

Roster of the People of Revolutionary Monmouth County

house burned by British Army, 6/28/78
Solomon, Job
   Private, State Troops
Solomon, John   Freehold
   Signer, Petition Favoring Quick Division of Prize Money, 12/79
   Signer, Petition Supporting Retaliation, 9/17/80
   Signer, Association for Opposing the Return of Tories, 1783
Solomon, John   Shrewsbury
   Private, Militia
Solomon, John, Jr.   Freehold
   Private, Militia, drafted into Continental Army 5/78
   Private, State Troops, enlists 5/78
   Private, Continental Army
Solomon, Joseph
   Signer, Petition Urging Action Against Disaffected
     & Favoring Retaliation, 5/12/81, opposes Retaliation clause
Solomon, Joshua
   Fifer, Militia
Sonnet, John   Upper Freehold
   schoolmaster
Soper, Joseph   Stafford and Dover
   Private, Militia
   Signer, Petition Urging Action Against the Pine Robbers, 12/27/81
Soper, Richard   Shrewsbury
   Private, Militia, delinquent 8/80
Soper, Right   Dover
   Signer, Petition Urging Action Against the Pine Robbers, 12/27/81
Soper, Reuben   Stafford
   Private, Militia
Southard, Amos   Stafford
   indicted for Misdemeanor, 1/81
Southard, John   Stafford
   Constable, 1779-80, fined L150 for missing court in 1779
     fined L140 for missing court in 1780
Southard, Zachariah   Stafford
   Private, Militia
Spargg, Uriah   Dover
Spargg, George   Freehold
Sperry, Joseph
   Signer, Petition Favoring Quick Division of Prize Money, 12/79
Sprague, *see* Spargg *and* Sproule
Spray, John

indicted for Misdemeanor, 7/83
Spray, Michael
    indicted for Misdemeanor, 7/83
Springer, John
    Private, New Jersey Volunteers
Springsteen, John   Freehold
Sproule, William
    Private, New Jersey Volunteers
Staates, Isaac   Shrewsbury and Middletown
    Private, Militia
    Private, State Troops, enlists 6/80
    Signer, Articles of Retaliation, 6/79
    Signer, Petition Favoring Quick Division of Prize Money, 12/79
    present at the capture of the British ship, Britannia, 12/31/79
    Signer, Petition Opposing the Return of Tories 6/10/83
Staates, John
    Signer, Petition Supporting Retaliation, 9/17/80
Staates, Mary
    witness at Monmouth Court, 1778
Staatesor, *see* Staates
Stacey, Matthew
    Refugee in New York, 1782
Stack, Peter
    Private, New Jersey Volunteers, captured prior to 1779
Stackhouse, Peter
    Private, New Jersey Volunteers
Stackhouse, Robert
    Private, New Jersey Volunteers
Stafford, Peter
    Private, New Jersey Volunteers
Stansbury, Jonathan   Upper Freehold
    indicted for Assault, 11/81
Starkey, Hezekiah
    Private, New Jersey Volunteers
Starkey, Matthew
    Private, New Jersey Volunteers, enlisted 2/14/77 deserts 8/12/77
Starkey, Mordecai
    Private, New Jersey Volunteers
Starkey, Nathan   Upper Freehold
Starkey, William
    Private, Militia
    Private, State Troops

    Private, Continental Army
States, *see* Staates
Steath, Robert
    Private, Militia
Steele, John   Shrewsbury
    schoolmaster
Steele, William
    Private, New Jersey Volunteers, captured 10/3/77
Stevens, Benjamin
    indicted for Misdemeanor, 1/81
Stevens, John, Esq.   Upper Freehold
Stevens, John
    Private, New Jersey Volunteers, enlisted 7/5/77 dead 8/29/77
Stevens, Nicholas   Freehold
    Private, Continental Army
Stevens, Samuel
    Private, New Jersey Volunteers, enlisted 7/5/77 deserted 7/20/77
Stevens, Thomas   Upper Freehold
    schoolmaster
Stevenson, Ann   Middletown
    household head
Stevenson, Daniel   Middletown
Stevenson, James   Middletown
    estate confiscated
Stevenson, John
    indicted for Misdemeanor, 5/82
Stevenson, Rebecca   Middletown
    household head
Stevenson, Samuel   Middletown
    estate confiscated
Stevenson, Shore   Middletown
    indicted for Burglary, 11/82
    estate confiscated
Stevenson, Thomas
    indicted for Misdemeanor, 5/82
Stevenson, William   Middletown
    Lieutenant, New Jersey Volunteers
    estate confiscated
Stewart, Alexander   Upper Freehold
    Private, Militia, drafted into Continental Army 5/78
    Private, Continental Army
Stewart, Bickley   Upper Freehold

takes oath to New Jersey Government, 3/19/77
Stewart, Cornelius
   Signer, Articles of Retaliation
Stewart, James
   Sergeant, New Jersey Volunteers
Stewart, Jonathan   Upper Freehold
Stewart, Josiah   Upper Freehold
Stewart, Malcolm
   Corporal, New Jersey Volunteers
Stewart, William   Dover
   Private, Militia
   Signer, Petition to Better Defend Toms River Area, 5/18/77
Stiles, John   Upper Freehold
   Militia Volunteer, Prior to the First General Militia Muster, 6/76
Still, Elisha
   Private, Militia
Still, Isaac   Dover
Stillwagon, Arthur
   Signer, Petition Supporting Quick Division of Militia Prizes, no date
Stillwagon, Jacob
   Private, Militia
   Private, State Troops
Stillwagon, Peter   Shrewsbury
   Private, Militia
   indicted for Petty Larceny, 8/79
Stillwell, Elias   Shrewsbury
Stillwell, Garret   Middletown
   Private, Militia, delinquent 6/79
   Private, Militia Dragoons, delinquent one tour
   Signer, Petition Favoring Quick Division of Prize Money, 12/79
   present at the capture of the British ship, Britannia, 12/31/79
   Signer, Petition Urging Compensation for Inflated Money, 5/22/83
   Signer, Petition Opposing the Return of Tories 6/10/83
Stillwell, Gershom   Middletown
   Private, Militia, hires substitute, 2/10/78
   indicted for Misdemeanor, 6/78
   sells produce to Continental Army, 7/80
Stillwell, James   Middletown
   estate inquisitioned for Forfeiture, 7/27/77
   estate confiscated, 9/79
Stillwell, Jarritt (Jared)
   Private, Militia

Signer, Articles of Retaliation, 6/79
Stillwell, Jeremiah (Jeremy)   Middletown
  Signer, Petition Opposing Slave Manumission, 2/2/74
Stillwell, John   Middletown
  Quartermaster, Militia
  Overseer of Highways, 1772-3
  Commissioner of Appeals, 1772-7 and 1782
  Signer, Petition Opposing Slave Manumission, 2/2/74
  Highway Surveyor, 1778-81
  rented Confiscated Tory estate, prior to 5/79
  Signer, Articles of Retaliation, 6/79
  Juror, Court of Oyer and Terminer, 12/80
    fined L3 for missing all or some of jury duty
  sells produce to Continental Army, 5/80
  Signer, Petition Encouraging Free Trade, 5/12/81
  Signer, Petition for Renewing Guard at Toms River, 12/10/81
  Signer, Petition Opposing the Return of Tories 6/10/83
Stillwell, John   Middletown
  Private, Militia, captured 2/13/77
  Signer, Petition Opposing Slave Manumission, 2/2/74
  present at the capture of the British ship, Britannia, 12/31/79
Stillwell, Joseph   Freehold
Stillwell, Joseph   Middletown
  Commissioner of Appeals, 1772-3
  Captain, State Troops, detached to Sandy Hook, 6/76
  Signer, Petition Calling for Action Against the Disaffected, 2/21/77
  Signer, Petition Urging Action Against the Disaffected, 3/14/77
  Signer, Petition to Better Provision Militia, 2/25/78
  Assistant to the Tax Assessor, 1779-83
  present at the capture of the British ship, Britannia, 12/31/79
  sells produce to Continental Army, 5/80
  sells produce to Continental Army, 7/80
  Signer, Petition for Renewing Guard at Toms River, 12/10/81
  Justice of the Court of Oyer and Terminer, 11/82
  donates to Charity Fund for the Stevenson Family, 5/83
  Signer, Petition Opposing the Return of Tories 6/10/83
Stillwell, Joseph   Middletown
  Baptist
  Lieutenant, Militia
Stillwell, Joseph   Middletown
  Private, Militia, hires substitute 2/10/78
    delinquent 11/29/78, delinquent 6/11/80

Stillwell, Joseph　　　　　Shrewsbury
　　Private, New Jersey Volunteers, enlisted 3/30/77 deserts 5/12/77
　　indicted on two counts of Trespass, 1/20/78
　　Private, Militia, hires substitute, 2/10/78
　　indicted for Riot & Trespass, 6/78
Stillwell, Lydia　　　　　Middletown
　　household head
　　indicted for Misdemeanor, 11/82
Stillwell, Mary　　　　　Middletown
　　household head
Stillwell, Obadiah
　　Private, Militia, captured 2/13/77, dies in prison
Stillwell, Phoebe　　　　Middletown
　　household head
Stillwell, Samuel　　　　Upper Freehold
　　Accused of Being Active in Tory Uprising of 12/76
　　estate inquisitioned for Forfeiture, 7/29/79
　　estate confiscated
Stillwell, Thomas　　　　Middletown
　　Private, Militia
　　Signer, Articles of Retaliation, 6/79
Stillwell, William　　　　Middletown
　　Constable, 1778
　　substitute, Militia, 2/10/78
Stillwell, William　　　　Shrewsbury
　　Private, Militia, deserts 6/79
Stimits, Jesse　　　　　Middletown
　　Signer, Petition Opposing the Return of Tories 6/10/83
Stimits, John　　　　　Middletown
　　Private, Militia
　　Signer, Petition Opposing the Return of Tories 6/10/83
Stimits, Peter　　　　　Middletown
　　Private, Militia
　　Signer, Petition Opposing Slave Manumission, 2/2/74
　　present at the capture of the British ship, Britannia, 12/31/79
　　Chosen Freeholder, 1780
Stimits, William　　　　Middletown
　　Signer, Petition Opposing the Return of Tories 6/10/83
Stine, Jacob　　　　　Upper Freehold
Stine, John　　　　　Upper Freehold
　　Private, New Jersey Volunteers
Stine, Martin　　　　　Upper Freehold

Stine, Mathias   Upper Freehold
    Private, Militia
Stiner, see Stine
Stipy, Richard   Upper Freehold
Stockton, Abraham
    indicted for Misdemeanor, 11/81
Stockton, Charles
    Ensign, New Jersey Volunteers, captured prior to 1779
Stockton, William
    Private, New Jersey Volunteers
Stoneker, John
    sells produce to Continental Army, 5/80
Storer, Storey, see Story
Story, John   Freehold
    Private, Militia
    Signer, Petition for Stricter Militia Law, 5/31/79
    Signer, Association for Opposing the Return of Tories, 1783
Story, Luke   Upper Freehold
    Sergeant, State Troops
Story, Samuel   Freehold
Story, Samuel   Upper Freehold
    Private, Militia
Story, Seth   Upper Freehold
    Private, Militia
    Private, State Troops
Story, Thomas   Upper Freehold
Story, William   Upper Freehold
    Private, Militia
Stout, Abram (Abraham)   Middletown
    Private, New Jersey Volunteers
    indicted for Misdemeanor, 8/79
    indicted for Misdemeanor, 1/81
    indicted for Misdemeanor, 11/81
    indicted for Misdemeanor, 5/82
    estate confiscated
Stout, Benjamin
    indicted for Misdemeanor, 1/81
Stout, Catherine   Shrewsbury
Stout, Charity
    indicted for Misdemeanor, 11/81
    indicted for Misdemeanor, 5/82

Stout, Cornelius
   Signer, Petition Supporting Retaliation, 9/17/80
Stout, Daniel
   Signer, Petition Against Association for Retaliation 12/81
Stout, David   Freehold
   Private, Militia, hires substitute, 2/10/78
Stout, David   Middletown
   Convicted of High Treason, 4/25/82
   estate confiscated
Stout, Elisha
   Private, Continental Army
Stout, Elisha, Jr.   Shrewsbury
   Private, Militia, delinquent 8/80
Stout, Jacob   Shrewsbury
   Private, Militia, delinquent 8/80
   Signer, Petition Favoring Quick Division of Prize Money, 12/79
Stout, Jacob, Jr.   Shrewsbury
   Private, Militia, delinquent 9/80
Stout, James
   Private, Militia
Stout, Jehu   Middletown
Stout, Jeremiah
   Private, Militia
Stout, John   Dover
   Signer, Petition Against Association for Retaliation 12/81
   Township Overseer of the Poor, 1783
Stout, John   Middletown
   estate confiscated
Stout, John   Shrewsbury
   Private, Militia, delinquent 8/80
Stout, John, Jr.   Middletown
   Private, Militia, hires substitute, 2/10/78
Stout, Jonathan   Middletown
   estate inquisitioned for Forfeiture, 7/2/77
   estate confiscated
Stout, Jonathan   Shrewsbury
   Private, Militia
Stout, Jonathan
   son of Richard
   indicted for Misdemeanor, 1/78
   convicted of Assault, 6/3/78
   convicted of Misdemeanor, 1/81

Stout, Leah — Middletown
   household head
Stout, Lewis — Middletown
   estate confiscated, 1784
Stout, Mary — Middletown
   household head
Stout, Mary — Middletown
   household head
Stout, Peter — Middletown
   Laborer, Pennsylvania Salt Works
   estate inquisitioned for Forfeiture, 7/2/77
   indicted for Misdemeanor, 8/79
   indicted for Misdemeanor and Horse Stealing, 1/81
   estate confiscated
Stout, Richard — Freehold
   Laborer, Pennsylvania Salt Works, intermittent 8/76-6/77
Stout, Richard — Middletown
   Overseer of Highways, 1770
   Overseer of the Poor, 1778
   Signer, Petition Opposing the Return of Tories 6/10/83
   two slaves run away and join Black Brigade
Stout, Richard — Shrewsbury
   estate confiscated
Stout, Robert — Shrewsbury
   Private, New Jersey Volunteers
   estate confiscated
   Signer, Petition Opposing Slave Manumission, 2/2/74
   Laborer, Pennsylvania Salt Works, intermittent 8/76-6/77
Stout, Thomas — Middletown
   Private, Militia
   present at the capture of the British ship, Britannia, 12/31/79
Stout, William — Middletown
   indicted for Misdemeanor, 8/79
   estate confiscated
Stover, Peter
   Private, New Jersey Volunteers
Stover, Richard
   sells produce to Continental Army, 5/80
Strickland, *see* Stricklen
Stricklen, Henry — Freehold
   Sergeant, Militia
   Private, State Troops

Roster of the People of Revolutionary Monmouth County

    Juror, Court of Oyer and Terminer, 12/80
      fined L3 for missing all or some of jury duty
    sells produce to Continental Army, 5/80
Stricklen, Henry, Jr.   Freehold
    indicted for Misdemeanor and Assault, 5/82
Stricklen, Thomas
    Private, Militia
Striker, Adam   Middletown
    Private, Militia
    rented Confiscated Tory estate, prior to 5/79
    Signer, Articles of Retaliation, 6/79
    present at the capture of the British ship, Britannia, 12/31/79
Striker, Henry   Middletown
    Ensign, Militia
    Signer, Articles of Retaliation, 6/79
    Signer, Petition Favoring Quick Division of Prize Money, 12/79
    Signer, Petition for Renewing Guard at Toms River, 12/10/81
Striker, Henry, Jr.   Middletown
    Private, Militia Dragoons, delinquent one tour
    Private, State Troops
    present at the capture of the British ship, Britannia, 12/31/79
Strong, William   Shrewsbury
    recipient of poor relief
Stryker, *see* Striker
Stuart, *see* Stewart
Stubbs, David
    Private, State Troops
Stucky, Daniel
    accused of being active in Tory Rebellions of 12/76
Stucky, Jacob   Shrewsbury
Studham, Samuel
    Private, New Jersey Volunteers
Studson, Joshua   Dover
    Lieutenant, Militia
    Captain, Privateer vessel
    Signer, Articles of Retaliation, 6/79
Stymits, *see* Stimits
Sullivan, John   Freehold
    Corporal, New Jersey Volunteers
    Private, Continental Army
Sullivan, Joshua (Joseph)
    Fifer, Continental Army

Sutfin, *see* Sutphin
Sutphin, *see also* Zutphin
Sutphin, Aaron
    Signer, Articles of Retaliation, 6/79
Sutphin, Abraham   Freehold
    Private, Militia
    Signer, Petition Urging Compensation for Inflated Money, 5/22/83
Sutphin, Benjamin   Freehold
    Signer, Articles of Retaliation, 6/79
    Signer, Association for Opposing the Return of Tories, 1783
Sutphin, Benjamin
    Signer, Association for Opposing the Return of Tories, 1783
Sutphin, Cornelius   Freehold
    Signer, Articles of Retaliation, 6/79
    Signer, Association for Opposing the Return of Tories, 1783
Sutphin, David
    Private, Militia
    Private, State Troops, enlisted 6/80
    Signer, Articles of Retaliation, 6/79
    Signer, Association for Opposing the Return of Tories, 1783
Sutphin, Derrick   Freehold
    Sergeant, Militia
    Private, State Troops
    Signer, Articles of Retaliation, 6/79
    present at the capture of the British ship, Britannia, 12/31/79
    sells produce to Continental Army, 5/80
Sutphin, Derrick   Freehold
    Militia Volunteer, Prior to the First General Militia Muster, 6/76
    Signer, Articles of Retaliation, 6/79
    sells produce to Continental Army, 5/80
    Signer, Petition Encouraging Free Trade, 5/12/81
    Signer, Petition Urging Compensation for Inflated Money, 5/22/83
Sutphin, Isaac
    Signer, Petition Supporting Issuing of New Jersey Currency, 1771
Sutphin, Job
    Private, Militia
Sutphin, John   Freehold
    Signer, Articles of Retaliation, 6/79
    Private, Militia
    Private, State Troops, enlisted 6/80
Sutphin, John   Middletown
    Private, Militia

Signer, Petition Opposing Slave Manumission, 2/2/74
Signer, Articles of Retaliation, 6/79
Grand Juror, Court of Oyer and Terminer, 8/79
Signer, Petition Favoring Quick Division of Prize Money, 12/79
Signer, Petition for Renewing Guard at Toms River, 12/10/81
Grand Juror, Court of Oyer and Terminer, 11/82
Signer, Petition Urging Compensation for Inflated Money, 5/22/83
Sutphin, John
   Private, Militia, "dies of wounds"
Sutphin, Joseph   Freehold
   Private, Militia
   Private, State Troops, enlisted 6/80
   Signer, Articles of Retaliation, 6/79
   Signer, Petition Supporting Retaliation, 9/17/80
   Signer, Petition Urging Compensation for Inflated Money, 5/22/83
Sutphin, Koert
   Militia Volunteer, Prior to the First General Militia Muster, 6/76
   Corporal, Militia, captured 2/13/77
Sutphin, Koert
   Private, Militia
Sutphin, Peter
   Private, Militia
Sutphin, Richard   Freehold
Sutphin, Richard   Shrewsbury
   Private, Militia, delinquent 8/80
Sutphin, William   Freehold
Sutphin, William   Middletown
   Private, State Troops, enlists 5/78
Sutten, James
   Private, Militia, drafted into Continental Army 5/78
Sutten, Jonas
   Private, Militia
   Private, Continental Army
Sutten, Leary   Stafford
   Private, Militia
Sutten, Lewis   Shrewsbury
   Signer, Petition Urging Action Against the Pine Robbers, 12/27/81
Sutten, Nathan
   arrested for Disaffection, 11/76
   accused of being active in Tory Rebellions of 12/76
Sutten, Richard   Shrewsbury and Upper Freehold
   Private, Militia

Suydam, Richard   Middletown
    Private, Militia
Swain, Aaron   Dover
    Signer, Petition Urging Action Against the Pine Robbers, 12/27/81
Swain, Andrew   Shrewsbury
    Private, Militia, delinquent 8/80
Swain, Anthony   Shrewsbury
    Private, Militia, delinquent 9/80
Swangle, Isaac   Upper Freehold
Swart, Cornelius   Middletown
    sells produce to Continental Army, 5/80
Swart, Hans
    indicted for Misdemeanor, 1/81
Swart, John   Shrewsbury
Sweaze, Caleb
    indicted for Murder, 5/82
Sweaze, Isaac
    indicted for Murder, 5/82
Sweetman, Henderson   Freehold
    sells produce to Continental Army, 5/80
    Juror, Court of Oyer and Terminer, 11/82
Sweetman, Michael   Freehold and Shrewsbury
    Captain, Militia
    Signer, Petition Urging Action Against the Disaffected, 3/14/77
    Signer, Articles of Retaliation, 6/79
    Signer, Petition for Renewing Guard at Toms River, 12/10/81
    Grand Juror, Court of Oyer and Terminer, 11/82
    Signer, Association for Opposing the Return of Tories, 1783
Sweetman, Michael   Upper Freehold
    witness at Monmouth Court, 1778
Swem, Anthony   Upper Freehold
Swem, Jesse
    Private, Militia, drafted into Continental Army 5/78
    Private, Continental Army
Swem, John   Upper Freehold
Swem, Vincent
    Private, New Jersey Volunteers, captured 6/26/78
Swimm, *see* Swem
Swink, Henry   Shrewsbury
Syckles, *see* Sickles
Sylvester, Obadiah   Freehold
    Private, Militia

Roster of the People of Revolutionary Monmouth County
Private, State Troops

T

Tabor, Daniel
    convicted of Misdemeanor, 12/80
Tabor, Jesse
    Private, New Jersey Volunteers
Tabor, John
    indicted for Misdemeanor, 1/81
Tabor, Nash   Shrewsbury
Tabor, Noah   Shrewsbury
    Private, Militia
Tabor, Tucker
    Sergeant, New Jersey Volunteers
Tallman, *see* Talman
Talman, Christopher   Shrewsbury
    estate inquisitioned for Forfeiture, 7/2/77
    estate confiscated
Talman, Daniel   Shrewsbury
    Signer, Petition Supporting Retaliation, 9/17/80
Talman, Deborah
    indicted for Misdemeanor, 8/79
    indicted for Misdemeanor, 1/81
Talman, Gideon   Shrewsbury
    Private, Militia
Talman, James   Shrewsbury
    Private, Militia
    Private, New Jersey Volunteers
    indicted for Misdemeanor, 11/82
Talman, James   Shrewsbury
    of Pumpkin Point
    Private, Militia
Talman, Jeremiah   Shrewsbury
    indicted for Misdemeanor, 8/79
Talman, Jeremiah, Jr.   Shrewsbury
    Private, New Jersey Volunteers, enlisted 2/5/77 deserted 8/17/77
Talman, John   Shrewsbury
    indicted for Misdemeanor, 11/81
    Signer, Petition Urging Compensation for Inflated Money, 5/22/83
Talman, Joseph   Shrewsbury
    doctor

Talman, Joseph   Shrewsbury
Talman, Oliver   Shrewsbury
    Private, Militia
    indicted for Misdemeanor, 8/79
Talman, Oliver   Shrewsbury
    Private, New Jersey Volunteers, captured 7/1/78
    estate inquisitioned for Forfeiture, 4/1/80
    estate confiscated
Talman, Peter
    Lieutenant, Continental Army
Talman, Samuel   Shrewsbury
Talman, Stephen   Shrewsbury
    arrested for disaffection 11/76 and 1777
    accused of being active in Tory Rebellions of 12/76
    indicted for Misdemeanor, 5/82
    estate confiscated
Talman, Stephen
    sells produce to Continental Army, 5/80
Talman, William
    Private, Militia
    Private, Continental Army
Tanner, Peter   Middletown
    Private, Militia
    Signer, Articles of Retaliation, 6/79
    present at the capture of the British ship, Britannia, 12/31/79
Tapscott, James   Freehold
    Private, Militia
    Private, State Troops, enlisted 6/80
    Coroner, 1778
    Signer, Articles of Retaliation, 6/79
    sells produce to Continental Army, 5/80
    Signer, Petition Encouraging Free Trade, 5/12/81
    Grand Juror, Court of Oyer and Terminer, 7/83
    Signer, Petition Supporting Quick Division of Militia Prizes, no date
Tapscott, William, Esq.   Upper Freehold
    witness at Monmouth Court, 1778
    Signer, Petition for Stricter Militia Law, 5/31/79
    Juror, Court of Oyer and Terminer, 8/79
        fined L30 for missing all or some of jury duty
    Justice of the Peace, 1780-3
Tapscott, William, Jr.   Upper Freehold
    Signer, Petition Urging Action Against Disaffected

& Favoring Retaliation, 5/12/81
Grand Juror, Court of Oyer and Terminer, 7/83
Tatum, Charles
   Private, Militia
Taylor, Asher   Shrewsbury
   flees to New York, dead 1776
Taylor, Conrad
   Signer, Petition Against Association for Retaliation 12/81
Taylor, David   Shrewsbury
   Signer, Petition Opposing Slave Manumission, 2/2/74
   flees to New York
   indicted for Riot & Trespass, 1/20/78
   indicted for Misdemeanor, 1/81
Taylor, Deborah   Middletown
   wife of George Taylor
   household head
   convicted of Misdemeanor, 1/20/78
Taylor, Edward, Esq.   Middletown
   Baptist
   mill owner
   Delegate, New Jersey Provincial Congress
   Overseer of Highways, 1773
   Signer, Petition Opposing Slave Manumission, 2/2/74
   arrested for disaffection 1777, placed under house arrest
   convicted of Misdemeanor, 12/80
   indicted for Misdemeanor, 11/81
   indicted for Perjury, 5/82
   Signer, Petition from Victims of the Association for Retaliation 9/82
Taylor, Edward   Middletown
   Signer, Petition Opposing Slave Manumission, 2/2/74
   sells produce to Continental Army, 5/80
   Juror, Court of Oyer and Terminer, 11/82
Taylor, Edward   Upper Freehold
   Private, Militia
Taylor, Fenwick   Upper Freehold
Taylor, George   Middletown
   Vestryman, Anglican Christ Church, 1772-6 and 1780
   Signer, Articles of Retaliation, 6/79
   sells produce to Continental Army, 5/80
Taylor, George   Middletown and Shrewsbury
   Colonel, Militia
   Township Assessor, 1772-6

    Signer, Petition Opposing Slave Manumission, 2/2/74
    flees to Sandy Hook
    Captain, New Jersey Volunteers
    estate inquisitioned for Forfeiture, 3/22/79
Taylor, George, Jr.   Middletown and Shrewsbury
    Private, New Jersey Volunteers
    Signer, Petition Opposing Slave Manumission, 2/2/74
    estate confiscated
Taylor, Henry
    Private, New Jersey Volunteers
Taylor, James   Freehold
    Private, Militia
    Private, Militia Dragoons, delinquent one tour
    Private, State Troops
    Signer, Petition for Renewing Guard at Toms River, 12/10/81
    Juror, Court of Oyer and Terminer, 5/82
    Juror, Court of Oyer and Terminer, 11/82
Taylor, James
    Sergeant, New Jersey Volunteers
Taylor, John, Esq.   Middletown
    Baptist
    Royal Sheriff, Monmouth County
    "High Commissioner" for issuing loyalty oaths to British, 1776
    arrested for Disaffection, 1777
    parts of estate "Applied for Publick Use"
    indicted for Misdemeanor, 1/78
    indicted for Misdemeanor, 6/3/78, acquitted
    Signer, Petition Against Association for Retaliation 12/81
    donates to Charity Fund for the Stevenson Family, 5/83
Taylor, John   Shrewsbury
    Captain, New Jersey Volunteers
        commands company at Sandy Hook Lighthouse, 4/78
    Captain, New York Volunteers
    estate inquisitioned for Forfeiture, 6/30/77
    estate confiscated
Taylor, John   Shrewsbury
    Militia Volunteer, Prior to the First General Militia Muster, 6/76
    Private, Militia
    Signer, Petition Opposing Slave Manumission, 2/2/74
    indicted for Misdemeanor, 6/78
    flees to New York 6/79
    estate confiscated

Roster of the People of Revolutionary Monmouth County

Taylor, John   Middletown
    son of Edward
    Private, New Jersey Volunteers
    indicted for Misdemeanor, 5/82
    indicted for Misdemeanor, 11/82
Taylor, John, Jr.   Middletown
    Private, Militia
    Signer, Petition Opposing Slave Manumission, 2/2/74
    donates to Charity Fund for the Stevenson Family, 5/83
Taylor, Joseph   Middletown
    estate inquisitioned for Forfeiture, 6/30/77
    estate confiscated
Taylor, Joseph   Upper Freehold
    Private, Militia, wounded at Battle of Germantown
    Signer, Petition Opposing Slave Manumission, 2/2/74
    Juror, Court of Oyer and Terminer, 1/78
        fined L5 for not attending all or part of Jury duty
    Juror, Court of Oyer and Terminer, 12/80
        fined L3 for missing all or some of jury duty
    Juror, Court of Oyer and Terminer, 5/82
        fined for missing jury duty
    Juror, Court of Oyer and Terminer, 11/82
Taylor, Lawrence   Upper Freehold and Freehold
    Lieutenant, Militia
    tavern owner
    indicted for Misdemeanor, 1/78
    Signer, Petition Favoring Quick Division of Prize Money, 12/79
Taylor, Morford   Shrewsbury
    arrested for Disaffection, 11/76
    accused of being active in Tory Rebellions of 12/76
    flees to New York
    estate inquisitioned for Forfeiture, 6/30/77
    killed off Sandy Hook while in a fishing boat 1782
    estate confiscated
Taylor, Nathaniel   Shrewsbury
    flees to New York, dies 1776
Taylor, Phoenix   Upper Freehold
    Private, Militia
Taylor, Samuel
    escapes from Freehold jail, 1780
Taylor, Thomas   Shrewsbury
    Signer, Petition Favoring Quick Division of Prize Money, 12/79

Taylor, William   Freehold
    lawyer
    leads petition drive against Declaration of Independence, 6/76
    arrested 11/76
    estate inquisitioned for Forfeiture, 7/4/77
    indicted for Riot, 1/78
    sells produce to Continental Army, 5/80
Taylor, William   Upper Freehold
    Private, Militia
    sells produce to Continental Army, 5/80
    Signer, Petition in Favor of Daniel Longstreet, 11/21/80
    Juror, Court of Oyer and Terminer, 11/82
Taylor, William, Jr.   Middletown and Freehold
    Private, Militia, delinquent 2/10/78
    sells produce to Continental Army, 7/80
    indicted for Misdemeanor, 1/81
    indicted for Misdemeanor, 11/81
    Overseer of Highways, 1783
Tears, William
    accused of being active in Tory Rebellions of 12/76
Telfair, David   Upper Freehold
    Minister
Ten Eyck, Alexander
    Signer, Articles of Retaliation, 6/79
Ten Eyck, Jacob
    Captain, Militia
Ten Eyck, John
    Ensign, Militia, killed 6/17/77
Tennent, William
    Private, State Troops
Tenney, George   Shrewsbury
    Private, Militia, delinquent 2/10/78
    convicted of Misdemeanor, 12/80
Tenney, Margaret   Upper Freehold
    household head
Tenny, *see* Tenney
Test, John   Freehold
Tharp, *see also* Throp
Tharp, Abel
    Private, Continental Army
Tharp, Abner   Shrewsbury
Tharp, Benjamin   Middletown

    Private, Militia
    Private, Continental Army
Tharp, Daniel   Middletown
Tharp, Isaac   Shrewsbury
Tharp, Robert
    Private, State Troops, enlisted 6/80
Thomas   Upper Freehold
    free black householder
    formerly belonged to Potts family
Thomas, Alexander
    Private, New Jersey Volunteers
Thomas, Andrew   Shrewsbury
Thomas, Ezekiel
    Private, New Jersey Volunteers
Thomas, John   Upper Freehold
Thomas, Richard
    Private, Militia
Thomas, Robert
    Private, Militia
Thomas, Thomas
    teamster for Militia company near Navesink Highlands, 8/76
Thomas, William   Upper Freehold
    Militia Volunteer, Prior to the First General Militia Muster, 6/76
Thompson, *see* Thomson
Thomson, Ana
    indicted for Misdemeanor, 11/81
Thomson, Benjamin
    Private, Militia
Thomson, Catherine   Freehold
    daughter of Cornelius
    convicted of Seditious Words, 6/3/78
Thomson, Cornelius   Freehold
    Paymaster, New Jersey Volunteers
Thomson, Cornelius
    Private, Militia, hires substitute, 2/10/78, delinquent 3/11/78
Thomson, David   Freehold
    Corporal, Militia
    Private, Militia, hires substitute, 2/10/78, delinquent 3/11/78
Thomson, Eleck   Dover
Thomson, Euphame   Shrewsbury
    listed as having a "lame foot"
    recipient of poor relief

Roster of the People of Revolutionary Monmouth County

Thomson, John   Dover
    Private, New Jersey Volunteers, enlisted 12/4/76 deserted 3/6/77
    accused of being active in Tory Rebellions of 12/76
    indicted for Felony, 11/81
Thomson, John
    Militia Volunteer, Prior to the First General Militia Muster, 6/76
    Ensign, New Jersey Volunteers
    estate inquisitioned for Forfeiture, 3/1/79
Thomson, John   Shrewsbury
    Militia Volunteer, Prior to the First General Militia Muster, 6/76
    Private, Militia
    helps keep the poor
Thomson, Joseph   Freehold
    Private, Militia
Thomson, Joseph   Upper Freehold
    arrested for Disaffection, 11/76
    convicted on two counts of Riot, 1/20/78
    sells produce to Continental Army, 5/80
    leased horse team to Continental Quarter Master 12/81
Thomson, Lewis   Freehold
    Militia Volunteer, Prior to the First General Militia Muster, 6/76
    Ensign, New Jersey Volunteers
    estate confiscated
Thomson, Lewis
    Private, Militia
Thomson, Robert   Upper Freehold
    indicted for High Treason, 1/20/78, convicted 6/78
Thomson, Samuel   Upper Freehold
Thomson, Thomas, Sr.   Freehold
    arrested for disaffection, 1777
    Private, Militia, hires substitute 2/10/78
    indicted for Seditious Words, 6/78
    indicted for High Treason, 8/79
    sells produce to Continental Army, 5/80
Thomson, Thomas, Jr.   Freehold
    arrested on four counts Riot and one count of Trespass, 1/20/78
    sells produce to Continental Army, 5/80
    leased horse team to Continental Quarter Master 12/81
Thomson, William   Middletown
    arrested for Disaffection, 1/77
    joins Continental Army in exchange for Pardon, 5/23/77
    Private, Militia, delinquent 11/29/78, delinquent 6/11/80

present at the capture of the British ship, Britannia, 12/31/79
Thorn, John   Middletown
   estate confiscated
Thorn, Robert   Middletown
   Delegate, Friends' Quarterly Meeting, 1774
Thorn, Samuel   Middletown
   estate confiscated
Thorn, Thomas   Middletown
   estate inquisitioned for Forfeiture, 3/23/79
   estate confiscated
   Signer, Petition Opposing Slave Manumission, 2/2/74
   Signer, Articles of Retaliation, 6/79
Thorp, see Tharp or Thorn or Throp
Throckmorton, Holmes   Freehold
   Private, New Jersey Volunteers, deserted prior to 1779
   Private, Continental Army
Throckmorton, Jacob
   sells produce to Continental Army, 5/80
Throckmorton, James   Shrewsbury
   Militia Volunteer, Prior to the First General Militia Muster, 6/76
   Private, Continental Army
Throckmorton, James   Upper Freehold
Throckmorton, Job   Shrewsbury and Freehold
   Private, Militia
   Signer, Articles of Retaliation, 6/79
   converts to Methodism, 1780
Throckmorton, John   Freehold
   Signer, Petition Supporting Issuing of New Jersey Currency, 1771
   merchant
   Signer, Petition Opposing Slave Manumission, 2/2/74
   arrested for Disaffection, 1/77
   Lieutenant, New Jersey Volunteers, captured 8/22/77
   Lieutenant, Militia
   Lieutenant, Roger's Kings Rangers
   estate confiscated
Throckmorton, John
   Corporal of Militia, Prior to the First General Militia Muster, 6/76
Throckmorton, Joseph   Shrewsbury
   Member, Shrewsbury Committee of Observation
   Vestryman, Anglican Christ Church, 1777-82,
      Warden, 1778
   sells produce to Continental Army, 5/80

Throckmorton, Joseph   Shrewsbury
  Private, Militia
  helps keep the poor
  sells produce to Continental Army, 5/80
Throckmorton, Mary   Freehold
  household head
Throckmorton, Rosina
  indicted for Misdemeanor, 11/82
Throckmorton, Samuel
  Signer, Petition Supporting Issuing of New Jersey Currency, 1771
  Militia Volunteer, Prior to the First General Militia Muster, 6/76
  Sergeant, Militia
Throckmorton, Samuel   Shrewsbury
  Private, Militia
Throp, *see also* Tharp
Throp, Abel   Upper Freehold
  Private, New Jersey Volunteers, deserted 7/2/77
  Private, Continental Army
Throp, Benjamin   Freehold
  Private, Continental Army
Throp, Judiah   Upper Freehold
Throp, Samuel   Upper Freehold
Throp, William   Upper Freehold
  arrested for Disaffection, 1/77
Thurman, Richard
  Signer, Petition Against Association for Retaliation 12/81
Thurman, Thomas
  two slaves run away and join Black Brigade
Tice, Ann
  witness at Monmouth Court, 1778
Tice, Elisha
  Private, Continental Army
Tice, Jacob   Freehold and Middletown
  Lieutenant, Militia (Monmouth and Middlesex County)
  Signer, Petition Against Loyalist Auction Commissioners, 3/24/79
  Signer, Petition Favoring Quick Division of Prize Money, 12/79
  present at the capture of the British ship, Britannia, 12/31/79
  indicted for Misdemeanor, 11/81
  Signer, Petition Against Association for Retaliation 12/81
  indicted for Misdemeanor, 5/82
Tice, John   Freehold and Middletown
  Signer, Petition Opposing Slave Manumission, 2/2/74

    Signer, Petition Against Loyalist Auction Commissioners, 3/24/79
    Signer, Petition for Stricter Militia Law, 5/31/79
    sells produce to Continental Army, 5/80
    Signer, Petition Against Association for Retaliation 12/81
    Juror, Court of Oyer and Terminer, 5/82
        fined for missing jury duty

Tice, John   Freehold
    sells clothing to Continental Army, 3/78

Tice, John   Shrewsbury

Tice, Joseph
    sells produce to Continental Army, 5/80

Tice, Mathias
    Signer, Articles of Retaliation, 6/79
    Signer, Petition Urging Compensation for Inflated Money, 5/22/83

Tice, Richard   Freehold
    Private, Militia, captured 2/13/77
    Signer, Articles of Retaliation, 6/79

Tice, William   Dover
    Militia Volunteer, Prior to the First General Militia Muster, 6/76
    Private, Militia

Tie, William
    accused of being active in Tory Rebellions of 12/76
    Private, New Jersey Volunteers, dead 12/14/77

Tilton, Benjamin   Upper Freehold
    Private, Militia

Tilton, Benjamin, Jr.   Middletown
    Private, Militia
    present at the capture of the British ship, Britannia, 12/31/79

Tilton, Clayton   Shrewsbury
    flees to New York, 10/76
    estate inquisitioned for Forfeiture, 7/3/77
    indicted for Murder, 1/81
    Captain of Associated Loyalists, 1/15/81
    estate confiscated

Tilton, Clayton, Jr.   Shrewsbury
    Laborer, Pennsylvania Salt Works, intermittent 8/76-6/77

Tilton, David   Shrewsbury

Tilton, Edward
    Private, Militia
    donates to Charity Fund for the Stevenson Family, 5/83

Tilton, Esther   Upper Freehold
    household head

Tilton, Ezekiel   Middletown
    indicted for Burglary, 11/82
    estate inquisitioned for Forfeiture, 4/1/80
    estate confiscated
Tilton, Hezekiah
    Laborer, Pennsylvania Salt Works, intermittent 8/76-6/77
Tilton, Increase   Shrewsbury
    Delegate, Friends' Quarterly Meeting, 1775-81
Tilton, Jacob   Dover
    Militia Volunteer, Prior to the First General Militia Muster, 6/76
    Laborer, Pennsylvania Salt Works, intermittent 8/76-6/77
    Signer, Articles of Retaliation, 6/79
    Signer, Petition Urging Action Against the Pine Robbers, 12/27/81
    Juror, Court of Oyer and Terminer, 5/82
        fined for missing jury duty
    Juror, Court of Oyer and Terminer, 11/82
Tilton, Jeremiah
    indicted for Misdemeanor, 11/82
Tilton, John   Dover and Shrewsbury
    Militia Volunteer, Prior to the First General Militia Muster, 6/76
    Signer, Petition Urging Action Against the Pine Robbers, 12/27/81
    Refugee in New York, 1782
Tilton, John   Middletown
    Militia Volunteer, Prior to the First General Militia Muster, 6/76
    estate confiscated
Tilton, John   Middletown
    rented Confiscated Tory estate, prior to 5/79
    Signer, Articles of Retaliation, 6/79
    Signer, Petition Supporting Retaliation, 9/17/80
    Signer, Petition Opposing the Return of Tories 6/10/83
    Signer, Association for Opposing the Return of Tories, 1783
Tilton, John   Middletown
    Captain, Associated Loyalists
    estate inquisitioned for Forfeiture, 4/1/80
    estate confiscated
Tilton, John   Shrewsbury
    Private, Militia, delinquent 8/80
    indicted for Misdemeanor, 11/82
Tilton, John   Shrewsbury
    Signer, Articles of Retaliation, 6/79
Tilton, John, Jr.   Dover
    Private, Militia

    Signer, Petition Urging Action Against the Pine Robbers, 12/27/81
Tilton, John, Jr.   Middletown
    Signer, Articles of Retaliation, 6/79
    Signer, Petition Opposing the Return of Tories 6/10/83
Tilton, Joseph   Shrewsbury
    witness at Monmouth Court, 1778
    Private, Militia, delinquent 9/80
Tilton, Nathan   Middletown
    Private, Militia, hires substitute 2/10/78
Tilton, Nathaniel   Middletown
    Delegate, Friends' Quarterly Meeting, 1774-81
Tilton, Nehemiah   Freehold
    Signer, Articles of Retaliation, 6/79
Tilton, Obadiah   Shrewsbury
    Delegate, Friends' Quarterly Meeting, 1776-8, 1783
    sells produce to Continental Army, 5/80
Tilton, Peter   Middletown
Tilton, Phoebe   Middletown
    household head
Tilton, Phineas   Upper Freehold
    Militia Volunteer, Prior to the First General Militia Muster, 6/76
Tilton, Robert   Upper Freehold
    Signer, Petition Against Association for Retaliation 12/81
Tilton, Samuel   Middletown
Tilton, Thomas   Middletown
Tilton, Thomas   Middletown
Tilton, Thomas   Shrewsbury
    Delegate, Friends' Quarterly Meeting, 1774-7
Tilton, William   Middletown
    Private, Militia, hires substitute
    Delegate, Friends' Quarterly Meeting, 1778, 180, 1782
Timer, *see* Tinner
Tinner, Peter
    Private, Militia
Tinney, *see* Tenney
Tipperly, Christian
    Private, New Jersey Volunteers, enlisted 12/1/76
        discharged 2/13/77
Titus, John
    Private, New Jersey Volunteers, enlisted 1/7/77 dead 6/11/77
Titus, Silas
    Private, Militia, delinquent 2/10/78

witness at Monmouth Court, 1778
Toby, Warden   Upper Freehold
Toole, Thomas
    Private, New Jersey Volunteers
Tole, Richard   Shrewsbury
    Private, Militia
Trafford, Samuel   Shrewsbury
    helps keep the poor
Trafford, Samuel, Jr.   Shrewsbury
Traxler, John   Upper Freehold
Trevase, Abraham   Dover
    Militia Volunteer, Prior to the First General Militia Muster, 6/76
Tribit, John
    Private, Militia
Tribute, John   Upper Freehold
Trout, John   Upper Freehold
Trout, Peter   Upper Freehold
    Private, Militia
Truax, Abraham
    Private, Militia
Truax, Cornelius
    Private, Militia
Truax, Jacob
    Private, Militia
Truax, John   Middletown
    Overseer of Highways, 1771
    Signer, Articles of Retaliation, 6/79
    Juror, Court of Oyer and Terminer, 12/80
        fined L3 for missing all or some of jury duty
Truax, John   Shrewsbury
Truax, Ruliff   Shrewsbury
    Signer, Petition Opposing Slave Manumission, 2/2/74
    Private, New Jersey Volunteers, died in hospital 11/24/77
Truax, Samuel   Middletown
    Private, Militia
    present at the capture of the British ship, Britannia, 12/31/79
Truax, Samuel
    Private, Militia
Truax, Susannah   Middletown
    household head
Truax, William
    Private, Militia, captured 2/13/77

Tucker, Bishop — Upper Freehold
Tucker, James
    Delegate, Friends' Quarterly Meeting, 1774-5
    indicted for High Treason, 1/81
    indicted for Misdemeanor and High Treason, 11/82
Tucker, John — Shrewsbury
    Delegate, Friends' Quarterly Meeting, 1774-83
Tucker, Samuel — Shrewsbury
    sells produce to Continental Army, 5/80
    Signer, Petition from Victims of the Association for Retaliation 9/82
Tunis, Henry — Middletown
Tunis, Henry — Middletown
    Private, Militia, captured 2/13/77
    Signer, Petition Opposing the Return of Tories 6/10/83
Tunis, Jonathan — Middletown
    Signer, Petition Opposing the Return of Tories 6/10/83
Tunis, Moses — Middletown
    Signer, Petition Opposing the Return of Tories 6/10/83
Tunis, Sarah — Middletown
    household head
Tunison, Cornelius
    Private, Militia
Turvey, Nathaniel
    Private, New Jersey Volunteers, enlisted 5/5/77 dead 7/19/77
Tyson, John — Middletown
Tyson, John, Jr. — Middletown
    Private, Militia
    present at the capture of the British ship, Britannia, 12/31/79
    Signer, Petition Opposing the Return of Tories 6/10/83
Tyson, Mathias
    Private, Militia
    present at the capture of the British ship, Britannia, 12/31/79

U

Underwood, John
    Private, New Jersey Volunteers, enlisted 4/1/77 dead 8/15/77

V

Vail, Henry
    Signer, Petition Favoring Quick Division of Prize Money, 12/79

Valentine, William
   arrested for Disaffection, 11/76
   accused of being active in Tory Rebellions of 12/76
   indicted for Misdemeanor, 11/81
   indicted for Misdemeanor, 5/82
Van, Henry
   Private, State Troops
Van Aartsdalen, *see* Van Artsdalen
Van Arsdall, Cornelius
   sells produce to Continental Army, 5/80
Van Arsdall, Oake
   sells produce to Continental Army, 5/80
Van Artsdalen, Jacob
   Private, Militia
Van Blarkin, David   Shrewsbury
   Private, Militia, delinquent 6/79
Van Brackle, John   Freehold and Middletown
   Private, Militia
   Signer, Articles of Retaliation, 6/79
   Signer, Petition Opposing the Return of Tories 6/10/83
Van Brackle, John, Jr.   Freehold
Van Brackle, Mathias   Middletown
   Signer, Petition Opposing the Return of Tories 6/10/83
Van Brackle, Stephen   Freehold
   Private, Militia
Van Brackle, Stephen   Middletown
   Private, Militia
   present at the capture of the British ship, Britannia, 12/31/79
   Signer, Petition Opposing the Return of Tories 6/10/83
Van Brackle, Stephen   Shrewsbury and Middletown
   Signer, Petition Opposing Slave Manumission, 2/2/74
   Signer, Petition Against Loyalist Auction Commissioners, 3/24/79
   Grand Juror, Court of Oyer and Terminer, 8/79
   donates to Charity Fund for the Stevenson Family, 5/83
   Signer, Petition Opposing the Return of Tories 6/10/83
Van Brunt, Cornelius   Shrewsbury
   Private, Militia, delinquent 8/17/80
Van Brunt, Hendrick   Shrewsbury
   Private, Militia, delinquent 8/17/80
Van Brunt, Hendrick   Shrewsbury
   Lieutenant, Militia
   Signer, Petition to Better Provision Militia, 2/25/78

Roster of the People of Revolutionary Monmouth County

Van Brunt, Hendrick   Shrewsbury
  Major, Militia, captured 1780
  Signer, Petition Opposing Slave Manumission, 2/2/74
  Signer, Petition Calling for Action Against the Disaffected, 2/21/77
  Signer, Petition Urging Action Against the Disaffected, 3/14/77
  Signer, Petition to Better Provision Militia, 2/25/78
  sells produce to Continental Army, 5/80

Van Brunt, Joseph   Shrewsbury
  Corporal, Militia

Van Brunt, Nicholas, Jr.   Shrewsbury
  Private, Militia, delinquent 6/11/80
  Signer, Petition Opposing Slave Manumission, 2/2/74

Van Brunt, Nicholas   Shrewsbury
  Minister
  Member, Shrewsbury Committee of Observation
  Sheriff, 1777-9
  Captain, Militia
  Signer, Petition Opposing Slave Manumission, 2/2/74
  Signer, Petition Calling for Action Against the Disaffected, 2/21/77
  Signer, Petition Urging Action Against the Disaffected, 3/14/77
  Signer, Petition for Stricter Militia Law, 5/31/79
  Signer, Articles of Retaliation, 6/79
  Grand Juror, Court of Oyer and Terminer, 5/82
  Juror, Court of Oyer and Terminer, 11/82
  Signer, Association for Opposing the Return of Tories, 1783

Vance, Samuel   Middletown

Van Cleaf, Benjamin   Freehold
  house burned by British Army, 6/28/78
  Signer, Articles of Retaliation, 6/79
  Signer, Petition Favoring Quick Division of Prize Money, 12/79
  Signer, Petition for Renewing Guard at Toms River, 12/10/81
  Juror, Court of Oyer and Terminer, 5/82
    fined for missing jury duty

Van Cleaf, Benjamin   Middletown
  Captain, Militia
  Signer, Petition to Better Provision Militia, 2/25/78
  Signer, Articles of Retaliation, 6/79
  Signer, Petition Favoring Quick Division of Prize Money, 12/79
  Grand Juror, Court of Oyer and Terminer, 12/80
  Grand Juror, Court of Oyer and Terminer, 5/82
  Grand Juror, Court of Oyer and Terminer, 11/82
  Signer, Association for Opposing the Return of Tories, 1783

Van Cleaf, Benjamin   Middletown
Private, Militia, delinquent 6/11/80
Signer, Petition Supporting Quick Division of Militia Prizes, no date

Van Cleaf, Elizabeth   Freehold
household head

Van Cleaf, Jacob
Signer, Articles of Retaliation, 6/79

Van Cleaf, John   Freehold
Private, Militia
Signer, Association for Opposing the Return of Tories, 1783

Van Cleaf, John   Freehold and Shrewsbury
Captain, Militia
Signer, Petition Supporting Issuing of New Jersey Currency, 1771
Signer, Petition Opposing Slave Manumission, 2/2/74
Signer, Petition for Stricter Militia Law, 5/31/79
Signer, Articles of Retaliation, 6/79
Signer, Association for Opposing the Return of Tories, 1783
Signer, Petition Supporting Quick Division of Militia Prizes, no date

Van Cleaf, Joseph   Freehold
Private, Militia
Signer, Articles of Retaliation, 6/79

Van Cleaf, Peter   Freehold
Private, Militia
Private, Continental Army, enlisted 1/11/81
Signer, Articles of Retaliation, 6/79
Signer, Petition Urging Compensation for Inflated Money, 5/22/83

Van Cleaf, Sarah   Freehold
household head

Van Cleaf, William   Middletown
Baptist
Signer, Petition Supporting Issuing of New Jersey Currency, 1771
Captain, Militia, captured 2/13/77
Signer, Petition Calling for Action Against the Disaffected, 2/21/77
Signer, Petition to Better Provision Militia, 2/25/78
Signer, Petition Against Association for Retaliation 12/81
Signer, Association for Opposing the Return of Tories, 1783
Signer, Petition Supporting Quick Division of Militia Prizes, no date

Van Cleaf, William   Shrewsbury
Private, Militia

Van Cleaff, Van Cleave, Van Cleve, *see* Van Cleaf

Van Court, John   Freehold
Private, Militia, serves as substitute 2/10/78

fined $50 for Militia delinquency, 3/11/78
Signer, Petition Favoring Quick Division of Prize Money, 12/79
indicted for Misdemeanor, 11/81
Van Deripe, John   Freehold
Van Deripe, Mathias
    Signer, Articles of Retaliation, 6/79
Van Dike, Abraham   Shrewsbury
    exempt from Militia service, 2/10/78
Van Dike, Charles   Shrewsbury
    convicted of Trespass, 1/20/78
    indicted for Misdemeanor, 6/78
Van Dike, Isaac   Shrewsbury
    Private, Militia
    sells produce to Continental Army, 7/80
Van Dike, John   Shrewsbury
    Private, New Jersey Volunteers
    Private, Militia
    indicted for Misdemeanor, 1/81
    indicted for Misdemeanor, 5/82
Van Dike, Joseph   Shrewsbury
    Captain, Militia
Van Dike, Martin   Shrewsbury
Van Dike, Thomas
    Private, New Jersey Volunteers
Van Dine, Dennis (Denice)   Middletown
    Private, Militia
    indicted for Misdemeanor, 8/79
    estate confiscated
Van Dine, Hendrick   Middletown
    indicted for Misdemeanor, 8/79
    estate confiscated
Van Dine, John
    Private, Militia
Van Dine, Ruliff (Ralph)   Middletown
    Laborer, Pennsylvania Salt Works, intermittent 8/76-6/77
Van Dorn, Benjamin   Middletown
    Signer, Petition Opposing the Return of Tories 6/10/83
Van Dorn, Cornelius   Middletown
    Signer, Petition Opposing the Return of Tories 6/10/83
Van Dorn, Esek
    Private, Continental Army
Van Dorn, Isaac   Middletown

Private, Militia
Signer, Petition Supporting Issuing of New Jersey Currency, 1771
present at the capture of the British ship, Britannia, 12/31/79
Signer, Petition for Renewing Guard at Toms River, 12/10/81
Signer, Petition Opposing the Return of Tories 6/10/83
Van Dorn, Isaac
  Private, Militia
  Laborer, Pennsylvania Salt Works
Van Dorn, Jacob   Freehold
  sells clothing to Continental Army, 3/78
  Signer, Petition for Renewing Guard at Toms River, 12/10/81
  Juror, Court of Oyer and Terminer, 5/82
    fined for missing jury duty
  Juror, Court of Oyer and Terminer, 11/82
Van Dorn, Nicholas
  Private, Militia
  Overseer of Highways, 1771 and 1782
  Signer, Petition Opposing Slave Manumission, 2/2/74
Van Dorn, Peter
  Signer, Articles of Retaliation, 6/79
  Signer, Association for Opposing the Return of Tories, 1783
Van Dorn, Thomas
  Private, New Jersey Volunteers
Van Dyke, *see* Van Dike
Van Emburgh, John
  sells goods to Pennsylvania Salt Works, 8/76-10/76
Van Gelder, Abraham
  Signer, Articles of Retaliation
Van Gordon, Benjamin
  Private, New Jersey Volunteers, killed 6/28/78
Van Hice, Abraham
  sells produce to Continental Army, 5/80
Van Hice, Aucke (Oakey)
  Private, New Jersey Volunteers
Van Hise, Van Hoice, *see* Van Hice
Van Horn, Cornelius
  Signer, Association for Opposing the Return of Tories, 1783
Van Horn, Mathias   Freehold
  Signer, Association for Opposing the Return of Tories, 1783
Van Hyce, *see* Van Hice
Van Kaitch, Casler   Freehold
Van Kaitch, Robert   Freehold

Van Kirk, James   Freehold
 Juror, Court of Oyer and Terminer, 1/78
  fined L5 for not attending all or part of Jury duty
 sells clothing to Continental Army, 3/78
 Signer, Articles of Retaliation, 6/79
 Juror, Court of Oyer and Terminer, 12/80
  fined L3 for missing all or some of jury duty
 Signer, Petition Encouraging Free Trade, 5/12/81
 Signer, Association for Opposing the Return of Tories, 1783
Van Kirk, Jemison
 Private, Militia
Van Kirk, John
 Private, Militia
Van Kirk, Mathias   Shrewsbury
Van Kirk, Peter   Shrewsbury
 Private, Militia, delinquent 8/80
Van Kirk, Stephen   Shrewsbury and Middletown
 Private, Militia
 holds tavern license, 1775
 Signer, Petition Favoring Quick Division of Prize Money, 12/79
 Juror, Court of Oyer and Terminer, 5/82
  fined for missing jury duty
 Juror, Court of Oyer and Terminer, 11/82
 Signer, Petition Opposing the Return of Tories 6/10/83
Van Kirk, William
 Private, Militia
Van Law, John
 indicted for Misdemeanor, 6/78
Van Law, Judiah
 indicted for Misdemeanor, 1/78
Van Loo, *see* Van Law
Van Mater, Benjamin   Middletown and Shrewsbury
 Signer, Petition Supporting Issuing of New Jersey Currency, 1771
 holds tavern license, 1775
 Militia Volunteer, Prior to the First General Militia Muster, 6/76
 Signer, Articles of Retaliation, 6/79
 Signer, Petition Favoring Quick Division of Prize Money, 12/79
Van Mater, Benjamin   Middletown
 Private, Militia Dragoons, delinquent one tour
 present at the capture of the British ship, Britannia, 12/31/79
Van Mater, Chrineyonce   Middletown
 mill owner and horse breeder

Overseer of the Poor, 1771
Overseer of Highways, 1776
Private, Militia, 4/76
indicted for Misdemeanor, 6/78
estate inquisitioned for Forfeiture, 7/4/77
fined and jailed 1778
estate confiscated
Refugee in New York, 1782
indicted for High Treason, 8/79, case held over to 5/82 and 11/82

Van Mater, Clarence (Chrineyonce) Middletown
Signer, Petition Supporting Issuing of New Jersey Currency, 1771
Signer, Petition Opposing Slave Manumission, 2/2/74
Militia Volunteer, Prior to the First General Militia Muster, 6/76
Overseer of Highways, 1779
sells produce to Continental Army, 7/80
indicted for Misdemeanor, 1/81
Overseer of the Poor, 1783

Van Mater, Clarence Middletown
Private, Militia
estate confiscated

Van Mater, Cornelius Shrewsbury
holds tavern license, 1775
Captain, Militia
Signer, Petition Opposing Slave Manumission, 2/2/74
sells produce to Continental Army, 5/80
indicted for Misdemeanor, 11/81

Van Mater, Cyrenus Middletown
Signer, Petition Supporting Issuing of New Jersey Currency, 1771
Militia Volunteer, Prior to the First General Militia Muster, 6/76
Private, Militia
sells produce to Continental Army, 5/80

Van Mater, Daniel Freehold
New Jersey Volunteers, 1/77
estate inquisitioned for Forfeiture, 3/24/79
estate confiscated

Van Mater, Guisebert (Gilbert) Freehold and Middletown
Private, Militia
Signer, Petition Supporting Issuing of New Jersey Currency, 1771
Signer, Petition Opposing Slave Manumission, 2/2/74
Refugee in New York, 1782
Convicted of High Treason, 4/25/82

Van Mater, Hendrick Shrewsbury

Roster of the People of Revolutionary Monmouth County

    arrested and jailed in Maryland for six months, beginning 11/76
    estate inquisitioned for Forfeiture, 3/19/79
    estate confiscated
Van Mater, Huldah
    wife of Chrineyonce Van Mater
    convicted of Misdemeanor, 1/20/78
Van Mater, Jacob   Middletown
    Private, New Jersey Volunteers
    Signer, Petition Opposing Slave Manumission, 2/2/74
Van Mater, John   Freehold
    Signer, Petition Favoring Quick Division of Prize Money, 12/79
    sells produce to Continental Army, 5/80
Van Mater, John   Middletown
    refuses loyalty oath to Continental Government, jailed, 11/76
    accused of being active in Tory Rebellions of 12/76
    Signer, Petition Supporting Issuing of New Jersey Currency, 1771
    indicted for Misdemeanor, 8/79
    convicted of Misdemeanor, 1/81
Van Mater, John   Shrewsbury
    Signer, Petition Opposing Slave Manumission, 2/2/74
Van Mater, Joseph   Middletown
    Signer, Petition from Victims of the Association for Retaliation 9/82
Van Mater, Richard   Freehold
    Signer, Petition Supporting Issuing of New Jersey Currency, 1771
    Signer, Petition for Settlement of Quartermaster Debts, 9/6/77
    Juror, Court of Oyer and Terminer, 1/78
        fined L5 for not attending all or part of Jury duty
    Juror, Court of Oyer and Terminer, 12/80
        fined L3 for missing all or some of jury duty
    Juror, Court of Oyer and Terminer, 5/82
        fined for missing jury duty
    Juror, Court of Oyer and Terminer, 11/82
    lost slaves during the war
Van Mater, Ruliff   Shrewsbury
Van Mater, Ryche   Middletown
    Overseer of the Poor, 1775-6
Van Norman, James
    Private, Militia
    Private, State Troops
    Private, Continental Army
Van Nort, see Van Nortwick and Van Note
Van Nortwick, Alexander   Freehold

Van Nortwick, Martin   Freehold
   Private, Militia
Van Note, Cornelius
   indicted for Misdemeanor, 11/81
   indicted for Misdemeanor, 5/82
Van Note, Jacob   Shrewsbury
   Signer, Association for Opposing the Return of Tories, 1783
Van Note, Jacob
   arrested for Robbery, 1/20/78
   indicted for Murder, 8/79
Van Note, John
   Private, Militia
   Private, New Jersey Volunteers
Van Note, Joseph   Shrewsbury
   Private, Militia
   Signer, Articles of Retaliation, 6/79
Van Note, Peter   Shrewsbury
   estate confiscated
Van Note, Peter
   Private, New Jersey Volunteers, enlisted 4/6/77 dead 10/4/77
   estate inquisitioned for Forfeiture, 7/4/77
Van Note, Rebecca   Shrewsbury
   household head
Van Note, Thomas   Dover
   Militia Volunteer, Prior to the First General Militia Muster, 6/76
   Township Overseer of Highways, 1783
Van Note, William
   indicted for Murder, 8/79
Van Pelt, Aaron   Middletown
   Private, Militia
Van Pelt, Alexander
   Private, Militia
   Private, State Troops
   present at the capture of the British ship, Britannia, 12/31/79
Van Pelt, Christopher
   Private, Militia
   present at the capture of the British ship, Britannia, 12/31/79
   leased horse team to Continental Quarter Master 12/81
   Signer, Petition Opposing the Return of Tories 6/10/83
Van Pelt, Hance   Middletown
   Private, Militia
Van Pelt, Hendrick   Middletown

Private, Militia
Private, State Troops, enlists 6/80
present at the capture of the British ship, Britannia, 12/31/79
Signer, Petition Opposing the Return of Tories 6/10/83
Van Pelt, Hendrick   Middletown
Signer, Articles of Retaliation, 6/79
Signer, Petition Opposing the Return of Tories 6/10/83
Van Pelt, Jacob   Middletown
Private, Militia
Signer, Articles of Retaliation, 6/79
present at the capture of the British ship, Britannia, 12/31/79
Van Pelt, Johannes
Private, Militia
present at the capture of the British ship, Britannia, 12/31/79
Van Pelt, John   Middletown
Van Pelt, Peter   Middletown
Private, Militia
Van Pelt, Sanders   Middletown
Signer, Petition Opposing the Return of Tories 6/10/83
Van Pelt, Thomas   Middletown
Signer, Petition Opposing the Return of Tories 6/10/83
Van Pelt, Tunis   Middletown
Private, Militia, captured 2/13/77
Signer, Articles of Retaliation, 6/79
present at the capture of the British ship, Britannia, 12/31/79
Van Pelt, Walter   Middletown
Private, Militia
Private, State Troops, enlists 6/80
Signer, Articles of Retaliation, 6/79
present at the capture of the British ship, Britannia, 12/31/79
Signer, Petition Opposing the Return of Tories 6/10/83
Van Pelt, William   Middletown
Private, Militia
Private, State Troops
present at the capture of the British ship, Britannia, 12/31/79
Van Schoick, Benjamin   Upper Freehold
Private, Militia
Van Schoick, David   Shrewsbury
Signer, Petition for Stricter Militia Law, 5/31/79
Van Schoick, John   Freehold
Signer, Articles of Retaliation, 6/79
Van Schoick, John   Freehold

Van Schoick, Jonah
   Private, Militia
Van Schoick, Josiah   Upper Freehold
   Private, Militia
   Signer, Petition Supporting Retaliation, 1780
Van Schoick, Koert   Freehold
   Private, Militia
   Signer, Articles of Retaliation, 6/79
   present at the capture of the British ship, Britannia, 12/31/79
Van Schoick, Peter   Shrewsbury
Van Schoick, Robert   Upper Freehold
   Private, Militia
   Signer, Articles of Retaliation, 6/79
   Signer, Petition Supporting Retaliation, 9/17/80
Van Schoick, William   Freehold
   Signer, Petition for Settlement of Quartermaster Debts, 9/6/77
   Signer, Articles of Retaliation, 6/79
   Juror, Court of Oyer and Terminer, 8/79
      fined L30 for missing all or some of jury duty
   Juror, Court of Oyer and Terminer, 5/82
Van Sickles, see Sickles
Van Skoik, see Van Schoick
Van Teneyck, see Ten Eyck
Van Wickley, Simon
   sells produce to Continental Army, 5/80
Vanderbelt, Aaron   Freehold
   Signer, Petition Opposing Slave Manumission, 2/2/74
   Signer, Petition Against Loyalist Auction Commissioners, 3/24/79
   Signer, Petition for Renewing Guard at Toms River, 12/10/81
   Juror, Court of Oyer and Terminer, 11/82
   donates to Charity Fund for the Stevenson Family, 5/83
   Signer, Petition Opposing the Return of Tories 6/10/83
Vanderbelt, Amos
   witness at Monmouth Court, 1778
Vanderbelt, Aurt   Middletown
Vanderbelt, Cornelius   Freehold
Vanderbelt, Cornelius   Middletown
   Overseer of Highways, 1779
   Signer, Petition Opposing the Return of Tories 6/10/83
Vanderbelt, Hendrick   Freehold
   Sergeant, Militia
   Signer, Articles of Retaliation, 6/79

present at the capture of the British ship, Britannia, 12/31/79
   Signer, Association for Opposing the Return of Tories, 1783
Vanderbelt, Jacob
   Private, Militia
   indicted for Misdemeanor, 8/79
Vanderbelt, John   Freehold
Vanderhall, Abraham
   Private, Militia
   Private, Continental Army
Vanderhall, Cornelius   Middletown
   Private, Militia
   Private, State Troops
   present at the capture of the British ship, Britannia, 12/31/79
   sells produce to Continental Army, 5/80
Vanderhoff, Cornelius   Freehold
   Private, Militia, captured 2/13/77
   Private, State Troops, enlists 6/80
   Signer, Articles of Retaliation, 6/79
   present at the capture of the British ship, Britannia, 12/31/79
Vanderhoff, John
   Private, Militia
Vanderhoff, Michael   Freehold
Vanderhoff, Peter   Middletown
   Ensign and Quartermaster, Militia
   Signer, Petition Against Loyalist Auction Commissioners, 3/24/79
   Signer, Petition Against Confiscation Commissioners, 5/8/79
   Signer, Articles of Retaliation, 6/79
   Signer, Petition Against Association for Retaliation 12/81
   leased horse team to Continental Quarter Master 12/81
Vanderhoff, Peter
   leased horse team to Continental Quarter Master 12/81
Vanderhoof, Vanderhuff *see* Vanderhoff
Vanderhoven, Peter
   indicted for Perjury, 1/81
   indicted for Misdemeanor, 11/81
Vanderhull, *see* Vanderhall *or* Vanderule
Vanderhule, *see* Vanderule
Vanderule, Abram
   Militia Volunteer, Prior to the First General Militia Muster, 6/76
   Private, Militia
   Sergeant, Continental Army, Jonathan Forman's Company, 10/77
Vanderule, Cornelius   Middletown

Signer, Petition Opposing Slave Manumission, 2/2/74
Vanderule, Greshom
   Private, Militia, dies from wounds at Battle of Germantown, 10/77
Vanderule, Henry   Middletown
   Private, Militia
   Private, State Troops
   Signer, Petition Opposing Slave Manumission, 2/2/74
Vandervander, Christopher
   Laborer, Pennsylvania Salt Works, intermittent 8/76-6/77
Vandervander, Peter   Middletown
   Private, Militia
Vanderveer, Cornelius   Freehold
   Private, Militia
   sells produce to Continental Army, 5/80
Vanderveer, Cornelius   Middletown
Vanderveer, Cornelius   Shrewsbury
   Member, Shrewsbury Committee of Observation
   Signer, Petition Favoring Quick Division of Prize Money, 12/79
   Grand Juror, Court of Oyer and Terminer, 5/82
Vanderveer, Cornelius, Jr.   Shrewsbury
   Private, Militia
Vanderveer, David   Shrewsbury and Freehold
   Signer, Petition Opposing Slave Manumission, 2/2/74
   sells clothing to Continental Army, 3/78
   Signer, Articles of Retaliation, 6/79
   Grand Juror, Court of Oyer and Terminer, 5/82
Vanderveer, Dominicus   Middletown
Vanderveer, Garret   Freehold
   house burned by British Army, 6/28/78
   Signer, Petition for Stricter Militia Law, 5/31/79
   Signer, Articles of Retaliation, 6/79
   Signer, Petition Supporting Retaliation, 9/17/80
   sells produce to Continental Army, 5/80
   Juror, Court of Oyer and Terminer, 11/82
Vanderveer, Hendrick   Shrewsbury
   Ensign, Militia
   Signer, Petition to Better Provision Militia, 2/25/78
   Signer, Petition for Stricter Militia Law, 5/31/79
   Signer, Articles of Retaliation, 6/79
   Signer, Petition Favoring Quick Division of Prize Money, 12/79
   sells produce to Continental Army, 5/80
Vanderveer, Jacob   Freehold

Signer, Articles of Retaliation, 6/79
Vanderveer, Isaac
   sells produce to Continental Army, 5/80
Vanderveer, John   Freehold
   Private, Militia
   Signer, Petition for Settlement of Quartermaster Debts, 9/6/77
   Coroner, 1778
   sells produce to Continental Army, 5/80
   Signer, Petition Encouraging Free Trade, 5/12/81
   Signer, Articles of Retaliation, 6/79
   Coroner, 1782
   Juror, Court of Oyer and Terminer, 5/82
      fined for missing jury duty
   Grand Juror, Court of Oyer and Terminer, 11/82
   Grand Juror, Court of Oyer and Terminer, 7/83
   lost slaves during the war
Vanderveer, Joseph   Middletown
   Private, Militia
   Signer, Articles of Retaliation, 6/79
   present at the capture of the British ship, Britannia, 12/31/79
   Signer, Petition Opposing the Return of Tories 6/10/83
Vanderveer, Peter
   indicted for Misdemeanor, 11/81
Vanderveer, Tunis   Middletown
   Lieutenant, Militia, delinquent 6/11/80
   Signer, Petition Favoring Quick Division of Prize Money, 12/79
   present at the capture of the British ship, Britannia, 12/31/79
   Grand Juror, Court of Oyer and Terminer, 12/80
   Grand Juror, Court of Oyer and Terminer, 11/82
   Signer, Petition Supporting Quick Division of Militia Prizes, no date
Vanderveer, Tunis   Freehold
   Sergeant, Militia
   Private, State Troops, enlists 6/80
   Signer, Articles of Retaliation, 6/79
   sells produce to Continental Army, 5/80
Vanderveer, Tunis
   witness at Monmouth Court, 1778
   Signer, Petition for Stricter Militia Law, 5/31/79
   Signer, Articles of Retaliation, 6/79
   Grand Juror, Court of Oyer and Terminer, 8/79
   Signer, Petition Favoring Quick Division of Prize Money, 12/79
   Signer, Petition Supporting Retaliation, 1780

sells produce to Continental Army, 5/80
  Signer, Petition for Renewing Guard at Toms River, 12/10/81
  Juror, Court of Oyer and Terminer, 11/82
  Signer, Association for Opposing the Return of Tories, 1783
Vanderveer, Tunis, Jr.   Freehold
  Private, Militia, captured 2/13/77
  Private, State Troops, enlists 6/80
  Signer, Articles of Retaliation, 6/79
  Signer, Petition Favoring Quick Division of Prize Money, 12/79
Vanderventer, see Vandervander
Vandervoort, Ann   Middletown
  household head
Vantwicke, John
  Private, Militia
  Private, Continental Army
Vantwicke, Joseph
  Private, Militia
  Private, Continental Army
Vargisson, William   Dover
Varrick, see Warrick
Vaughan, Francis   Upper Freehold
Vaughan, Isaac   Upper Freehold
  Militia Volunteer, Prior to the First General Militia Muster, 6/76
Vaughan, James   Upper Freehold
  Plundered by Tories, 12/76
Vaughan, John   Upper Freehold
  Private, Militia
Vaughan, John   Upper Freehold
  Militia Volunteer, Prior to the First General Militia Muster, 6/76
  Signer, Petition Against Association for Retaliation 12/81
  Juror, Court of Oyer and Terminer, 5/82
    fined for missing jury duty
Vaughan, Micajah   Upper Freehold
  Private, Militia
Vaughan, Robert   Upper Freehold
  Private, Militia
Vaughan, Samuel   Upper Freehold
  Private, Militia
Vinson, Oliver   Freehold
  runaway slave
  Private, Black Brigade
Vorhees, Garret   Freehold

Signer, Articles of Retaliation, 6/79
Vorhees, Hendrick (Henry) Freehold
Militia Volunteer, Prior to the First General Militia Muster, 6/76
Private, Militia
Private, Continental Army
Signer, Petition for Stricter Militia Law, 5/31/79
Signer, Articles of Retaliation, 6/79
Signer, Petition Encouraging Free Trade, 5/12/81
leased horse team to Continental Quarter Master 12/81
Signer, Petition for Renewing Guard at Toms River, 12/10/81
Vorhees, Jacques
Private, Militia
Vorhees, James
sells produce to Continental Army, 5/80
indicted for Misdemeanor, 11/82
Vorhees, Lucas
Private, Militia
Vorhees, Tunis Freehold
Private, Militia
Signer, Articles of Retaliation, 6/79
present at the capture of the British ship, Britannia, 12/31/79
Vorhees, William Freehold
Militia Volunteer, Prior to the First General Militia Muster, 6/76
Private, Militia
Signer, Articles of Retaliation, 6/79
Vought, John Shrewsbury
Lieutenant, New Jersey Volunteers, 12/76
Captain, New Jersey Volunteers, 7/78
Vunck, Hendrick Freehold
Signer, Articles of Retaliation, 6/79
Vunck, Henry
Corporal, Militia, captured 2/13/77
Vunck, Peter Freehold
Signer, Articles of Retaliation, 6/79

W

Waddell, Waddle, *see* Wardell
Waddington, John
Sergeant, New Jersey Volunteers
Wade, Humphrey
convicted of Horse Stealing, 1/81

Wainwright, Daniel   Freehold and Shrewsbury
    indicted for Murder, 5/82
    Constable, 1779
Wainwright, Daniel, Jr.   Shrewsbury
Wainwright, Elizabeth   Shrewsbury
    helps keep the poor
Wainwright, John   Shrewsbury
    son of Vincent
    Private, Militia
    Private, State Troops
    indicted for Misdemeanor, 1/81
    indicted for Misdemeanor, 11/81
Wainwright, Joseph   Shrewsbury
    helps keep the poor
Wainwright, Thomas   Shrewsbury
    Captain, Militia
    helps keep the poor
    Signer, Petition Opposing Slave Manumission, 2/2/74
    Signer, Petition Urging Action Against the Disaffected, 3/14/77
    Signer, Petition to Better Provision Militia, 2/25/78
    Signer, Petition Favoring Quick Division of Prize Money, 12/79
    Signer, Petition for Renewing Guard at Toms River, 12/10/81
    leased horse team to Continental Quarter Master 12/81
Wainwright, Vincent   Shrewsbury
    Private, Militia
    Signer, Petition Favoring Quick Division of Prize Money, 12/79
    sells produce to Continental Army, 5/80
    Signer, Petition for Renewing Guard at Toms River, 12/10/81
    leased horse team to Continental Quarter Master 12/81
Walker, Aaron
    Drummer, State Troops
Walker, Forman   Freehold
    Private, Militia
    Drummer, Militia
    sells produce to Continental Army, 5/80
Walker, George   Freehold
    Militia Volunteer, Prior to the First General Militia Muster, 6/76
    Private, Militia
    Laborer, Pennsylvania Salt Works, intermittent 8/76-6/77
    house burned by British Army, 6/28/78
    Signer, Petition for Stricter Militia Law, 5/31/79
    Signer, Petition Encouraging Free Trade, 5/12/81

Wall, Garret   Middletown
    Signer, Petition for Renewing Guard at Toms River, 12/10/81
    Chosen Freeholder, 1770-6
Wall, Humphrey   Middletown
    Overseer of the Poor, 1774
Wall, Humphrey   Upper Freehold
Wall, James   Freehold and Middletown
    Lieutenant, Militia
    Sergeant, State Troops
    Township Collector, 1772
    Signer, Petition Urging Action Against the Disaffected, 3/14/77
    Signer, Petition to Better Provision Militia, 2/25/78
    indicted for Misdemeanor, 6/78
    Signer, Petition for Stricter Militia Law, 5/31/79
    Signer, Petition Favoring Quick Division of Prize Money, 12/79
    sells produce to Continental Army, 5/80
    present at the capture of the British ship, Britannia, 12/31/79
    Signer, Petition Opposing the Return of Tories 6/10/83
Wall, John   Freehold
    Signer, Petition for Stricter Militia Law, 5/31/79
Wall, John   Middletown
    Baptist
    Overseer of the Poor, 1771-4
    Township Collector, 1773-4
    Signer, Petition Opposing Slave Manumission, 2/2/74
    Town Clerk, 1777-8
    Juror, Court of Oyer and Terminer, 12/80
       fined L3 for missing all or some of jury duty
    donates to Charity Fund for Stevenson Family, 5/83
    Signer, Petition Opposing the Return of Tories 6/10/83
Wall, John, Jr.   Middletown
    Signer, Petition Opposing Slave Manumission, 2/2/74
    Commissioner for Appeals, 1779-83
    Chosen Freeholder, 1779 and 1781
    Town Clerk, 1779-83
Walling, Benjamin
    Captain, Militia
Walling, Carhart   Middletown
    Private, Militia
    present at the capture of the British ship, Britannia, 12/31/79
    Constable, 1782
Walling, Daniel

Private, Militia
present at the capture of the British ship, Britannia, 12/31/79
Walling, Gershom Middletown
Signer, Petition Opposing Slave Manumission, 2/2/74
Constable, 1779
Walling, James Freehold
Lieutenant, Militia
Signer, Petition Against Confiscation Commissioners, 5/8/79
present at the capture of the British ship, Britannia, 12/31/79
donates to Charity Fund for Stevenson Family, 5/83
Walling, James Middletown
Baptist
Walling, James, Jr. Middletown
Private, Militia
Baptist
present at the capture of the British ship, Britannia, 12/31/79
Walling, John Middletown
Baptist
Overseer of Highways, 1773
Signer, Petition Opposing Slave Manumission, 2/2/74
Chosen Freeholder, 1780
Commissioner for Appeals, 1783
Walling, John, Jr. Middletown
Private, Militia
present at the capture of the British ship, Britannia, 12/31/79
indicted for Misdemeanor, 7/83
Walling, Joseph Middletown
Private, Militia
present at the capture of the British ship, Britannia, 12/31/79
Walling, Lewis
Captain, Militia
Walling, Philip
Private, Militia, wounded at Middletown, 6/21/81
present at the capture of the British ship, Britannia, 12/31/79
Signer, Association for Opposing the Return of Tories, 1783
Walling, Thomas Middletown
Captain, Militia
Signer, Petition Opposing Slave Manumission, 2/2/74
Signer, Articles of Retaliation, 6/79
Signer, Petition Favoring Quick Division of Prize Money, 12/79
present at the capture of the British ship, Britannia, 12/31/79
Signer, Petition for Renewing Guard at Toms River, 12/10/81

Chosen Freeholder, 1782
Juror, Court of Oyer and Terminer, 11/82
Walling, Thomas   Middletown
    Private, Militia
Walling, William   Middletown
    Private, Militia
    present at the capture of the British ship, Britannia, 12/31/79
    Signer, Petition Opposing the Return of Tories 6/10/83
Waln, James   Upper Freehold
    Under Sheriff [?], 1779
Waln, Richard   Upper Freehold
Walsh, see Welsh
Walton, Elisha   Freehold
    Major, Militia
    Delegate, New Jersey Legislature, Upper House, 1783
    Signer, Petition Urging Action Against the Disaffected, 3/14/77
    Signer, Petition to Better Provision Militia, 2/25/78
    Signer, Articles of Retaliation, 6/79
    Signer, Petition Favoring Quick Division of Prize Money, 12/79
    Signer, Petition in Favor of Daniel Longstreet, 11/21/80
    Signer, Petition Encouraging Free Trade, 5/12/81
    Signer, Petition for Renewing Guard at Toms River, 12/10/81
    Grand Juror, Court of Oyer and Terminer, 11/82
    Signer, Petition Supporting Quick Division of Militia Prizes, no date
Walton, James
    Private, Militia, hires substitute
Walton, John   Freehold
    Captain, Militia
    Captain, State Troops, 1780, 1782, dies 1782
    Signer, Petition Urging Action Against the Disaffected, 3/14/77
    Signer, Petition to Better Provision Militia, 2/25/78
    Signer, Articles of Retaliation, 6/79
    Signer, Petition Favoring Quick Division of Prize Money, 12/79
    present at the capture of the British ship, Britannia, 12/31/79
    sells produce to Continental Army, 5/80
    Signer, Petition Encouraging Free Trade, 5/12/81
    Signer, Petition for Renewing Guard at Toms River, 12/10/81
    Grand Juror, Court of Oyer and Terminer, 11/82
    Signer, Petition Supporting Quick Division of Militia Prizes, no date
Walton, Margaret   Freehold
    wife of Captain John Walton
        signs troop return for his company after his death

Walton, William — Shrewsbury
    household head, 1782
    estate inquisitioned for Forfeiture, 3/30/79
    estate confiscated
Walton, William — Upper Freehold
    Sergeant, Militia
    Signer, Petition Against Association for Retaliation 12/81
Wamsley, Sarah — Middletown
    household head
Ward, John — Shrewsbury
    Private, New Jersey Volunteers
    estate confiscated
Ward, William
    Private, Militia
    Private, State Troops
Wardell, Cornelius
    Private, New Jersey Volunteers
Wardell, Daniel — Shrewsbury
    Delegate, Friends' Quarterly Meeting, 1782
Wardell, Ebenezer — Shrewsbury
    Captain, New Jersey Volunteers
    estate inquisitioned for Forfeiture, 10/5/77
    estate confiscated
Wardell, Elizabeth — Shrewsbury
    wife of Ebenezer
    indicted for Misdemeanor, 8/79
    convicted of Misdemeanor, 12/80
Wardell, Hannah — Shrewsbury
    Delegate, Friends' Quarterly Meeting, 1774-81
    listed on Militia return 6/29/80
Wardell, Henry — Shrewsbury
    Minister
    Captain of Militia, Prior to the First General Militia Muster, 6/76
    Captain, Militia, resigns 7/2/76
    joins British Army at Trenton, 12/76
    arrest warrant issued for his capture, 1777
Wardell, Jacob — Shrewsbury
    of Long Branch
    arrested for spying, 1776
    arrested for Seditious Words, 1/20/78
Wardell, Jacob — Shrewsbury
    son of Joseph

Roster of the People of Revolutionary Monmouth County

    Private, New Jersey Volunteers
    indicted for Misdemeanor, 11/81
Wardell, James   Shrewsbury
    of Snag Swamp
    Private, Militia
    indicted for Misdemeanor and Seditious Words, 5/82
Wardell, John   Shrewsbury
    of Long Branch
    Judge, Royal Court of Common Pleas
    Vestryman, Anglican Christ Church, 1770-6
    arrested for disaffection, 11/76
    estate inquisitioned for Forfeiture, 3/31/79
    indicted for Seditious Words, 1/81
    Signer, Petition from Victims of the Association for Retaliation 9/82
Wardell, John   Shrewsbury
    Private, Militia
Wardell, Joseph   Shrewsbury
    of Long Branch
    blacksmith
    arrested for disaffection, 1776
    indicted for Misdemeanor, 8/79
    estate confiscated
Wardell, Joseph, Jr.   Shrewsbury
    of Rumson
    Delegate, Friends' Quarterly Meeting, 1775-82
    convicted of Misdemeanor, 6/3/78
    indicted for Misdemeanor, 8/79
    indicted for Misdemeanor, 1/81
Wardell, Joseph   Shrewsbury
    of Snag Swamp
    indicted for Misdemeanor, 1/81
Wardell, Mary   Shrewsbury
    of Long Branch
    household head
Wardell, Meribah   Shrewsbury
    Delegate, Friends' Quarterly Meeting, 1778, 1780, 1782
Wardell, Michael
    Private, New Jersey Volunteers
Wardell, Nathan
    Private, New Jersey Volunteers
Wardell, Peter   Shrewsbury
    of Long Branch

    indicted for Misdemeanor, 8/79
    indicted for Misdemeanor, 1/81
    indicted for Misdemeanor, 11/81
    indicted for Misdemeanor, 11/82
    estate confiscated
Wardell, Samuel   Shrewsbury
Wardell, Sarah   Shrewsbury
    indicted for Seditious Words, 1/81
Wardell, Solomon   Shrewsbury
    convicted of Misdemeanor, 12/80
Wardell, Stephen
    indicted for Misdemeanor, 1/81
Wardell, Thomas
    Captain, Militia
Wardell, William   Shrewsbury
    accused of being active in Loyalist Rebellion of 12/76
    indicted for Misdemeanor, 5/82
    indicted for Misdemeanor and Seditious Words, 11/82
    estate confiscated
Warell, see Wardell or Worell
Warden, Daniel   Freehold
Warden, John   Shrewsbury
    Militia Volunteer, Prior to the First General Militia Muster, 6/76
    arrested for Disaffection, 11/76
    accused of being active in Tory Rebellions of 12/76
    indicted for Misdemeanor, 7/83
Warden, Joshua   Dover
Warden, William
    Private, New Jersey Volunteers, enlisted 7/2/77 deserted 9/24/78
Warne, George   Middletown
    Private, Militia
Warne, Godfrey
    Signer, Articles of Retaliation, 6/79
Warne, John   Upper Freehold
Warner, see Warne
Warren, James   Upper Freehold
Warrick, Matthew   Upper Freehold
    Signer, Petition in Favor of Daniel Longstreet, 11/21/80
Warwick, John   Upper Freehold
Warwick, John, Jr.   Upper Freehold
    Private, Militia
Watson, James

substitute, Militia, 2/78, 3/78
Watson, John   Shrewsbury
   Private, Militia, delinquent 8/80
Watson, Joshua
   Private, New Jersey Volunteers, deserted 10/17/77
Watson, William   Upper Freehold
   Private, Militia, drafted into Continental Army 5/78
   Private, Continental Army
Weatherall, John   Upper Freehold
   Militia Volunteer, Prior to the First General Militia Muster, 6/76
   sells produce to Continental Army, 5/80
   indicted for Misdemeanor, 1/81
Weatherby, Benjamin
   Captain, Continental Army
Weatherby, Bennett
   indicted for Misdemeanor, 1/81
Weatherby, Henry   Shrewsbury
   accused of being part of Samuel Wright's Tory Association 11/76
   arrested for Disaffection, 11/76
   accused of being active in Tory Rebellions of 12/76
   flees to Sandy Hook, 1777
Weatherby, Matthew
   Private, New Jersey Volunteers, captured 8/22/77
Weatherby, William   Shrewsbury
   arrested for Disaffection, 10/76
   accused of being part of Samuel Wright's Tory Association 11/76
Weatherhill, *see* Weatherall
Webb, John   Upper Freehold
   Laborer, Pennsylvania Salt Works, intermittent 8/76-6/77
   indicted for Misdemeanor, 11/81
Webb, Joseph   Upper Freehold
Webb, Thomas
   Private, State Troops, enlists 4/81
Webster, Hugh   Shrewsbury
   Delegate, Friends' Quarterly Meeting, 1775

Webster, John   Shrewsbury
   Delegate, Friends' Quarterly Meeting, 1775
Webster, Richard
   indicted for Misdemeanor, 7/83
Weed, John
   Private, New Jersey Volunteers, captured prior to 1779

Weeks, Arthur — Upper Freehold
  Private, Militia
Weeks, Nathan — Upper Freehold
Weer, *see* Weir
Weir, Timothy — Shrewsbury
Wells, Carvil
  Private, New Jersey Volunteers, enlisted 12/19/76 deserts 2/13/77
Wells, Elizabeth — Freehold
  household head
Welsh, Aaron
  Signer, Articles of Retaliation, 6/79
Welsh, Valentine — Freehold
  Private, State Troops, enlisted 6/80
Welsh, William — Upper Freehold
Wescott, Richard
  Laborer, Pennsylvania Salt Works, intermittent 8/76-6/77
West, Arthur — Shrewsbury
West, Asher
  Vestryman, Anglican Christ Church, 1778-82
  sells produce to Continental Army, 5/80
  Signer, Petition for Renewing Guard at Toms River, 12/10/81
West, Daniel — Shrewsbury
  Private, Militia
West, Jacob — Freehold
  arrested on two counts of Riot, 1/20/78
  sells produce to Continental Army, 5/80
West, James — Shrewsbury
  Private, Militia
  Vestryman, Anglican Christ Church, 1778-82
  indicted for Misdemeanor, 6/78
  sells produce to Continental Army, 5/80
  lost slaves during the war
West, John — Upper Freehold
  Private, State Troops, enlisted 6/80
West, John — Middletown
  Laborer, Pennsylvania Salt Works, intermittent 8/76-6/77
West, John — Shrewsbury
  son of James
  holds tavern license, 1775
  Private, Militia
  indicted for Misdemeanor, 8/79
West, Jonathan

    Pine Robber, killed
West, Joseph   Shrewsbury
    of Fresh Pond
    helps keep the poor
    Private, Militia, delinquent, 8/17/80
West, Joseph   Shrewsbury
    of Long Branch
    Private, Militia
West, Josiah   Freehold
    Signer, Petition Against Loyalist Auction Commissioners, 3/24/79
    Signer, Articles of Retaliation, 6/79
West, Josiah   Middletown
    Private, Militia, captured 2/13/77
    donates to Charity fund for Stevenson family, 5/83
    Signer, Petition Opposing the Return of Tories 6/10/83
West, Lydia   Shrewsbury
    household head
West, Obriah   Shrewsbury
    indicted for Misdemeanor, 12/80
West, Rebecca   Shrewsbury
    household head
West, Samuel   Shrewsbury
    Vestryman, Anglican Christ Church, 1783
West, Stephen   Shrewsbury
    Militia Volunteer, Prior to the First General Militia Muster, 6/76
    Private, Militia
    indicted for two counts of Riot & Trespass, 6/3/78
    Pine Robber, killed 1778
West, Thomas   Freehold
    Signer, Articles of Retaliation, 6/79
West, Thomas   Shrewsbury
    helps keep the poor
    Private, Militia
West, Uriah   Shrewsbury
    helps keep the poor
    indicted for High Treason, 6/3/78
    Private, Militia, delinquent 8/17/80
West, Walter
    convicted of Misdemeanor, 1/81
    indicted for Misdemeanor, 11/82
West, William   Freehold
    indicted for Misdemeanor and Contraband Trading, 1/81

West, William	Upper Freehold
Wetherall, see Weatherall
Wetherby, see Weatherby
Weymouth, Peter
    sells produce to Continental Army, 5/80
Wheaton, Peter
    Private, Continental Army, Jonathan Forman's Company, 10/77
White, Amos	Shrewsbury
    exempt from Militia service, 2/10/78
    sells produce to Continental Army, 5/80
White, Benjamin	Shrewsbury
White, Briton	Shrewsbury
    helps keep the poor
    Refugee in New York, 1782
    estate inquisitioned for Forfeiture, 6/1/78
    estate confiscated
White, Dinah	Shrewsbury
    household head
    Delegate, Friends' Quarterly Meeting, 1775, 1777
White, Francis	Shrewsbury
White, George	Shrewsbury
    Private, Militia
White, Hannah	Shrewsbury
    widow
    recipient of poor relief
White, Henry	Shrewsbury
    Private, New Jersey Volunteers, deserted 6/29/77
    indicted for Trespass, 1/78
White, Henry	Shrewsbury
    Private, Militia
    Signer, Petition Favoring Quick Division of Prize Money, 12/79
    Signer, Petition Encouraging Free Trade, 5/12/81
    Signer, Petition Supporting Retaliation, 9/17/80
White, Jacob	Shrewsbury
    sells produce to Continental Army, 5/80
White, James
    Private, New Jersey Volunteers
White, Jane	Shrewsbury
    household head
White, John	Shrewsbury
    weaver
    Private, Militia

indicted for Misdemeanor, 11/82
White, John						Shrewsbury
    convicted of Misdemeanor, 6/3/78
    indicted for High Treason, 1/81
White, John						Shrewsbury
    of Rumson
    indicted for High Treason, 11/82
White, Jonathan					Shrewsbury
    Delegate, Friends' Quarterly Meeting, 1777-83
White, Joseph, Jr.				Shrewsbury
    Private, Militia
    indicted for Contraband Trading, 1/81
White, Joseph					Shrewsbury
    Private, Militia, delinquent 8/9/80
    indicted for Misdemeanor, 1/81
White, Josiah
    Corporal, New Jersey Volunteers
    indicted for Misdemeanor, 8/79
    estate confiscated
White, Levi						Shrewsbury
    Private, Militia
White, Lewis					Shrewsbury
    Private, Militia, delinquent 8/17/80
White, Lydia					Shrewsbury
    recipient of poor relief
White, Mary						Shrewsbury
    household head
White, Michael			Shrewsbury
    indicted for Misdemeanor, 8/79
    indicted for Misdemeanor, 1/81
White, Peter					Shrewsbury
    Private, Militia
White, Peter					Shrewsbury
    Delegate, Friends' Quarterly Meeting, 1782-3
White, Peter, Jr.				Shrewsbury
White, Philip					Shrewsbury
    Private, Militia
White, Philip					Shrewsbury
    convicted of Misdemeanor, 6/3/78
    refugee, killed 3/82
White, Rachel					Shrewsbury
    household head

White, Robert   Shrewsbury
    mason
White, Robert   Shrewsbury
    carpenter
    Delegate, Friends' Quarterly Meeting, 1783
White, Samuel   Shrewsbury
White, Sarah
    daughter of Amos
    indicted for Misdemeanor, 8/79
White, Thomas   Shrewsbury
    son of John
    of Shark River
    Laborer, Pennsylvania Salt Works, intermittent 8/76-6/77
    Corporal, New Jersey Volunteers
    indicted for Misdemeanor, 8/79
    indicted for Misdemeanor, 5/82
    indicted for Misdemeanor, 11/82
White, Thomas   Shrewsbury
    son of Peter
    of Rumson
    holds tavern license, 1775
    indicted for Misdemeanor, 11/81
    Signer, Petition from Victims of the Association for Retaliation 9/82
White, Thomas, Jr.   Shrewsbury
    shoemaker
    sells shoes to Continental Army, 5/80
    indicted for Misdemeanor, 11/82
White, Thomas   Shrewsbury
    son of Levi
    Private, Militia
White, Vincent (Vinson)
    Private, New Jersey Volunteers
White, William   Dover
    Militia Volunteer, Prior to the First General Militia Muster, 6/76
    Private, New Jersey Volunteers
    Refugee in New York, 1782
White, William
    Private, Militia
White, William
    Private, New Jersey Volunteers, dead 10/16/77
White, Zephaniah   Middletown
    Signer, Petition Opposing the Return of Tories 6/10/83

Whitehall, Jacob
   Private, Continental Army, Jonathan Forman's Company, 10/77
Whitlock, Ephraim
   Lieutenant, Cont. Army, Jonathan Forman's Company, 10/77
Whitlock, James
   Major, Militia, captured 6/79 exchanged 12/22/80
Whitlock, James
   Ensign, Militia, captured 2/13/77 at Navesink, paroled 8/78
   present at the capture of the British ship, Britannia, 12/31/79
Whitlock, James, Jr.
   Private, Militia, captured 2/13/77
Whitlock, Mary   Middletown
   household head
Whitney, Joseph
   Private, New Jersey Volunteers, captured 8/22/77
Whitney, Joshua
   Private, New Jersey Volunteers, captured 8/22/77
Whitsell, Andrew
   Private, New Jersey Volunteers
Whitsell, John
   Private, New Jersey Volunteers, captured 8/22/77
Wickson, Isaiah   Dover
   Militia Volunteer, Prior to the First General Militia Muster, 6/76
Wickson, Josiah   Dover
   Signer, Petition to Better Defend Toms River Area, 5/18/77
Wikoff, Aucke   Shrewsbury
   Lt. Colonel, Militia, captured
   holds tavern license, 1775
   Signer, Petition Calling for Action Against the Disaffected, 2/21/77
   Signer, Petition Urging Action Against the Disaffected, 3/14/77
   Signer, Petition to Better Provision Militia, 2/25/78
   captured again, paroled to Long Island, 8/78
   rented Confiscated Tory estate, prior to 5/79
Wikoff, Garret   Freehold
   Private, Militia, captured 2/13/77
   Signer, Articles of Retaliation, 6/79
   Signer, Petition Supporting Retaliation, 9/17/80
   Signer, Petition in Favor of Daniel Longstreet, 11/21/80
   Signer, Petition Urging Compensation for Inflated Money, 5/22/83
Wikoff, Isaac
   sells produce to Continental Army, 5/80
Wikoff, Jacob   Freehold

Roster of the People of Revolutionary Monmouth County

Wikoff, Jacob   Middletown
   Private, Militia
   Signer, Petition Opposing Slave Manumission, 2/2/74
   Signer, Petition for Settlement of Quartermaster Debts, 9/6/77
   sells produce to Continental Army, 5/80
   Signer, Petition Encouraging Free Trade, 5/12/81
   Signer, Petition for Stricter Militia Law, 5/31/79
   Signer, Articles of Retaliation, 6/79
   Juror, Court of Oyer and Terminer, 11/82
Wikoff, Patience   Freehold
   household head
   Signer, Petition for Settlement of Quartermaster Debts, 9/6/77
Wikoff, Peter   Upper Freehold
   sells goods to Pennsylvania Salt Works, 8/76-10/76
   Captain, Militia
   Signer, Petition Urging Action Against the Disaffected, 3/14/77
   Signer, Petition to Better Provision Militia, 2/25/78
   Signer, Petition Urging Action Against Disaffected
      & Favoring Retaliation, 5/12/81, opposes Retaliation Clause
   Signer, Petition for Renewing Guard at Toms River, 12/10/81
   Juror, Court of Oyer and Terminer, 11/82
   Grand Juror, Court of Oyer and Terminer, 7/83
   Signer, Association for Opposing the Return of Tories, 1783
Wikoff, Samuel   Upper Freehold
   Private, Militia
   Juror, Court of Oyer and Terminer, 11/82
   Grand Juror, Court of Oyer and Terminer, 7/83
Wikoff, Sarah
   sells produce to Continental Army, 5/80
Wikoff, William   Freehold
   Private, Militia
   indicted for Trespass, 1/78
   Signer, Articles of Retaliation, 6/79
   Signer, Association for Opposing the Return of Tories, 1783
   lost slaves during the war
Wikoff, William   Freehold
   Corporal of Militia, Prior to the First General Militia Muster, 6/76
Wilber, *see* Wilbur
Wilbur, Edward   Dover
   Militia Volunteer, Prior to the First General Militia Muster, 6/76
   sells goods to Pennsylvania Salt Works, 8/76-10/76
   Signer, Petition to Better Defend Toms River Area, 5/18/77

Constable, 1778-80, misses Court due to illness, 1778
    fined L140 for missing Court of Oyer and Terminer, 1780
Wilbur, John
    Laborer, Pennsylvania Salt Works, intermittent 8/76-6/77
    Private, Militia
    Private, State Troops
Wilbur, Margaret
    sells goods to Pennsylvania Salt Works, 8/76-10/76
Wilbur, Mary
    sells goods to Pennsylvania Salt Works, 8/76-10/76
Wilbur, William   Dover
    Militia Volunteer, Prior to the First General Militia Muster, 6/76
    Private, Militia
    Signer, Articles of Retaliation, 6/79
    indicted for Misdemeanor, 11/81
Wilcox, William   Freehold
Wiley, John
    Private, Militia
    Private, Continental Army
Wilgus, John   Upper Freehold
Wilgus, Richard   Upper Freehold
    Militia Volunteer, Prior to the First General Militia Muster, 6/76
Wilgus, William   Upper Freehold
    witness at Monmouth Court, 1778
    Private, Militia
    Constable, 1782-3
Wilkinson, James
    Private, Militia
Wilkinson, John   Upper Freehold
    Plundered by Tories, 12/76
    Signer, Articles of Retaliation, 6/79
    Signer, Association for Opposing the Return of Tories, 1783
Wilkinson, Peter   Upper Freehold
Willets, see Willett
Willett, Ann   Middletown
    household head
Willett, Humphrey   Middletown
    Private, Militia
    Signer, Articles of Retaliation, 6/79
    present at the capture of the British ship, Britannia, 12/31/79
Willett, John   Middletown
    Sergeant, Militia

Signer, Petition Opposing Slave Manumission, 2/2/74
Signer, Articles of Retaliation, 6/79
indicted for Misdemeanor, 11/81
Signer, Petition Opposing the Return of Tories 6/10/83
Willett, John, Jr.   Middletown
   Signer, Petition Opposing the Return of Tories 6/10/83
Willett, Joseph   Middletown
   Private, Militia
   Signer, Articles of Retaliation, 6/79
   present at the capture of the British ship, Britannia, 12/31/79
   Signer, Petition Opposing the Return of Tories 6/10/83
Willett, Mary   Middletown
   household head
Willett, Peter
   sells produce to Continental Army, 5/80
Willett, Thomas   Middletown
   Overseer of the Poor, 1770
   indicted for Misdemeanor, 8/79
   estate inquisitioned for Forfeiture, 7/2/77
   estate confiscated
Willett, Valentine
   Private, Militia
Willetts, *see* Willett
Williams, Ann   Shrewsbury
   Delegate, Friends' Quarterly Meeting, 1778-82
   listed on Militia return 6/29/80
Williams, Chiles   Dover
Williams, Daniel   Shrewsbury
   Private, Militia
   Laborer, Pennsylvania Salt Works, intermittent 8/76-6/77
   arrested while attempting to flee to Sandy Hook, 1777
   Sergeant, New Jersey Volunteers
   indicted for Misdemeanor, 11/82
Williams, Deborah   Shrewsbury
   listed on Militia return 6/29/80
Williams, Edmund   Middletown
Williams, Edmund   Shrewsbury
   Delegate, Friends' Quarterly Meeting, 1776-83
   arrested 1777, escapes
   sells produce to Continental Army, 5/80
   Private, Militia, delinquent 8/9/80
Williams, Elihu   Shrewsbury

Delegate, Friends' Quarterly Meeting, 1775-81
Williams, Elizabeth   Shrewsbury
    Delegate, Friends' Quarterly Meeting, 1774-82
Williams, Ezekiel   Shrewsbury
    Laborer, Pennsylvania Salt Works, intermittent 8/76-6/77
    Private, New Jersey Volunteers, enlisted 1/1/77
        discharged 11/14/78
    Pine Robber, killed 1779
Williams, George   Shrewsbury
    indicted for Misdemeanor, 8/79
    convicted of Perjury and Misdemeanor, 12/80
Williams, Giles   Shrewsbury
    flees to New York, 1777
Williams, Hannah
    witness at Monmouth Court, 1778
Williams, Henry
    Private, New Jersey Volunteers
Williams, Humphrey   Shrewsbury
Williams, James   Shrewsbury
    Private, Militia
    Delegate, Friends' Quarterly Meeting, 1775
    indicted for Misdemeanor, 1/81
Williams, John, Sr.   Shrewsbury
    Captain, New Jersey Volunteers
    estate inquisitioned for Forfeiture, 7/2/77
    estate confiscated
Williams, John   Shrewsbury
    son of Joseph
    arrested for Disaffection 11/76 and 1777
    indicted for two counts of Riot, 6/78
    killed on his farm
Williams, John   Upper Freehold
    Accused of Being Active in Tory Uprising of 12/76
    arrest warrant issued for his capture, 1777
    Private, New Jersey Volunteers, captured prior to 1779
Williams, John   Shrewsbury
    Corporal, New Jersey Volunteers
Williams, John, Jr.   Shrewsbury
    accused of being active in Tory Rebellions of 12/76
    indicted for Riot and Trespass, 6/3/78
    estate inquisitioned for Forfeiture, 3/31/79
    estate confiscated

Williams, Joseph   Shrewsbury
    Private, New Jersey Volunteers, enlisted 12/26/76   dead 4/30/77
Williams, Joseph   Shrewsbury
    Private, New Jersey Volunteers
    Private (?), Associated Loyalists
    indicted for Horse Stealing, 1/81
    Convicted of High Treason, 4/25/82
    indicted of Murder, 5/82
    estate confiscated when his wife dies, 1783
Williams, Obadiah   Shrewsbury
    Private, Militia, delinquent 8/9/80
    indicted for Misdemeanor, 1/81
Williams, Obadiah   Shrewsbury
    arrested, dies in jail at Freehold
Williams, Obadiah   Shrewsbury
    estate confiscated, 1782
Williams, Samuel   Middletown
Williams, William   Upper Freehold
    Militia Volunteer, Prior to the First General Militia Muster, 6/76
    indicted for Misdemeanor, 6/3/78
    indicted for Misdemeanor, 8/79
Williams, William   Upper Freehold
Williamson, Albert   Middletown
Williamson, Arthur   Freehold
    Private, Militia
    sells produce to Continental Army, 5/80
    Signer, Association for Opposing the Return of Tories, 1783
Williamson, David
    sells produce to Continental Army, 5/80
Williamson, Elbert   Freehold
Williamson, Hannah   Shrewsbury
Williamson, Hendrick   Freehold
    Private, Militia, captured 2/13/77
    Signer, Articles of Retaliation, 6/79
Williamson, John   Middletown
Williamson, Tunis
    Refugee, in New York 1782
Williamson, William   Freehold
    Private, Militia
Williamson, William   Freehold
    sells clothing to Continental Army, 3/78
    Signer, Association for Opposing the Return of Tories, 1783

Willin, Henry
    Private, Militia
    Private, Continental Army
Willis, Micajah
    indicted for Misdemeanor, 1/81
Willis, Richard
    indicted for Misdemeanor, 1/81
    indicted for Misdemeanor, 5/82
Willis, Robert   Shrewsbury
    Delegate, Friends' Quarterly Meeting, 1774-5
Willocks, Lydia   Freehold
    household head
Willocks, Thomas   Freehold
Willocks, William
    Signer, Articles of Retaliation, 6/79
    sells produce to Continental Army, 5/80
    Signer, Petition for Renewing Guard at Toms River, 12/10/81
Willox, *see* Willocks
Wilson, Alexander   Upper Freehold
    Militia Volunteer, Prior to the First General Militia Muster, 6/76
Wilson, Andrew   Middletown
    Private, Militia
    indicted for Misdemeanor, 6/3/78
Wilson, Andrew   Upper Freehold
    Private, Militia
    Corporal, Continental Army, Jonathan Forman's Company, 10/77
    Signer, Association for Opposing the Return of Tories, 1783
Wilson, Benjamin   Middletown
    Private, Militia
    arrested for Disaffection, 11/76
    accused of being active in Tory Rebellions of 12/76
    present at the capture of the British ship, Britannia, 12/31/79
    indicted for Misdemeanor, 11/81
    indicted for Misdemeanor, 5/82
    indicted for Assault, 7/83
Wilson, Daniel   Upper Freehold
    Private, Militia
    sells goods to Pennsylvania Salt Works, 8/76-10/76
    indicted for Misdemeanor, 5/82
Wilson, Esther
    wife of Andrew
    indicted for Seditious Words, 6/78

indicted for Misdemeanor, 11/81
indicted for Misdemeanor, 5/82
Wilson, George   Shrewsbury
    exempt from Militia service, 2/10/78
Wilson, Jacob   Middletown
    Private, New Jersey Volunteers
    Private, Militia
    Signer, Petition Opposing the Return of Tories 6/10/83
Wilson, James   Freehold
    Constable, 1778
    Signer, Petition Urging Compensation for Raid Victims, 5/25/79
    Signer, Petition for Stricter Militia Law, 5/31/79
    Signer, Petition Favoring Quick Division of Prize Money, 12/79
    sells produce to Continental Army, 5/80
    Grand Juror, Court of Oyer and Terminer, 12/80
    Grand Juror, Court of Oyer and Terminer, 5/82
    Juror, Court of Oyer and Terminer, 11/82
    Grand Juror, Court of Oyer and Terminer, 7/83
Wilson, James   Freehold
    Private, Militia
    Private, State Troops
Wilson, James   Middletown
    indicted for Misdemeanor, 11/81
    indicted for Contraband Trading, Seditious Words, Petty Larceny,
        and Boarding an Enemy Vessel -- all 5/82
Wilson, John   Middletown
    Private, Militia
Wilson, Joseph   Middletown
    Private, New Jersey Volunteers
Wilson, Joseph   Upper Freehold
    Private, Militia
    sells produce to Continental Army, 5/80
Wilson, Peter   Freehold
    Private, Militia, hires substitute, 2/10/78, delinquent 3/11/78
Wilson, Richard
    flees to New York, 1777
Wilson, Robert
    Private, New Jersey Volunteers
    sells produce to Continental Army, 5/80
Wilson, Roger
    Private, New Jersey Volunteers, captured 6/26/78
Wilson, Sarah

wife of Benjamin
indicted for Misdemeanor, 1/81
Wilson, William   Freehold
Private, Militia, delinquent 2/10/78
Laborer, Pennsylvania Salt Works, intermittent 8/76-6/77
Signer, Petition Supporting Quick Division of Militia Prizes, no date
Wing, John   Freehold
Winant, Winnant, Winnants, *see* Wynnant
Winnerite, Joseph   Dover
Winter, James   Dover
Militia Volunteer, Prior to the First General Militia Muster, 6/76
Private, Militia, captured 2/13/77, dies in prison in New York 3/4/77
Winter, Joseph   Dover
Private, Militia, drafted into Continental Army 5/78
Winter, Joseph, Jr.   Dover
Laborer, Pennsylvania Salt Works
Winter, Mary   Middletown
household head
Winter, Wilbur   Middletown
Constable, 1780
Witchell, Jacob
Private, Militia
Private, Continental Army
Witsel, *see* Whitsell
Wixson, *see* Wickson
Wolcott, *see* Woolcott
Wolfe, Matthew   Middletown
Private, Militia
Signer, Petition Opposing Slave Manumission, 2/2/74
indicted for Misdemeanor, 11/81
indicted for Misdemeanor, 5/82
Wolverston, Stephen
Signer, Petition Against Association for Retaliation 12/81
Wood, Aaron
Private, Continental Army
Wood, Benjamin
Private, Militia
Wood, George
Private, Militia
Wood, George
Private, New Jersey Volunteers, enlisted 12/15/76 dead 4/25/77
Wood, Jacob

Private, New Jersey Volunteers, captured prior to 1779
Wood, John
    convicted of Robbery, 6/3/78
    Pine Robber
Wood, Joseph   Upper Freehold
Wood, Mathias (Matthew)
    Private, Militia
    indicted for Misdemeanor, 5/82
    indicted for Misdemeanor, 11/82
Wood, Obadiah
    Private, New Jersey Volunteers
Wood, Stephen
    Private, New Jersey Volunteers, enlisted 12/16/76 dead 3/29/77
Woodcock, William
    indicted for Petty Larceny, 8/79
Woodhull, John   Freehold
    Minister, Tennent Church
    sells produce to Continental Army, 5/80
    Signer, Petition Supporting Retaliation, 9/17/80
Woodley, George
    Private, New Jersey Volunteers
Woodmancy, Asa   Dover
    Private, Militia
Woodmancy, David   Dover
    Private, Militia
    Township Town Clerk & Freeholder of Appeals, 1783
    indicted for Misdemeanor, 11/81
    indicted for Misdemeanor, 7/83
Woodmancy, David, Jr.   Shrewsbury
    indicted for Seditious Words, 1/20/78
    indicted for Misdemeanor, 11/81
    indicted for Misdemeanor, 7/83
Woodmancy, Gabriel   Dover
    indicted for Seditious Words, 6/78
    Township Assessor & Chosen Freeholder, 1783
Woodmancy, James   Dover
    Private, Militia
    Juror, Court of Oyer and Terminer, 1/78
        fined L5 for not attending all or part of Jury duty
    Township Collector, 1783
Woodmancy, John   Dover
    Juror, Court of Oyer and Terminer, 12/80

fined L3 for missing all or some of jury duty
Constable, 1783
Woodmancy, John, Jr.　　　Shrewsbury
　　indicted for Misdemeanor, 7/83
Woodmancy, Joseph　　　Upper Freehold
　　plundered by Tories, 12/76
Woodmancy, Samuel　　　Dover
　　Constable, 1782
Woodmancy, Thomas　　　Shrewsbury
　　Private, New Jersey Volunteers
　　indicted for Misdemeanor, 8/79
Woodmansee, see Woodmancy
Woodruff, Benjamin　　　Middletown
Woodson, Patrick
　　indicted for Misdemeanor, 6/78
Woodward, Abraham
　　sells produce to Continental Army, 5/80
Woodward, Anthony　　　Upper Freehold
　　Accused of Being Active in Tory Uprising of 12/76
Woodward, Anthony, Jr.　　　Upper Freehold
　　accused of being active in Loyalist Rebellion of 12/76
　　Accused of Being Active in Tory Uprising of 12/76
　　flees to British Army, 1/77
　　convicted on two counts of Riot in absentia, 1778
Woodward, Apollo　　　Upper Freehold
Woodward, Deborah　　　Upper Freehold
　　household head
Woodward, George
　　sells produce to Continental Army, 5/80
Woodward, Israel　　　Upper Freehold
Woodward, James　　　Upper Freehold
　　plundered by Tories, 12/76
　　Juror, Court of Oyer and Terminer, 1/78
　　　　fined L5 for not attending all or part of Jury duty
Woodward, Jesse　　　Upper Freehold
　　Accused of Being Active in Tory Uprising of 12/76
　　convicted on four counts of Riot, 1/20/78
Woodward, Jesse Tomson　　　Upper Freehold
　　Private, State Troops
　　sells produce to Continental Army, 5/80
Woodward, John　　　Upper Freehold
　　Ensign, New Jersey Volunteers

Roster of the People of Revolutionary Monmouth County

    Accused of Being Active in Tory Uprising of 12/76
    indicted for Horse Stealing, 5/82
Woodward, Joseph   Upper Freehold
Woodward, Peter   Upper Freehold
    Private, New Jersey Volunteers
Woodward, Primus   Upper Freehold
    free black householder
Woodward, Robert   Upper Freehold
    accused of being active in Loyalist Rebellion of 12/76
    Ensign, New Jersey Volunteers
    indicted for Horse Stealing, 5/82
Woodward, Samuel   Upper Freehold
    Accused of Being Active in Tory Uprising of 12/76
    convicted on two counts of Riot, 1/20/78
    indicted for Murder, 5/82
Woodward, Thomas   Upper Freehold
Woodward, Thomas   Upper Freehold
    son of Anthony
    accused of being active in Loyalist Rebellion of 12/76
    indicted for Riot, 1/20/78
Woodward, William   Upper Freehold
    accused of being active in Loyalist Rebellion of 12/76
Woodward, William, Jr   Upper Freehold
Woodworth, Charles   Freehold
Wool, Jeremiah   Middletown
    Signer, Petition Opposing the Return of Tories 6/10/83
Wool, Josiah   Middletown
    Signer, Petition Opposing the Return of Tories 6/10/83
Woolcott, Benjamin   Shrewsbury
    Private, Militia
    Delegate, Friends' Quarterly Meeting, 1775-80
Woolcott, Benjamin   Shrewsbury
    Private, Militia
    exempt from Militia service, 2/10/78
Woolcott, Henry   Shrewsbury
    exempt from Militia service, 2/10/78
    indicted for Misdemeanor, 11/82
Woolcott, Jacob   Shrewsbury
    Delegate, Friends' Quarterly Meeting, 1775
    Signer, Articles of Retaliation, 6/79
    Signer, Petition Favoring Quick Division of Prize Money, 12/79
    sells produce to Continental Army, 5/80

Woolcott, Peter   Shrewsbury
    Private, Militia
Wooley, see Woolley
Woolley, Abraham   Shrewsbury and Freehold
    Sergeant, Militia
    Private, State Troops
    Signer, Petition Encouraging Free Trade, 5/12/81
    Signer, Petition for Renewing Guard at Toms River, 12/10/81
    Signer, Petition Urging Action Against the Pine Robbers, 12/27/81
Woolley, Adam   Shrewsbury
    Private, New Jersey Volunteers, enlisted 12/6/76 deserts 12/15/76
Woolley, Amos
    Private, New Jersey Volunteers, enlisted 12/17/76 dead 3/4/77
Woolley, Anthony   Shrewsbury
Woolley, Assail
    indicted for Murder, 5/82
Woolley, Benjamin   Shrewsbury
    Delegate, Friends' Quarterly Meeting, 1776-7, 1781-3
    arrested for Disaffection, 1/77
    estate inquisitioned for Forfeiture, 6/1/78
    estate confiscated
Wooley, Daniel   Shrewsbury
    Private, Militia
    Private, New Jersey Volunteers
Woolley, David
    Private, New Jersey Volunteers
Woolley, Elihu   Shrewsbury
    Private, New Jersey Volunteers
    Private, Militia
Woolley, Jacob
    son of Silas
    indicted for Misdemeanor, 1/81
Woolley, James   Shrewsbury
    Private, New Jersey Volunteers, enlisted 12/16/76 dead 7/30/77
Woolley, James   Shrewsbury
    Lieutenant, Militia
    Signer, Petition Opposing Slave Manumission, 2/2/74
    Signer, Petition to Better Provision Militia, 2/25/78
Woolley, Jedediah
    Private, Continental Army
Woolley, Joel   Shrewsbury
    indicted for Misdemeanor, 5/82

Woolley, John Freehold
  weaver
  Signer, Association for Opposing the Return of Tories, 1783
Woolley, John Shrewsbury
  Private, New Jersey Volunteers
Woolley, John Shrewsbury
  of Rumson
Woolley, Joseph
  Private, Militia
  Signer, Articles of Retaliation, 6/79
  Signer, Association for Opposing the Return of Tories, 1783
Woolley, Levi Shrewsbury
  Private, New Jersey Volunteers, enlisted 12/21/76 deserts 7/4/77
Woolley, Montellion Shrewsbury
  Private, Militia
Woolley, Nathan Shrewsbury
  accused of being part of Samuel Wright's Tory Association 11/76
  exempt from Militia service, 2/10/78
  convicted of Misdemeanor, 6/3/78, going to Phila. without a pass
  sells produce to Continental Army, 5/80
  Signer, Petition from Victims of the Association for Retaliation 9/82
Woolley, Peter Freehold
Woolley, Randle (Randal)
  Private, New Jersey Volunteers
Woolley, Ruth Shrewsbury
  recipient of poor relief
Woolley, Silas Shrewsbury
  indicted for Misdemeanor, 8/79
  convicted of Misdemeanor, 12/80
Woolley, Stephen Shrewsbury
  Private, Militia
  indicted for Misdemeanor, 8/79
Woolley, Thomas
  Private, New Jersey Volunteers
  arrested for Disaffection, 11/76
  accused of being active in Tory Rebellions of 12/76
Woolley, Thomas Shrewsbury
  sells produce to Continental Army, 5/80
Woolley, William Middletown
  arrested for Disaffection, 11/76
  accused of being active in Tory Rebellions of 12/76
  estate confiscated

Woolley, William   Shrewsbury
  Private, Militia
  Signer, Petition Supporting Retaliation, 9/17/80
Woolley, William   Shrewsbury
  Militia Volunteer, Prior to the First General Militia Muster, 6/76
  accused of being part of Samuel Wright's Tory Association 11/76
  Private, New Jersey Volunteers, enlisted 12/19/76   dead 5/10/77
Woolf, see Wolfe
Worell, John
  Private, New Jersey Volunteers
Worell, Nicholas   Shrewsbury
  Private, Militia
  present at the capture of the British ship, Britannia, 12/31/79
  Signer, Association for Opposing the Return of Tories, 1783
Worell, Ryckes   Middletown
Worell, William
  Private, New Jersey Volunteers
Worth, Alexander   Dover
  arrested for acting as British spy, jailed in Freehold, 1778
Worth, Edward
  sells goods to the Pennsylvania Salt Works, 8/76-10/76
  Signer, Petition Against Association for Retaliation 12/81
Worth, Green   Dover
  Signer, Petition Against Association for Retaliation 12/81
Worth, Henry   Dover
  Signer, Petition Against Association for Retaliation 12/81
Worth, Henry   Dover
Worth, John   Freehold
  Private, Militia
  Private, State Troops, enlists 5/80
Worth, John   Dover
  Private, New Jersey Volunteers
Worth, Peterson   Dover
  Signer, Petition Against Association for Retaliation 12/81
Worth, William   Dover
  Private, Militia
  Private, Continental Army
  Signer, Petition Against Association for Retaliation 12/81
Worthly, John
  indicted for Misdemeanor, 1/81
Worthly, Philip
  Sergeant, New Jersey Volunteers

Worthly, Richard — Shrewsbury
Wright, Aaron — Upper Freehold
  accused of being active in Loyalist Rebellion of 12/76
Wright, Alexander
  Private, New Jersey Volunteers
Wright, David — Upper Freehold
Wright, Elizabeth
  indicted for Misdemeanor, 11/81
Wright, John
  arrested for Disaffection, 1/77
Wright, Jonathan — Shrewsbury
  Private, Militia
  Delegate, Friends' Quarterly Meeting, 1778
Wright, Nathan — Upper Freehold
Wright, Robert — Upper Freehold
  accused of being active in Loyalist Rebellion of 12/76
Wright, Samuel — Upper Freehold
  accused of being active in Loyalist Rebellion of 12/76
Wright, Samuel — Shrewsbury
  arrested for disaffection, 11/76
  indicted for Murder, 8/79
Wright, Sarah — Upper Freehold
  household head
Wyckoff, Wykoff, *see* Wikoff
Wynnant, Cornelius — Shrewsbury
Wynnant, Nicholas — Shrewsbury
  Private, Militia
  helps keep the poor

Y

Yateman, Esek — Freehold
  Signer, Petition Urging Compensation for Inflated Money, 5/22/83
Yateman, James — Freehold
  Signer, Articles of Retaliation, 6/79
  Signer, Association for Opposing the Return of Tories, 1783
Yateman, John — Freehold
  Signer, Articles of Retaliation, 6/79
  Signer, Petition Encouraging Free Trade, 5/12/81
  Signer, Petition Urging Compensation for Inflated Money, 5/22/83
Yateman, John, Jr. — Freehold
  Private, Militia, captured 2/13/77

Signer, Articles of Retaliation, 6/79
Signer, Petition Urging Compensation for Inflated Money, 5/22/83
Yateman, Peter   Freehold
    Corporal, Militia, captured 2/13/77
Yates, Benjamin   Upper Freehold
    Private, Militia
Yates, William   Upper Freehold
    Private, Militia
    Private, State Troops
Yetman, *see* Yateman
Yerricks, Cornelius
    Private, New Jersey Volunteers, enlisted 4/4/77   dead 8/15/77
Young, Christopher
    Private, New Jersey Volunteers, captured prior to 1779
Young, David
    Corporal, New Jersey Volunteers
Young, Enoch
    Private, New Jersey Volunteers, enlisted 4/12/77 deserts 12/11/78
Young, James   Middletown
    Signer, Petition Opposing the Return of Tories 6/10/83
Young, James   Middletown
    Signer, Petition Opposing the Return of Tories 6/10/83
Young, John   Middletown
    Signer, Petition Opposing the Return of Tories 6/10/83
Youngs, *see* Young

Z

Zutphin, *see also* Sutphin
Zutphin, Aurt   Middletown
    Signer, Articles of Retaliation, 6/79
Zutphin, Derrick   Middletown
Zutphin, John   Middletown

Roster of the People of Revolutionary Monmouth County

This Roster was Compiled from:

Petitions and Associations: Petitions and voluntary associations are excellent sources for compiling lists of persons and gauging their political and personal leanings. However, petition and association signatures were often solicited at public places and some individuals may have been coerced by mobs or pressured by peers to sign documents that they did not wholeheartedly support. Still, even with this caveat in mind, petitions are probably the most valuable single source for attempting to figure out the political and personal leanings of an individual.

Fortunately, approximately half of the petitions from Revolutionary era Monmouth County seem to have survived into the present day. This estimate is based on the fact that slightly more than half of the petitions recorded in the *Votes and Proceedings of the New Jersey Assembly* (at the New Jersey State Library, Trenton, and the Library Company, Philadelphia) still exist. Since these petitions frequently had very long titles, or no title at all, the compiler has attempted to summarize their principal mission (written in italics).

Supporting the Issuance of New Jersey Currency, New Jersey State Archives, 1771, Bureau of Archives and History, Manuscripts Collection, box 19, #31.

Opposing Slave Manumission, February 2, 1774, New Jersey State Archives, Bureau of Archives and History, Manuscripts Collection, box 14, #17.

Supporting William Barton, January 31, 1776, Massachusetts Historical Society, manuscript number #9532.

Supporting Richard Lloyd, January 31, 1776, Monmouth County Historical Association, Collections Alphabetical, folder: William Barclay Parsons.

Calling for Action Against the Disaffected, February 21, 1777, New Jersey State Archives, Department of Defense, Numbered Manuscripts, #10336.

Affirming Loyalty of Moses Ivins, March 12, 1777, New Jersey State

Archives, Bureau of Archives and History, Manuscripts Collection, box 38, #87.

Urging Action Against the Disaffected, March 14, 1777, New Jersey State Archives, Department of Defense, Numbered Manuscripts, #1141.

To Form Special Militia Company for the Defense of Toms River, May 18, 1777, Monmouth County Historical Association, J. Amory Haskell Collection, Folder 22.

Urging Settlement of Quartermaster Department Debts, September 6, 1777, New Jersey State Archives, Collective Series, Revolutionary War Documents, #52.

To Better Provision the Militia, February 25, 1778, National Society of the Daughters of the American Revolution Library, File Cabinet, Folder: John Lloyd of New Jersey.

Against Monmouth County Auction Commissioners, March 29, 1779, New Jersey State Archives, Bureau of Archives and History, Manuscripts Collection, box 14, #41.

Against Monmouth County Auction Commissioners, May 8, 1779, New Jersey State Archives, Bureau of Archives and History, Manuscripts Collection, box 14, #46.

Urging Compensation for War Victims, May 25, 1779, New Jersey State Archives, Collective Series, Revolutionary War Documents, #76.

For Stricter Militia Law, May 31, 1779, Monmouth County Historical Association, J. Amory Haskell Collection, Folder 22.

Articles of Retaliation (Association for Retaliation), June 1779, Barber, John W. and Henry Howe, <u>Historical Collections of New Jersey</u>, New Haven, Connecticut: John Barber, 1868, pp. 371-4.

Favoring Quick Division of Prize Money, December 1779, New Jersey State Archives, Bureau of Archives and History, Manuscripts Collection, box 14, #51.

Supporting Retaliation, 1780, New Jersey Historical Society, MG 14,

Ely Collection.

Supporting Retaliation, September 17, 1780, Tilton, LeRoy W. "New Jersey Petition of 1780, Concerning Retaliation," <u>National Genealogical Society Quarterly</u>, vol. 34, Spring 1946, pp. 75-6.

In Favor of Daniel Longstreet, November 21, 1780, National Archives, Collection #881, reel 593.

Encouraging Free Trade, May 12, 1781, New Jersey State Archives, Bureau of Archives and History, Manuscripts Collection, box 14, #65.

Urging Action Against Disaffected & Favoring Retaliation, May 12, 1781, New Jersey State Archives, Department of Defense, Revolutionary War, Numbered Manuscripts, #11037.

Against Association for Retaliation, December 1781, New Jersey State Archives, Department of Defense, Revolutionary War, Numbered Manuscripts, #11036, #10948, and Collective Series, Revolutionary War Documents, #114.

For Renewing Guard at Toms River, December 10, 1781, Library of Congress, MMC, Monmouth County, New Jersey, Oversize Cabinet 2, Drawer 7.

Urging a Guard Against the Pine Robbers, December 27, 1781, Massachusetts Historical Society, Monmouth County, New Jersey, Petition.

From Victims of the Association for Retaliation, September, 1782, New Jersey State Archives, Collective Series, Revolutionary War Documents, #121.

Urging Compensation for Inflated Money, May 22, 1783, New Jersey State Archives, Bureau of Archives and History, Manuscripts Collection, box 15, #38.

Opposing the Return of Tories, June 10, 1783, New Jersey State Archives, Collective Series, Revolutionary War Documents, #132-5.

Association for Opposing the Return of Tories, 1783, New York Public Library, New Jersey Collection, Monmouth County.

Roster of the People of Revolutionary Monmouth County

Supporting Quick Division of Prizes, no date, New Jersey State Archives, Bureau of Archives and History, Manuscripts Collection, box 19, #30.

Militia Rolls, Pay Lists, and other Militia Listings: Militia rolls (often called returns), and pay lists are invaluable sources of names and a good indication of those who served in the Revolutionary militia. Yet attempting to determine a person's politics based on a single listing in a militia company is a reckless proposition, and the prudent use of militia returns is limited by the following three factors.

- First, militia service was compulsory. A great many disaffected persons are listed on individual militia rolls because at certain times these disaffected persons expected fines or retribution for not turning out.
- Second, because militia service was dangerous and clashed with business and agricultural interests, some relatively affluent Whigs accepted fines for delinquency despite being supporters of the Revolution.
- Third, those militia returns compiled through May 1776 were made before the citizenry in many parts of Monmouth County was effectively mustered into militia companies, and before the militia's role was redefined to support American independence. As such, these early militia returns are largely confined to those leading Whigs, and their sons, who voluntarily mustered themselves. These early returns also contain a great many Whig-Loyalists, persons who supported the Whig cause prior to the Revolution, but subsequently became Loyalists when the Whig cause became a Revolutionary cause.

With these limitations in mind, militia returns may still be useful in another way. Militia rolls are an excellent way of assessing an individual's standing within his local community. Militia officers were elected by the men of the company, and officers (and non-commissioned officers to a lesser degree) were invariably among most respected and/or affluent men in their communities.

It is also worth noting that Monmouth County's Revolutionary militia included a cavalry and an artillery company. These companies, originally mustered in 1777 under Captains Jacob Covenhoven and Barnes Smock, were comprised of volunteers and served more often than regular militia companies. Thus it would be safe to assume that the men who joined these two companies were generally faithful supporters of the Revolution.

The following returns, in addition to William S. Stryker's *Officers and Men of New Jersey in the American Revolution* (Baltimore: Genealogical Publishing Company, 1967) were used in compiling this roster. They are listed chronologically, with the commanding officer, when known.

Volunteer Militia Return, November 1775, Captain Thomas Cook, New Jersey State Archives, Department of Defense, Numbered Manuscripts, #1095.

Volunteer Militia Return, March 1776, Captain Barzilla Grover, New Jersey State Archives, Department of Defense, Numbered Manuscripts, #1103.

Volunteer Militia Return, April 1776, Captain Henry Waddle, New Jersey State Archives, Department of Defense, Numbered Manuscripts, #1133.

Volunteer Militia Return for Company of Grenadiers, April 1776, Captain Henry Waddle, New Jersey Historical Society, Revolutionary War Collection, Collection #4, item #7.

Militia Return, November 1776, Captain Reuben Randolph, New Jersey State Archives, Department of Defense, Revolutionary War, #1128.

Militia Return, November 1776, Captain Michael Sweetman, Monmouth County Historical Association, Subjects Alphabetical Collection, Revolution, folder #1.

Militia Pay List, November 1776, Captain Cornelius Covenhoven, Monmouth County Historical Association, J. Amory Haskell Collection, box 1, folder #10, document D.

List of Militia Prisoners Captured February 13, 1777, Lieutenant Colonel Nathaniel Scudder, Raser, Edward, "American Prisoners Taken at the Battle of the Navesink," Genealogical Magazine of New Jersey, vol. 45, n. 2, May 1970, pp. 49-61.

Roster of the People of Revolutionary Monmouth County

Militia Return for Company of Light Horse, January 1778, Captain Daniel Hendrickson, Monmouth County Historical Association, J. Amory Haskell Collection, folder 10.

Militia Return, June 1778, Captain Stephen Fleming, New Jersey Historical Society, Holmes Papers, box 5, folder 1.

List of Persons Present at the Capture of the Brig Britannia, December 1779, Colonel Asher Holmes, New Jersey State Archives, Department of Defense, Revolutionary War, Numbered Manuscripts, #10089-98.

Militia Return, June 1780, Captain James Green, Stryker-Rodda, Harriet, "Militia Women of 1780, Monmouth County, New Jersey," N.S.D.A.R. Magazine, vol. 113, n. 4, April 1979, pp. 308-12.

Militia Return, July 1780, Captain John Covenhoven, New Jersey State Archives, Department of Defense, Revolutionary War, Numbered Manuscripts, #1100.

Rolls of State Troops and Continental Soldiers from Monmouth County: In addition to militia service, a great many Monmouthers served their country in the State Troops and the Continental Army.

The State Troops of Monmouth County -- State troops were voluntarily enlisted and drafted from existing militia companies for fixed amounts of time (typically one year or six months) to defend the state against British/Tory raids from New York. As such, State Troops were different from both Continental soldiers and militia. In Monmouth County, a company of State Troops was raised and posted in the Navesink Highlands within days of the British occupation of Sandy Hook, in May 1776. Other State Troops companies were raised and deployed on or near the shores every other year of the war through 1782. Generally, State Troops were promised comparable pay and equipment as Continental Troops.

The Continental Soldiers of Monmouth County -- Contrary to common perceptions, the Continental Army was actually composed of a wide array of units, raised under a wide variety of laws and serving under different command structures with different missions.
 The Continental Line: The Continental Army was the army of the

national government and the majority of Continentals served in regular regiments organized by state, known as the state's "Continental Line". The first company of Monmouth County Continentals was raised in late 1775, under Captain Elias Longstreet, and marched off to take part in the disastrous Canadian campaign of 1775-6. Unfortunately, no rolls for this company have survived. By 1777, another company of Monmouthers was serving in the First Regiment of the New Jersey Line under Captain Jonathan Forman and many other Monmouthers were recruited into other New Jersey companies. By 1779, two companies of Monmouthers under Major John Burrowes were annexed to Colonel Oliver Spencer's Fourth Regiment of the New Jersey Line, after the dissolution of David Forman's Additional Regiment (see below). A few muster rolls of Jonathan Forman's and Major John Burrowes' companies have survived and are listed below.

Flying Camp: The difference between Flying Camp and State Troops (discussed above) is subtle. Both were raised from existing militia companies for defined amounts of time, and promised pay and accouterments comparable to Continental soldiers of the state line. The difference is that State Troops were assigned for local defense, while Flying Camp were annexed to the Continental Army and placed under the Continental command structure. In May 1776, a regiment of "Flying Camp" was raised from Monmouth and Middlesex Counties, under the command of Colonel David Forman. Forman's regiment served with the Continental Army through November 1776; it dissolved when the six month term of enlistment of the soldiers expired at the end of November. While some records of Forman's Flying Camp have survived, no enlistment rolls still exist.

Additional Regiments: Additional regiments were parts of the Continental Army raised with the mission of defending particularly vulnerable localities. As such, these regiments were stationary and largely outside of the Continental command structure. Of the many additional regiments chartered during the war, few ever reached full strength and most seem to have had rather inglorious tenures. Colonel David Forman was authorized to raise an Additional Regiment in Monmouth County in January 1777, but recruiting went so badly that Forman was also allowed to recruit from Delaware and Maryland. It appears that Forman's regiment never exceeded two hundred-fifty men (less than half of full strength). After spending a scandal-plagued year as commander of his Additional Regiment, David Forman was forced to relinquish command of his regiment, and this incomplete regiment was formally merged with the Fourth

Regiment of the New Jersey Line in 1778. Unfortunately, none of Forman's muster rolls have survived, but many of Forman's men appear subsequently in the rolls of Colonel Oliver Spencer's Fourth Regiment of the New Jersey Line.

While some recruits into the State Troops and Continental Army were, no doubt, passionate supporters of the Revolutionary cause, or children of passionate supporters, most New Jersey recruits were persons of modest wealth, lured to service by generous bounties. As such, persons listed on the forthcoming lists may or may not have been sterling patriots, but almost all were of modest social status.

The rolls are listed chronologically.

Monmouth Continentals under Captain Jonathan Forman, November 1777, Massachusetts Historical Society, manuscript number #9534.

Recruits for State Troops, May-June 1778, New Jersey State Archives, Department of Defense, Revolutionary War, Numbered Manuscripts, #3363.

Monmouth Militiamen Drafted into Continental Army, May-June 1778, New Jersey State Archives, Department of Defense, Revolutionary War, Numbered Manuscripts, #3625-30.

List of Men in Captain John Burrowes' Company, August 1779, Stryker, William S., <u>New Jersey Continental Line in the Indian Campaign of 1779</u>, Trenton: W.S. Sharp, 1885.

State Troops Present at the Capture of the British Brig Britannia, December 1779, New Jersey State Archives, Department of Defense, Revolutionary War, Numbered Manuscripts, #10089-10098.

Recruits for State Troops, June 1780, National Archives, Collection 881, reels 593 and 640.

List of Men Serving in the State Troops, June 1780, New Jersey State Archives, Bureau of Archives and History, box 35, #32.

Monmouthers in Oliver Spencer's Continental Regiment, January 11, 1781, New Jersey State Archives, Department of Defense, Revolutionary War, Numbered Manuscripts, #2391 (oversize).

Roster of the People of Revolutionary Monmouth County

Monmouth Militiamen Drafted into Continental Army, April-June 1781, New Jersey State Archives, Department of Defense, Revolutionary War, Numbered Manuscripts, #3625-30.

Recruits for State Troops, May 1781, New Jersey State Archives, Department of Defense, Revolutionary War, Numbered Manuscripts, #3621-2.

Recruits for State Troops, February 1782, New Jersey State Archives, Bureau of Archives and History, box 35, #32.

Monmouth Continentals, undated, New Jersey State Archives, Department of Defense, Numbered Manuscripts, #3776-7.

Monmouth State Troops, undated, New Jersey State Archives, Department of Defense, Revolutionary War, Numbered Manuscripts, #3844-5, 3852, 3856A.

<u>Lists of Officeholders:</u> Lists of officeholders are generally reliable indicators of the people who assumed leadership roles in the local Revolutionary movement. Unfortunately, only a modest number of such lists of officeholders have survived, and there will forever be a great many gaps in the knowledge of Monmouth County's Revolutionary era officeholders.

The first Whig officeholders compiled in this roster are the persons who served on local Whig committees, so-called Committeemen. By April 1776, each of Monmouth County's townships (except perhaps Stafford) had Committees of Correspondence (to guide local Whig activities and share information with Whigs in other areas) and Committees of Observation (to enforce the boycott on British goods). In addition, there was a Monmouth County Committee of Correspondence. Collectively, these various committees coordinated the Whig movement in Monmouth County into August 1776, when these committees seem to have faded from prominence. It is safe to assume that no outright Tories ever served on these quasi-legal committees, but many so-called Whig-Loyalists certainly did.

By 1777, an infrastructure of local civil officers formed the foundation of the local Revolutionary government in Monmouth County. Many of these offices were not popularly elected, and it appears that the popularly elected offices were limited to: certain township officers and overseers, sheriff, coroners, and state legislators. Other officers, including judges of the courts, justices of the peace (often known as magistrates), tax collectors, forage masters, and commissioners appointed for various specific tasks were appointed by the state legislature. As such, persons who served in appointed offices were probably allied with the state government and the Revolutionary movement. Elected officers were more likely to reflect the ambiguous attitudes of the public at large. As such, in the Whig Township of Freehold, officeholders were generally strong supporters of state government and the Revolutionary movement. However, in the largely disaffected Atlantic shore townships (Shrewsbury, Dover, and Stafford) it is safe to assume that most of the elected officeholders were moderate/neutral to the Revolutionary cause, and some may have even had Tory leanings.

The following lists of officeholders are listed chronologically:

Jurors of the Court of Common Pleas, 1769-75, Monmouth County Archives, Common Pleas Minutes (bound).

Middletown Township Officers, 1770-83, Middletown *Town Book*, Monmouth County Historical Association, Vault, Shelf 6.

Members of the Freehold and Shrewsbury Committees of Correspondence, 1775-6, "Proceedings of the Committees of Freehold and Shrewsbury," Proceedings of the New Jersey Historical Society, 1st Series, vol. 1, pp. 190-1.

Middletown Township Committee of Correspondence, circa 1776, Resolve to Support Continental and Provincial Congress, Monmouth County Historical Association, Curator's Files, Marlpit Hall, folder: Taylor Family Association.

Monmouth County State Legislators and Sheriffs, 1776-83, Ellis, Franklin, History of Monmouth County, Philadelphia: R.T. Peck & Company, 1885, pp. 108-111.

Officers of the Court (Justices, Magistrates, Constables, Coroners, Grand Jurors, and Jurors), January 1778, New Jersey State Archives, Judicial Records, Court of Oyer and Terminer, Monmouth County, box 2, folder: January 1778.

Officers of the Court (Justices, Magistrates, Constables, Coroners, Grand Jurors, and Jurors), June 1778, New Jersey State Archives, Judicial Records, Court of Oyer and Terminer, Monmouth County, box 2, folder: June 1778.

Officers of the Court (Justices, Magistrates, Constables, Coroners, Grand Jurors, and Jurors), August 1779, New Jersey State Archives, Judicial Records, Court of Oyer and Terminer, Monmouth County, box 2, folder: August 1779.

Officers of the Court (Justices, Magistrates, Constables, Coroners, Grand Jurors, and Jurors), December 1780, New Jersey State Archives, Judicial Records, Court of Oyer and Terminer, Monmouth County, box 2, folder: December 1780.

Officers of the Court (Justices, Magistrates, Constables, Coroners, Grand Jurors, and Jurors), November 1781, New Jersey State Archives, Judicial Records, Court of Oyer and Terminer, Monmouth County, box 2, folder: November 1781.

Officers of the Court (Justices, Magistrates, Constables, Coroners, Grand Jurors, and Jurors), May 1782, New Jersey State Archives, Judicial Records, Court of Oyer and Terminer, Monmouth County, box 2, folder: May 1782.

Officers of the Court (Justices, Magistrates, Constables, Coroners, Grand Jurors, and Jurors), November 1782, New Jersey State Archives, Judicial Records, Court of Oyer and Terminer, Monmouth County, box 2, folder: November 1782.

Officers of the Court (Justices, Magistrates, Constables, Coroners, Grand Jurors, and Jurors), July 1783, New Jersey State Archives, Judicial Records, Court of Oyer and Terminer, Monmouth County, box 2, folder: July 1783.

Dover Township Officials, March 1783, Salter, Edwin, History of Monmouth and Ocean Counties, Bayonne, New Jersey: E. Gardner & Sons, 1890, p. 352.

Church and Charity Lists: Church lists are a good source of names and, of course, religious affiliation. This is important because religious

affiliation generally correlated with politics in Revolutionary New Jersey. Dennis Ryan and other historians of Revolutionary New Jersey have made the following generalizations about the position taken by the state's major religious denominations during the Revolution:
- Presbyterians -- large majority supported the Revolution.
- Dutch Reformed -- majority supported the Revolution.
- Baptists -- slight majority supported the Revolution.
- Quakers -- slight majority either disaffected or actively Loyalist.
- Anglicans -- majority either disaffected or actively Loyalist.

With regard to Monmouth County, the above generalizations seem be reasonably accurate, with two slight exceptions. First, it should be noted that a great many of Monmouth County's ethnic Dutch were being absorbed into Presbyterian congregations at the time of the Revolution -- thus the line in between Dutch Reformed and Presbyterian in Monmouth County is blurry. The result is that the vast majority of Monmouth County's Dutch supported the Revolution. Second, the inhabitants of the lower Monmouth County shore (between the villages of Toms River and Tuckerton) are difficult to classify in terms of religious denomination, since there were no regular religious meetings in this area. Most were of English descent, and it is probably safe to assume that most were either Quakers or Anglicans. However, this remains an assumption that cannot be proven. Not surprisingly, this was Monmouth County's most solidly disaffected region.

A problem with Church lists is that they do not reflect the devoutness of listed individuals or the standing of those persons within the congregations (unless the person in question is listed as a church officer or was disciplined by the congregation). It would be fair to state that less devout members of congregations are less likely to conform to the generalizations listed above. As such, church lists -- though somewhat valuable -- should not be treated as binding in determining a person's likely politics. At best, these are indicative of an inclination toward supporting or opposing the Revolution.

Charity lists may be a stronger indicator of an individual's personal politics. Due to the voluntary nature of charitable contributions, it is safe to assume that charitable contributors tended to support the cause or recipient of the charity. Thus, when the cause in question can be strongly linked with a family or group that supported or opposed the Revolution, a strong inference can be drawn about the cause's supporters.

Church lists typically include genealogically important information (baptisms, marriages, etc.) of little value to historians. This genealogical knowledge is not indicated on this roster. As such, genealogists may wish to seek out the original copies of these lists.

The church and charity lists captured in this roster are arranged chronologically.

Church Officers and Elders of the Christ Church of Shrewsbury (Anglican), 1770-83, Vestry Book, Monmouth County Historical Association, Vault, Shelf 4.

Delegates to Friends' (Quakers) Quarterly Meetings, 1774-83, Friends Historical Library (at Swarthmore College), Shrewsbury Meeting Minutes, reels MR PH 51, 585, and 587.

Keepers of the Poor and Persons on Poor Relief, 1776-83, Shrewsbury Township, New York Historical Society, BV Shrewsbury, Town Poor & Road Book.

Baptists of Middletown, 1777, Stillwell, John, Historical and Genealogical Miscellany, Baltimore: Genealogical Publishing Company, 1970, vol. 2, p 273.

Charity List for the Relief of Daniel Stevenson's family, Middletown, May 1783, Monmouth County Historical Association, Cherry Hall Papers, box 15, folder 11.

Tax Lists and Indicators of Economic Activity with Governmental Entities: Tax lists (ratables) and other indicators of economic activity, such as account books, ledgers, and quartermaster records, are excellent sources of names and good indicators of the wealth of the individuals listed. Fortunately, a great many such records have survived, including the full compilation of tax receipts for Monmouth County for the years 1778-9. In addition, some fairly comprehensive account books and quartermaster records for Monmouth County have also survived.

The value of these documents in assessing an individual's political views is uneven. Tax lists, for example, should be of little value in

Roster of the People of Revolutionary Monmouth County

determining a person's attachment to the Revolutionary movement since paying taxes was mandated by law. However, tax collectors dared not venture into large parts of Shrewsbury, Dover and Stafford townships throughout most of the Revolution, so it might be safe to assume that the people in those townships who did pay taxes must have been friendly to the new government. Of course, no neighborhood was totally homogenous, so some disaffected residents in well-affected neighborhoods paid taxes and vice versa. And of course, a single listing on a tax roll gives no indication of whether that person paid taxes any other year, nor does it reflect local factors (such as the short-term presence of troops in the area) that may have made it impossible to avoid paying taxes for a particular year. In short, tax lists are, at best, only a weak indicator of political orientation.

Slightly more valuable are lists of voluntary economic activity with governmental entities. With more autonomy, it is logical to assume that disaffected persons would choose to avoid supporting the Revolutionary cause. Unfortunately, personal motivations are not one dimensional, and an individual's economic best interest frequently over-ruled political principles. As such, a great many mildly disaffected persons probably sold goods to Continental Quartermasters and state commissaries -- at least when those officers were offering high prices. Conversely, a great many supporters of the Revolution probably withheld goods from Continental and state officers when those officers could not offer sufficient compensation for the requested goods. Thus, listings of economic activity can be very valuable in determining an individual's support for the Revolution, but must be scrutinized closely to make certain that economics did not present an overwhelming counter-incentive for the people in question.

The following tax lists and indicators of economic activity were used in compiling this roster and are listed chronologically. The Pennsylvania Salt Works are included because they were co-owned by the Pennsylvania government and were strongly identified with the Continental cause.

Persons Paying Excise Tax for Tavern License, Shrewsbury Township, December 1775, New York Historical Society, BV Shrewsbury, Town Poor & Road Book.

Account Books, Pennsylvania Salt Works, kept by Thomas Savadge, 1776-9, Historical Society of Pennsylvania, Pennsylvania Salt Works Account Books.

Roster of the People of Revolutionary Monmouth County
Ledger of Persons Who Sold Clothing for the Use of the Continental Army, kept by David Forman, June 1778, Princeton University Special Collections, CO 140, David Forman.

Renters of Forfeited Loyalist Estates, 1779, New Jersey State Archives, Commissioners of Forfeited Estates, box 5, folder 2.2.

Account of Books of Persons Who Sold Produce to Continental Quartermaster, kept by David Rhea, Monmouth County Quartermaster, May-July 1780, New Jersey State Archives, Department of Defense, Revolutionary War, Numbered Manuscripts, #4429.

List of Persons Who Sold Goods to John Lloyd, Monmouth County Contractor, July 1780, in Stratford, Dorothy Agans, Certificates and Receipts of Revolutionary New Jersey, Lambertville, New Jersey: Hunterdon House, 1996, pp. 242-4.

List of Persons Who Sold Sheep to Continental Quartermaster, kept by David Rhea, Quartermaster for Monmouth County, New Jersey State Archives, Department of Defense, Revolutionary War, Numbered Manuscripts, #8219-33.

Ledger of Persons Who Leased Horse Teams to Quartermaster's Department, kept by David Rhea, December 1781, New Jersey State Archives, Department of Defense, Revolutionary War, Numbered Manuscripts, #5934.

Tax Ratables, 1779, Stryker-Rodda, Kenn, The Revolutionary Census of New Jersey, New Orleans: Polyanthus, 1972.

Lists of Active Tories: In November and December 1776, large numbers of Monmouthers, emboldened by the advance of the British Army into New Jersey, began mustering and challenging Continental authority. In November, parties of Monmouth Tories, embodying under Samuel Wright in the Long Branch area and William Taylor in Freehold, were exposed and arrested by Continental detachments under General Adam Stephen and Colonel David Forman respectively. However, the Tory insurrections continued, and by Christmas 1776, Monmouth Tories were in control of much of Monmouth County, including: 1. western Upper Freehold Township, 2. Middletown and most of the Raritan Bayshore, 3. The Atlantic shore

Roster of the People of Revolutionary Monmouth County from Shrewsbury to Toms River. Only Pleasant Valley (a collection of neighborhoods between Freehold and Middletown), the village of Freehold and perhaps the interior villages of Colts Neck and Tinton Falls remained under Whig control by late December. However, the Tory uprisings -- loosely coordinated at best -- were largely local events. An attempt to raise a county-wide Tory Militia met with disaster on January 2, 1777, when the two hundred Tory recruits were dispersed by a Continental detachment under Lt. Colonel Francis Gurney. Within days of that crucial event, each of the isolated Tory associations were scattered by the same detachment of Pennsylvania Continental soldiers.

The principal actions of the Tory Associations, while in power, seems to have been: issuing loyalty oaths to Monmouthers, seizing militarily important goods, such as guns and horses, from Whig neighbors, and mustering Tory recruits into the New Jersey Volunteers -- a Provincial Corps of the British Army. Fortunately, there is fairly good documentation of the arrests made following the collapse of the Tory Associations. However, it should be noted that many of the persons arrested for being active in the Tory associations quickly recanted once arrested. Thus, it would be safe to assume that many of the Tory associators were persons of ambiguous commitment to the Tory counter-insurrections. Many of these Tory associators apparently joined based on promises of material gain. So while the people listed in this section were active Tories, their level of commitment is less clear.

It also should be noted that many of the most disaffected persons, such as the Quakers of northern Shrewsbury Township and the shore residents south of Toms River, were not active in these Tory associations, and remained destabilizing forces in Monmouth County long after the Tory associations were broken up. Furthermore, many of the genuinely committed Tories escaped arrest and went off to serve in the New Jersey Volunteers -- thereby escaping Continental authorities. In general, these other types of active Tories are not listed in this section, though many are listed in subsequent sections.

The lists of persons active in the Tory insurrections of late 1776 are presented by geographic area.

Freehold, William Taylor's Association, November 1776
List of Monmouth Tories in Prison in Philadelphia, taken by Colonel David Forman, compiled December 18, 1776, National Archives,

Roster of the People of Revolutionary Monmouth County
Papers of the Continental Congress, reel 84, item 70, pp. 115-7.

Freehold, Tory Militia Recruits, recruited by John Morris and Elisha Lawrence, Dispersed and Captured January 2, 1777
List of Recruits for New Jersey Volunteers, at January 2, 1777, captured by Lt. Colonel Francis Gurney, Prince, Carl, The Papers of William Livingston, Trenton: New Jersey Historical Commission, 1979, vol. 1, pp. 337-8.

Long Branch - Manasquan - Shark River, Samuel Wright's Association, November 1776
List of Persons Active in Samuel Wright's Tory Association, November 1776, as identified by Samuel Knott, New Jersey State Archives, Collective Series, Revolutionary Documents, #32.

Upper Freehold, Anthony and Jesse Woodward's Association, December 1776
List of Persons Active in Woodward Insurrection, December 1776, as identified by Thomas Fowler, New Jersey State Archives, Bureau of Archives and History, Manuscript Collection, Manuscripts, box 38, #36-7.

List of Persons Active in Woodward Insurrection, Took Loyalty Oaths to New Jersey Government, March 19, 1777, Minutes of the Council of Safety of the State of New Jersey, Jersey City: John H. Lyon, p 7.

List of Persons Active in Woodward Insurrection, December 1776, as identified by James Ferell and Isaiah Horner, Princeton University, Rare Books and Special Collections, Barricklo Collection, CO 387, box 1, folder Miscellaneous.

Miscellaneous and Multiple Association Lists
List of Tory Prisoners from Monmouth County in Philadelphia Jail, circa January 1777, Historical Society of Pennsylvania, Records of the Pennsylvania Revolutionary Government, reel 25, frame 691.

List of Persons Subpoenaed, Issued to Suspected Tory Leaders, April 1777, by New Jersey Council of Safety, Minutes of the Council of Safety of the State of New Jersey, Jersey City: John H. Lyon, 1872, p 14.

List of Monmouth Tories in Jail Who Agree to Join Continental Army in Exchange for Pardon, May 23, 1777, Minutes of the Council of the

Roster of the People of Revolutionary Monmouth County Safety of New Jersey, Jersey City: John H. Lyon, 1872, p 53.

List of Persons Active Samuel Wright's Association and Middletown Tories, undated, Princeton University, Rare Books and Special Collections, Barricklo Collection, CO 387, box 1, folder Miscellaneous.

Lists of Criminals: There can be no doubt that criminal activity increased in Monmouth County during the Revolution. There are two general reasons for this increase:

- Economic dislocation caused by war-related activities, impressment of property and goods for military use, and destruction of private property and loss of life due to the war itself.
- Political disaffection from the Revolutionary government caused by mandatory militia service and ideological opposition to the Revolutionary cause.

Most information on criminal activities is provided through court records. Following the decline and expiration of the New Jersey Council of Safety in early 1778, the county courts became the principal vehicles for prosecuting political and common criminals. The Revolutionary era court system in New Jersey was multi-layered, and consisted of three distinct courts, the Court of Common Pleas, the Court of General (Quarterly) Sessions, and the Court of Oyer and Terminer.

- The Court of Common Pleas met four to six times a year and generally heard civil suits, usually regarding debts between citizens.
- The Court of General Sessions (sometimes called the Court of Quarterly Sessions) met four times a year, and existed to hear criminal cases, such as charges of petty larceny, trespass, assault, and various misdemeanors.
- The Court of Oyer and Terminer was only held at the Governor's order and was presided over by the Chief Justice of the New Jersey Supreme Court. The Court of Oyer and Terminer existed to hear criminal felony cases, such as murders, burglaries, and horse stealing, and to hear cases regarding political crimes, such as seditious words, riot, and high treason charges.

However, the jurisdiction of these three courts was rarely precise, and the various courts often heard cases that seemingly should have been heard before other courts.

It should also be noted that some of courts records (though by far the best source for information on criminals) provide confusing and even contradictory information. For example, each of the three different documents that list indictments from the January 1778 session of the Monmouth Court of Oyer and Terminer differ slightly in terms of persons indicted and charges against them. Many court records include unusual spellings of names and unreadable or archaic phrases. Equally frustrating, because certain cases were carried over from one court session to another, it is difficult to determine whether a person indicted at consecutive court sessions was being tried on new charges, or re-tried on old charges. Finally, most of the criminal indictments in all of the court records are for unspecified misdemeanors, a broad charge that included such diverse crimes as: seditious speech, illegally traveling inside enemy lines, refusing Continental currency, tax evasion, and trading with agents of the enemy. Only rarely is the specific misdemeanor charge listed in court records. The compiler adopted two general rules when dealing with conflicting or confusing information:
1. When in doubt, list too much rather than too little information -- meaning that certain persons who are listed as indicted several different times may actually have been indicted on fewer charges, and had their cases re-heard at different court sessions.
2. When information in certain court records is contradicted in more reliable documents (including more carefully compiled court records), the compiler chose not include the more suspect information.

Absent from this list are most of the civil suits filed in the Courts of Common Pleas, including all of those concerning privates debts. Such cases provide little or no information on political disposition or criminal activity, and need not be included in this roster.
Fortunately, the records of most of Monmouth County's Revolutionary era courts still exist. The following returns, listed chronologically, are apparently the only records to survive.

Indictments at the Court of Quarterly Sessions, 1774-83, Monmouth County Archives, Miscellaneous Unbound Records.

Significant Indictments at the Court of Common Pleas, 1776-82, Monmouth County Archives, box: Common Pleas/Court Papers.

Roster of the People of Revolutionary Monmouth County
Persons Indicted for Crimes at the Monmouth Court of Oyer and Terminer, January and June, 1778, David Library of the American Revolution, Morristown National Historical Park Collection, reel 39.

Persons Indicted for Crimes at the Monmouth Court of Oyer and Terminer, January 1778, New Jersey State Archives, Judicial Records, Court of Oyer and Terminer, box 2, folder: January 1778.

Persons Indicted for Crimes at the Monmouth Court of Oyer and Terminer, June 1778, New Jersey State Archives, Judicial Records, Court of Oyer and Terminer, box 2, folder: June 1778.

Persons Indicted for Crimes at the Monmouth Court of Oyer and Terminer, August 1779, New Jersey State Archives, Judicial Records, Court of Oyer and Terminer, box 2, folder: August 1779.

Persons Indicted for Crimes at the Monmouth Court of Oyer and Terminer, December 1780-January 1781, New Jersey State Archives, Judicial Records, Court of Oyer and Terminer, box 2, folder: December 1780-January 1781.

Persons Indicted for Crimes at the Monmouth Court of Oyer and Terminer, November 1781, New Jersey State Archives, Judicial Records, Court of Oyer and Terminer, box 2, folder: November 1781.

Persons Convicted of Crimes at the Monmouth Court of Oyer and Terminer, January 3, 1781, New Jersey Archives, Extracts from American Newspapers, Trenton: State Gazette Publishing, 1917, vol. 5, p 167.

Persons Convicted of Crimes at the Monmouth Court of Oyer and Terminer, February 7, 1781, New Jersey Archives, Extracts from American Newspapers, Trenton: State Gazette Publishing, 1917, vol. 5, p 191.

Persons Indicted for Crimes at the Monmouth Court of Oyer and Terminer, May-June 1782, New Jersey State Archives, Judicial Records, Court of Oyer and Terminer, box 2, folder: May-June 1782.

Persons Convicted of Treasonable Practices at the Monmouth Court of Oyer and Terminer, June 6, 1782, New Jersey Archives, Extracts from American Newspapers, Trenton: State Gazette Publishing, 1917, vol. 5, p 461.

Roster of the People of Revolutionary Monmouth County

Persons Indicted for Crimes at the Monmouth Court of Oyer and Terminer, November 1782, New Jersey State Archives, Judicial Records, Court of Oyer and Terminer, box 2, folder: November 1782.

Persons Indicted for Crimes at the Monmouth Court of Oyer and Terminer, July 1783, New Jersey State Archives, Judicial Records, Court of Oyer and Terminer, box 2, folder: July 1783.

List of Militia Delinquents, Substitutes, and Exemptions: While militia service was mandatory, there is little doubt that militia delinquency was widespread throughout most of Monmouth County, over the course of the entire Revolution. Militia delinquents were frequently disaffected from the Revolutionary cause, but a great number were also Quakers who did not serve due to religious convictions, and some were men who gladly chose to pay the fines for delinquency and attend to their business interests, rather than risk their lives in the militia. As such, militia delinquency, by itself, is not a strong indicator of a person's attachment to the Revolutionary cause -- though it would be safe to assume that most delinquents were less than devoted patriots.

In addition, militiamen could be excused from militia service for two reasons. First, they could hire a substitute to serve in their stead. Second, throughout the Revolution, certain professions were exempted from militia service, including: educators, office holders, students, and clergymen. Laborers in certain war-related industries, such as foundries and salt works, were also exempted at times during the war. In addition, individuals were occasionally excused from militia duty to attend to family emergencies.

The following lists of delinquents are listed chronologically, with the commanding officer, when known:

List of Militia Delinquents, Colonel Asher Holmes, February 10, 1778, Monmouth County Historical Association, Cherry Hall Papers, box 15, folder 7.

List of Militia Delinquents, Substitutes, and Exemptions, commanding officer unknown, February 10, 1778, New Jersey State Archives, Department of Defense, Revolutionary War, Numbered Manuscripts, #1147.

Roster of the People of Revolutionary Monmouth County

List of Militia Delinquents and Substitutes, Captain Jonathan Holmes, March 11, 1778, Monmouth County Historical Association, Cherry Hall Papers, box 6, folder 6.

List of Militia Delinquents, Captain Benjamin Van Cleaf, November 29, 1778, New Jersey State Archives, Department of Defense, Revolutionary War, Numbered Manuscripts, #1130.

List of Militia Delinquents, Captain Barnes Smock and Captain Benjamin Van Cleaf, June 11, 1780, National Archives, Collection #881, reels 593 and 640.

List of Militia Delinquents, Captain Stephen Fleming, August 11, 1780, New Jersey State Archives, Department of Defense, Revolutionary War, Numbered Manuscripts, #1125.

List of Militia Delinquents from Alarm, commanding officer unknown, August 17, 1780, New Jersey Historical Society, Holmes Family Papers, box 4, folder 2.

List of Militia Delinquents, Captain Daniel Hampton, September 25, 1780, New Jersey State Archives, Department of Defense, Revolutionary War, Numbered Manuscripts, #1140.

List of Militia Delinquents, Captain Jacob Fleming, October 9, 1780, Rutgers University Special Collections, "S" Collection.

List of Militia Delinquents, Captain John Burrowes, April 1782, Monmouth County Historical Association, J. Amory Haskell Collection, folder 13.

List of Militia Substitutes, Captain James Green, undated, Monmouth County Historical Association, J. Amory Haskell Collection, folder 10.

List of Militia Dragoon Delinquents, Captain Barnes Smock, June 13, 17[?], New Jersey State Archives, Department of Defense, Revolutionary War, Numbered Manuscripts, #1111.

<u>Lists of Loyalist Refugees:</u> Due to their opposition to the Revolutionary government, large numbers of Monmouth County loyalists left Monmouth County and sought British protection on Sandy Hook or Staten Island. Eventually, most of these so-called refugees

ended up in New York City or western Long Island, where most spent the war under-employed and a good deal less comfortable than they had been before the war. All of the people listed in this section risked imprisonment, confiscation of property, and long-term separation from family and community. Given the size of the risks and sacrifices that were made, it is safe to assume that the people listed in this section were ardently opposed to the Revolution.

The documentation on the Monmouth Loyalists who went into the British lines is incomplete for all but two groups of refugees, Loyalists who enlisted into the New Jersey Volunteers and prominent Loyalists whose estates were confiscated. But while documentation for these two groups is abundant, it must be noted that there were certainly a large number of refugees who never served in the New Jersey Volunteers and who either did not own estates, or whose estates were never confiscated. Some reference to these refugees may be found in the preceding sections.

Rolls of the New Jersey Volunteers
Compiled Rolls of First and Second Battalion of the New Jersey Volunteers, January 1777-June 1778, Rutgers University Libraries, Special Collections, Muster Rolls of the New Jersey Volunteers, 2 boxes, compiled by Joseph Donohue.

Muster Roll of 2nd Battalion of New Jersey Volunteers, Lt. William Drummond, February 25, 1778, Library of Congress, MMC, Courtland Skinner, box 1.

Muster Roll of 1st Battalion of New Jersey Volunteers, Captain John Taylor, April 24, 1778, Rutgers University Special Collections, New Jersey Volunteers, Muster Rolls.

Schedule of Loyalist Forces with British Army at the Battle of Monmouth (including 2nd Battalion of New Jersey Volunteers), July 1778, Monmouth Battlefield State Park, Research Files, folder: Loyalist Forces.

Recruits into First Battalion of New Jersey Volunteers, Captain Thomas Crowell, Library of Congress, MMC, Cortland Skinner, box 1.

Lists of Loyalist Refugees
Executions and Inquisitions Against Loyalist Estates, 1776-81, Monmouth County Archives, Revolutionary War Papers, box 1, folders

1-3.

Executions Against Loyalist Estates, 1778-87, Monmouth County Archives, Bound Book #1.

Loyalist Estates Confiscated, compiled February 18, 1779, New Jersey Archives, Extracts from American Newspapers, Trenton: State Gazette Publishing, 1917, vol. 3, p 89.

Loyalist Estates Confiscated, May 1779, Ellis, Franklin, History of Monmouth County, Philadelphia: R.T. Peck & Company, 1885, pp. 226-7.

Loyalist Estates Confiscated, May 1779-1784, New Jersey State Archives, Commissioners of Forfeited Estates, box 5, folder 4.1.

Petition of Monmouth Loyalists in New York to Sir Guy Carleton, July 18, 1782, David Library of the American Revolution, British Headquarters Papers, reel 14, #5098.

Roster of the Black Brigade (including several Monmouth County African-Americans), April 16, 1783, National Archives, Papers of the Continental Congress, reel 66, item 53, frames 276-94.